John Hancock

Image credit: Old Print Shop, New York, NY

JOHN HANCOCK,

John Hancock

Merchant King and American Patriot

HARLOW GILES UNGER

CASTLE BOOKS

This edition published in 2005 by
CASTLE BOOKS ®
A division of Book Sales, Inc.
114 Northfield Avenue
Edison, NJ 08837

This edition published by arrangement with and permission of
John Wiley & Sons, Inc.
111 River Street
Hoboken, New Jersey 07030

Library of Congress Cataloging-in-Publication Data:

Unger, Harlow G.
John Hancock : merchant king and American patriot / Harlow Giles Unger.
p. cm.
Includes bibliographical references and index.
1. Hancock, John, 1737-1793. 2. Statesmen—United States—Biography.
3. United States. Declaration of Independence—Signers—Biography.
4. United States. Continental Congress—Presidents—Biography.
5. United States—Politics and government—1775-1783.
6. Massachusetts—Politics and government—1775-1783.
I. Title.
E302.6.H23 U53   2000
973.3'092—dc21   99-057092

ISBN-13: 978-0-7858-2026-0
ISBN-10: 0-7858-2026-4

Printed in the United States of America

To my dear friends
Kathleen and Ronald Potier
and, as always,
to my son, Richard

Contents

List of Illustrations

Acknowledgments

I COULD NOT have produced this book without the enthusiastic and generous help of a host of skilled editors, librarians, researchers, and friends. Chief among these were my editor, Hana Umlauf Lane, senior editor at John Wiley & Sons, and my friend and agent, Edward Knappman, of New England Publishing Associates. My sincerest thanks, too, to Diane Aronson and her colleagues—especially Chuck Antony, copyeditor—at John Wiley & Sons for the wonderful work they did in copyediting and preparing this book for publication. The beautiful design and typeface choice are the work of Sona Lachina of Lachina Publishing Services. Bravo. I also want to thank Maia Keech and her colleagues at the Library of Congress; Joann Huddleston, Corporate Archives, John Hancock Mutual Life Insurance Company; Douglas Southerd, librarian at the Bostonian Society; William Faucon, curator of manuscripts, and R. Eugene Zepp, Rare Books and Manuscripts, Boston Public Library; Louise Jones, librarian at the Yale Club of New York City; and the staff at the Massachusetts Historical Society, the Houghton Library at Harvard University, the New England Historical and Genealogical Society, and the Boston Athenaeum. Many friends also helped me with this book by responding to my inevitable calls for help, as they always do, with cheer and personal support. They included Eleanora von Dehsen, in New York; Francis Everett and Richard Everett III, in Boston; Randi Ladenheim Gil, in New York; Carol Kneeland, in Pawling, New York; Douglas Kneeland, at Swarthmore College, in Pennsylvania; Tracie Byrd, American Paintings and Sculpture, Yale

University Art Gallery, in New Haven; Carol Haines, Concord Museum, Concord, Massachusetts; André Mandel, in Paris, France; and Kathleen Potier and Ronald Potier, in Lancaster, Pennsylvania; and I owe especial thanks to my patient friend (and cousin) Joshua Mostkoff Unger, who not only helped simplify my work with his guidance in computer operations but contributed some research material and was always ready to respond to my every call for help. To everyone: thank you.

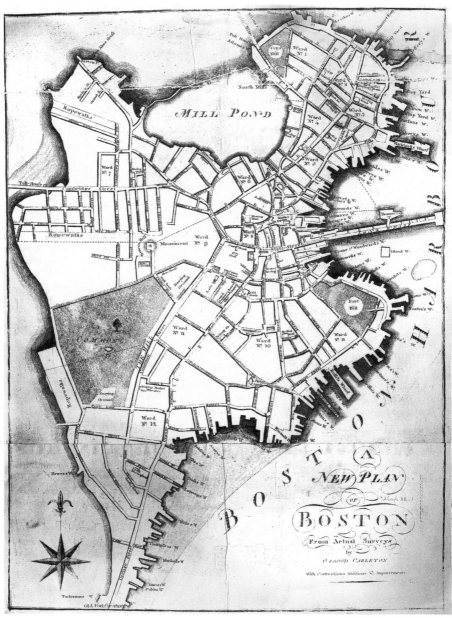

Boston, 1814. A virtual island, Boston is connected to the mainland by narrow Boston Neck. Hancock Wharf is on the upper right, above Long Wharf. Although not depicted, Hancock House stood above and overlooking the Common. Griffin's Wharf, the site of the Boston Tea Party, can be seen protruding below Fort Hill, near the large letter *N* in BOSTON. (*Bostonian Society*)

Chronology

1724   Thomas Hancock founds House of Hancock.

1737   January 12. John Hancock born in Braintree, Massachusetts.

1744   Uncle Thomas "adopts" JH; takes him to Boston as heir to House of Hancock.

1754   JH graduates from Harvard. French and Indian War (Seven Years War) begins.

1759   British crush French at Quebec.

1764   Thomas Hancock dies. JH inherits House of Hancock.

1765   British pass Stamp Act. JH protests.

1766   Parliament repeals Stamp Act. JH hailed as hero; elected to legislature.

1767   British pass Townshend Acts. Hancock leads merchant boycott of British goods.

1768   British seize Hancock sloop *Liberty;* send troops to Boston. JH tried as smuggler.

1770   Boston Massacre. Parliament repeals Townshend Acts.

1773   Boston Tea Party.

1774   JH leads Boston revolution. Parliament passes Coercive Acts. First Continental Congress meets in Philadelphia; declares rights to "life, liberty and property."

1775   Revolutionary War begins. Continental Congress names JH president. British victory at Bunker Hill. JH marries.

1776   British evacuate Boston. JH signs Declaration of Independence, July 4, and becomes first president of the United States; named commander of Massachusetts militia. British occupy New York. House of Hancock liquidated. First child, Lydia Henchman Hancock, is born.

1777   Americans crush Burgoyne at Saratoga. France recognizes U.S. independence. Daughter, Lydia, dies.

1778   JH ends his presidency. French join war. Son, John George Washington Hancock, is born. General Hancock's militia defeated at Newport. JH salvages French military alliance.

1780   JH elected first Massachusetts governor.

1781   Cornwallis surrenders at Yorktown. Revolutionary War ends.

1783   Treaty of Paris ratified, April 15. Britain recognizes U.S. independence.

1785   JH resigns as governor.

1786   Shays's Rebellion in Massachusetts.

1787   Son dies in accident. Governor Bowdoin sends militia to crush Shays's Rebellion. People demand Hancock's return; reelect him governor. Constitutional Convention opens in Philadelphia.

1788   JH assures ratification of Constitution; proposes nine Conciliatory Amendments as Bill of Rights.

1789   Washington elected president. First Congress convenes. JH reelected governor.

1793   October 8. John Hancock dies in Boston at fifty-seven.

Introduction

JOHN HANCOCK did not set out to be a rebel, let alone found a new nation. He was quite happy with the old one, which had made him rich and powerful—the head of one of North America's largest mercantile empires and all but certain to become the first Lord Hancock. Hancock loved wealth. He reveled in it. He adored all the foppish trappings it could buy: the fashionable wigs, frilled shirts, silk and velvet jackets and breeches—and the shoes with silver or gold buckles that sparkled as he strode along Boston's Hancock Wharf. He envisioned a monumental estate in Britain to go with his title—a castle, perhaps, or even a palace, overlooking an expanse of formal French gardens and a wide allée of meticulously shaped plane trees . . .

There simply was no doubt about it: John Hancock was the least likely man in Boston to start a revolution.

Then, in a series of arrogant miscalculations, Parliament tried to refill the English treasury's empty war chests by dipping its collective hands into John Hancock's pockets and those of other colonial merchants and planters. Gradually and reluctantly, the colonists turned against king and country. Hancock and the others would gladly—eagerly—have relented; all were loyal British subjects and wanted to remain so. But a few prideful English politicians, many of them now long forgotten, rejected every opportunity to compromise. The American Revolution had more to do with money than with liberty, though some colonial leaders disguised their lust for power in the philosophical glories of the Age of Enlightenment. George Washington, one of the South's wealthiest planters, was more honest than most. He expressed his motive for rebellion in simple terms: "They have no right to put their hands in my pockets."[1]

In the North, John Hancock reacted the same way when Parliament "thrust their dirty hands" into his coffers. Hancock was a merchant—one of an unyielding plutocracy that had ruled Boston and exploited New England's wealth for decades. Like other eighteenth-century merchants, Hancock's business empire encompassed far more than retail stores. Merchants' enterprises were the conglomerates of their era. Hancock was a wholesaler, warehouser, importer, exporter, shipbuilder, shipowner and operator, investment banker, and realty developer and manager. Like other merchants, he and his uncle (who built the House of Hancock into Boston's largest business) mercilessly manipulated markets, beat down suppliers, held up buyers, and extracted every penny they could from the latter two. And every last one of them smuggled and bribed customs inspectors to avoid paying import duties, thus depriving Britain of a basic source of revenues from the colonies.

The Hancocks were no different from other merchants; they were just better at the game—more daring, more willing to take risks, and sometimes more clever at analyzing market conditions and minimizing those risks. The game began each day at dawn, as frontiersmen, farmers, and assorted peddlers brought their goods to market. Boston was America's most important city and port— the closest to England and, therefore, the most important way station for goods traveling to and from the colonies. More than five hundred ships a year sailed in and out of Boston Harbor, carrying goods to and from all parts of the world. Boston's maze of crooked little streets shook each day with the rumble of wagons and horses on the cobblestoned main ways. The smaller alleys echoed with cries and curses of tradesmen as their wagon wheels slipped and snapped in rutted pools of mud and dung. By midday they were gone, replaced by a crowd of merchants arguing, lying, bargaining, dealing, shaking hands (and fists), cursing, and after all was said and done, buying and selling the goods that had been all but stolen from the farmers earlier that day. They bought low, sold high, and traded anything and everything that could be bought, sold, or traded for a profit. They bought rum and traded it for black men and women and children, whom they sold into slavery to buy molasses to make more rum to buy more Africans . . .

By noon they were up at the Town House, the government center, bribing whatever officials needed bribing to let their business deals go through. A collective midafternoon thirst drew the merchants into the taverns that lined the waterfront and every nearby street. There were 150 of them, each a cherished temple for a specific element of Boston society and all but closed to everyone else. Every craft had its tavern—every profession, every occupation, every merchant group and political faction. Freemasons went to the Green Dragon, clergymen and magistrates to the Blue Anchor, seamen and drunks to the Ship Tavern. The Hancocks and other merchants went to the Merchants Club or the luxurious Royal Exchange near the Town House to continue their business games at dinner and into the night.

The winners—and the Hancocks were the biggest—believed, as most winners do, that they had earned, and deserved to keep, every penny of profit they collected. Although none liked the idea, some even made a show of paying some of the taxes they owed. Britain had tried taxing colonists with import duties for more than a century, but merchants simply bribed customs officials or smuggled goods in duty free. A century of wars with France and Spain finally bankrupted Britain, however, and Parliament decided it would have to increase taxes in America and enforce tax collection more strictly—at bayonet point, if necessary.

At first, Hancock, like other politically conservative merchants, was certain that saner voices in Parliament—or at least the king—would renounce the idea. It was only after Parliament rejected all compromise and even introduced a state tea monopoly to drive colonial merchants out of business that he gradually and reluctantly threw his lot in with Boston's so-called patriots. From the first, Hancock feared and despised them. Although Harvard graduates like him, they were hotheads—pseudointellectuals who used the idea of independence and specious constitutional arguments to further their own personal ambitions.

Hancock favored mediation and reconciliation, but he found himself sitting on a shaky fence in a society polarized by the arrogance of an impolitic Parliament and venomous cries for vengeance by angry, often irrational, colonial rebels. To side with the English would mean the loss of his property to angry colonists; to side with the rebels would mean treason and possible death on the gallows in England. He decided to join the rebels, but rather than leave his fate in their hands, he gradually seized control of the rebellion from the bloodthirsty madmen who had ignited the insurrections. Once in control, he directed that rebellion in a way that most benefited himself, of course, but in the end assured the people of Massachusetts self-rule under a stable, independent government.

The Revolution cost him most of his fortune—a large portion of it buying arms and ammunition for minutemen. It almost cost him his life as well, but in the end he won enormous political power, international fame, and the deep love of the people of his state.

Although John Hancock's bold signature on the Declaration of Independence is a national symbol—indeed, his name is a synonym for the word "signature"—Hancock remains among the least known of America's founding fathers. A huge Boston life insurance company emblazons his name on its glass skyscraper,[2] a World War II aircraft carrier carried his name into battle on its bow, and thousands of Americans walk along Hancock Streets and Avenues—but few know much, if anything, about him. Only a handful of historians have bothered to write his biography; most history texts ignore him; and even the state he led and the wife he adored all but forgot him after he died. His widow laid his body in an unmarked grave in the Old Granary Burying Ground in Boston, adding only a small sandstone slab on the wall nearby with the inscription *No. 16, Tomb of Hancock.* The state did not honor its great son and first governor until a century later, when a great-grandniece unveiled a simple granite shaft above his grave.

One of the most paradoxical figures of his time, John Hancock himself bears some of the responsibility for his own historical obscurity. Throughout much of his life he was a foppish pseudo-aristocrat—a bachelor merchant king who lived alone with a widowed aunt in an isolated hilltop mansion on Beacon Hill, over-looking Boston. He owned Beacon Hill. His land covered its crest, and his was the only house there. His vain behavior and garish display of wealth earned him few close friends. He might never have married if his aunt had not arranged a union for him—with a prominent young lady who agreed to live with him and his aunt in their mansion but would never love him.

Hancock suffered the disdain and mockery of some of the other leaders of Boston's revolution. They despised his lavish entertainments on Beacon Hill, his gilded coach and four with its liveried servants and garish Hancock coat of arms emblazoned on its doors. But without his wealth to buy arms and ammunition, they knew, they could not fulfill their dreams for rebellion against royal rule and for independence from England. So they swallowed their pride, fed his vanity, and wooed him to their cause. But they did not like him or understand him, and in the end they hated him for usurping their dream, inserting himself as its hero, and rele-gating them to secondary roles. And above all, the rebel leaders hated him for being rich. Confusing cultural equality with politi-cal equality, they cast away their lace-frilled shirts and velvet breeches in favor of the yeoman's coarse linens and flannels; they adopted foul language and habits; and they ignored their Harvard educations to pose as common men. Hancock refused—and saw no practical reason—to do the same. He loved English culture and fashions, not to mention fine French wines. He did not believe his love of luxury would have the slightest effect on the struggle for American independence and the rights of man—and it did not.

So, during the Revolution and after, he continued to live as an aristocrat—even in the face of enemy cannon fire—and he contin-ued to ride through Boston in his splendid, gilded coach and four, with his four liveried riders and the elegant Hancock arms embla-zoned on its doors. In contrast to the Harvard intellectuals among the rebels, the ordinary people of Boston and the rest of Massachusetts—the minutemen who did the fighting instead of the dreaming—adored him and his aristocratic trappings. Even as they burned the homes of other aristocrats, they embraced John Hancock as their hero, inexplicably, irresistibly. And from the beginning he repaid that veneration by devoting his life to them and sacrificing one of the largest fortunes in the colonies to underwrite their welfare and independence. He became America's first great philanthropist and humanitarian. He put hundreds to work in his own company and set up others in their own businesses; he delivered firewood and food to the poor during Boston's bitter winters; he rebuilt whole neighborhoods devastated by Boston's periodic fires; he supported widows and orphans—even sent them to college at his own expense, and paid churches to assure that the poor had seats of their own; he bought the city its first fire engine; built a concert hall; and maintained and improved—all at his own expense— the city's magnificent Common, a park that was open to all the people of Boston, rich and poor alike, to use and enjoy.

After the Boston Massacre, he stepped from his regal chariot to issue the first stirring cry for independence to the American people. After the Boston Tea Party, he ignored a warrant for his arrest and rode to Lexington a day before the battle, and then to the Continental Congress in Philadelphia to preside over deliberations. A year later, he was first to sign the Declaration of Independence, and, in effect, sign his own death warrant for treason against England. As president of Congress, John Hancock became the first "president of the united States," thirteen years before Washington. Then, as major general and commander of the Massachusetts militia, he marched to battle in Rhode Island. Later he helped repair Franco-American military relations and assure victory and independence. After independence, the people of Massachusetts hailed him as their hero and elected him their first governor—and they continued to elect him until he died, during his ninth term. Some would have continued electing him even after his death.

Since the day of his death, bewildered historians have unsuccessfully struggled to understand the Hancock paradox. He was, without question, one of early America's greatest heroes, if only by circumstance—far more so than Paul Revere or others of greater note whom some history texts have elevated to unwarranted pseudoheroism. At one and the same time Hancock could be haughty and humble, vain and meek, petulant and composed, selfish and generous, garish and modest, pompous and retiring, aloof and deeply loving and caring. He was unpredictably predictable and predictably unpredictable. He grew up in unimaginable luxury, lived as an aristocrat, won renown as a democrat, and earned the trust, admiration, and even adoration of ordinary men—not only the minutemen who went to war with him but the clerks, longshoremen, laborers, and seamen who toiled for his far-flung enterprises. A member of Boston's Revolutionary leadership, he faced constant opposition from his coconspirators, who nonetheless tapped his fortune unhesitatingly to assure the success of their enterprise. He has proved so puzzling a figure that no one—then or since—can agree even on his height or size. "Gov. Hancock was nearly six feet in stature, and of thin person," said one observer;[3] "nearly six feet tall and sturdily built," said another;[4] "not tall," said a third. After measuring the governor's inauguration clothes that were preserved in the State House in Boston, one historian insisted that "John Hancock was approximately five feet, four inches tall, neck fourteen and a half inches; sleeve, thirty-three inches; waist, thirty-one and a half inches; and chest thirty-eight inches."[5] Another historian modifies these findings by suggesting that "if we allow for shrinkage of the garments caused by cleaning, we can arrive at an approximate height of Hancock as five feet, six inches tall. In his day, this was an encouraging height."[6]

In 1817, John Adams—a childhood playmate of Hancock, but later a harsh critic, and finally a reluctant admirer—declared that Hancock's personality was too complex to detail in a biography. "His biography," said Adams, "would fill as many volumes as Marshall's *Washington*."[7] Although Adams conceded that a Hancock biography would be "instructive and entertaining," he went on to say, "his life will, however, not ever be written." More than a century later, historian James Truslow Adams (1878–1949) wrote despairingly of Hancock that he could "only patch and guess toward a conception of an enigmatic character." Abandoning the task himself, Adams then asked, "Will the biography of him that [John] Adams said would never be written yet come into being?"[8] I hope this volume will be that biography.

John Hancock's transformation from Tory patrician to fiery rebel is one of the least-known stories of the Revolution. It is the story of a man who was no less flawed and no more perfect than his fellowman, but who, unlike many, displayed his flaws for all to see—brazenly, sometimes maddeningly. Never letting modesty temper or cloak his ambitions for wealth and political power, he was, perhaps, the consummate American hero.

1

The Boy on Beacon Hill

(1737-1750)

JOHN HANCOCK was the third of his line to carry that name, and from the moment he was born, his family had little doubt that he would follow the first and second John Hancock—his grandfather and father—to the pulpit of the Congregational Church. In the towns near Boston, the Hancocks *were* the Congregational Church and had been since the beginning of the eighteenth century. The first John Hancock assumed the pulpit of the North Precinct Church in Cambridge in 1698, when power over church and town was indivisible in Massachusetts. After fifteen years in command, the first Reverend Hancock led a tax revolt in the North Precinct, which was ten miles from central Cambridge. He declared the North Precinct and its church independent—a perfectly legal procedure under the Cambridge Platform of 1648, which gave every Congregational church the right to total autonomy. Despite protests from Cambridge, the North Precinct became Lexington, Massachusetts. Its parishioners kept their taxes in their own pockets and made the first John Hancock their all but absolute monarch.

Quickly dubbed the "Bishop of Lexington," he brooked no opposition to his ironfisted rule. Although Congregationalists ordained no bishops, he ruled like a Roman Catholic bishop. His power, like that of all Congregationalist ministers of the time, stemmed from the determination of early Puritan settlers to found a "Bible commonwealth" in the Massachusetts Bay Colony. They limited free speech and political privileges and reimposed in New England the same religious discrimination that Anglicans had imposed on them in old England. They limited voting rights to propertied male members of the Congregational Church and converted town after town into theocracies, where ministers ruled the spiritual world and deacons and elders ruled the material world.

"Bishop" John Hancock was the first of his family to join the ruling class. His grandfather Nathaniel was an English Puritan farmer[1] who landed in America in 1634, a dozen years after the *Mayflower*, and settled in Cambridge (then New Towne). His only surviving son, also Nathaniel, inherited fourteen acres to farm, but he sired thirteen children and had to supplement his income as a shoemaker and town constable. He also became a church deacon, an office that assured his sons instruction by the minister and preparation for Harvard College, the wellspring of New England spiritual power. His second son—the future Bishop—entered Harvard in 1685 but ranked only thirteenth in a class of fourteen boys under Harvard's humiliating system of gradation by family social rank. The son of a Massachusetts governor or Harvard president stood, marched, or sat at the head of his class in processions, in church, in recitation rooms, and at meals. Next in rank came grandsons of governors, sons of trustees, sons of large landowners, and so on. Sons of farmers ranked last.

Whatever Harvard may have taught him about social rank, it also taught him theology, along with the logic, argumentation, and rhetoric that gave his booming voice and strong personality the wherewithal to overwhelm those who questioned his judgment.

From the beginning he ruled firmly but fairly. He was powerfully built, with a dour face that brooked little or no discussion. Every parishioner knew to accept his every suggestion as a command. Asked to resolve a long-standing dispute between two parishioners over property lines, the Bishop ordered each to cut some stakes and plant them in the ground several feet apart from

"Bishop" John Hancock, minister of the Congregational Church at Lexington, Massachusetts, and grandfather of the patriot. (*Lexington Historical Society*)

each other. He drew a line in the earth and told them, "Your line runs there, and there let it run forever. . . . And let us have no more quarreling about this matter." The issue was settled.[2]

And later, when two church deacons protested his failure to consult them on church decisions, he told them that saddling his horse and holding his bridle was all "I ever can consent to let the ruling elders do for me."[3] Although no one ever again bothered to seek election as elder, his despotic rule provided nothing but wealth for the members of his church and community—especially after he freed them from heavy Cambridge taxes by making Lexington independent. In the end, the town rewarded him with handsome wage increases, about fifty acres of land, and the right to cut timber from common land. More important, they retained him—and his despotic ways—for fifty-four years, until his death, in 1752, at eighty-two.

The Bishop of Lexington was no less a despot at home than he was at church. He married Elizabeth Clarke, the daughter of the Reverend Thomas Clarke, also a Harvard graduate, and beginning in 1702, they produced a quick succession of five children. His tyranny all but crushed the spirit of his firstborn—the second John Hancock—but his second son, Thomas, inherited his father's strong personality, and at fourteen he willingly traded his father's tyranny for near bondage as an indentured apprentice in a bookseller's shop.

The second John Hancock grew up a meek little chap who obediently followed his father's footsteps through Harvard and, eventually, to the pulpit, although his lack of sparkle delayed his ordination by several years. "Mr. Hancock," wrote one of his classmates, "has no great Character for his Abilities Either Naturale or Acquired. The professor told me He . . . could make a very handsome bow, and if the first did not suit He'd Bow Lower a Second time." Unable to obtain a ministry, John took a job as librarian at Harvard, while Thomas completed the apprenticeship that channeled his passions in the world of trading, where he amassed one of America's great fortunes.

Despite the Bishop's ambitions, the second John Hancock languished at the Harvard library for three years, until the winter of 1726, when the tiny North Parish in Braintree (now Quincy), Massachusetts, invited the shy young man to their dilapidated little meetinghouse. Built in 1666, the little stone church had all but collapsed, and during Hancock's first winter, "cartloads of snow" drifted into the building for him to shovel out before he could conduct Sunday morning services.

Braintree was, nonetheless, a prosperous community, with several large, established farms and families. The Adams family had fifty acres, and the Quincys had even more. Both families had ties to Boston's merchant community. The Adamses were cousins of Deacon Samuel Adams, the Boston brewer, who was a church leader and powerful political boss. The patriarch of the Braintree Quincys was Col. Josiah Quincy, who was a merchant and trader as well as a farmer, with political ties to the royal governor. Aware of the wealth that farm families disguised with plain clothes and simple houses, Bishop Hancock set out to negotiate a handsome contract for his son from the reluctant parishioners. In a thundering sermon at his son's ordination, the Bishop told them, "Those who are called by office to preach the word of God have power of rule, also. . . . And therefore are the keys of the kingdom to be committed unto them. Not only the key of doctrine but of discipline. The keys are an emblem of power. I might have added—their power to ask and receive wages for this their service. . . . And the laws of Christ have given them this power to take wages for their work and to take it not as alms or charity but as justice."[4]

The Bishop cowed his son's parishioners into building their minister a new house, ceding him a few acres of farmland, giving him £200 for resettlement, and paying him a salary of £110 a year—£10 more than his predecessor and slightly more than the average annual income of skilled tradesmen. The Bishop concluded his son's ordination with a homily: "He that desires the office of a bishop desires a good work. You are where God would have you be . . . you have not begged the office nor invaded it nor shuffled yourself into it . . . but have tarried till a wide . . . door is opened unto you."[5]

In December of 1733, the younger Reverend Hancock married Mary Hawke, a local farmer's daughter, and in the spring of 1735 their first child, a daughter, was born. Their first son, who would bear his father's and grandfather's name, was born eighteen months later, on January 12, 1737; their third and last child, Ebenezer, followed in November 1741.

The Reverend Hancock's church stood by the village green, the geographic, spiritual, social, and governmental center of a community of about forty families. Most of the town's three hundred people lived on farms tied to town by long ribbons of dirt wagon trails. Six homes shared the green with the Hancock manse and the meetinghouse. The old, unused stocks stood silent vigil nearby to warn those who would violate the laws of God. Free of his domineering father's influence, the gentle minister of Braintree served more as mediator than governor. He earned the town's love and respect by letting church deacons deal with secular governance while he concentrated on baptisms, marriages, and funerals. Only fifteen months before baptizing his own son, John, he baptized the Adams family's newborn son, John Adams, the future president.

When the third John Hancock was born, Braintree farmers had stripped the land of most of the oaks, elms, and maples that once covered the slopes to the bay, across from Boston. Farmhouses, barns, and an assortment of variously shaped outbuildings dotted the land. Farmers spent their days slogging behind their horses or oxen, and cows grazed on whatever grass they could find along the fields' edges. Most farms grew wheat, corn, oats, barley, hay, or flax to sell in Boston markets, although some had orchards and all had kitchen gardens nestled close to their houses to provide food for the family. Indian-corn meal was a staple that supplemented the typical diet of fruits and vegetables. Fresh meat was a luxury, as was flour. Most families salted down a slaughtered pig or a side of beef each fall to assure themselves some meat through the winter. In 1740 a brewery opened in Braintree, to quench community thirst with a steady flow of ale and rum. Braintree and the rest of New England had been at peace for more than twenty years. The Peace of Utrecht had ended Queen Anne's War in 1713 and pushed the French too far inland for them and their Indian allies to stage the deadly raids that had terrorized the New England frontier for so long.

Living on the village green, young John Hancock grew up free of tiresome farm chores, but he was often alone with little to do. His father was either away visiting parishioners or busy writing sermons, and his mother tended to dote over John's older sister, Mary. Jeffrey, the gentle slave, was the only member of the household who had no option but to listen to the boy's chatter. As he grew more independent, Hancock took to following older farm boys. John Adams and the Quincy boys Edmund and Samuel went on frequent gambols through the woods to the stream for a swim or up to the crest of a ruined old fort to fire imaginary rifles at phantom Indian raiders. Some Indians actually came into their sights, but they were harmless Punkapoags from the reservation at Stoughton, who came to fish in the Neponset or buy goods in town. The Quincy boys' father, Col. Josiah Quincy, was agent for the few Indians the colonists had not killed.[6]

Adams and the others had mixed feelings about their young hanger-on, but the Reverend John Hancock was the town's most exalted citizen and only Harvard graduate—and could send bad little boys to hell! So John Adams and the others tolerated the minister's son, but they did not like him. As Adams later wrote of Hancock, "He inherited from his father, though one of the most amiable and beloved of men, a certain sensibility, a keenness of feeling, or—in more familiar language—a peevishness that sometimes disgusted and afflicted his friends."[7]

When he reached the summer of his fifth year—in 1742— Hancock followed Adams and the other boys to Mrs. Belcher's "dame school." Massachusetts had made universal education compulsory a century earlier. Under the School Act of 1647, communities with fifty or more householders were required to establish formal petty (or elementary) schools, and communities with a hundred or more householders had to establish Latin grammar (or secondary) schools.

In small communities without schoolhouses, educated ladies like Dame Belcher ran petty schools in their kitchens to teach local children elementary reading, writing, and arithmetic.[8] If Hancock had completed his studies, he would have moved to the town's Latin grammar school to prepare for Harvard and the pulpit, with four to seven years of Latin, Greek, history, geography, geometry, algebra, and trigonometry.

In the spring of 1744, however, Hancock's father became ill and died, just three weeks short of his forty-second birthday. His wife and three children faced poverty and homelessness until they received a letter from the old Bishop. At seventy-four, he still preached in Lexington and lived with his wife in a large manse.[9] The rooms that once housed his own children were empty, and he invited his daughter-in-law and three children to move in. The old man looked forward to molding his grandson into the greatest Reverend John Hancock of them all.

Before the Bishop could devour his grandson, however, another, equally forceful Hancock appeared at the manse in Lexington in an English-built gilt-edged coach and four, attended by four liveried servants. A silver-and-ivory coat of arms emblazoned its doors—three fighting cocks, the topmost with a dragon's tail, above a raised hand of protest[10]—which the owner believed was his due, if not his verifiable birthright. Beneath it heraldic gold script proclaimed, *Nul Plaisir Sans Peine* (no pleasure without pain). Thomas Hancock, the Bishop's second son, who had left home at the age of fourteen, had returned after twenty-seven years. He had left as an indentured apprentice and now reappeared as one of America's richest, most powerful merchants, owner of Boston's prestigious, world-renowned House of Hancock.

Like many powerful eighteenth-century merchants', Hancock's enterprise was a conglomerate that included retailing, wholesaling, importing, exporting, warehousing, ship and wharf ownership, investment banking, and real estate investing. What made Thomas Hancock different was that he was more successful than most other merchants, and he had succeeded in Boston, then the richest city in the New World. Although no one had a firm idea of all the things Hancock traded, everyone knew that whatever in the world one might want, one could find it at Thomas Hancock's, and if he didn't have it, he could get it for a price. Every bit as overwhelming as his father, the Bishop, Thomas Hancock could buy anything he wanted; and what he wanted more than anything else in the world when he strode into his father's house in Lexington in the summer of 1744— and what he intended to buy at any price—was a son and heir to the House of Hancock.

Thomas Hancock had spent twenty-seven years building his commercial empire and he was not about to let it fall into the hands of strangers after his death. He and his wife, Lydia—"as ladylike person as ever lived"[11]—had been married in 1731, but after thirteen years had been unable to have the children they both craved so much. His older brother's death provided the first opportunity to adopt an acceptable child. At seventy-four, the Bishop was too old to raise three small children and did not earn enough to send two boys to Harvard. Thomas pledged to provide lifelong security in the most generous fashion for his father, his brother's widow, Mary, and all three children—if Mary would allow him to raise the older boy, John, as his own in Boston. His uncle would assure him the finest schooling, culminating at Harvard, where he would follow in his father's and grandfather's educational footsteps. Mary Hancock and the Bishop had little choice but to yield to the forceful merchant king and to watch as her little boy, the third and soon to be the greatest John Hancock, left the manse in Lexington and waved good-bye from his uncle's stately carriage.

They were an incongruous sight, the merchant king and his new son. The little country boy was dressed in an ill-fitting washed-out gray suit his mother had made. His hair flowed back to a little bobtail, and his skin glowed red from the scrubbing his mother had administered early that morning. His uncle was built as powerfully as the Bishop, but his face was less dour. It bore a benign smile, whose inscrutability had lured many traders into deals that plunged them into financial oblivion while increasing the House of Hancock's varied assets.

Although Thomas Hancock lacked the Harvard credentials of Boston's other aristocrats, he had impeccable personal taste, from his immaculate, carefully powdered wig to his silver shoe buckles. Embroidered ruffled shirt cuffs flared from the ends of his jacket sleeves and embraced his soft, puffy hands. The rest of his costume—the magnificent knee-length velvet coat and the shirt frills that peeked discreetly from the front of his jacket—showed the care he took to compensate for his academic deficiencies with well-displayed evidence of his wealth, power, and high standing. A gold chain held a magnificently fashioned watch. It was his most prized

Thomas Hancock, uncle of the patriot and founder of the House of Hancock, one of the great mercantile empires in the American colonies. From a portrait by John Singleton Copley in the Fogg Museum of Art at Harvard University. (*Courtesy of the Harvard Portrait Collection, President and Fellows of Harvard College. Gift of John Hancock to Harvard College, 1766. Photo by David Mathews. Image copyright, President and Fellows of Harvard College, Harvard University*)

personal possession. To little John Hancock, even the great robes of the church that his father and grandfather wore on Sundays had never looked so grand as the clothes of his uncle the merchant king. He was simply splendid.

The horses of Thomas Hancock's coach stepped out slowly at first, carefully avoiding the deep ruts of the parched country road, but as the road improved at the approaches to Boston they picked up their pace, until they reached the town gate on Boston Neck, a narrow little strip of land that connected the city to the mainland. Colonial Boston was almost an island, an outcropping at the end of a narrow, hilly spit. All the hills except Beacon Hill would later be carved away to fill the surrounding marshes and mudflats that separated the town from the mainland. From above, eighteenth-century Boston lay in the water like a fallen bird, its stubby wings outspread. One wing lay in the Charles River, on the northwest, while the opposite wing lay in the harbor. A short neck connected the body of the bird to its head, or North End. At high tide the Charles River estuary flooded the mudflats and salt marshes to the west of the city and formed the Back Bay. On the east, or harbor side, endless finger piers reached into the water, side by side, embracing the hundreds of ships that sailed in and out of the busy harbor (see Map, page xiii).

After entering the town gate, Hancock's carriage passed the gallows before trotting onto Orange, Newbury, and Marlborough Streets (all, now, Washington Street). They passed Province House, the magnificent mansion of the royal governor, and turned left up School Street. Simple two-story wood and brick houses lined both sides of the way, sometimes separated by tiny alleys. Dismal little workshops and stores lay inside most of the dark entries. A handful of church steeples towered above, but none higher than Christ Church (Old North Church), whose steeple reached more than 190 feet above the town. After forging their way through a swamp of horse dung, Hancock's team reached the bottom of Beacon Hill and slowly hauled the coach up to the edge of the Common, at the peak of the hill on the left. A gateway opposite the Common opened on the grandest home the little country

A painting of Hancock House, the palatial Beacon Hill mansion of Thomas and Lydia Hancock and their nephew John Hancock. It was torn down in 1863. (*Bostonian Society. Photo by Richard Merrill*)

boy—and indeed most of Boston—had ever seen, a Georgian palace three stories tall, including roof dormers.

Built of square-cut granite blocks and trimmed at each corner with brownstone quoins, the mansion had two large windows on either side of a central entrance on the ground floor and a large balcony above that provided a breathtaking view across the entire Common, the city, harbor, and sea beyond, and across the surrounding countryside. In all, the house had fifty-three windows, including those in the dormers, lighted by 480 squares of the best crown glass from London. Hancock's London agent had taken "particular care about my window glass, that it be the best and every square cut exactly to the size."[12] Outside, a two-acre landscaped green bore a variety of shade trees and elegant gardens. At the far end, a small orchard included mulberry, peach, and apricot trees from Spain. A gardening enthusiast, Hancock ordered many trees and plants from English nurseries and unwittingly enriched the entire New England landscape with species of trees, shrubs, and flowers that were new to North America: all originated from windblown seeds from Thomas Hancock's gardens on Beacon Hill.

He told one horticulturist "to procure for me two or three dozen Yew trees, some Hollys and Jessamine vines; and if you have any particular curious things . . . [that] will beautify a Flower Garden, send a sample. . . . Pray send me a Catalogue of that Fruit you have that are Dwarf Trees and Espaliers. . . . My Gardens all Lye on the South Side of a hill, with the most beautifull Assent to the Top; and its Allowed on all hands the Kingdom of England don't afford so fine a Prospect as I have both of Land and Water. Neither do I intend to Spare any cost or pains in making my Gardens beautifull or Profitable."[13] Hancock's gardens were the most beautiful and most envied in Boston.

Inside his house, a wide, paneled central entrance hall reached through to a set of rear doors that looked onto the formal gardens. Delicately carved spiral balusters bounded a broad staircase that rose along the left wall of the main hall. A ten-foot-tall "Chiming Clock" topped with sculpted figures "Gilt with Burnished Gold" stood against the opposite wall. Oil portraits of important men, in uniform or formal clothes, stared out from large gilded frames on the walls in the rooms off the hall, casting silent judgments on all who entered. The great parlor, or drawing room, lay off the hall to the right as one entered the house, and the family sitting room sat opposite. Mahogany furniture filled the parlor, upholstered in luxurious damask that matched the drapes. Imported green-and-scarlet "Flockwork" from England—a "very Rich & Beautiful fine Cloth" wallpaper ornamented with tufts of wool and cotton—covered the walls. Elegant brass candlesticks sparkled with reflected light from the marble hearth—one of three downstairs. The servants kept fires burning in every room during the cold Boston winters. Across the hall, English wallpaper in the family room displayed a panorama of brightly colored "Birds Peacocks Macoys [macaws] Squirrells Fruit & Flowers" that Hancock described as "better than paintings done in oyl."[14] Beyond the family room

Article from *Harper's Weekly* (1859?) with engravings showing the interiors and exterior of Hancock House, with the State House in the background. The article incorrectly asserts that Hancock received Washington there, but the president rejected Hancock's invitation and never set foot in the mansion. (*Bostonian Society*)

were the dining room and kitchen, which included "a Jack of three Guineas price, with a wheel-fly and Spitt-Chain to it." One of the smaller rooms behind housed Hancock's huge china collection, while the others served as lodgings for servants and slaves.

Hancock stocked his cellar with Madeira wines that he bought "without regard to price provided the quality answers to it." He also bought a docile slave named Cambridge for £160 to help serve his and Lydia Hancock's many guests from "6 Quart Decanters" and "2 doz. handsom, new fash'd wine glasses," made of the finest rock crystal from London.[15]

Upstairs, above the parlor, lay the huge guest bedroom, with furnishings and matching draperies in yellow damask. Years later its canopied four-poster would sleep, among others, Sir William Howe, commanding general of the British army in America during Washington's siege of Boston in the winter of 1775–76. Opposite the guest room stretched the master bedroom, done in crimson. Two other, smaller bedrooms lay on the second floor, with storage and servants' quarters scattered above beneath the roof.[16]

"We live Pretty comfortable here on Beacon Hill,"[17] said Thomas Hancock modestly.

WITHIN HOURS of entering his new home on the hill, little John Hancock began a year of intensive training with a private tutor, who transformed the country boy into a sophisticate with impeccable manners, speech, and behavior—a model of mid-eighteenth-century Anglo-Boston society. His doting aunt Lydia groomed and dressed him in velvet breeches, with a satin shirt richly embroidered with lace ruffles at the front and cuffs. His shoes bore the same sparkling silver buckles as his uncle's. Thomas Hancock was immensely proud of his new son's good looks, and as quickly as the boy's bearing and manners permitted, he made a ceremony of introducing him to the scores of military and government leaders, including the royal governor, who constantly came to pay court to the great merchant and dine at his wife's fine table.

In July 1745, John Hancock was ready to enroll in the prestigious Boston Public Latin School (later, Boston Latin School),[18] on School Street, at the bottom of Beacon Hill behind the Anglican King's Chapel. A two-story wooden building with a neat peaked roof and belfry, Boston Public Latin was the academic gateway to Harvard College and leadership in church, business, or government—and often all three. It was no place for a rebel. Thirty years earlier, ten-year-old Benjamin Franklin, bridling under the harsh discipline, dropped out of Boston Latin after only two years there.

Headed by Tory martinet John Lovell, the school put John Hancock through five years of torturous studies, stretching from seven in the morning to five in the afternoon four days a week, and from seven to noon on Saturdays. There was no school on Thursdays, Sundays, and fast days, or on Saturday afternoons. School ran the year round, with only a week's vacation at Thanksgiving and at Christmas and three weeks off in August. In the end, Hancock and other survivors of Lovell's brutal pedagogy learned to venerate the king and to read, write, and speak fluent Latin and Greek; to read and cite the Old and New Testaments in Latin and Greek; and to read and cite the works of Julius Caesar, Cicero, Virgil, Xenophon, and Homer. The boys spent the last hour of every day of those five years mending quills and perfecting their handwriting, which in Hancock's case produced his magnificent signature.[19] Headmaster Lovell punished recalcitrant students with a sharp slap across one or both hands with his ferule, a wooden stick much like a ruler. His idea of a reward was to allow students to work in his garden.[20]

Hancock had little time for play and did not win many friends, arriving at school and leaving as he did each day in his uncle's gilded coach and four, pampered by liveried servants. Quite simply, the boy's sudden access to such vast and almost indescribable wealth and privilege provoked envy among other boys at school—much as his uncle's sudden access to wealth had provoked envy among their parents. Only seven years earlier, Thomas Hancock and his wife had lived with everyone else among the crooked little dung-filled streets and alleys of Boston, dodging the buckets of slop that rained on passersby each morning. Then, suddenly, for next to nothing, he acquired the idyllic pasture on Beacon Hill, fronting Boston Common, and the masons began raising the granite shell of his palace. Hancock kept buying property until he owned the entire crest of Beacon Hill[21] and half the town below, including the massive Clark's Wharf, Boston's second-largest wharf.

"He had raised a great estate with such rapidity," wrote Gov. Thomas Hutchinson, himself one of Boston's most successful merchants when Hancock was building his fortune, "that it was commonly believed that he had purchased a valuable diamond for a small sum, and sold it at its full price."[22]

Occasionally, Uncle Thomas took his nephew to Clark's Wharf to see the great sailing ships and visit the House of Hancock, where the huge silver-and-ivory Hancock seal emblazoned the forbidding door to the great compting room. Several times, his uncle let him peer in wonder at the faceless clerks amid mountains of ledgers, journals, and letter books that held the secrets of the House of Hancock. One day, his uncle assured him, those secrets—and the vast wealth of the House of Hancock—would all be his.

2

The Merchant King

(1724-1750)

ALMOST EVERYONE in Boston in the 1720s had come for one thing: money. Unlike their Puritan forebears, Bostonians no longer faced English religious or political persecution. Congregational and Anglican churches stood peacefully side by side, and political control had passed from the hands of a theocracy to a plutocracy of wealthy merchants. Only freemen—property owners—could vote, which limited voting to a few hundred white men, who voted themselves into the bicameral legislature, known as the General Court. Women, children, slaves, and most servants were chattel, with no rights. The equivalent of a middle class—small shop-keepers and craftsmen—usually rented their stores and living quarters and did not qualify as property owners or voters. Although the merchants shared power with a royally appointed governor, the powerful London Board of Trade invariably convinced the king that it was in everyone's best interest to appoint a Boston merchant to that post to ensure the growth of trade.

Boston's merchant plutocracy turned their city into a mercan-tile utopia. It was by far the busiest, most important, and best-developed port in the colonies, with a well-protected harbor that lay less than six weeks away, on the shortest transatlantic trade route, from England. More than five hundred ships sailed out of the harbor each year, carrying America's resources to European lands that had long earlier depleted their own. From the New World sailed cured fish from America's bottomless seas, bales of pelts and furs from vast herds of animals, stacks of lumber from virgin forests that stretched to the horizon, ores from lodes that snaked their way endlessly through the rich earth, and vital illuminating and lubricating oil from the enormous pods of whales that thronged the coastal waters. In exchange, ships brought back spices from the Orient, tea, silks, satins, velvet, damasks, silver, china, crystal, handcrafted English and French furniture and paneling, works of art, and other luxuries that America's increasingly wealthy merchants and government officials sought for the stately homes they built to replicate English and European aristocratic life.

Unlike Britain, where class barriers frustrated the ambitions of those seeking wealth, the colonies offered access to wealth to almost any talented hardworking man, regardless of class origins—provided, of course, he fit easily into the community racial and religious makeup. Thomas Hancock had only just finished a seven-year apprenticeship when he founded the House of Hancock, on July 1, 1724.[1] His father, Bishop John Hancock, did not have the money to send both his boys to Harvard, so he lavished his available resources on his oldest son's ministerial training and indentured the second boy to a bookseller. It was a good choice in a colony that, from its beginnings, made education and the teaching of literacy compulsory and created a population that depended on reading as its major leisure activity. Besides the scriptures, booksellers carried tracts and sermons of virtually every minister of note—all sold in clumsy, uncut, unbound sheets. Recognizing the need for bookbinding facilities in Boston's growing publishing industry, Thomas Hancock became a master bookbinder, and when his apprenticeship ended, he solicited bookbinding orders from Boston's many booksellers, who were elated to turn the jumble of unprinted sheets into rows of easy-to-find bound books. Hancock accepted payment in stocks of stationery and printed materials as well as cash, and by the end of six months he had accumulated enough of all three to open his own shop, the Stationer's Arms, on Ann Street. Sixty days later he had so many bookbinding orders he had to subcontract surplus orders to another bookbinder. Meanwhile he advertised heavily and built book sales so high that he had to subcontract sales of three thousand books to another dealer on a 6 percent commission.

Only one constraint slowed his breathtaking race to riches—the lack of cash. There simply wasn't much of it in Massachusetts, and of course, there were no banks. The monetary system had broken down, replaced largely by barter. Some men traded their labor or handiwork for food, lodging, and other necessities; others hunted, fished, and farmed to survive. Merchants routinely accepted produce, livestock, pelts, and other goods as currency. Hancock was no exception, accepting a wide range of items (and sometimes labor) in payment for stationery or books. As he accumulated nonstationery items, his stationery store evolved into a general store.

By 1727, after only three years, Hancock's purchases of books and materials totaled £5,000 a year, at a time when the most skilled craftsman earned about £100 a year. His stock had expanded to include "Bibles large and small, Testaments, Psalters, Psalm Books with tunes or without, Singing-books, School-books . . . Books in Divinity, Philosophy, History, Navigation, Physics, Mathematics, Poetry." In addition, he sold a full line of stationery and supplies: "Writing Paper, Books for Accounts or Records, Ink, Quills, Sealing-wax, . . . Inkhorns, Spectacles, Letter-cases, with other Stationery wares."[2]

The following year he exhausted his credit, but he had become a master at solving money problems. He approached a larger bookseller, Daniel Henchman, then "the most eminent and enterprising bookseller . . . in Boston, or indeed in British North America."[3] Henchman was one of Boston's most socially and politically prominent merchants—a church deacon, lieutenant colonel in the militia, justice of the peace, and generous donor to the poor. He had immaculate credit, and young Hancock convinced Henchman they could reduce purchase costs by combining orders and obtaining volume discounts. The scheme proved so successful that the two not only bought together, they undertook a series of joint ventures, including publishing and paper manufacturing. Their ventures led to a warm friendship that Hancock quickly extended to include Henchman's fourteen-year-old daughter, Lydia. In 1730, two years after he and Henchman had first met, the twenty-seven-year-old merchant married sixteen-year-old Lydia Henchman, and Thomas Hancock took his place among Boston's leading merchant families.

By 1736 Hancock's was Boston's most prosperous general store, offering a wide variety of cloth (calico, chintz, muslin, cotton, buckram, taffetas, damasks, and silks), along with thread, fans, girdles, "and sundry other sorts of Haberdashery," according to an advertisement in the *Boston News-Letter*. The ad also listed "silk Shoes, Mens and Womens Hose," millinery, compasses, hourglasses, leather, cutlery, and such staples as sugar, tea, and corn[4] — in addition to books and stationery supplies. He was a brilliant merchant. He was the first to organize his store into departments and offer volume discounts. He advertised heavily and stocked his shelves according to seasonal needs, selling off one season's goods before the new season began, to avoid accumulating shopworn inventories. He harbored an innate sense of what would and would not sell from one season to the next. His advertisements were clever for his era:

Excellent good Bohea Tea, imported in the last ship from London: sold by Tho. Hancock

N.B. If it don't suit the ladies' taste, they may return the tea and receive their money again.[5]

His dress department was his largest, with cloth, ribbons, knee and shoe buckles, hats, fans, and other items. The hardware department offered brass compasses, fire steels, larding pins, swords, and other items that provided about 10 percent of total sales. Rum and similar provisions contributed a similar percentage of sales, while tea accounted for about 1 percent and coal and ships' stores another 1 percent. Stationery and books provided a mere six-tenths of 1 percent of sales in his expanded general store. Few shoppers could not buy what they needed at Hancock's. Everyone in Boston and flocks of country people filled his store each day. As annual sales soared to £10,000, Hancock was able to buy in larger quantities at lower costs and expand into wholesaling. He added a warehouse that supplied other merchants—and even the government.

The leap from retailing into wholesaling was vital to the growth of every merchant, because it permitted so-called commodity barter—the exchange of large quantities of commodities with merchants in other colonies without any need for cash. None of the colonies accepted the others' cash. In effect, each colony was an independent nation, and none trusted the value of the others' paper money. Rhode Island money, for example, was worthless in Massachusetts, and vice versa, and merchants from the two colonies paid either with gold or silver coins or with commodities. A Rhode Island merchant wrote Hancock, "As my son John Jenks is now bound to Boston in order to buy two hundred small arms for our force and two hundred blankets for them & our currency will not pass at Boston I prepare to pay for the above articles in molasses."[6] Samuel Bradley, a Connecticut merchant, sent Henchman eighty-three bushels of oats and eighteen bushels of rye as payment for two dozen Psalters, and one dozen each of "testements" and "Scotch bibels small common sort."[7]

When the values of commodities exchanged in a trade were unequal, one merchant simply gave the other "change" in the form of nonperishable staples, such as gunpowder, molasses, corn, or most commonly, salted fish. Thomas Hancock bought a shipment of corn, tea, sugar, rum, and *fish* in exchange for salt, paper, wood, whale oil, skins, ducks—and also *fish*. The curious trading of fish for fish represented "commodity money," to replace cash as change in the transactions.

In addition to his marketing skills, Hancock had an uncanny mastery of bartering techniques, which he raised to an art form with scrupulous bookkeeping. While other merchants kept much of their business in their heads or on scraps of paper, Hancock noted every transaction in journals and ledgers that revealed every penny that others owed him or that he owed others. "Two prs of Breeches for yr Nepue [nephew John]" at £1.6.8 each, read one tailor's bill to Hancock, and "A pr of breeches mended for D[itt]o" at £0.2.4. Also listed was "A pr of Breeches newseated and mended for yr Sarvant" at £0.2.8, bringing the total to £2.18.4. On the debit side of the ledger were the tailor's purchases, for £2.17.8½, of tea, a quire of paper, and "1 doze women's glazed Lamb Gloves" at Hancock's store.[8] As obvious as it may seem today, bookkeeping barter was a new concept in Boston. Although friendly handshakes sealed most business transactions, bookkeeping barter prevented bad memory, misplaced bills, and other human frailties from eroding merchant profits, and it proved a key to Hancock's dazzlingly rapid success.

Each advance Hancock made into the realm of merchant trading opened opportunities for further advances. He expanded from retailing to wholesaling to intercolonial commodity barter, and once established as a major intercolonial commodity trader, he moved into a still more profitable area: international triangular barter, involving huge, complex, three-way trades. Triangular barter automatically carried him into investment banking because trades often involved letters of credit. In triangular barter, Hancock accepted goods or a letter of credit from one firm, which he then used to purchase more goods (or more letters of credit) from a second firm. Often triangular barter expanded into four-way or five-way deals that were far too complex without efficient record keeping. In one deal, Hancock sent New England salted fish to the French West Indies, where his agent traded it for low-cost molasses to send to Holland for distillation into cheap rum that he bought and shipped back to New England. Careless bookkeeping could easily scuttle such deals, but Hancock's ledgers show gross profits of almost 100 percent on each leg of every voyage. Triangular trade was big business that bankrupted some merchants and made fortunes for others. Only ten years after finishing his apprenticeship, Thomas Hancock found himself among the latter.[9]

As an investment banker, Hancock took advantage of every major profit opportunity, including the huge, rough-and-tumble London market for whale oil and whalebone. The oil was used for both illumination and lubrication, and the long, dark days of winter all but depleted London's supplies. The bone (or fins) was resilient cartilaginous strips for making corset stays, cap stiffeners, buggy whips, and similar items. The first boats to England with spring supplies made the most money, and Hancock found a way to be first. While other merchants waited for whalers to bring their catch to Boston for transport to London, Hancock sent his ships to isolated whaling settlements along the shores of northern New England and Newfoundland, near the hunting grounds and closer to England. There he traded much-needed clothing, tools, foodstuffs, and rum for oil and bone, which he carried off to London before other whalers had off-loaded their catch in Boston.

Once in London with their cargo, sailors on his ships—who earned a percentage of the proceeds for each load—drove bidding to a fever pitch by spreading rumors that theirs might be the last oil cargo to reach port for months. Hancock's first ship sailed from Boston in 1729, only five years after he had started his little stationery store. The ship carried rum, beef, cotton, hemp, and other commodities to whaling towns in New England and Newfoundland, picked up whale oil and bone along the way, and when it was full, sailed to London, where his agent awaited with eager customers. Hancock paid his agent 3 percent of the proceeds, gave 8 percent to his captain and crew, and kept the rest—89 percent—either to pocket or to buy goods to bring back to Boston, to make more money.

Thomas Hancock's oil ventures made him rich beyond his wildest dreams. Within five years he had commissioned five ships to handle his trade, ordering five thousand or more gallons of rum at a time from New England distillers to fill the demand along coastal fishing ports. In turn, he picked up enough cargoes of whale oil and bone for England—along with a dozen or more paying passengers on each trip—to produce a mountain of sterling. As his trade expanded, he discovered foreign markets for other products, such as sealskins and dried fish—the latter especially valuable after poor fish catches in Europe.

He expanded his trade routes and sent ships to Amsterdam, Bilbao, Lisbon, Malaga, Madeira, and other European ports. By 1732 he had agents in virtually every major western European port. He had the good sense to pick as his London agent the son-in-law of one of London's major merchant bankers, which consequently extended him almost unlimited credit. To cut shipping costs and reduce dependence on the sailing schedules and trade routes of vessels owned by other merchants, he bought his own ships, which he sold at will whenever profits from such sales exceeded the potential profits from available cargoes for return voyages. Hancock owned shares in well over a dozen ships between 1732 and 1738 but kept none of them for more than a year or two. In 1737, when a poor whaling season sent oil costs soaring from less than £10 a ton to £48, he simply dropped out of the oil trade, sold his ships, and invested the money in land and income-producing properties. He bought twenty thousand acres of timberland in Connecticut, Massachusetts, and Maine (then part of Massachusetts). In Boston he bought a number of rental properties and a three-eighths share in Clark's Wharf, the city's longest and busiest finger pier after Long Wharf. It lay in the North End, extending into the harbor from Fish Street and the silver shop where Paul Revere sold silver and copper engravings, carved picture frames, music sheets, surgical instruments, dental plates, and his own crude drawings. Although only half the length of Long Wharf, Clark's Wharf—Boston soon called it Hancock Wharf—dwarfed the wharves of the Belchers, Hutchinsons, Olivers, and other great merchant families.

Among his other investments in 1737, Thomas Hancock bought two acres on the crest of Beacon Hill to build a palace for himself and his wife, Lydia. Two years later they began a life of splendor never before seen in New England. Lydia Hancock became Boston's most celebrated hostess. A large woman, almost

Lydia Henchman Hancock (1714–76), wife of merchant
Thomas Hancock, doting aunt and surrogate mother of
young John Hancock. Aunt Lydia raised the patriot as her
son from age seven and served as his official hostess in
Hancock House for more than twenty years. From a minia-
ture portrait by John Singleton Copley. (*National Portrait
Gallery, Smithsonian Institution*)

obese, with a face that exuded nothing close to beauty, Lydia was
nevertheless handsomely pleasant—and her exquisite taste enriched
every aspect of her own and her husband's lives: clothes, home
decor, table settings, food. She entertained brilliantly, and her
home became the essential gathering place for Boston's social elite.
Hancock adored fine wines and collected a wine cellar that drew
gasps of envy from even the wealthiest French noblemen. Every
member of Boston's aristocracy—including the royal governor—

salivated in anticipation of a treasured invitation to one of Lydia Hancock's lavish dinner parties on Beacon Hill.

With wealth came power, of course, and in 1740, a year after moving into his home atop Boston, Thomas Hancock joined four of the town's great merchants—Thomas Hutchinson, Andrew Oliver, Thomas Cushing, and the brewer Samuel Adams—as one of five selectmen who, with the provincial governor, ruled Boston. Almost always Harvard graduates from the highest ranks of the city's merchant plutocracy, the selectmen were both legislators and executives, with control over city finances and commerce and, indirectly, the rest of the colony. They held the financial destiny of virtually every business in their hands. As with elections to the General Court (the provincial legislature), voting was limited to Boston's six-hundred-odd freemen—the white propertied males who made up about 4 percent of the population and who depended on the most powerful merchants for their economic survival. It was in every merchant's best interests to retain them in power. Thomas Hutchinson was a direct descendant of Anne Hutchinson, the early-seventeenth-century American religious leader.[10] He graduated from Harvard in 1727 before entering his father's huge mercantile house—the largest in Boston before Thomas Hancock came along. His brother-in-law Andrew Oliver graduated from Harvard three years earlier and was also heir to a great mercantile establishment. The provincial governor, Jonathan Belcher, was also a graduate of Harvard, class of 1699, and he, too, was the son of a prosperous merchant. Besides power, a selectman's post gave each first claim to the most lucrative government contracts—made all the richer by the nonchalance with which the provincial governor parceled them out without competitive bids or price negotiations. With his election as selectman, Thomas Hancock began amassing a fortune in government contracts.

WAR—or preparations for war—had been a virtual constant somewhere in the American colonial world since 1613—in New England, Canada, the Ohio country or along the Mississippi, in the Floridas or the West Indies, and along the South American coasts.

It had largely been a three-way affair between England, France, and Spain—with Indian tribes joining one side or the other, depending on which seemed strongest and which seemed likeliest to serve Indian interests. Occasionally the three combatants declared a truce, but because of the wealth of the colonies, each leaped at the slightest provocation to resume hostilities and gain an advantage over the other two. The Hancocks had lived on Beacon Hill only a few months when British king George II declared war on Spain after British merchant captain Robert Jenkins claimed the Spanish had seized his ship eight years earlier and cut off his ear—and he displayed what looked like an ear to a committee of Parliament.[11] In fact, the British had been raiding Spain's forests in Central America and Florida for a decade; Jenkins's ear provided an excuse for England to seize the territories. In January 1740, James Edward Oglethorpe, founder of Georgia, invaded Florida. In Boston, Gov. Jonathan Belcher organized an expedition to raid Spanish cities in the Caribbean. A thousand eager New Englanders—a huge force for a city of only fifteen thousand—signed up, and Belcher, who had built a fortune as a merchant before securing the governorship in 1730, turned to his new friend Selectman Thomas Hancock to supply the troops with beef, pork, clothing, tents, and other basics. As the troops trained on the Common, Hancock watched from his balcony on Beacon Hill and glowed with "the pleasure of Seeing 'em Disciplined every Day from 5 in the morning till night[.] Before our house many Gentlemen & others Daily fill the Common[.] Wee have not the Less Company for it (but a quicker draft for Wine & Cyder)."[12]

Hancock found other ways to profit from the conflict, by buying shares in two privateers—privately owned ships with government licenses, or letters of marque, to seize and plunder enemy merchant vessels on the high seas. Such letters of marque distinguished privateers from pirate vessels in that they complemented their nation's navies by attacking enemy cargo ships. As compensation, privateers kept the goods and ships they seized and sold them on the open market. Col. Josiah Quincy and his brother

Edmund moved into Boston from Braintree and built a privateer that returned with a Spanish vessel containing a lifetime of riches—161 chests of silver, two of gold and other valuables.[13]

Hancock bought shares in two privateers, one of them a 105-ton two-master with four four-pound cannons. Before they sailed, Hancock sent orders to the captain and crew to

> lett those whom you may conquer . . . know that you are blest with the most noble Virtue, Courage tempered with mercy . . . as the cause your going on must be accounted by the Laws of God & Man Just & honorable, so you are in the way of your Duty to your King & Country, & therefore may put up your Petitions . . . that it may please the Almighty to give you Victory over our Enemies, and that you may return again in Safety is not only the hearty Wishes but sincere Prayers of
>
> Your Friends & Owners[14]

As England spilled its treasure into the ocean conflict over Jenkins's ear, much of it—£55,000—washed ashore onto Hancock Wharf, where British expeditions bought supplies. In March 1744, the French joined Spain and enlarged the conflict into the more global War of the Austrian Succession, or King George's War, as it was known in America. As the war expanded, so did Hancock's profits. A new royal governor in Massachusetts, William Shirley, believed that Boston's safety depended on capturing the French fortress at Louisbourg, on Cape Breton Island. He organized the largest military expedition ever undertaken in the colonies—a fleet of about a hundred vessels to carry a force of four thousand New England militiamen and their British commanders. On the recommendation of his predecessor, he appointed Hancock to round up the ships and supply the entire expeditionary force with food, clothing, arms, ammunition, and all other materials for as long as the force remained in Canada. Louisbourg earned Hancock almost £100,000 and made him Boston's—and possibly America's—richest man, a mere twenty-one years after finishing his apprenticeship as a bookseller.

He was now past forty, however, and he and his wife lamented their failure to produce an heir. With the death of his brother in May 1744, they decided to adopt the oldest of the three orphaned children, and so, in July, seven-year-old John Hancock arrived on Beacon Hill and began his transformation from a country lad to a young aristocrat. At first he saw little of his uncle, who spent almost every waking hour organizing the enormous Louisbourg expedition. It was not until March 1745 that the expedition finally sailed from Boston Harbor; and in July, when news arrived of its victory, Boston erupted in celebration: church bells rang, bonfires blazed into the night sky, and joyful Bostonians sang and danced on the Common, as Hancock, his wife, and their eight-year-old nephew cheered from their balcony on Beacon Hill. The victory and subsequent occupation of Louisbourg would mean years of profits for Hancock from supplying the British military establishment.

With his wealth and political and social prominence came social responsibility, and Hancock undertook at his own expense the care and maintenance of the entire Boston Common—the forty-five-acre park that stretched from his front door, down Beacon Hill, to the heart of the city. He had the Frog Pond cleaned regularly to prevent stagnation, planted a grove of elm trees to shade the park, and continually saw to the upkeep of all the public areas. He also made generous gifts to the church. He added several acres of Beacon Hill property to his own, and as his coach became a daily presence outside the governor's mansion, he decided his social position required an appropriate emblem. Accordingly, he ordered his London agent "to look into the Herald Office & take out My Arms. Let it be well Cutt Crest & Arms in Silver & fixt to Ivory for use of a Compting Room."[15] He also ordered a new coach for himself and the family and a smaller chaise for short rides for Lydia when he was using the larger vehicle.

"Let it be a new, neat, and very good one," he wrote to his agent in London, "a neat, roomy, genteel Chariot . . . with a pack carriage, the Doors to have double slides for Glass and Canvas Sashes; the lining of a good light cloth or scarlet, which[ever] is most Fashionable; one neat Seat, Cloth with a handsome fringe; one ditto, plain for common use and bad weather, one pair Harness . . . of the best leather and strong; one pair of spare worsted reins; two or three whips; four dozen harness bells fixed on wires to put on in winter. . . . Since it will last for Life, let everything be of the best and Fashionable." Then, to temper what might be perceived as garishness, Hancock added, "I hope you won't think it savours too much of Vanity in all this, as its all for the Benefitt of Mrs. Hancock's health." As an afterthought, he asked whether his London agent might not send over "a good coachman, sober and honest and one that understands a kitchen garden, to keep from being idle . . . not an overgrown fatt fellow, nor an old one . . . not younger than twenty-six or twenty-eight nor older than thirty to thirty-six."[16]

The carriage—but not the coachman—arrived in the spring of 1750, in time for young John Hancock's graduation from Boston Public Latin. Tory headmaster Lovell would remain at his post for nearly twenty-five years afterward—until the day in April 1775 when he watched British troops march by on their way to Lexington and Concord. He turned to his students and abruptly dismissed the class, saying only, "War's begun and school's done. *Deponite libros*."[17] A year later, when the last British troops evacuated Boston and sailed for England, Lovell sailed with them, having educated more than two thousand boys from Boston's elite families.[18] To his deep distress, many of them were leading the rebellion against his beloved England, and three months after his departure, they would help found a new and independent nation.

3

The Merchant Prince

(1750-1764)

JOHN HANCOCK easily passed his Harvard entrance examinations in the summer of 1750. The Bishop, his grandfather, still believed his grandson would prepare for the ministry. His uncle had different ideas and had never hidden them from his nephew, who as a result never displayed the studious approach to academics that preparation for the ministry required. He was, in fact, far from the best student in his class at Boston Latin, but Headmaster Lovell's standards were so high that even the poorest students ranked among the academic elite of those who applied to Harvard; and so, in the autumn of 1750, John Hancock enrolled as a freshman at the age of thirteen and a half. He was the second youngest in his class of twenty but ranked fifth under the gradation system, based on his uncle's wealth, political power, and social standing in Boston, and John's own heritage as the son and grandson of Harvard alumni.[1] The prospect of a generous legacy to the college from Thomas Hancock certainly did not hurt John's ranking, which gave him the appropriate preference in seating in church, the classroom, and the refectory.

With no bridges across the river from Boston to Cambridge, the ride to Harvard was too long and circuitous to travel each day.

Because of his age, however, John's aunt and uncle decided he should lodge off campus at the home of a Congregational minister in Cambridge who earned extra income by boarding several freshmen. Like Hancock, they were usually younger boys whose parents wanted to spare them the cruel hazing that upperclassmen inflicted on freshmen. Freshmen served as "slaves" to older students, polishing their shoes, keeping their fireplaces supplied with wood, cleaning their rooms, fetching food and drink, running errands, and performing other menial chores. Although more than two years older than Hancock, Benjamin Church, who was preparing to be a physician, also boarded at the minister's home, within sight of Harvard.

Harvard was America's oldest and most prestigious college. It was founded in 1636, only sixteen years after the landing at Plymouth, and evolved into one of the most remarkable institutions in American colonial history—and indeed, in the history of Western civilization, given that church and crown had perpetuated illiteracy as a weapon to enslave their peoples. "After God had carried us safe to New England," wrote two early Puritan historians, "and we had builded our houses, provided necessaries for our livelihood, reared convenient places for God's worship, and settled the civil government: one of the next things we longed for, and looked after was to advance learning and perpetuate it to posterity."[2] That the founding of a college should have been so high a priority for a group of settlers facing the exigencies of life in the wilderness reflected the high level of education among colonial leaders. At least a hundred had studied at England's Cambridge University, and thirty-two at Oxford. Of these, almost all were part-time farmers by necessity, but three also practiced medicine, fifteen taught, twenty-seven were public officials, and ninety-eight served in the ministry, which involved instructing the young and training would-be ministers. Not unlike Oxford or Cambridge, Harvard housed as many as fifty students in a collegial atmosphere presided over by the president, a professor, and four tutors, all served by a steward, cook, butler, and several other servants. The average age of students varied from fifteen to eighteen and included boys from other colonies as well as new arrivals from England.

When John Hancock enrolled, Pres. Edward Holyoke, a liberal Congregational minister, had turned Harvard into one of the most forward-looking institutions in the world. A firm believer in toleration and the separation of church and state, Holyoke replaced obsolete texts with works by Watts, Newton, Locke, and many controversial tomes that had emerged during the Age of Enlightenment. He modernized scientific instruction and added a host of new courses, including oratory—a course of public debates, dialogues, and orations by the two upper classes on the most controversial issues of the day. Harvard—and the atmosphere of discussion and debate that Holyoke introduced—produced every leader of the American Revolution in Massachusetts. In 1743 Samuel Adams, a brewer's son and future leader of the Revolution against England, argued the legality, under certain circumstances, of resisting the king. Four years later Thomas Cushing, a merchant's son who would later join Samuel Adams, argued that "Civil Government Originate[s] from Compact." Other debaters included John Adams, Elbridge Gerry, James Otis, Robert Treat Paine, James Warren, John Warren, and of course, John Hancock, and the topics they debated included the right of "Faithful Subjects" to evade "Prohibitary Duties."[3]

The Reverend Holyoke liberalized life at Harvard as well as thought, by reducing the length of the school year. Students at Yale, which remained tied to Puritan orthodoxy, went to school the entire year, with meager two-week "vacancies" at the end of each quarter. Harvard gave students a six-week vacation in summer and a five-week vacation in winter, with a four-day break during each month of the school year.

In August 1750 the Hancocks—young John, his aunt, and uncle—pulled up in their splendid carriage to the Massachusetts Avenue gateway of Harvard College for commencement exercises. At the time, commencement did indeed mark the festive beginning of the school year rather than its end. Although the president awarded degrees to graduates and delivered a farewell valedictory, the primary purpose of commencement was to welcome incoming

Harvard College. Engraving of the college buildings in the eighteenth century, when John Hancock and other Massachusetts patriots were in attendance. Hancock lived in Massachusetts Hall, on the right. Founded in 1636, Harvard was America's first college. Its original buildings burned and were replaced by Harvard Hall, on the left, in 1675; Stoughton Hall, center, in 1699; and Massachusetts Hall, in 1720. (*Library of Congress*)

freshmen and returning students with a salutatory address. Commencement transformed the Cambridge green into a country fair. Shops closed everywhere in the Boston area. Farmers from miles around crowded with Boston sophisticates at colorfully decorated booths to buy food, candy, cakes, wine, rum, ale, toys, and tickets for games of chance. Acrobats tumbled, jugglers juggled, and fairgoers danced and sang until the church bells tolled to signal the start of the solemn academic procession to the meetinghouse.

The scholars led the procession, walking two by two in their academic robes. Bachelor of arts candidates led the way; master of arts recipients[4] came behind. President Holyoke followed, in his velvet-and-silk ceremonial robe and ermine collar, the mace of office cradled in his arms. Then came members of the corporation (trustees), with tutors marching next, ahead of the governor and the Governor's Council. Last in the procession came "the rest of the gentlemen"—city and state dignitaries, including Selectman Thomas Hancock. The ceremonies included dissertations in Latin by the leading scholars, followed by an English oration. After the ceremonies, incoming students began celebrating with families and friends until "they seem to be all drunkeness and confusion."[5]

For Hancock and other undergraduates, reality set in the following morning at five-thirty, when they arose for required chapel services at six, followed by breakfast. College regulations promised "that there shall always be chocolate, tea, coffee and milk for breakfast, with bread, biscuit and butter." The college provided each student with a pewter plate, but students usually brought their own spoons, knives, and mugs. Classes began at eight with a lecture, either by the president or by the school's one professor, John Winthrop, the world-renowned astronomer and mathematician, who taught the range of sciences, along with algebra and calculus.[6] After lecture, Harvard students spent the rest of the morning studying or in recitations with their class tutor. Lunch at noon was the big meal of the day—meat or fish, vegetables, bread, and beer or cider. Students returned to their studies in the afternoon until evening prayers at five and a light supper at seven-thirty—usually hasty pudding (a rye, corn, or wheat flour porridge), along with pie, fruit, beer, cider, or metheglin (mead). After-dinner study was all but impossible during the long, dark winter months, and many upperclassmen spent evenings drinking—an option not open to Hancock at the minister's off-campus home. Living off campus, however, had at least one advantage: Hancock escaped much of the humiliation heaped on freshmen by upperclassmen—although he still had to doff his hat to seniors in town, and like other freshmen he was forbidden to wear a hat on campus "except it rains, snows, or hails, or he be on horseback or hath both hands full."[7]

Despite Holyoke's curricular reforms, he did not dare alienate the Calvinist community, which provided half the funds Harvard needed to sustain itself, and he retained studies of the scriptures as a basic element of the curriculum, with Saturdays devoted entirely to the study of theology. Hancock's freshman curriculum consisted of Greek, Latin, logic, rhetoric, physics, Bible studies, theology, mathematics, and geometry. Believing—indeed, knowing—that its graduates would lead the nation, Harvard placed particular emphasis on rhetoric, "the art of speaking and writing with elegance."[8] Sophomores added "natural philosophy" (science) to their course load, while juniors added moral philosophy, metaphysics, geography, and oratory. Seniors expanded their studies to include geometry and higher mathematics, and they engaged in formal debating. Harvard classes were still led by tutors, each of whom instructed his class for the entire four years, in all courses.[9]

At the beginning of his sophomore year, Hancock moved into Massachusetts Hall in Harvard Yard and wasted little time taking advantage of the first moments of independence he had ever experienced: he got drunk. Harvard expected students to lead "sober, righteous & Godly lives." The rules banned drinking in student quarters, along with "rudeness at meals," "firing guns or pistols in the college yard," "abominable lasciviousness," and the "atrocious crime . . . of fornication." Hancock not only drank regularly, he joined four other students—one of them his childhood friend Sam Quincy from Braintree—in a "drinking frolic" in which they made the slave of a former Harvard president "drunk . . . to Such a Degree as greatly indanger'd his Life." The rules gave President Holyoke and the tutors little choice but to discipline Hancock by degrading him four places—the first of three generations of Hancocks to be so disgraced.[10]

Although John Hancock escaped further degrading, he continued drinking—even after being fined at least once for missing early morning chapel. He liked drinking. It was far more exhilarating than study, and in any case, most of the other students drank—as did his uncle Thomas and his uncle's distinguished friends. Indeed, most Americans drank heavily, and his uncle's wealth was based at least in part on importing tons of molasses for making rum. Although his uncle preferred Madeira and other fine wines, the rest of New England loved rum, consuming a million and a quarter gallons a year—four gallons a year for every man, woman, and child. They could not get enough of it. Neither the

House of Hancock nor other merchants could import enough molasses to quench New England's thirst for rum.

At the beginning of his sophomore year, Hancock ran into his childhood friend from Braintree John Adams, who despite being fifteen months older, had just enrolled in Harvard as a freshman. His late arrival demonstrated the advantage of Boston Public Latin School over country schools. Indeed, Adams might never have gained entry to Harvard had his father not withdrawn him from Braintree Latin and hired a tutor to give him private instruction. After eighteen months he passed his entrance examinations, in the spring of 1751, and enrolled that August, with Hancock a year ahead. Even more humiliating for the farm boy Adams was his low social ranking—sixteenth.

Hancock graduated from Harvard in July 1754—the third in a direct line of John Hancocks to achieve that distinction, but the first not to enter the ministry. His uncle and aunt attended the boy's graduation, of course, along with his mother, older sister, and younger brother, Ebenezer. Only his grandfather the Bishop was missing. He had died in 1752 at his Lexington manse, never knowing that his grandson would not follow in his footsteps to the pulpit. Although John's life at Harvard—and prior to that on Beacon Hill—had not permitted much contact with the Bishop and his immediate family, his feelings for them had never diminished. Indeed, there are indications he often longed for them.

Harvard College, May 1st 1754

Dear Sister,

I Believe Time slips very easie with you. I wish you would spend one Hour in writing me, I do assure you I should take it as great favor. There was, nay now is, a report that you are going to be married very soon, I should be Glad to know to whom. I hope you will give me an Invitation. . . .

Accept my kind Love to you, I hope you are well, and I am,

Dear Sister,
Your Loving Brother,
Till Death shall separate us.
John Hancock [11]

Whether Mary answered him or not, she appeared at Cambridge with her mother and brother Ebenezer at John's graduation in July. Now seventeen, John had grown into a handsome, sophisticated young man, with carefully groomed brown hair and impeccably tailored clothes—an amazing contrast to the seven-year-old country boy that Thomas Hancock had carried off to Boston a decade earlier. The same holiday atmosphere prevailed in Cambridge at John Hancock's graduation—the booths sprouted on the green as they had at previous commencements, and people from the entire Boston area took the day off to watch the splendid pageantry and procession. John's class was an undistinguished lot. All received bachelor's degrees with him, but only he would rise to national prominence.

Besides his degree—and the right to be called "Sir Hancock" by all Harvard undergraduates—John Hancock received no academic honors at Harvard, but he needed none. His uncle had not sent him to Harvard for academic honors, nor had John ever pretended any deep interest in academics. Indeed, he never bothered to obtain his master's degree—then a routine award to all Harvard graduates who presented a dissertation three or more years after graduation, with no required on-campus study or presence. Like many of his classmates who entered family businesses after graduation, John Hancock was content to glean Harvard's cultural veneer and such practical business skills as higher mathematics, logic, public speaking, and debating. In effect, Harvard taught him to think quickly, logically, and decisively. Moreover, a Harvard degree commanded respect and all but guaranteed entry into the tightly knit circle of aristocratic Harvard alumni who governed New England political, economic, and social affairs. His uncle, of course, was the equal of—perhaps even superior to—every other member of Boston's aristocracy, but for one credential: a Harvard degree. Now his nephew had that degree, and between the two of them, Thomas Hancock envisioned building the House of Hancock into one of the world's great trading companies.

After John Hancock graduated from Harvard, his uncle began training him for eventual partnership. He started in the compting room, with its silver-and-ivory coat of arms on the door bearing the ironic motto *Nul Plaisir Sans Peine*. More *peine* than *plaisir* seemed to radiate from the owl-like stares of the gray-faced clerks hovering over their ledgers as John and his uncle entered. Thomas Hancock, and now John Hancock, were the only ones with access to all the books and complex transactions that revealed the secrets of how Thomas Hancock had built the House of Hancock into one of America's largest merchant banking and trading houses. Thomas Hancock had set up the books so that no one clerk could put the entire puzzle together and become a competitor.

Business had slowed just enough to give the elder Hancock time to teach his nephew every aspect of the business, which he turned into a school for the young man's benefit. "And what a school this was," John Adams recalled years later. "Four large ships constantly plying between Boston and London and other business in proportion."[12]

Thomas Hancock explained all the complex transactions of the House of Hancock to his nephew and taught him basic negotiating skills—in the store, with buyers; in the marketplace, with other merchants and traders; and along the waterfront, with shipbuilders, shipowners, captains, and ordinary seamen. Wherever Thomas Hancock went, John Hancock was at his side—a virtual appendage—listening carefully and politely, and learning. Hancock dressed his nephew in the same elegant clothes that he himself enjoyed, planned his every move, and paraded the young man through the throngs of government officials, merchants, military men, and other important Bostonians who peopled the morning markets in and about Faneuil Hall and the Town House (now the Old State House). The ground floor of the Town House was a midday gathering place for merchants to argue and trade after the markets had closed. The General Court, or colonial legislature, sat just above them.

By midafternoon Boston's business elite moved their debates to the taverns and coffeehouses, and with more than 150 of the former and untold numbers of the latter, it was important that Thomas Hancock take his nephew to the elegant Royal Exchange, near the Town House, and the Merchants Club. Day by day the young man formed the best business associations in Boston. They spent a good deal of time eating—huge quantities by today's standards. Midafternoon was dinnertime—the main meal of the day was served, with no starter but with ample wine and huge platters of meat, poultry, venison or game, turtle, and salmon or other fish. Vegetables were largely ignored, although peas were popular, and the favorite desserts were cherry, strawberry, or other fruit pies or plum cake. Dinners began with toasts to the king, the queen, the royal family, Parliament, the ministry, various noblemen and military figures, to continued good trade, and to the health of everyone present[13]—until diners staggered home for a light supper, usually around nine.

The merchant king gave generously to the city and spent considerable time teaching his heir apparent the civic responsibilities of a community leader. As a selectman, Thomas Hancock helped supervise almshouses, schools, roads, and public properties ranging from the granary to the town's cemeteries, as well as the Common that blanketed the slope of Beacon Hill, beneath the balcony of his home—his men repaired fences to prevent incursions by wandering livestock, and they constantly filled in washed-out areas to combat erosion. Although Thomas Hancock was not interested in Calvinist spiritualism, he nevertheless was an active member of the relatively liberal Brattle Square Church,[14] to which he contributed generously, and where the Hancocks had bought a family pew.

Evenings often saw Thomas Hancock and his nephew dine at the Royal Exchange or at Province House, the governor's mansion, where Thomas Hancock had to attend official functions as a selectman and, subsequently, a member of the Council, the upper house of the General Court. Lydia Hancock staged elaborate banquets designed to further her husband's mercantile interests. The Hancocks expected John to attend and allowed their nephew little or no privacy or life of his own. In that respect, however, they were no different from other proper Boston parents whose children had yet to attain their majority—then still the age of twenty-one.

By the end of his first year at the House of Hancock, John, still only eighteen, had grown into a tall, slim, and graceful—if not effeminate—young man. He had learned his first year's lessons well—social as well as practical—and was on his way to setting Boston's standards for dress as well as conduct in business. His dress was impeccable; he loved beautiful clothes as much as his uncle did, and with the latter's guidance, he ordered from London a huge wardrobe of frilled shirts, silver-buckled shoes, and a variety of gilt-edged jackets and breeches that would number in the hundreds as he reached his maturity. He ordered one jacket of scarlet velvet that sent Boston aristocracy scrambling to find similar cloth.

If he was somewhat of a social dandy, he grew into an indefatigable worker at business; when he was not in the shadow of his uncle in the market or at social functions, he labored long and hard to master the lessons in his uncle's ledgers and letter books. John Adams recalled that John Hancock "became an example to all the young men of the town. Wholly devoted to business, he was as regular and punctual at his store as the sun in his course."

Before the end of John Hancock's first year at his uncle's business, England and France had resumed their hostilities in what had now become a second Hundred Years War.[15] A westward migration by settlers from Pennsylvania and Virginia into the Ohio territory had provoked the French into fortifying the area to reaffirm their sovereignty. Twenty-one-year-old George Washington planted the seeds of the war in February 1754, while John Hancock was in his last year at Harvard. Then a lieutenant colonel in the Virginia militia, Washington led a small force into the Ohio territory to protect Virginia's claims at the Forks of the Ohio (now Pittsburgh), where the Allegheny and Monongahela Rivers meet. After winning an initial skirmish with a French reconnaissance party, he retreated before a larger French force, and by the end of the year the British and French were at it once again, with the British intent on dislodging their enemy from North America once and for all.

Uncanny in his ability to sense political and economic change, Thomas Hancock had added six hundred half barrels of pistol powder to his December 1753 merchandise order from London—two months before the George Washington incident. Then he gave orders to sell all his ships to avoid risks of seizure by the French navy if war broke out. Within days a secret message arrived from Governor Lawrence of Nova Scotia with plans for a surprise attack on the French stronghold at Fort Beauséjour, on the isthmus connecting Nova Scotia with Acadia (now New Brunswick). Lawrence offered Hancock a monopoly for military supplies in exchange for unlimited credit. Hancock agreed and sent an urgent order to his London agent and merchant bank for £20,000 of credit for arms, powder, blankets, and other materials—and a man-of-war to deliver the order. He explained only that he was rendering "certain services not yet Publick." He ordered huge quantities of clothing, stockings, shoes, and foodstuffs from New England suppliers and a load of wheat from Philadelphia, then rounded up wagons for transport and chartered ships. It was the second time in a decade Hancock had provisioned a large expeditionary force, and he was quite adept. By summer 1754, his warehouse overflowed with military supplies, and his nephew John, who had just graduated from Harvard, worked as he never had before, attempting to keep track of the huge inventories and register them in appropriate account books.

One of John's key clerical tasks in the compting room was to copy his uncle's hastily scribbled letters in careful handwriting—once as a duplicate for Hancock's own records, and often six or more times to send on different ships, to ensure that at least one survived the storms at sea or seizure by privateers and reached its destination. John copied the most confidential letters in the magnificent handwriting he had learned at Boston Public Latin and at Harvard. The letters themselves provided training in the conduct of business and politics.

By early June 1755 the Hancocks had assembled thirty-one ships in Boston Harbor, and two regiments of New Englanders—about two thousand men—set sail for Canada. On June 19 the expedition overwhelmed Fort Beauséjour in a surprise attack that left the entire French garrison dead or captured. By the end of the month the British had captured the entire Bay of Fundy and the lands along its shores, including settlements with about six thousand French-speaking Catholic Acadians, whom Governor Lawrence adjudged potential rebels. Lawrence ordered them to swear allegiance to the English crown or be expelled and scattered throughout the British colonies far from Acadia. He employed eighteen of Hancock's chartered ships, and his troops forced three thousand men, women, and children to board at bayonet point and watch as other troops burned their homes and villages. The dispersal went on for months, with the House of Hancock sending bills for "digging graves" and the "burying of 2 French children."[16] In a letter that John transcribed, Thomas Hancock expressed satisfaction to his British agent that Nova Scotia was "pretty clear of those vermin. . . . For God's sake, then let us Root the French Blood out of America." As quartermaster general, in effect, for two enormously successful British military enterprises, Thomas Hancock had become an outspoken British imperialist.

In February 1757 the British government appointed Cambridge-educated Thomas Pownall, a former deputy governor of New Jersey, as governor of Massachusetts. He immediately conferred with Boston's business leaders—Thomas Hancock foremost among them—to develop a plan for pursuing the war more vigorously. A champion of a more aggressive policy toward the French and the Indians, Hancock offered Pownall his full political and logistical support. Expulsion of the French from America, Hancock had long enthused, "will be the salvation of England[,] for in 40 years this very America will absolutely take of all the manufactury of England, a Noble Return for their assistance[,] a Good Interest 40 per Cent for their Outsett at Least . . . whoever keeps America will in the End (whether French or English) have the Kingdom of England."[17] He had good reason to be enthusiastic: he was already earning more than £30,000 a year from the war, and the new governor now asked him to help raise and supply an additional militia of seven thousand men.

Hancock's zeal for punishing Acadians seemed to wane, however—especially after seeing a pitiful group that was captured in

Boston trying to make their way home from the Carolinas. While they languished in prison awaiting transport back to exile in North Carolina, the Governor's Council, or upper house of the legislature, asked Hancock to provide them with food. During that time Hancock experienced a change of heart and asked the Council to be "compassionate [about] their unhappy circumstances" and free them. The Council complied.

By 1758 Hancock had become the primary financier and procurement officer in America for the British military, and the defense ministry at Whitehall in London appointed him His Majesty's agent for transports, thus putting an official cachet on the unofficial role he had played for a decade. The appointment extended Hancock's authority beyond procurement to include payment of enlistment bounties to seamen, provisioning the fleet, chartering cargo ships for the military, and handling payrolls. Generals and civilian governors were to turn to the House of Hancock for all supplies and payrolls. For his efforts, Thomas Hancock would end up with a 5 percent commission for his services during the French and Indian War from 1754 to 1760—and an appointment in 1758 to the Governor's Council, which handled most of the colony's finances. The huge burden of work forced him to turn over more responsibilities to his nephew John, who had worked for the firm for five years by then and whose own name now appeared on orders with increasing regularity.

By 1759 the English were well on their way to victory. In July they captured Fort Niagara, while another force moved up Lake Champlain toward the St. Lawrence. The fatal strike came on September 13, when Gen. James Wolfe captured the Plains of Abraham surrounding Quebec. The House of Hancock supplied draught oxen and recruited teamsters for Wolfe's artillery. After a pitched battle—which claimed Wolfe's life as well as that of French commander Louis-Joseph, marquis de Montcalm—the city of Quebec surrendered on September 18. In midwinter the French surrendered Canada to the British and ended the French and Indian War.

The war's end sent Massachusetts trade with England plunging, along with revenues. House of Hancock revenues dropped

50 percent. A spring drought only added to New England's economic woes by forcing farmers and consumers to cut spending to a minimum. For the first time in Thomas Hancock's career, the always ebullient, aggressive merchant seemed tired. The frenetic pace he had set during the war years had taken its toll on his health and depleted his energy. Severe gout had produced painful swelling in his wrists and ankles, and at fifty-seven what he described as a "nervous disorder" left him with little energy to reorganize his business for peacetime trade. With an immense personal fortune at his command, he decided the time had come to begin turning the business over to John and plan his own retirement.

First he would send his nephew to spend a year in London to meet and establish close ties with House of Hancock agents and to collect outstanding debts and pay overdue bills. Thomas Hancock believed the experience would teach his nephew negotiating skills. Moreover, both Thomas and Lydia Hancock wanted John to add some cultural polish to his formal education by taking the grand tour of Europe that was so fashionable among the young men of America's distinguished families. Thomas Hancock had already prepared the way for his nephew's visit with a letter to his primary agent in London: "I have given my Nephew Mr. John Hancock, who has been with me many years in Business, an Oppor'y of Going to London, to see my Friends & Settle my Acc'ts . . . & I am to desire you to be so kind as to provide him with good Lodgings where you think will be most convenient for him with Reputable People."[18] At the same time, he gave John personal letters of introduction to all other House of Hancock business connections in London, describing his nephew as "a sober, modest young Gentleman" whose "Industry[,] Go[o]d behaviour[,] and ability has Recommended him to me in such Manner that on his return from England I propose to Take him a Partner with me in my Business."[19]

Aunt Lydia was heartbroken at losing her beloved Johnny, and even Uncle Thomas had qualms about his nephew's risking a voyage through swarms of privateers and enemy naval vessels. He sent him on a ship with Thomas Pownall, who had resigned as Massachusetts governor and was returning home to England. Hancock gave Pownall instructions for negotiating a ransom with any captors who might seize the ship, and he sent a letter to his London agent ordering him to provide ransom for John's release if he were captured by the French.

The two branches of the legislature gathered at the waterfront with the Hancock family on June 3, 1760, to bid the popular governor and his young charge good-bye. Thomas Hancock and a few sturdy legislators joined Pownall and John Hancock on the "gaily decorated barge, whose oarsmen carried them out to Nantasket Roads to the province ship *King George,* where they spent the late afternoon feasting and toasting. Toward dusk, as the tide turned, the entourage transferred to the merchantman *Benjamin and Samuel,* and at 8:00 P.M. she hoisted sail and headed out past harbor islands, bound east to England."[20] Thomas Hancock gave his nephew his treasured watch as a parting gift.

"After you sailed," wrote the nervous uncle in the first of two emotional letters to John in London, "we had E. & N.W. Winds & Dirt. Mrs. Hancock was very uneasy, I told her all was well, Our best Respects to Gov'r Pow[nall], hope to hear you had a good Passage."[21]

In the second he wrote, "This goes by way of Lisbon. . . . Your Aunt had been much Concerned for you, & I have been put to it to keep up her Spirits. . . . Take Care of yourself and observe the advice to a son [he quotes Polonius speaking to Laertes in *Hamlet*].[22] . . . Let me know who receives you with respect. Write me how the World goes on yr Side of the Water, be frugal of Expences, do Honor to your Country & furnish Your Mind with all wise Improvements. Keep the Pickpockets from my Watch. God Bless you & believe me, Your Loving Uncle."[23]

After thirty-seven uneventful days, John Hancock arrived in London. After life in a city of fifteen thousand, the English capital, with its population of 650,000, all but overwhelmed the young Bostonian—not just by its size but by the startling contrast between its stately churches, mansions, and government buildings, on the one hand, and on the other, its narrow, filthy streets and the choking stench of effluent in the open channel beneath his coach. London was the world's busiest port, with vessels all but obscuring the thick, black, open sewer some called the Thames. Dockside was a bedlam of shouts and cries from the army of brutes maneuvering huge crates and casks and baskets onto and off an armada of bobbing ships and barges. Freight wagons trembled and rocked under mountainous loads at pierside, then squeaked and rumbled off into the tunnel-like streets nearby, menacing anyone in their way.

But London was also the financial and cultural center of the empire, and John Hancock lost no time in taking advantage of both aspects of the city after first visiting his uncle's agent and settling into nearby quarters. After settling some of his uncle's debts and placing orders for new supplies, he visited his uncle's agents and suppliers in Bristol and Manchester with much the same purpose, but at the same time letting them know whom they would be dealing with in the future. Most were smart enough to write obsequious letters to Thomas Hancock that his nephew was "winning all hearts" in the English business world.[24]

John then turned to London's social and cultural life, breaking out—in explosive fashion—of the Puritan fetters that had restrained him in Boston. His extravagance would make him the target of harsh criticism for the rest of his life. He dined at London's most fashionable restaurants, haunted art galleries, concert halls, and taverns, and enlarged his wardrobe to preposterous levels. He spent hundreds of pounds on the most fashionable clothes, attracting attention at every tea and even while strolling through the Ranelagh or Vauxhall Gardens. By the time his year in London came to an end, he would spend more than £500, or five times what the most skilled craftsman could expect to earn in a year.

Just after he arrived in London, his younger brother, Ebenezer, graduated from Harvard College. Thomas Hancock had fulfilled his pledge to look after his brother's widow and children and had paid all the costs of Ebenezer's education. After an undistinguished academic career and a brief flirtation with the ministry, Ebenezer chose to go into business, and Thomas Hancock put the boy to work in the firm's warehouse. John sent his brother a few self-righteous words of advice:

London August 30, 1760

My Dear Brother

It is now almost two Months since I arrived in London, and in all the Time I have only wrote you one short Letter just to tell you I was Safe here & Promis'd to write you more at large in my Next. This Next is now begun but [I] know not how to go on[.] Should I attempt to tell you how I have spent my time & what I have seen. Description would not be able to perform what little imagination could supply here with. I intend in a few days to Take a Tour & see as much of the country as I can while the Season lasts & Store up all the Curiosities against that happy day when I shall have the pleasure to meet you & all my Dear Friends in Boston, which with all its pleasures & my happy connections there I should think not an ill exchange for London.

John expressed disappointment that Ebenezer had abandoned plans to enter the ministry, saying he had expected him to "make a figure in a Pulpit." But John had learned

you rather chuse to Shine in the Mercantile way. I shall be glad to hear that my uncle has fix'd you in his Store. I hope your conduct will be so pleasing to him, as in some measure to answer his many Indulgences. A close application to business . . . will soon make it a pleasure, without which you can never expect to succeed. I need not tell you it is for your own interest to please your Uncle & Aunt & when you consider that your sole Dependence is upon them & that you are under the strongest obligations, that, I should think, must induce you to strive all in your power so to conduct as they may have no reason to think their indulgencies are lost upon you. Be very cautious in the choice of your company and don't give way to a loose behaviour. Establish a good character at first by which you will gain the esteem of Mankind. Treat your Uncle & Aunt with great respect & and be sure to do nothing to forfeit their favour.

Pay my best respect to my Uncle & Aunt, from whom
I long to hear . . . and Remember my dutiful regards to my
Mother & Love to my Sister.[25]

On October 25 the death of King George II put an end to John
Hancock's revelries, as London and England went into mourning.
"I am very busy in getting myself mourning upon the Occasion of
the Death of his late Majesty King George the 2d, to which every
person of any Note here Conforms even to the deepest mourning,"
Hancock wrote in a letter for his mother. "Everything here is now
very dull. All plays are stopped, and no Diversions are going forward so that I am at a loss how to dispose of myself. On Sunday
last the Prince of Wales was proclaim'd King thro' the City with
great Pomp and Joy. His Coronation . . . will not be till April [so]
that I can't yet determine whether I shall stay to see it, but rather
think I shall, as it is the grandest thing I shall ever meet with."[26]

John escaped London's sorrow by traveling to Amsterdam and
Hamburg, where he cemented relationships with House of Hancock agents. On his return he fell ill, and as Christmas approached,
the business agent's son invited him to his home, where a "Remarkably Tender and Kind" young servant girl was assigned to nurse
him.[27] Her remarkably tender care would come back to haunt Hancock twelve years later, in 1772, when a bookseller, John Mein,
published a book assailing America's proindependence movement
and tarring its leaders. "In London about twelve years ago," Mein
wrote of Hancock, "he was the laughing-stock and contempt of all
his acquaintances. . . . He kept sneaking and lurking about the
kitchen of his uncle's correspondent, drank tea every day with the
housemaid, and on Sunday escorted her to White Conduit House
[a social and cricket club on the edge of the city] . . . but his old
school fellows and intimates knew that, though nature had bestowed upon him a human figure, she had denied him the powers
of manhood. The girl was therefore in perfect safety."[28]

After recovering from his illness, Hancock received a stern
letter from his uncle about his spending. He replied in apologetic
terms that appealed to his uncle's own addiction to fine clothes:

I observe in your Letter a Circumstance in Regard to my
Dress. I hope it did not Arise from your hearing I was too
Extravagant that way, which I think they can't Tax me with.
At the same time I am not Remarkable for the Plainess of my
Dress, upon proper Occasions I dress as Genteel as any one,
and can't say I am without Lace. I endeavor in all my Conduct
not to Exceed your Expectations in Regard to my Expences,
but to Appear in Character I am obliged to be pretty Expensive. I find Money some way or other goes very fast, but I
think I can Reflect it has been spent with Satisfaction and to
my own honour. I fear if you was to see my Tailor's Bill, you
would think I was not a very plain Dressing person. . . . I shall
be mindful to send by the first Opportunity the Mitts for my
Aunt and the Shoes for you, with a Cane if I can find one
Suitable.[29]

Somewhat taken aback by his uncle's disapproving tone, the
young Hancock stepped up his attention to business, consolidating
his uncle's accounts with fewer but more powerful agents, who
thus stood to profit more from the higher volume and could offer
better terms. He also went to the British Board of Ordnance to
establish personal contacts and gather intelligence on the award of
war contracts. He signed a contract for the House of Hancock to
serve as primary American supplier for the British contractor for
all troop supplies in Nova Scotia.

The London winter's endless gray rain and black fog frequently sent young Hancock reeling with coughing fits, however,
and as he lay in his sickbed, longing for home welled from time to
time, as when he wrote to his mother that he was "almost satiated
with London and . . . shall with satisfaction, bid Adieu to this
grand Place, with all its pleasurable enjoyments and tempting
Scenes, for the most substantial Pleasures . . . in the enjoyment of
my friends in America . . . whom I prefer to the . . . superficial, flat-
tering sincerity of many here. . . . A man of Fortune might live here
as happy as possible, but for me . . . the greatest Estate in England
would be but a poor Temptation . . . to spend my days here." Hancock nevertheless looked forward to the April coronation, after

which he fully expected to be presented at court before returning home to America.[30]

In March 1761, however, the palace announced George III's engagement to Charlotte of Mecklenburg, and the coronation was postponed until September 22, two weeks after the marriage was to take place. John wrote to his uncle asking permission to extend his stay in Britain to witness the events. At first his uncle approved, but he changed his mind because of the risks that autumn hurricanes posed to shipping. In addition, Daniel Henchman, Aunt Lydia's father and Uncle Thomas's mentor, patron, and close friend, had fallen ill and died. Both Thomas and Lydia Hancock were despondent and grew deeply lonely for their Johnny to console them. Thomas Hancock was getting—and feeling—older. He longed for his nephew to take over the exhausting day-to-day work at the House of Hancock.

"Mrs. Hancock and I have been willing you should stay for the coronation, and I have given you leave," he wrote. "But on our maturely . . . considering it to be late in the fall before you can reach New England, and the many dangers that will attend a fall voyage, we . . . desire your return . . . may be as soon as possible. . . . I fear Aunt and I am much concerned for you! [W]e are sorry to hear that you have been Confined. [S]he longs to have you at home & so do I, and Indeed I want you much."[31] John Hancock made immediate plans to sail home.

With the Seven Years War still raging on land and sea, passage proved difficult to arrange. Merchant ships routinely postponed sailing until they could find warships to escort them through the shoals of enemy warships, privateers, and pirate vessels. Young Hancock was unable to book passage until July and languished in Portsmouth until late August, waiting for his ship to sail. In July he sent his uncle a letter of explanation by one of the smaller packets that routinely braved the seas alone:

Honored Sir,

I have not Time as I am Engag'd in preparing my Voyage to write a long Letter, and this is a saving way, that I can only Acquaint you I long since Agreed . . . for a passage, and

Expected by this to have been half way to Boston, but unexpected Detentions have Arisen, both with Respect to want of
Goods and Convoy, however, can now say I am in great hopes
we shall soon sail, she falls down river on Tuesday, and I shall
set out for Portsmouth by Land on Thursday, and if we are
not Detained there in waiting for Convoy, shall in a week be
on our Passage, which in Compliance with your orders, I am
very earnest for, and my assiduous Endeavours have not been
wanting to get a Passage sooner, but hope all's for the best. . . .

    You will please to present my most Dutifull Regards
to my Dear Aunt[,] Mrs. Hinchman [*sic*], and Respectful
Compliments to all my Friends, with whom I hope to be soon.

    My earnest wishes for your Health and Happiness,
Concludes me in great haste, with utmost Gratitude, Honored
Sir, Your most obliged and most Dutiful Nephew.

    My Things are all going on board Monday.[32]

By the end of the summer of 1761, Thomas Hancock longed
deeply for his nephew John Hancock's quick return from England. The elder Hancock had overcome some of his lethargy
of the previous year and had set to work rebuilding the firm's
fallen revenues. Although military revenues remained substantially below those of the war years, Hancock's London agent had
written excitedly of anticipated whale oil shortages in England.
The war had crippled American whaling, and prices, which had
dropped to unprofitably low levels of less than £15 a ton before
the war, had soared to £23 a ton for "the common brown stuff"
and £25 a ton for pure, white oil. As an old hand in the whale oil
trade, Hancock was eager to renew his whale oil business but recognized that it would require building new ships, and at his age
the venture would be too difficult without his nephew's help.

    While his nephew sat in Portsmouth, Hancock's London agent
sent Uncle Thomas the bill for John's stay in London. "If his expenses while here has been more than you may have expected," the
agent wrote, "I am sure you'll excuse it; for I can assure you no
gentleman I know of, from any part of America, has laid it out
with more propriety and frugality, always keeping up such a character as was agreeable to the connections you were pleased to grant

him. He is a very worthy, well-disposed young gentleman and despises the thing that is mean and low; and I doubt not he will be a comfort both to you and Mrs. Hancock."[33]

John Hancock did not arrive in Boston until October 3,[34] and whatever fears he may have harbored of a reprimand for his high spending were quickly dispelled by his aunt and uncle's embraces and tears of joy. He brought gifts for everyone, including a cap and French horn for Cato, his uncle's slave, but was shocked by his uncle's appearance. Uncle Thomas seemed far older than his fifty-eight years. His wrists and ankles were swollen with gout, and he complained that "we are all Just Creeping about pretty poorly."[35]

The day after John's return, Thomas Hancock began preparations to hand the reins of his huge commercial empire to his nephew. After a torrent of orders from 1754 to 1760, the fall of Canada had reduced his military trade to a few hundred pounds a year. Overseas commercial trade was also declining because of French privateers, who were seizing so many vessels that insurers were "frightened and will not touch anything without a very high premium."[36] The previous year's drought had left farmers unable to pay their bills or buy new merchandise. A Hancock request to one farmer for payment of his debts brought a letter describing "the distress the People in the Country amongst us are in at present[.] Crops Cut Short Last Summer by Drought followed with a Long Severe Winter[,] A great Scarcity of provisions[,] and fodder Stocks Dying and Dead and money Scarce Beyond account[,] the people Not able to Raise money at present which Renders it very Difficult to pay you the hard Cash . . . hope you will at this time Deal Tenderly with me who are your very Humble Servant, David Barber."[37]

In the months following his return to Boston, John Hancock immersed himself in House of Hancock business. During the winter of 1762, Thomas Hancock fell ill, and after three months in a sickbed, he had aged dramatically. He grew "incapable of doing hardly any business,"[38] and by midsummer he had grown despondent and said he did not "expect to be able to attend to . . . business again."[39] John took more and more control of the business. With his uncle ailing and unable to provide companionship, John sought fellowship among Harvard graduates by joining the Masonic Lodge of St. Andrews in October 1762. At year's end, the still-ailing Thomas Hancock drafted a letter to all business associates of the far-flung House of Hancock trading empire:

Boston, January 1st, 1763.

Gent'n

I am to acquaint you that I have at last Got my affairs into such a Scituation, as that I have this Day Taken my Nephew Mr. John Hancock, into Partnership with me having had long Experience of his Uprightness & great Abilities for Business, as that I can heartily Recommend him to Your Friendship and Correspondence, which wish may be long & happy. . . .

I wish You the Compliments of the Season, & am with much Respect

Your most Obed't Serv't

Thomas Hancock[40]

The appointment came as the exhausting Seven Years War with France and Spain at last came to an end. The warring nations had signed a preliminary treaty in November 1762, and parliamentary approval would assure formal acceptance in February 1763. With John Hancock's elevation to full partnership, the House of Hancock, whose assets consisted of a large warehouse and several stores in Boston, along with a fleet of six oceangoing ships, changed its name to Thomas Hancock & Nephew. John Hancock immediately began asserting his authority—with the constant encouragement of his increasingly sick uncle. The surrender of French Canada opened the frontier to unimpeded migration, and as a result, New England property values fell sharply. John Hancock took full advantage, snapping up as much property as he could in Boston and in the farmlands and forests of Massachusetts and Connecticut. He and several investors also bought a large tract of land across Boston Harbor on Point Shirley (now Winthrop) to develop as a major fishing port and processing facility. In town he bought the remaining shares in Clark's Wharf, together with its dozen-odd stores, and changed the signs to read *Hancock Wharf*. Store rentals and wharfage fees would provide the young man with substantial, stable income for the remainder of his life. With the seas safe to sail again, the Hancocks also set up an international trust to corner the whale oil market with their London agent and a third firm, in Nantucket. The Hancocks began building a fleet of transports. The first was the biggest, most costly ship they had ever built—a full-rigged ship of 160 tons, with the dual purpose of carrying oil on the outgoing voyage and conventional cargo on the return trip. Thomas Hancock took a deep interest in the construction, which was "to be done in the best manner, shall aim to have her a prime going Ship, handsome and to carry well, plain but neat."[41] The wily old merchant even came up with a scheme to partition the hold in thirds to carry other cargo if the Nantucket partner was unable to fill the entire ship with whale oil. Unlike their other ships, the Hancocks had no intention of selling the new ship. They called it the *Boston Packet* and envisioned it as the first in a new, modern fleet offering regular transatlantic shipping service. They called the second ship in the fleet the *Lydia*.

In late autumn John Hancock went to Nantucket to corner the market for the spring catch with pledges to outbid all other buyers. By the time he returned to Boston, an epidemic of smallpox had cast a pall over the normally festive pre-Christmas celebrations. In January 1764 the epidemic reached such deadly proportions that the governor and the General Court, including the Hancocks, fled to Cambridge. Harvard postponed the beginning of the winter term, and the government took up residence in the college. In typical Hancock fashion, John and his uncle installed themselves in regal fashion, transferring their huge wardrobes and many valuable possessions, including linens, dining room service, and everything else needed to make their quarters as homelike as possible.

At midnight on January 24 they awoke to the muffled cries of "Fire," in the midst of what Harvard president Holyoke's daughter described as "the severest snowstorm I ever remember. . . . One moment brought me to the window, when I saw old Harvard College on fire; and it was with the greatest difficulty they saved the other buildings."[42] The fire destroyed the college library and cost Thomas Hancock, who "lodged out on account of the storm . . . everything except the clothes he had on. . . . The Governor and a great number of the Court assisted in extinguishing the fire." The next day "our worthy Court" voted first to appropriate £2,000 to begin rebuilding the college, and as its next order of business voted "a sum to Mr. Hancock to repair his loss, which, with what of money, plate, etc., they have found in the ruins, I hope will make his loss light." That the legislature appropriated public funds to replace a member's personal losses indicates both the power of the Hancocks and how profoundly self-serving the merchant-controlled provincial government really was.

The epidemic raged throughout the winter, and by mid-March, one-third of Boston's population had fled to the country. Although the General Court had at first banned the new inoculation, just then coming into vogue, it relented by late spring, and the epidemic began to recede. It is not clear whether Thomas Hancock was infected or not, but he returned to Boston in the spring of 1764 in weakened condition and took to his bed. John Hancock, meanwhile, returned to the task of creating a whale oil monopoly with his London partners. By the time the first whalers pulled into Nantucket, John Hancock had outbid every other oil merchant and cornered the market. He outbid all his competitors and drove prices up to £110 a ton—five times the previous year's levels. But he filled both the *Packet* and the *Lydia* with oil and sent them off to London while his competitors' ships bobbed in the harbor with empty holds, awaiting the next catch. His London agent commanded the highest prices of the year when the Hancock vessels arrived and put the Hancocks in a position to launch their new transatlantic shipping service.

Under the new partnership scheme, Hancock's London agents were to be ready with cargoes bound for America after the ships arrived in London and discharged their oil. The ships were to leave

London each year in March and August, with spring and autumn goods for Hancock's wholesale and retail operations, and return with whale oil. After its maiden trip to England, the *Packet* returned with twenty tons of hemp, which was in great demand by rope makers in Boston's huge shipbuilding industry.

On Wednesday, August 1, 1764, with business thriving again at Thomas Hancock & Nephew, Thomas Hancock walked down Beacon Hill to the Town House for a meeting of the Governor's Council. As the sixty-one-year-old merchant king entered the Council chamber at the top of the circular stairs, just after noon, he collapsed. Council members carried him back to his mansion on Beacon Hill, where he died "of apoplexy," a stroke, at about three o'clock,[43] leaving his twenty-seven-year-old nephew, John Hancock, as Boston's new merchant king and one of the wealthiest men in America.

4

Of Stamps and Taxes

❦

(1764-1765)

THOMAS HANCOCK left an estate worth £100,000, not including twenty-two thousand acres of undeveloped land in Connecticut and Massachusetts (the latter included present-day Maine) and innumerable parcels of developed properties and buildings in Boston and elsewhere in Suffolk County. He left his wife, Lydia, £10,000 sterling, the house on Beacon Hill, its furnishings, carriages, horses, and slaves, and all the lands around it. He divided an additional £8,000 and about 9,000 acres of his least valuable undeveloped lands along the Kennebec River in Maine among relatives and friends. He left his nephew Ebenezer a cash bequest of about £666 and thirty-two hundred acres of land in Maine. He established a £1,000 trust fund at Harvard to sustain a "professor of Oriental languages" of the "Protestant Reformed Religion," specializing in Hebrew. There were bequests of £600 to the city of Boston to build a hospital for the insane and of £700 to the Society for Propagating Christianity to sustain its Indian missionary program, and he left small gifts of £20 each, for Communion cups, to his father's church in Lexington and his own Brattle Square Church. He gave one of his slaves, Prince Holmes, a cash gift of

£20 and his other slave, Cato, the most generous gift of all—the promise of freedom when he reached thirty, if he behaved.[1]

He left the remainder of his estate to his nephew John Hancock—the boy he had loved as a son. John Hancock thus inherited the entire House of Hancock, its warehouses, shops, ships, and inventory, and all of the properties in Boston and the surrounding areas of Suffolk County, including Hancock Wharf and the Point Shirley development, across the harbor. He also inherited the most valuable of the twenty-two thousand acres of New England wilderness.

John Hancock buried his uncle on the Monday after his death, and five days later, on Friday, to his utter bewilderment, his aunt Lydia handed him the deed to the mansion and land on Beacon Hill, with title to all its furnishings that she had inherited from her husband. In signing it over to her nephew, she asked only that he permit her to spend the rest of her own life there.

In contrast to his carefree behavior when he broke away from parental controls in London, John Hancock assumed his position as family patriarch and head of the House of Hancock with dignity and authority, riding to work each day in his uncle's carriage and striding into his offices with the confidence of a mature, successful merchant. He was unquestionably Boston's best-dressed young man—trim, handsome, with dark brown hair, which he now covered more and more frequently with a fashionable London wig. His wardrobe—all from London—included red, blue, and violet gold-laced broadcloth coats; velvet breeches in green, lilac, blue, and other "harmonious colors"; lace-trimmed shirts; white silk stockings; and shoes topped with silver and gold buckles.[2] He routinely ordered "Ten Groce of best Quart Champaigne Bottles for own use" and 400 gallons of the best Madeira, admitting to his supplier, "I like pale Wine . . . I like rich wine."[3] To his great joy, his aunt Lydia continued taking complete charge of Hancock House, directing the household staff and organizing for her nephew, as she had for her husband, Boston's most elegant luncheons, teas, and dinners, with lavish arrays of meats, poultry, vegetables, fruits, sweets, and wines.

Hancock could not have inherited his uncle's business at a worse time, however. After writing to all his agents, customers, and suppliers of his intention "to carry on the business . . . by myself,"[4] he pressed ahead valiantly with his uncle's plans to expand the business, but the postwar economic slump had deteriorated into a full-scale depression. Many merchants had overstocked because of the seemingly endless demand that the war had created. As early as spring of 1763, six months after Britain had silenced her cannons, several major Boston mercantile houses had collapsed, while others trembled ominously on their foundations. Part of the problem lay in slow communications. Long before the first ship arrived from London with news that the war had ended, merchants had placed their orders for merchandise that would no longer be needed. Toward the end of 1763, another smallpox epidemic sent citizens fleeing the city, leaving merchants and shopkeepers crushed by piles of Christmas inventories and no one to buy them.

Despite the economic wreckage about him, Hancock pressed on. To maintain his advantage in the whale oil market, he sent Nantucket dealers unprecedented orders totaling £17,000 for oil and whalebone—enough to corner the market and fill the *Boston Packet,* the *Lydia,* and four other ships. He sent other ships out with potash and lumber, and when the economic slowdown undermined plans for the fish-processing plant at Point Shirley, he began working with other investors to turn the area into a summer retreat for Bostonians.

"No alteration appeared in Mr. Hancock," John Adams would later recall in his memoirs. At the time, Adams was a young Boston lawyer. "The same steady, regular, punctual, industrious, indefatigable man of business . . . not less than a thousand families were every day in the dependent on Mr. Hancock for their daily bread."[5]

Although he worked night and day, his efforts produced nothing but losses. Newer, faster ships sailed to London in less than four weeks, compared to the five to eight weeks it took his older vessels to get there. Although his high bids for oil sent his ships off to London first, faster vessels left with cheaper oil a little later

JOHN HANCOCK.

Engraved by J.B. Longacre from a Painting by Copley.

John Hancock, the young merchant king, in his imported wig and sartorial finery, in a portrait by John Singleton Copley. (*Library of Congress*)

and got to London first to win the highest bids. Adding to his troubles at sea, one of Hancock's six ships returned to Boston with one of its seamen infected with smallpox, and with the disease still prevalent, the ship was sent into quarantine, her cargo burned, and her outward-bound departure delayed for weeks.

Nor was he having much better luck on land. He had ordered a full line of Christmas merchandise for his stores, including a dozen pair of costly custom-made shoes from London. As his uncle had done, he advertised: a Christmas sale at "Store No. 4 at the east end of Faneuil Hall Market" offered "a general assortment of English and India goods; also choice Newcastle coals and Irish butter, cheap for cash." Because of poor economic conditions he hesitated to sell any goods on credit, but his customers had so little cash that if he refused credit, they would not have bought enough to allow him to remain in business. To raise cash he tried calling in old debts, asking "those persons who are still indebted to the estate of the late Hon. Thomas Hancock, Esq., deceased, to be speedy in paying their respective balances to prevent trouble."[6] His demand had little effect. Those who owed him money either had none or were bankrupt, and their failures had precipitated a wave of unemployment that sent more merchants into bankruptcy, and on and on. Some of the town's greatest merchants went under— one of them with debts of £170,000. Silversmith Paul Revere only barely managed to keep his shop open at the top of Hancock Wharf on Fish Street. A creditor tried to recover a debt of £10 by slapping a lien on the shop but finally settled out of court.[7]

Adding to Hancock's troubles, his brother, Ebenezer, refused to work for his older brother and used his inheritance from Uncle Thomas to set up his own retail hardware business with a partner. John Hancock had to begin training one of his clerks, William Palfrey, as a new assistant. At the beginning of 1765, Hancock wrote to his English agents to cancel his orders for the following spring: "The great uneasiness . . . here, owing to the failure of some persons of note has put us all into great anxiety, as trade has met with a most prodigious shock and the greatest losses to some people . . . ever known in this part of the world. . . . Times are very bad and precarious here; and take my word, my good friends, the times will be worse here."[8] Hancock confided that the wave of failures had left him reluctant to buy any more goods from England. "If we are not reliev'd at home we must live upon our own produce and manufactures," he warned.[9]

Like New England's other merchants, Hancock was simply not prepared for peace. For two centuries New England's economy had been based on war or the threat of war. Thomas Hancock had built the House of Hancock on war profits, and his nephew John—and Boston's other merchants—now discovered that peace was highly unprofitable in a frontier society where consumers can produce or derive most of the things they need from the wilderness. Barter made money—and merchants—all but unnecessary. Only the military relied on merchants on a regular basis, for arms, ammunition, clothing, food, and transport. Soldiers have no time to produce, grow, or hunt. The end of the Seven Years War, therefore, plunged the American colonies into economic stagnation—and it was that very moment the British government picked to raise taxes. Although their timing was terrible, the British had good reasons. The French and Indian War had left the government more than £145 million in debt, of which £1,150,000 had gone to the colonies for their part in the war. While colonial merchants such as the Hancocks had reaped fortunes, Parliament had crushed the English with an avalanche of taxes that swept forty thousand into debtors' prisons and provoked antitax riots by tens of thousands of workers across the face of England.

British prime minister George Grenville feared the regional tax uprisings would become a national rebellion unless he eased the tax burden. First lord of the treasury and chancellor of the exchequer, Grenville also became prime minister in April 1763. He inherited an annual budget that included nearly £1 million to support the king and his castles and £372,774 for supporting expanded military garrisons in America. Described as "one of the ablest men in Great Britain,"[10] he could do little about the king's spending, but he could at least force colonists to pay for their own defense. Taxes were not new in America. They had been in effect for forty years—mostly indirect taxes, or import duties that merchants were supposed to pay but had evaded by smuggling or by bribing customs officials.

New England merchants—Hancock included—smuggled in an estimated 1.5 million gallons of molasses a year, on which they should have paid £37,500 in duties; but corrupt customs officials collected barely £2,000 a year—not even one-fourth of their own salaries. The merchants argued disingenuously that the duties would double retail prices of rum and leave colonists unable to afford a drop of their favorite drink, but in truth only greed lay behind their objection to duties. They distilled a gallon of molasses costing sixteen pence into a gallon of rum, for which they charged 192 pence—a gross profit of 1,100 percent! In all, New England merchants paid about £100,000 a year for molasses and earned gross revenues of about £1.25 million, on which they refused to pay a mere 3 percent—£37,500—in taxes. Although merchants in England routinely paid duties on imports, two centuries of unfettered free enterprise had left colonists not only evading duties but arrogantly smuggling in cheap sugar and molasses from the French West Indies—an enemy land—thus undermining the economic future of their fellow countrymen in the British West Indies.

Grenville decided to revise the tax code and add strict new enforcement measures. In the spring of 1764, Parliament had replaced the Molasses Act with a new American Revenue Act (often called the Sugar Act), which halved the tax on molasses to a minuscule three pence a gallon (to fend off merchant opposition) but banned imports of all foreign rum from French or Spanish territories. Grenville saw the new tax as a fair compromise that minimized effects on colonist consumers while protecting the interests of British West Indies sugar and molasses producers.

The few thousand pounds Grenville expected to collect from the sugar tax, however, would fall far short of the amount needed to pay for supporting the military in America. He therefore placed new or slightly higher duties on non-British textiles, coffee, and indigo, and he doubled duties on all other foreign goods, including Madeira and French wines. He also banned most direct trade between the colonies and foreign nations. Colonial merchants could still buy foreign products, but they had to buy them—at higher prices—from merchants in England, who had already paid duties on those products. Grenville estimated that the American Revenue Act would yield about £45,000 a year in annual revenues—hardly a burden.

In addition, Parliament gave Grenville special powers to enforce the American Revenue Act. He immediately reformed the customs service by stripping English appointees of the right to remain in England and name deputies in the colonies to do their jobs—usually fellow townsmen of the American merchants. He tightened ship inspection and registration procedures and banned shipowners and merchants from suing the customs service for illegal seizures. He placed the burden of proof for recovering seized ships and cargoes on merchants and shipowners, and he established a vice-admiralty court in Halifax to hear cases—as far from Boston, New York, and Philadelphia as possible. Thus, any merchant whose cargo or ship was seized would have to travel to Halifax to try to recover his property, in a court far from home where he had no influence.

At the same time, Parliament issued a little-noticed resolution suggesting "it may be proper to charge certain Stamp Duties in the said Colonies and Plantations."[11] English lawyers, insurance firms, merchants, publishers, and stationers routinely affixed government stamps, for which they paid a nominal sum, on legal documents of all types, including liquor licenses and other permits, wills, bails, ships' papers, bills of lading, bills of sale, insurance policies, appointments to office, and articles of apprenticeship. Stamps also had to be bought and affixed to university degrees, wine containers, newspapers, almanacs, pamphlets, publicly distributed leaflets, playing cards, and dice. The treasury believed the law should apply to the colonies. It was a small though effective revenue-raising measure that placed a minimum burden on the individual by spreading it across the entire spectrum of consumers.

Still the loyal British subject, Hancock did not balk at most of the new taxes in the American Revenue Act—certainly not at the insignificant duty on molasses—although he was "beginning to find the fussiness of the customs mildly irritating" and he found himself spending "an annoying amount of time filling out forms and writing to London for certificates."[12] Indeed, the new, tighter regulations benefited Hancock at first by grounding weaker fleets, which depended almost entirely on smuggling. Within months, the new regulations combined with the depression to reduce by 80 percent the number of ships traveling between the mainland colonies and the West Indies. Only the strongest fleets such as Hancock's continued to sail, but even he recognized the economic dangers of the new tax policies.

"The heavy taxes on the Colonies will be a great damp to Trade," he wrote to his English agent, who had ties to the all-powerful Board of Trade. "If such duties are laid and we must be Oblig'd to bear all, we shall have little or no Demand for Supplies from England, this ought to be Consider'd, and hope we Shall be Reliev'd, we are worth Saving in this part of the world."[13]

Jared Ingersoll, a major Connecticut distiller and the agent (essentially ambassador) for Connecticut in England, was more forceful in a letter to his friend Thomas Whately, one of the joint secretaries of the British treasury: "I think Parliament have over-shot their mark and you will not have any of your Expectations in any measure answered from the Provisions of the late Act." Ingersoll warned that not a single distiller trading with the French and Dutch West Indies had "the most Distant intention to pay the Dutys." He conceded that "a Seizure will be made of perhaps one Vessel in a Hundred," but it would have no effect on smuggling or on collecting duties. In terms of revenues, it would be "Burning a Barn to roast an Egg."[14]

The most dramatic response, however, came from James Otis, a firebrand attorney in the Massachusetts House of Representatives, the lower house of the General Court. He turned the tax controversy into a constitutional issue, charging that all British taxes "have a tendency to deprive the Colonies of some of their most essential Rights as British Subjects, and . . . particularly the right of assessing their own Taxes." In addition, he assailed Thomas Hutchinson and the wealthy plutocracy of Boston merchants "who grind the faces of the poor without remorse, eat the bread of oppression without fear, and wax fat upon the spoils of the people." He charged the merchants—especially Hutchinson—with "forging chains and shackles for the country."[15]

It was no coincidence that Otis singled out Hutchinson to attack—as opposed to Hancock, for example, or one of Boston's other great merchants. Otis loathed Hutchinson. His attack was personal; it had nothing to do with English taxes, but taxes were as good a platform as any from which to begin destroying the great merchant, who Otis believed had crippled his father's career and damaged the older man emotionally. Former governors Thomas Belcher and William Shirley had promised to appoint Otis's father, Col. James Otis, provincial chief justice as a reward for his loyal command of his county militia against the French and for his twenty-five years of service as judge in Barnstable, which he also represented in the General Court. Elected speaker of the House of Representatives, he was, in addition, leader of the bar in three rural counties and the logical and popular choice for chief justice. For reasons that remain unclear, Shirley's successor, Gov. Francis Bernard, had overruled Shirley and in 1760 appointed Hutchinson instead.

Several factors may have influenced Bernard's decision. Certainly, Hutchinson's polished demeanor appealed more to the Oxford-educated governor than the folk mannerisms of the self-educated country lawyer Colonel Otis. The Boston-born Hutchinson was a wealthy, exceptionally literate, Harvard-educated merchant who had been his province's representative in London and represented stability and loyalty to the crown. Bernard knew that Hutchinson would carry out the provisions of the controversial American Revenue Act. With his deep ties to rural populism, Otis may have seemed less predictable, and likely to be swayed by antitax sentiments of farmers. Whatever his motives for appointing Hutchinson, Bernard had made one of his most disastrous decisions as governor—by creating a bitter, outspoken, and influential enemy of royal rule in Boston. The decision was a heartbreaking disappointment for Colonel Otis, and it embittered his son James, who pledged to "set the province in flames" to avenge the governor's disavowal of the pledges of two previous governors to appoint his father to the Superior Court. "Upon the Governor's nominating me to Office," Hutchinson wrote, "one of the Gentlemen's sons who was solicitous for it swore revenge."[16]

James Otis, the young Boston lawyer whose personal hatred for the royal governor turned him into a leader of the Revolution. He later became insane. (*Library of Congress*)

Born in Barnstable in 1725, the younger James Otis graduated from Harvard in 1743, studied law, and after gaining admittance to the bar, moved to Boston in 1750. Five years later, he married a merchant's daughter. After the birth of their third child, he prepared to settle in as a member of Boston's plutocracy, serving as lawyer for his father-in-law's merchant friends. He joined the Merchants Club and the Masons, and in 1760 his influential friends rewarded the young man by getting him appointed advocate general of the same Superior Court he expected his father would one day head. After Governor Bernard frustrated his father's ambitions, young Otis resigned rather than serve under Hutchinson, and he waited for an opportunity to retaliate.

During the months that followed his resignation, Otis began sensing that British taxes represented an issue that would forge a bond between merchants and farmers and unite them in rebellion against the British governor he so despised and his judicial courtier Thomas Hutchinson. In a pamphlet he published in August 1764, entitled *The Rights of the British Colonies Asserted and Proved*, Otis raised the first specious cry against taxation without representation, conveniently overlooking the fact that few taxpayers in England had any representation in Parliament. Indeed, only 1 million of the 9 million adult males in Britain were entitled to vote.[17]

"Copyholders, leaseholders, and all men possessed of personal property only choose no representatives," explained one member of Parliament in defense of colonial taxation. "Manchester, Birmingham, and many more of our richest and most flourishing trading towns send no members of Parliament, consequently cannot consent by their representatives, because they choose none to represent them; yet are they not Englishmen? . . . Why does not their imaginary representation extend to America as well as over the whole island of Great Britain? If it can travel three hundred miles why not three thousand? If it can jump rivers and mountains, why cannot it sail over the ocean? If the towns of Manchester and Birmingham sending no representatives to Parliament are notwithstanding there represented, why are not the cities of Albany and Boston equally represented in the assembly?"[18]

Hancock paid little attention to the ramblings of Otis and certainly not to Otis's pamphlet. He had a great enterprise to run. Moreover, his company was still provisioning British troops in Nova Scotia with food and other supplies, and he was not about to alienate the chief justice, who was a fellow merchant, or the royal governor, who parceled out profitable contracts.

Early in 1765, Boston's tight little aristocracy rewarded Hancock's loyalty by giving him his uncle's seat as one of the city's five selectmen, which gave him a voice in regulating markets, law enforcement, schools, streets, and a city budget of about £10,000 a year. Although it pushed him to the edge of the political maelstrom, he showed no particular interest and simply listened attentively at town meetings, usually without responding. In his business life he was careful to pay his £300 to £400 taxes in sterling to the British government every year, convinced that he was paying as much as any Englishman of equal wealth in the mother country. In fact, he paid half as much on his declared revenues as comparably wealthy Englishmen, and he paid nothing, evading all duties, on contraband (mostly molasses, rum, or wines), which at times amounted to half his cargoes.

It was, therefore, somewhat startling to see him caught up in the outburst of hostility that greeted the news, in April 1765, that Grenville had asked Parliament to convert its resolution for a stamp tax into law. The tax would take effect the following November 1 and simply extend England's own seventy-year-old stamp tax to include the colonies. The tax raised about £300,000 a year in Britain, and Grenville estimated it would yield about £60,000 a year in America, at a cost of less than a shilling a day per capita, or less than three hours' earnings a year for a skilled artisan. When added to the £45,000 to be raised from the American Revenue Act, stamp tax collections would bring total tax revenues in America to about £105,000 a year, less than one-third of the cost of maintaining Britain's expanded army in America.

Hancock and other leading merchants had few objections to maintaining defensive military garrisons. Indeed, Andrew Rutledge, an influential South Carolina rice planter whose sons would help draft the Declaration of Independence, had suggested raising £100,000 to support four regiments on the frontier to protect the increasing number of white migrants. Because the end of the French and Indian War had stripped France of her Canadian possessions and ended the century-old French threat to the security of English settlers, colonists could now move westward to try their luck on the frontier, without fear of French assaults. The westward migration, however, brought settlers into conflict with Indians. In 1763, Ottawa chief Pontiac had gone to war to block

the white man's westward migration, destroying every British post
west of Niagara and laying siege to Detroit and Fort Pitt for five
months. Maj. Gen. Jeffrey Amherst prepared to send blankets
laden with smallpox germs into Pontiac's camp, but the British
commander in chief rejected the idea. After a series of bloody encounters, Pontiac offered the British a truce—but gave the British
government good reason for maintaining and even expanding its
military presence in North America.[19]

Colonist leaders argued, however, that the forces should be
American rather than British. In fact, at the beginning of the French
and Indian War, John Hancock's uncle Thomas had pointed out
the folly of English "parade ground tactics" in combating Indians
and asked his London agent to influence the British Board of
Ordnance to "let us fight them in their own way."[20] Other colonial—and even British—leaders realized that a militia made up of
colonists experienced in stalking forest game would be far more
skilled in fighting Indians.

In a widely circulated letter to newspapers in London and the
colonies, Benjamin Franklin, who was Pennsylvania's agent in
London, wrote, "If the Indians when at war march'd like the Euro-
peans, with great armies, heavy cannon, baggage and carriers, the
passes thro' which alone such armies could penetrate our country
or receive their supplies, being secur'd, all might be sufficiently
secur'd. . . . They pass easily between your forts undiscovered; and
. . . when they have surpriz'd separately, and murder'd and scalp'd
a dozen families they are gone. . . . The inhabitants of Hackney
[England] might as well rely on the Tower of London to secure
them from Highwaymen and housebreakers."[21]

English military leaders agreed. Col. Sir William Johnson, the
British superintendent of the Northern Indians, told the Board
of Trade in 1762 that "altho' our frontier Forts . . . may prove a
means of retarding the progress of an Army, or oppose an European force, they can in no wise prevent the Incursions of the Indians, who need not approach them in any of their inroads, and
can destroy the inhabitants and their Dwellings with very little
risque."[22]

By early spring in 1765, some colonists suspected that Grenville's motives for expanding the British military presence in America was not to fight Indians but to control colonists. Anger began to build. British motives became all too clear after Gen. Thomas Gage, the New York–based commander in chief of British forces in America, asked Parliament to pass a Quartering Act, requiring civil authorities in the colonies to supply barracks and provisions for British troops.

Even John Hancock grew annoyed, and he wrote to his agent in London suggesting that he lobby against passage of the Stamp Act. Calling the act "very cruel," he warned that British merchants would ultimately pay a higher price for the stamp tax than American merchants. "I hear the Stamp Act is like to take place," Hancock wrote. "We were before much burthened[.] We shall not now be able much longer to support trade, and in the end Great Britain must feel the effects of it. I wonder the merchants and friends of America don't make a stir for us."23

Hancock was not the only merchant writing to his London agents, of course, and indeed, a small force of merchants from Boston to Charleston, South Carolina—along with the agents representing each of the colonies before Parliament and the king's ministers—had vigorously opposed enactment of both the American Revenue Act and the Stamp Act. Despite claims to the contrary by American colonists, neither was passed unthinkingly or arbitrarily. Indeed, the debate was fierce, with future prime minister Charles Townshend calling the colonists "children planted by our Care, nourished up by our Indulgence . . . protected by our Arms." Col. Isaac Barre, M.P. for Chipping Wycombe and a veteran of the French and Indian War, responded,

> They planted by your Care? No! your Oppressions planted em in America. They fled from your Tyranny to a then uncultivated and unhospitable Country—where they exposed themselves to almost all the hardships to which human Nature is liable. . . .
>
> They nourished by *your* indulgence? They grew by your neglect of Em:—as soon as you began to care about Em, that

Care was exercised in sending persons to rule over Em, in one Department and another. . . .

They protected by *your* arms? They have nobly taken up Arms in your defence, have Exerted a Valor amidst their constant & Laborious industry for the defence of a Country, whose frontier, while drench'd in blood, its interior Parts have yielded all its little Savings to your Emolument. And believe me, remember I this Day told you so, that same Spirit of freedom which actuated that people at first, will accompany them still. . . . The people I believe are as truly Loyal as any Subjects the King has, but a people Jealous of their Lyberties and who will vindicate them, if ever they should be violated.[24]

Although "the whole house sat awhile as Amazed, intently Looking and without answering a Word,"[25] it voted 245 to 49 in favor of proceeding with the proposed tax.

After word arrived that Parliament had enacted the Stamp Act, Hancock initially accepted the inevitable. "I am heartily sorry for the great Burthen laid upon us," he wrote to his London agent. "We are not able to bear all things, but must submit to higher powers, these taxes will greatly affect us, our Trade will be ruined, and as it is, it's very dull." Then, turning to what remained for him a more important topic, he ordered "two pipes [about 125 gallons each] of the very best Madeira for my own Table. I don't stand at any price, let it be good, I like rich wine. You will use the same judgment in the choice of it as for my late uncle who had high opinions of your Fidelity."[26]

5

"Mad Rant and Porterly Reviling"

❧

(1765)

By the end of May 1765, economic depression was generating anger in almost every New England household, from Beacon Hill to the most humble frontier farm. Enforcement of customs collections and higher duties had slowed trade so much that cash all but disappeared from circulation. Importers collapsed under the weight of their debts to English suppliers. Shopkeepers and craftsmen closed their doors. Even the largest merchants struggled to stay in business. Hancock had only £2,000 in cash sterling left in his company account in London to cover £14,000 in debts. Although English firms owed him £3,000, his firm was still £9,000 in debt, and his agent began refusing new orders.[1] His personal fortune remained secure, however. Unlike many merchants, John Hancock, like his uncle Thomas before him, operated his business as a separate financial entity and never mingled his personal fortune with business funds. This left him always a rich man, even as his business faced imminent collapse.

Fueling anger over economic conditions were a spate of specious legal arguments against British taxes—largely derived from the original Otis rhetoric that taxation without representation was unconstitutional. The Otis argument was sheer propaganda that rabble-rousers were using to incite ignorant mobs, but it had no foundation in fact, either in the colonies or in England itself, where the vast majority of taxpayers went unrepresented in Parliament. Indeed, before considering the Stamp Act, Grenville had met with colonial agents and found that there were "many Reasons why they should not desire [representation]." For one thing, members of Parliament went unpaid. The colonies would, therefore, incur new costs to transport and support representatives in London. Second, the number of colonial representatives in Parliament would have been too small to have any influence—certainly not enough to overcome overwhelming English public opinion that colonists should pay their fair share of taxes.

Helping Otis generate his inflammatory propaganda was a fellow Harvard malcontent, the brewer's son Samuel Adams. A failure at every job he'd ever held, Adams blamed British rule for his miseries. As with Otis, his bitterness stemmed in part from wounds inflicted on his father by a royal governor. The elder Samuel Adams had used his brewery and its ties to the city's taverns to build political power, which he vested in a group of cronies he called the Boston Caucus. He used the economic depression to extend his power beyond Boston, across the farm regions, by backing a so-called land bank that printed and loaned its own paper money to farmers according to the value of their lands and crops. When Adams and the land bankers won a majority of seats in the House of Representatives in 1741, Hutchinson and other merchants convinced Governor Belcher, himself a merchant who needed little convincing, to veto the election. At Belcher's urging, Parliament then outlawed the land bank and its paper currency, adjudged its organizers to be criminals, and ordered them to buy back all land bank money with Massachusetts currency. The Massachusetts General Court spared Adams the disgrace of going to jail, but he lost almost all his life savings, and his son Samuel, then in his third year at Harvard, vowed revenge against Hutchinson. With his father nearly bankrupt, young Adams, who ranked fifth in his class of twenty-two under Harvard's system of social gradation, had to wait tables to pay for the rest of his college education. The humiliation did not prevent his graduating and gaining a master's degree, but it left him with a festering bitterness that made him incapable of success in any productive activity.

After leaving Harvard, he went to work for Thomas Cushing, a merchant friend of his father. Cushing soon dismissed the young man for writing political tracts instead of keeping the company ledgers. The elder Adams then gave his son some of his precious remaining savings to start a business, but young Sam loaned half the money to an irresponsible friend who lost it, and Sam promptly lost the rest on his own. Sam next went to work in the family brewery but ignored his job to found a political club with some young malcontents and write political diatribes in a newspaper they founded. It went bankrupt after a year. His father and mother died soon after, and although young Sam inherited the brewery and the family's fine home on Purchase Street, he allowed both to deteriorate so quickly that he sank deeply in debt. His father's political friends at the Boston Caucus bailed the young man out in 1756 by appointing him Boston tax collector. Within a short time he owed the town £8,000 for taxes that he either had failed to collect or had embezzled. He had married in 1749, but his wife died nine years later and left him with two children, a black slave girl, and a Newfoundland dog. They were all mired in poverty, struggling to survive his irresponsibility. His cousin John Adams sighed that Sam Adams "never looked forward in his life; never planned, laid a scheme, or formed a design for laying up anything for himself or others after him."[2] After fifteen years of failure at everything he tried, he festered with hatred for royal rule and the merchants who profited from it. He blamed them for all the ills of the world, including his own.

Between them, said the *Boston Evening Post,* James Otis and Samuel Adams filled Boston with "mad rant and porterly reviling"[3] against Hutchinson, Governor Bernard, and British rule. Helping them was James Otis's sister Mercy Otis, who was herself

Samuel Adams, the brewer's son and Revolutionary leader, whose business incompetence left him all but bankrupt and accused of embezzlement of public funds. From a portrait by John Singleton Copley. (*Library of Congress*)

a talented writer with a biting wit and gift for satire. The pro-British *Post* accused them of inculcating "pious countrymen" with the idea that "downright scurrility and gross impudence, was really the most exalted Patriotism, the most perfectly refined, disinterest Amor Patriae."[4] Adams and Otis found an outlet for their "scurrility" in the *Boston Gazette*, published by two antiroyalists, Benjamin Edes and John Gill. Together with Otis, Adams, and a dozen others, Edes and Gill helped found the Long Room Club, a secret society that met above their printing shop and spawned America's first political party, the Whigs.[5] Their number included ministers, lawyers, and two physicians—Dr. Joseph Warren and Dr. Benjamin Church, who had boarded off campus with Hancock during Hancock's freshman year at Harvard. All were Harvard alumni, with the exception of the successful silversmith Paul Revere, who never attended college. According to a rival newspaper, Edes's newspaper became "the most factious paper in America"; Adams became a master propagandist, "spit[ting] venom" in the *Gazette* and haranguing discontented workingmen in Boston taverns, while Otis aroused his fellow Masons at the Green Dragon tavern and the failing merchants at the Merchants Club.[6]

Otis and Adams were not the only colonists spitting venom, of course. Virginia's fiery Patrick Henry had invented an equally specious argument against the Stamp Act in the Virginia House of Burgesses. The people of Virginia, he had declared, were not bound by any tax laws other than those of their own legislature, and "any person who shall, by Speaking or Writing, assert or maintain That any Person or Persons, other than the General Assembly of this Colony . . . have any Right or Authority to lay or impose any Tax whatever on the Inhabitants thereof, shall be Deemed, an Enemy in his Majesty's Colony."[7]

The argument and his resolves had been sheer nonsense. Even Virginia's House of Burgesses rejected three of Henry's resolutions and moderated the language of the other four, with Henry later apologizing for "the tone" of his remarks.[8] In fact, both the royal governors and the Privy Council in London had the right to reject any resolution or law passed by colonial legislatures. Moreover, Parliament had controlled colonial trade and taxed imports and exports since 1660, with the passage of the Navigation Act and subsequent passage of at least twelve hundred more acts—some of them far harsher and costlier than the Stamp Act. Most had not provoked a whisper of protest. As John Adams pointed out, the American colonies bought commodities from Great Britain "that we could purchase cheaper elsewhere. This difference is a tax upon us for the good of the empire."[9]

Indeed, the sums involved in the Stamp Act were so trivial that, without the streams of invective by Otis, Sam Adams, and Henry, it alone could not have provoked the eruption of colonial anger that would burst across America in the summer of 1765. In mid-May, Governor Bernard of Massachusetts heard murmurs of opposition from the merchant plutocracy, who argued that the Stamp Act represented the first direct internal tax in the colonies imposed by Parliament—as opposed to external taxes such as duties. But the governor nevertheless believed they would ultimately submit to the act. He reminded the Massachusetts House of Representatives that "in an empire, extended and diversified as that of Great Britain, there must be a supreme legislature, to which all other powers must be subordinate. It is our happiness that our supreme legislature is the sanctuary of liberty and justice, and that the prince who presides over it, realizes the idea of a patriot king. Surely, then, we should submit our opinions to the determination of so august a body, and acquiesce, in a perfect confidence that the rights of the members of the British Empire will always be safe in the hands of the conservators of the liberties of the whole."[10]

Although the House received his message cordially, it nevertheless voted to consider "what dutiful, loyal and humble Address may be proper to make to our Gracious Sovereign and his Parliament in relation to the several Acts lately passed for levying Duties and Taxes on the Colonies." The House appointed a committee to invite delegates from other colonial assemblies "to consult together" in New York in October, and present "a General and united, loyal and humble representation of their Condition to his Majesty and the Parliament, [and] to implore relief."[11]

In mid-June, however, radical New England newspapers sounded "an Alarm Bell"[12] by publishing the original, inflammatory language of the Patrick Henry resolutions and saying that Virginia had passed them intact—a lie planted by Sam Adams. The *Newport Mercury* was first with the Henry rhetoric on June 24, and the radical *Boston Gazette* copied it on July 2. Although Hancock tried to remain aloof from the turmoil, he was not looking forward to the new tax burden of the Stamp Act. His agent had not

responded to his earlier pleas, so he wrote to former Massachusetts governor Pownall in London. Pownall had just published his
well-received work *The Administration of the Colonies*, suggesting
that in the interests of reconciliation and unity in the empire, Parliament permit the colonies to send representatives to the House of
Commons.

Hancock, whom Pownall had escorted to London five years
earlier, wrote his old friend: "I seldom meddle with Politicks and
indeed have not Time now to say anything on that head. I know the
goodness of your Disposition towards us, and I wish we could be
help'd out of our present Burthens & Difficulties, our Trade is
prodigiously Embarrassed, & must shortly be Ruin'd under the
present Circumstances, but we must Submit. . . . I, however, hope
we shall in some measure be Reliev'd, & Doubt not your good
influences to forward it."

On August 8 the British government published the names of
the colonial distributors who would sell stamps. The distributor for Massachusetts was Provincial Secretary Andrew Oliver, a
wealthy Boston merchant who was Chief Justice Thomas Hutchinson's brother-in-law. The appointment seemed proof positive of
James Otis's charges that wealthy merchants and the royal government were "forging chains and shackles for the country" and conspiring to "grind the faces of the poor without remorse, eat the
bread of oppression without fear, and wax fat upon the spoils of
the people."[13]

As one, Bostonians seemed to snap. Debts had piled high; there
was no work; shops had closed. With nothing left for rent or food,
many tramped off into the wilderness, hoping sadly that something would turn up. Early in the morning on August 14, an effigy
of Oliver dangled from the limb of an elm tree on High Street,
dubbed the Liberty Tree. As a crowd began gathering, Governor
Bernard ordered deputies to remove it, but they refused, saying
any effort would put them in "Imminent Danger of their Lives."
Sam Adams appeared with a group calling itself the Loyall Nine—
all of them members of the Boston Caucus. They included two
distillers and a ship's captain who had smuggled molasses until

customs shut them all down. Also in the group was the printer of the *Gazette*, Benjamin Edes. After Adams and the others had spoken, the mob began dispersing, only to re-form later in the day at Adams's invitation. The later rally, coming after working hours, attracted a rougher crowd of waterfront workers and laborers, who set to drinking and soon raged out of control. They tore down Oliver's effigy and carried it past the Town House and the governor's office, where they chanted defiantly, "Liberty, Property, and No Stamps." Growing in number, they moved toward a half-finished brick building near the waterfront, where Oliver planned "to let out shops." Believing it would house the stamp office, the mob tore it down and rushed to Oliver's beautiful estate. They beheaded and burned the straw dummy and began stoning the windows. Unsatisfied, they cried for a hangman's rope, broke down the mansion's doors, and when they realized Oliver had fled with his family, destroyed the magnificent furniture, art, and everything else they could lay hands on.[14] Chief Justice Hutchinson and the county sheriff tried reasoning with them, but they responded with volleys of epithets and stones and drove the two away. Governor Bernard ordered the colonel of the militia to summon his regiment, but the drummers who normally sounded the alarm were part of the mob, as were many of John Hancock's own employees.

"Everyone agrees," the governor wrote to the Board of Trade in London, "that this Riot had exceeded all others known here, both in the Vehemence of Action and Mischievousness of Intention and never had any Mob so many Abettors of Consequence as this is supposed to have had."[15] Although Samuel Adams was a familiar figure in Boston's taverns and certainly had been guilty of "mad rant and porterly reviling,"[16] there is no evidence he took part in the Oliver attack, either as a participant or an instigator, but he took full advantage of the proceedings by organizing a group he called the Sons of Liberty. The next morning an unidentified "group of gentlemen" warned Oliver that unless he resigned as stamp distributor, what was left of "his House would be immediately Destroyed and his Life [put] in Continual Danger." He signed a pledge to resign and told the group to announce his decision publicly.

Although Sam Adams said the night's events "ought to be forever remembered . . . [as] the happy Day, on which Liberty rose from a long Slumber,"[17] Hancock was appalled at the mob attack on one of his friends. Oliver, also a Harvard graduate, was the son of a great merchant, grandson of a prominent surgeon, and a ruling elder of the Boston church—the third generation in a distinguished Massachusetts family whose roots reached back to 1632, twelve years after the landing at Plymouth. But Hancock was also aware of the large number of near-bankrupt smaller merchants in the mob, and he suddenly found himself isolated in an increasingly polarized city. As a wholesaler he had strong ties to the small merchants, whom he often supplied. But his wealth made him a member of the plutocracy of large merchants like the Hutchinsons, Olivers, and other families with deep loyalties to England and the crown. Thinking he could influence events in England and turn the tide of rebellion, he again wrote to his London agent of the "general dissatisfaction here on account of the Stamp Act, which I pray may never be carried into Execution, it is a Cruel hardship upon us & unless we are Redressed we must be Ruined, our stamp officer has resigned . . . do Exert yourselves for us and promote our Interest with the Body of Merchants the fatal Effects of these Grievances you will feel very Sensibly; our Trade must decay & indeed already is very different. I can't therefore but hope we will be considered, & that some will rise up to exert themselves for us[.] We are worth saving but unless speedily relieved we shall be past remedy. Do think of us."[18]

Hancock's warnings proved all too accurate. The epidemic of mob violence spread to Newport, to towns along the Hudson River, to New York, Philadelphia, and Charleston. Rioting erupted again in Boston on August 26 when rumors swept through the city that the "whole body of [Boston] merchants had been represented as Smugglers" in depositions by the royal governor seeking their arrest.[19] Although Governor Bernard denied making any such charges, merchants "descended from the Top to the Bottom of the

Town" to the Town House. A mob gathered, lit a bonfire, and began drinking and shouting "Liberty and Property"—which Governor Bernard described as "the Usual Notice of their Intention to plunder and pull down a house."[20] The mob eventually marched to the home of the marshal of the vice-admiralty court, who saved his home by leading them to a tavern and buying a barrel of punch. Now drunker than before, they staggered to the home of another court official, broke down his doors, and burned all court records, before wrecking the house and its contents. A second mob smashed into the elegant new home of the comptroller of the customs, who had just arrived from England. After sacking the interior—and drinking all the wine in its cellar—one of the Loyall Nine, Ebenezer Mackintosh, a shoemaker and fire brigade commander, led both mobs to Thomas Hutchinson's.

One of the architectural jewels of North America, Hutchinson's palatial Inigo Jones–style residence bore Ionic pilasters on its facades; a delicate cupola crowned its roof. Warned of the mob's approach, he ordered his family to leave, while he confronted the mob. His daughter refused to leave without him, however, and they fled with Governor Bernard to the protection of British troops on Castle William, the island fortress in Boston Harbor. The mob broke down the massive doors and, room by room, destroyed everything they could lay their hands on, including Hutchinson's legendary collection of manuscripts—many of them significant public papers documenting the history of Massachusetts. It took the mob three hours to dislodge the cupola from the roof, and only fatigue and the rising sun put an end to the systematic destruction they wreaked on the Hutchinson home. Rumors swirled through Boston that the mob had a list of fifteen "prominent" gentlemen and contemplated "a War of Plunder, of general levelling & taking away the Distinction of rich & poor."[21]

Fearful for his own safety, Hancock joined other selectmen in refusing to bring the looters to justice. The governor convened the Council, the upper house of the state legislature, in the safety of Cambridge. They agreed that the previous night's rioting "had given such a turn to the Town that all Gentlemen in the Place were ready to support the Government in Detecting and publishing the Actors in the last horrid Scene."[22] Although the Council issued a warrant to arrest the shoemaker Mackintosh, Sam Adams led a group that demanded and won his release. After others were jailed, a mob broke into the jailer's house, seized his keys, and released the prisoners before they could be tried. They never were.

Again, Hancock tried to halt the tide of rebellion, clearly believing that Stamp Act repeal by Parliament would restore peace in Boston. "If the Stamp Act takes place," he warned his London agent, "we are a gone people—do help us all you can."[23]

BY THE END OF SEPTEMBER, events continued isolating John Hancock. Only the wealthiest merchants and men of great property—a tiny elite—remained united behind the royal governor. The base of those in opposition had broadened to include a sizable—and most respectable—majority, which included almost all the small merchants, as well as shipowners, printers, tavern owners, land speculators, smugglers, and ordinary citizens. All would have to pay stamp taxes on everything from playing cards to wills. For most it was the first direct tax they'd ever paid, although all paid indirect, hidden taxes such as customs duties, which merchants tacked onto wholesale and retail prices.

Publicly, Hancock sided with no one, and when a vacancy occurred in the House of Representatives, voters rejected him brusquely. He finished last on the list of candidates with a mere forty votes. Instead, they elected the outspoken James Otis and his embezzler friend Sam Adams—despite the prison term hanging over Adams's head. As titular leaders of the Whig majority, Otis and Adams seized control of every important committee in the House of Representatives. As Governor Bernard noted with dismay, the "Faction in perpetual opposition to Government" took complete control. "What with inflammatory Speeches within doors & the parades of the mob without," the governor wrote, the Otis-Adams radicals "entirely triumphed over the little remains of Government."

Hancock thus remained in a precarious position on the fence around his hilltop mansion. Rather than leave his property and personal safety at risk, he spent more time at the Merchants Club and at the Green Dragon tavern, where his fellow Masons assembled. Most, like Hancock, Otis, and Robert Treat Paine, were Harvard alumni, although the Freemasons did not exclude skilled craftsmen such as Paul Revere. Sam Adams was not a Mason, but he stopped by each day on his rounds of Boston taverns, and he gradually assumed leadership over the disparate elements of Boston's malcontents—the small merchants facing bankruptcy, the skilled artisans struggling to keep their shops open, and the out-of-work laborers, too poor to feed their children or heat their hovels. Nor did Adams forget the Utopians—the rich sons of Harvard who had studied and believed the works of John Locke.

According to his cousin John Adams, Sam Adams had the most thorough understanding of "the Temper and Character of the People,"[24] along with a gift for intellectual seduction. Although erudite, he spoke the common tongue and dressed in the common cloth—not miserably, but as a working artisan might after a day's work. Everywhere he went—in every tavern, on the streets—he recruited ceaselessly for his rebellion against royal rule and those who had destroyed his father. He "made it his constant rule," his cousin said, "to watch the rise of every brilliant genius, to seek his acquaintance, to court his friendship, to cultivate his natural feelings in favour of his native country, to warn him against the hostile designs of Great Britain."[25] His tactics varied with each recruit—flattery for one, cajolery for another, pledges and promises for yet another. From the moment he stepped into the General Court, he began organizing a group of powerful allies from rural districts to expand the power of his Caucus Club beyond Boston to the rest of the province. "The Caucus Club meets at certain times in the garrett of Tom Dawes," John Adams explained. "There they smoke tobacco till you cannot see. . . . There they drink flip, I suppose, and there they choose . . . selectmen, assessors, collectors, wardens, firewards, and representatives . . . before they are chosen in the town."[26]

Although he could count on a broad-based throng of rebels and wealthy young malcontents, Sam Adams had failed to recruit anyone from the merchant elite, and he knew he would never overturn the royal governor without the political and financial support of at least a few aristocrats to buy arms, ammunition, and rum for the mobs. His cousin John Adams called Sam a "designing person" who in public "affects to despize Riches, and not to dread Poverty, [but] no Man is more ambitious."

Sensing Hancock's fear and indecision, Sam Adams pounced on the young merchant. His technique of ingratiating himself was "the same manner that the Devil is represented seducing Eve, by a constant whispering at [the] Ear," according to Peter Oliver, whose brother's house had been gutted by the Adams mob. The seductive whispers left unsuspecting listeners "closely attached to the hindermost part of Mr. Adams as the rattles are affixed to the Tail of a rattlesnake." Whenever anyone tried to disengage himself from Adams's thrall, Oliver went on, Adams "like the Cuttlefish would discharge his muddy liquid, and darken the waters to such a hue that the other was lost."[27] Hancock listened closely to what Sam Adams had to say. Knowing that Adams was perhaps the only man in Boston who could guarantee the safety of his property, Hancock decided to pay for that guarantee—at least for a while—with financial support for Adams and his movement. Adams soon dug so deeply into Hancock's pockets that the merchant won the reputation of being Adams's "milch cow."

The fever for insurrection spread quickly across the colonies. The day after the destruction of the Hutchinson mansion, a mob in Newport, Rhode Island, set up a gallows for the stamp officer, who fled to a British warship in the harbor and promised to resign. As rioting spread, stamp officers resigned in New Hampshire, Connecticut, New York, New Jersey, Pennsylvania, Maryland, Virginia, North and South Carolina, Georgia, and even offshore in the Bahamas. In New York a mob of about two thousand marched through the city, broke open the governor's coach house, and seized the coach and his three other vehicles. After seating effigies of the governor and royal officials, they paraded the coaches through town, hung the effigies on a makeshift galley, and burned all the vehicles.

ON SEPTEMBER 23, 1765, fourteen boxes of stamps arrived in Boston, but with no stamp distributor to accept them, they went to the British garrison on Castle William. Boxes destined for Rhode Island and New Hampshire remained on board a ship guarded by two men-of-war. A few days later, stamps for other colonies arrived in Philadelphia and New York in anticipation of November 1, when the act would take effect. Calling the stamps "the most disagreeable commodity that were ever imported," Hancock continued appealing to influential friends in London, predicting that if the stamps were "carry'd into execution [they] will entirely Stagnate Trade here, for it is universally determined here never to submit to it, . . . & nothing but the repeal of the act will righten, the Consequence of its taking place will be bad, & I believe I may say more fatal to you than to us. For God's sake use your Interest to relieve us. I dread the Event."[28]

Five colonies—Connecticut, Rhode Island, Pennsylvania, Maryland, and South Carolina—had responded to the call of the Massachusetts General Court to meet in New York, and three other colonies that had failed to respond—New York, New Jersey, and Delaware—showed up anyway. The Stamp Act Congress, as the gathering was called, brought together for the first time leaders from all sections of the American colonies. From the opening session, on October 7, erudite moderates took control from radicals. Although James Otis headed the Massachusetts delegation, the congress rejected by one vote his nomination as chairman, in favor of a more moderate Massachusetts delegate.

After eleven days the congress approved a "Declaration of Rights and Grievances of the Colonists in America," written largely by Philadelphia's John Dickinson. The declaration maintained that the Stamp Act deprived colonists of "two privileges essential to freedom"—taxation by consent and trial by jury. Devoid of inflammatory language, the document reiterated the argument against taxation without representation by Parliament, but in effect agreed to taxation by the colonists' own legislatures if the Stamp Act were repealed. "The invaluable rights of taxing ourselves are not, we most humbly conceive, unconstitutional but confirmed by the Great Charter of English liberties."[29] The declaration also focused on the injustice of the vice-admiralty court in faraway Halifax overseeing trials of colonial shipowners and merchants for customs and tax violations. The declaration said that the vice-admiralty court deprived the colonists of the constitutional right of trial by jury. The document dissociated itself from antiroyalist radicals by asserting that colonists "glory in being subjects of the best of Kings having been born under the most perfect form of government. . . . That we esteem our connection with a dependence on Great Britain, as one of the great blessings, and apprehend the latter will be sufficiently secure, when it is considered that the inhabitants in the colonies have the most unbounded affection for his majesty's person, family and government, as well as for the mother country, and that their subordination to the parliament is universally acknowledged."[30]

Even the whimper with which the declaration ended could not convince delegates to affix their own names to the document, however. Only one signature appeared—that of the clerk of the congress—and only six colonies agreed to sponsor the petitions to king and Parliament. Otis was furious. He arrived in Boston railing irrationally against the Stamp Act, the British in general, and Thomas Hutchinson in particular. In what Otis's friends called "incoherent ravings," Otis urged the town meeting to march to the ruins of Hutchinson's home and destroy its remaining fragments. He challenged British prime minister George Grenville to one-on-one combat on the floor of the House of Commons to determine whether the colonies were to be free or be enslaved by British tyranny. Thomas Hutchinson responded by calling Otis "more fit for a madhouse than the House of Representatives."[31]

As the effective date of the Stamp Act approached, some merchants in New York, Philadelphia, and Boston agreed to stop importing all but a select list of goods from England on November 1. John Hancock recognized he would have little choice but to join the boycott. Not to do so would have been tantamount to pledging allegiance to the royal governor, and he surely would have had to flee to Castle William and abandon his beloved Beacon Hill property to Sam Adams's mob. In a letter designed for Sam Adams as much as his London agent, he wrote of his fears and his intention of joining the boycott. If his ships returned from England before November 1, he pledged to unload them, refill them with whale oil, and send them back to England. If the ships arrived after November 1, he said, he would remove their cargoes and haul the vessels ashore, and consequently cancel his orders for all spring goods.

"I now tell you, and you will find it come to pass, that the people of this Country will never Suffer themselves to be made slaves of by a Submission to the D——d act. But I shall now open to you my own Determinations," Hancock wrote.

> A thousand Guineas—nay, a much Larger sum—would be no Temptation to me to be able to be the first that should apply for a Stamp, for such is the aversion of the people to the Stamps that I should be sure to lose my property, if not my life. . . . Under this additional Burthen of the Stamp Act I cannot carry on business to any profit and we were before Cramp'd in our Trade & sufficiently Burthen'd, that any farther Taxes must Ruin us. . . . It is the united Resolution & Determination of the people here not to Carry on Business under a Stamp, we shall be in the utmost Confusion, here after the 1st Nov[emb]er & nothing but the Repeal of the Act can Retrieve our Trade again. . . . I would sooner Subject myself to the hardest Labour for a maintenance than carry on this Business as I now do under so great a Burthen, & I am Determin'd as soon as I know that they are Resolv'd to insist on this act to Sell my Stock in Trade & Shut up my Warehouse Doors. . . . I am very sorry for this occasion of writing so boldly, & of being obliged to come to such Resolutions, but the Safety of myself & the Country I have the honour to be a Native of require some Resolutions, I am free & Determin'd to be so & will not willingly & quietly Subject myself to Slavery.

Then, in a postscript that offered hard evidence of his attachment to the patriots, the still-unmarried merchant added, "This letter I propose to remain in my letterbook as a standing monument to posterity, and my children in particular, that I by no means consented . . . to this cruel act and that my best representations were not wanting in this matter."[32]

On October 31, two hundred New York City merchants signed an agreement to stop purchasing British and European goods until Parliament repealed the Stamp Act and modified the trade regulations of the 1764 American Revenue Act. About four hundred Philadelphia merchants followed suit the next day, and a month later, 250 Boston merchants, including John Hancock, did the same. The merchants hoped the boycott would so damage English trade that their agents and suppliers in England would force Parliament to repeal the Stamp Act.

As it turned out, Hancock had nothing to lose and everything to gain by supporting the boycott. Financially, it could not have come at a better time. In fact, he could not have bought another shilling's worth of goods even if he had wanted to. His credit had run out in London, and as he wrote, a letter from his London agent demanding payment of old bills stared up at him. The merchant boycott, therefore, gave him time to sell off inventories and accumulate some cash. Moreover, his inability to buy stamps left him unable to pay any London bills. All remittances, as well as other financial and legal documents, required stamps, and there were none to be had.

He began assailing the Stamp Act with enthusiasm. "There is not cash enough here to support it," he protested a week after the boycott began. "I believe that not a man in England, in proportion to estate, pays the tax that I do. What would a merchant in London think of paying £400 sterling annually, which my late uncle paid to this province and county? . . . And I now pay yearly . . . £300 sterling, besides all duties, imposts, ministers and many other additional taxes. . . . I will not be a slave. I have a right to the Libertys & Privileges of the English Constitution, & I as an Englishman will enjoy them."[33]

By the time the Stamp Act took effect, all stamp officers in the colonies had resigned, and with no stamps available, the act could not take effect. Americans nevertheless greeted November 1 as a day of mourning, with bells tolling throughout the day. The Sons of Liberty—Adams, Edes, and others—gathered at the Liberty Tree to hang the effigies of Grenville and another member of Parliament. That evening they put the effigies in a cart, and as thousands marched behind, they wheeled them past the Town House, where the General Court was sitting, and then to the gallows on Boston Neck, to be hung. The courts and customs houses had no choice but to close. Business came to a standstill.

After a few unanticipated days of festivity, however, Boston resumed its normal activities, ignoring the Stamp Act completely. Newspapers were published, courts heard cases, and stores reopened—all without stamps. The customs house also reopened and allowed goods to flow in and out normally. Hancock's ships from London arrived with autumn merchandise after the stamp tax deadline, and he simply refilled them with whale oil and sent them back to London as he had always done. Although he sent completed documents with his purchase orders for spring merchandise, he told his London agent not to fill them until Parliament repealed the Stamp Act. Excusing his inability to repay his outstanding debts, he pointed out that without stamps, he was legally unable to issue any remittances. He distanced himself from the violence that the Stamp Act had engendered but warned that he was unflagging in his support of the merchant boycott. "The injury that has been done to [Hutchinson] . . . is what I abhor and detest as much as any man breathing and would go to great lengths in repairing his loss. But an opposition to the stamp act is commendable."[34]

The boycott had terrible economic consequences for English merchants. Colonial merchants owed them about £4 million, but the flow of orders and cash from America was drying up. British exports dropped 14 percent, and goods piled up inside and outside British warehouses. Merchants in Bristol, Liverpool, Manchester, Leeds, Glasgow, and every other trading town in Britain inundated Parliament with petitions demanding repeal of the Stamp Act. London merchants asked Parliament to grant "every Ease and

Advantage the North Americans can with propriety desire."[35] For whatever reasons, Hancock's London agents had ignored his previous entreaties, but when he made good on his threat not to repay them or order any spring goods, they quickly joined the protest. In Virginia a prosperous planter in Mount Vernon could not resist poking fun at the miscalculations of Parliament and the British merchants. "I fancy the merchants of G. Britain trading to the Colonies," said George Washington, "will not be among the last to wish for a Repeal of it."[36]

6

A Hero by Circumstance

(1765-1768)

THE STAMP ACT took effect during the week before Pope's Day, which was Boston's version of Guy Fawkes Day, when England celebrated the execution of the leader of a Catholic conspiracy to blow up Parliament on November 5, 1605. Instead of encompassing a single, traditional parade with dancing and other festivities, however, Pope's Day had turned ugly in 1764, when two rival gangs—each a neighborhood crime family of sorts—staged parades that inevitably met head-on. After the bloodshed subsided, a little girl lay dead.

Sam Adams subsequently befriended the leaders of both gangs, and by the following summer he had united them into a single, powerful armed force that added physical power to his political protests. In August they had formed the core of the mob that sacked the homes of Andrew Oliver and Thomas Hutchinson—and frightened John Hancock off his political fence on Beacon Hill. On the evening before Pope's Day in November 1765, Adams staged a "Union Feast" for thugs from the two gangs to mingle with merchants and politicians "with Heart and Hand in flowing Bowls and bumping Glasses."[1] John Hancock was there—indeed, had not dared to stay away—and in the end, to Adams's delight and everyone else's cheers, he picked up the large tab for the entire dinner.[2]

Although Adams and Otis had whipped up crowd hatred against Boston's merchant kings, that hatred had never touched Hancock, who was a generous employer and well liked by the hundreds of colonists who depended on him for their livelihood. He had helped at least four of his own clerks, including his chief clerk, William Palfrey, set up their own shops, with innovative, fifty-fifty profit-sharing arrangements. In effect, Hancock established each as a franchisee, with about £1,500 worth of merchandise as opening inventory. Although Hancock remained the primary source of supply, each franchisee could buy anywhere and could stock goods that the House of Hancock warehouse did not carry. But it was usually easier for them to deal with Hancock; he was nearby, he could undersell everyone else, and in effect, he was each storekeeper's partner. Moreover, his terms were exceptionally generous for 1765, during an economic depression, when the young men he helped start in business might not have found work without heading for the frontier. Each also reaped the benefits of Hancock's business acumen and the Hancock name on their shops—as well as his friendship. Hancock served as mentor and generous friend to each of his "partners"—and a benevolent godparent to their children. They, in turn, would reciprocate with veneration and dogged loyalty to Hancock the remainder of their lives. Palfrey would gradually become Hancock's general partner and help manage the entire House of Hancock, as did another young partner-storekeeper, William Bant, an attorney.

So, when John Hancock showed up at the Green Dragon tavern, the men there already knew him as one of the rare Boston plutocrats whose employees sang his praises and who seemed to understand the plight of ordinary men. He did not, therefore, go to the tavern to win over the crowd. He went to win acceptance into the Adams-Otis political fold and prevent them from siccing their mad dogs on him and his property.

On Pope's Day, the following morning, Adams's "trained mob" marched in disciplined military formation before a startled governor and General Court at the Town House. To the governor's astonishment, the volatile leather worker Ebenezer Mackintosh led the force—marching in uniformed splendor—stride for stride and arm in arm with the colonel of the governor's own militia.[3] A few days later the governor wrote to England that he had "ordered some Companies of Militia to be mustered" to thwart the marchers, "but the militia refused to obey my orders; it was said that the People would have their shows."

Pope's Day 1765 marked a sharp turning point in Hancock's relationship with Boston radicals, and in the months that followed he drew closer and closer to them—always to preserve his life and property. It proved a wise move. Six weeks later, Adams's mob hauled poor Andrew Oliver down to the Liberty Tree, where, before all Boston, the mob forced him to make a public apology, stating that he detested the Stamp Act, and to swear never to attempt to enforce it. After the crowd released Oliver amid hoots of derision, Hancock left the scene of his friend's humiliation to sign another boycott agreement with 250 other Boston merchants. "In case the Stamp Act is not repealed my orders are that you will not . . . ship me one article," Hancock wrote to his London agents. He said his decision reflected the "united resolves of not only the principal merchants . . . of this town, but of those of the other trading towns of this province, and which I am determined to abide by."[4] A few days later, New York and Philadelphia merchants followed suit.

In mid-January 1766, Governor Bernard warned London that force would be required to restore order in Boston. He was, he said, "more & more assured that the People of this Town who have now got all the Power in their hands, will know no bounds, until the authority of Great Britain shall interpose with Effect."[5] Although Grenville had expressed his "Resentment and Indignation at the outrageous Tumults and Insurrections . . . in North America,"[6] he now faced a growing multitude of English merchants on the verge of financial ruin unless trade with the colonies resumed. They warned Parliament that the use of troops to enforce the Stamp Act would provoke rebellion. If Parliament wanted to tax the colonies, they counseled, it should continue the traditional practice of external taxation with hidden, indirect taxes such as import duties.[7]

By the end of February, the pressure for repeal grew over-whelming, and Parliament promised a group of thirty-nine leading English merchants that repeal was imminent. The merchants sent a circular letter to their American correspondents predicting repeal, but they warned against further rebellion and

> intemperate proceedings of various Ranks of People on your side the Water. . . .
>
> If therefore . . . you have a Mind to do credit to your Friends and strengthen the hands of your Advocates, hasten, we beseech you, to express filial Duty and Gratitude to your Parent Coun-try. Then will those who have been . . . your friends, plume them-selves on the restoration of Peace to the Colonies. . . . But if . . . [repeal of the stamp tax] is talked of as a Victory, If it is said the Parliament have yielded up the Right [to tax the colonies] then indeed your Enemies here will have a Complete Triumph. Your Friends must certainly lose all power to serve you. Your Taxmas-ters probably will be restored and such a train of ill consequence follow as are easier for you to imagine than for us to describe.[8]

Only four and a half months after it had taken effect, a chas-tened Parliament voted to repeal the Stamp Act, without a single stamp ever being affixed to a colonial document. It was a humili-ating defeat—particularly so because it had been inflicted by a constituency without a single direct vote in either the House of Commons or the House of Lords. In the end, the British govern-ment had collected no new taxes and had left its own treasury— and many British merchants—far poorer than they would have been had it never passed the act. Moreover, passage of the act created the first organized opposition to royal rule in the colonies—an opposition that rabble-rousers such as Sam Adams would convert into an unyielding movement for independence.

Tragically for England, the petty tyrants in Parliament who passed the Stamp Act refused to recognize defeat or seek reconcil-iation. Instead, they lit the fuse for the next colonial explosion with a Declaratory Act on the very day they repealed the Stamp Act. They asserted that "the Parliament of Great Britain had, hath and of right ought to have, full power and authority to make laws and statutes of sufficient force and validity to bind the colonies and people of America Subjects of the Crown of Great Britain in all cases whatsoever."

With news of repeal still weeks away, members of the Long Room Club believed Hancock had proved his loyalty by supporting the merchant boycott. Sam Adams recognized that as New England's most important merchant and a member of the mercantile elite, Hancock would add an important element then missing in the independence movement. On May 6, Adams's Boston Caucus assured Hancock's election to the General Court with 437 votes. By allying himself with the Whigs, Hancock believed he was espousing the cause of commercial freedom, but in fact, London believed his election had made him "one of the Leaders of the disaffected"—especially after he foolishly declared that he "would not suffer any of our [English customs] Officers to go even on board any of his London ships."9 On the afternoon of Hancock's election, Sam Adams walked with John Adams (who was still building his law practice) and is said to have told his younger cousin, "This town has done a wise thing today. They have made that young man's fortune their own."10

Ten days later, in one of the most fortuitous events of his political career, one of Hancock's ships brought him the official notice of repeal. London's merchants had selected him, as America's most important merchant, to announce the news to Boston at a selectmen's meeting. The selectmen cheered him and set aside the following day—Repeal Day—for celebration. At one in the afternoon, church bells—and every other bell in town—began pealing. Bostonians poured from their houses, firing guns in the air and shouting Hancock's name. As the shouts proliferated, they grew convinced—as he apparently did—that he had been the instigator of repeal instead of a simple messenger. Flags flew from every building in town, and bands marched through the city. Adams and the Sons of Liberty gathered at the Liberty Tree before parading to the debtors' prison with John Hancock's cash to buy the release of all the inmates.

Edes published a special Repeal Day issue of the *Gazette*:

> At one o'clock the Castle and Batteries and Train of Artillery fired a Royal Salute and the Afternoon was spent in Mirth and Jollity. In the Evening the whole Town was beautifully illuminated:— On the Common the Sons of Liberty erected a magnificent Pyramid, illuminated with 280 lamps. The four upper Stories of which were ornamented with the figures of their Majesties and fourteen worthy Patriots who have distinguished themselves by their Love of Liberty. On the Top of the Pyramid was fix'd a round Box of Fireworks horizontally. About one hundred Yards from the Pyramid the Sons of Liberty erected a Stage for the Exhibition of their Fireworks, near the Workhouse, in the lower Room of which they entertained the Gentlemen of the Town.[11]

Not to be outdone, Hancock set off his own, even larger display of fireworks on a huge stage in front of his mansion. All eyes turned toward the merchant king and his beautiful home, which he swathed in illuminations. Gradually the crowd worked its way up the Common to Hancock's gate, where he set up a pipe—a cask holding 125 gallons—of Madeira wine. When they emptied it, he sent out another. He came out on his balcony and waved to the cheering crowd, calling out greetings and looking every bit the hero of repeal. He not only convinced the crowd of his new role—he believed it himself. While the mob stood cheering and drinking outside, "John Hancock Esq. . . . gave a grand and elegant Entertainment to the genteel Part of the Town" inside the mansion.[12]

The celebration continued the next day. Hancock entertained twenty-nine merchants at the Bunch of Grapes, another popular merchants' tavern, at the corner of King and Kilby Streets, near the end of Long Wharf. At Province House, the governor's mansion on Marlborough Street, Governor Bernard celebrated Repeal Day with his Council by drinking His Majesty's health, before stepping out courageously to mingle with the rest of Boston. Bernard clearly thought Repeal Day marked the beginning of peace in the colonies.

For Otis and Adams, however, it was the beginning of war. They fired their first shot on May 28, in the House of Representatives, when the Boston Caucus took firm control. It named Otis speaker, Adams clerk, and antiroyalists, including Otis's father, to the Governor's Council, or upper house. Governor Bernard picked up the gauntlet and, under his charter powers, rejected Otis as speaker and vetoed the Council elections. Sam Adams responded sarcastically, "Had your Excellency been pleased in season to have favored us with a list [of councilors] and positive orders whom to choose, we should in your principles have been without excuse. But even the most abject slaves are not to be blamed for disobeying their master's will and pleasure, when it is wholly unknown to them."[13]

Adams replaced Otis as speaker with the pleasant, unassuming Thomas Cushing (the younger), who, like Hancock, had graduated from Harvard, inherited a huge mercantile empire, and been lured into the radical camp leadership by the siren songs of the cunning Sam Adams.

Bernard presented the General Court with a parliamentary demand to bring Stamp Act rioters to justice and force them to compensate those who had suffered losses in the riots. Caught unprepared, assembly radicals recognized that refusal might cost them the support of moderates who supported Stamp Act repeal but condemned violence. Otis and Adams finally pushed through a compromise bill that compensated riot victims but granted full amnesty to the rioters. In defying Parliament and the governor, Otis and Adams called the amnesty a victory, but it was a costly victory that turned moderates in England and the colonies against the Whigs for condoning criminal acts and failing to respect basic English law. What little warmth England retained for the colonists would disappear after Parliament was forced to raise English duties and taxes to compensate for American refusal to pay the stamp tax. "Grievous are the complaints of the poor in every part of the Kingdom," one newspaper would report, "on account of the extravagant price of provisions of all sorts. Every post brings fresh accounts of tumults, occasioned by the high price of bread. . . . There is nothing but Riots and Insurrections over the whole Country, on Account of the high Price of Provisions."[14]

John Hancock stayed out of the line of fire between Governor Bernard and the Otis forces. For him, Repeal Day had marked the beginning of new opportunities to expand his business and make money—and he set to work doing just that. He outbid the market for whale oil; he expanded exports to England, expanded the number of his retail stores, and ordered about £8,000 worth of new inventories to stock them. "He changed the course of his uncle's business, and built, and employed in trade, a great number of ships," wrote Thomas Hutchinson, "and in this way, and by building at the same time several houses, he found work for a great number of tradesmen, made himself popular, was chosen select man, representative, moderator of town meetings, etc."[15]

The expansion of his business expanded his spirit, and as his uncle had done, he became a major benefactor of his community. On May 22 he went to Cambridge, where he received enthusiastic applause at a pomp-filled public ceremony installing the first Hancock Professor of Oriental Languages, under the legacy of his uncle Thomas.[16] As business slowed for summer, he paid more attention to his new position as a member of the General Court. Its activities suddenly enthralled him, and he accepted posts on thirty different committees, whose functions ranged from regulating potash production to auditing the provincial treasurer's government accounts. Other Court members deferred to his knowledge and experience as the colony's most successful merchant and head of its largest enterprise. He discovered a gift for mediating differences, and delegates turned to him in increasing numbers for help in resolving disputes. His popularity grew daily—and nightly, at the lavish dinners he offered at various taverns and at Aunt Lydia's splendid feasts on Beacon Hill. To Sam Adams's consternation, Hancock was also accumulating power as a spokesman for Boston's shopkeepers and merchants and eroding Adams's own political base. Adams stepped up his personal propaganda in the *Gazette* and in public speeches. He staged demonstrations, parades, and fireworks to commemorate even the slightest triumph over royal governance.

"Otis and Adams," wrote John Adams, "are politic in promoting these festivals, for they tinge the minds of people; they impregnate them with the sentiments of liberty; they render the people fond of their leaders in the cause, and averse and bitter against all opposers. To the honor of the Sons [of Liberty], I did not see one person intoxicated, or near it."[17] In contrast, the Tories scorned those who marched in the Adams demonstrations as "the rabble," ignoring their importance because most could not vote.

In early 1767, John Hancock celebrated his thirtieth birthday at one of his never-ending entertainments that sealed his political position as leader of the important merchant faction. Otis and Adams had little choice but to offer him a seat at the inner circle of Whig power in Boston—the Long Room Club above Edes's print shop. Sam Adams's political star, meanwhile, began to lose a bit of its luster, as Tories[18] worked behind the scenes to produce some propaganda of their own, demeaning Adams as an embezzler of public funds. With Adams on the defensive, Hancock moved into the leadership breach, with coincidences continually working in his favor.

On the night of February 3, fire broke out in the bake house of one of his tenants. By morning it had razed more than twenty buildings, including many of his own, and left fifty families homeless. After the General Court appropriated £400 for their relief, Hancock added £400 of his own money to the fund, then saw to the distribution of huge stacks of free firewood to the poor throughout the city for the rest of what was one of the coldest winters in memory. Hancock constantly rode through town in his golden coach on the lookout for opportunities to relieve the most hard-pressed of Boston's underprivileged, both directly and indirectly. Boston had never seen any man of such evident wealth show such deep concern for the unfortunate. In addition to outright gifts of firewood, food, or free rent, he made substantial contributions to almost every church in the city, with seats and Bibles for the needy, window glass, Communion tables, and pulpits. He paid for a three-hundred-pound bell at one church and gave cash gifts to churches to minister to the needy. The ministers did not forget him in their sermons, and he gained a justifiable reputation as a great humanitarian with a deep devotion to his community and its citizens.

As the city's affection for Hancock increased, so did its disaffection with Sam Adams. In March the selectmen appointed a committee to examine the tax collector's books and found Sam Adams's collections for the province treasury short £2,300, while collections for the town were short £1,700. The people of Boston were outraged, and while the Boston Caucus was able to reelect Adams and Otis to the House of Representatives in the May elections, John Hancock outpolled them both with 618 votes—forty-four votes more than the tarnished Sam Adams. Hancock easily won reelection as selectman as well, and both Adams and Otis reluctantly recognized Hancock as a new and unexpected full partner in Boston politics.

As Hutchinson, Oliver, and Governor Bernard doubled over in uncontrollable laughter at the Adams predicament, the town meeting added to their delight by asking James Otis, of all people, as attorney for the town treasury, to charge his friend Adams with embezzlement. A year earlier, Otis had called Boston's electors "a pack of damned stupid fools," to which his enemies replied by calling him a "mad dictator."[19] A lower court jury of Boston Caucus loyalists acquitted Adams, but an appellate court reversed the decision and issued a judgment against him for £1,463, based on the total missing less the salary due him as tax collector. The court gave him nine months, until March 1768, to repay the city. Had a vengeful Parliament not acted just then, Otis and Adams might have disappeared from the political scene and left the moderate conciliator John Hancock to maneuver Boston's political machine between the conflicting interests of England and her colonists.

Antitax rioting in England, however, forced Parliament to cut English land taxes 25 percent. Government revenues fell £500,000, and Chancellor of the Exchequer Charles Townshend, a staunch defender of the Stamp Act, grew desperate for new sources of money. He sought to make colonists pay the costs of the British military in North America. No thought was given to reducing the size of the military or the king's £800,000-a-year allowance or to taxing the nobility more heavily. Townshend's opponents—those who had fought for Stamp Act repeal—urged the House of Commons not to sow further seeds of discontent in America, but those seeking to avenge the humiliation of repeal insisted that Massachusetts had usurped the powers of the king by granting amnesty to Stamp Act rioters. Although Townshend scoffed openly at the distinction between external and internal taxes, he agreed, in a speech filled with sarcasm, to impose only new external taxes.

At the end of June 1767, Pariament began passing the Townshend Acts, imposing import duties on glass, lead, paint, paper, and tea, worth about £40,000 a year, for defending the colonies and "defraying the charge of the administration of justice and the support of the civil government." In addition to levying new taxes, the acts empowered the courts to issue writs of assistance—search-and-seizure warrants to break in anywhere to ferret out smugglers and seize their property—and they created new vice-admiralty courts to try violators without juries. A third, more insidious measure in the Townshend Acts called for direct payment of crown-appointed judges and governors by Parliament rather than by colonial legislatures, thus making them independent of colonial influence. Townshend himself died before the acts took effect on November 20, and he never saw the havoc his vengeful scheme would wreak on the British empire.

News of the Townshend Acts arrived in early August and spread consternation across the colonies. Hancock was as furious as everyone else. Like other merchants, he believed Stamp Act repeal had been a Parliamentary mandate for merchants to conduct and expand colonial trade without further government interference. Repeal had encouraged him to expand, and he had looked forward to a growth in trade and prosperity that the Townshend Acts would prevent. He called together the town's merchants to urge reimposing a partial boycott of English imports—especially luxury goods that provided English merchants with the most profits but that colonists could easily do without.

"It is suprizing to me," he wrote to a London associate, "that so many attempts are made on your side to Cramp our Trade[,] new Duties every day increasing[.] In short we are in a fair way of being Ruin'd [.] We have nothing to do but unite & come under a Solemn agreement to stop importing any goods from England."[20] He made it clear that he would not allow English customs officials to board his ships or enter his stores and warehouses without proper warrants.

On October 28, James Otis chaired the Boston town meeting as Boston's merchants approved Hancock's proposal for a partial boycott of British luxury goods—expensive products such as gloves, shoes, gold and silver thread, and silks. The limited scope of the boycott reflected Hancock's views that a moderate approach would be more likely to bring Parliament to its senses and more likely, as well, to win support from merchants elsewhere in the colonies. At the same time, Hancock pushed through a resolution urging colonists to reduce their dependence on other British goods by making their own clothing, jewelry, watches, cheeses, sugar, malt liquors, cordage, and anchors. England had forbidden colonial production of such goods to prevent competition with similar manufactures in Britain. Thus, Boston now threatened a virtual end to trade with Britain by adding a nonconsumption agreement to the nonimportation agreement. Even Tory merchants such as the Hutchinsons, Olivers, and Clarkes could not continue importing if American customers refused to buy their goods. The nonconsumption agreement amounted to a declaration of commercial independence and cleared the first barrier to political independence.

A month later the *Pennsylvania Chronicle* published the first of twelve stirring essays by the brilliant John Dickinson, the London-educated Philadelphia lawyer and member of the Pennsylvania assembly who had drafted the declarations at the Stamp Act Congress. His essays appeared in twenty of the twenty-six newspapers published in the thirteen colonies (and in pamphlet form in 1768). They united American opposition to the Townshend Acts by supporting Boston's declaration of commercial independence and calling the debate over external and internal taxes meaningless. Dickinson charged that Britain could bleed the colonies as effectively with external as with internal taxes and that there was no difference between the Townshend Acts and the Stamp Act. Both, he said, burdened the colonies with unconstitutional taxes.

"If Britain can order us to come to her for necessities we want, and can order us to pay what taxes she pleases before we take them away, or when we land them here, we are . . . slaves," he wrote. There was no need for Americans to pay taxes for military protection, he said, because the colonies had already compensated Britain with commercial benefits from trade. The colonists were "pouring the fruits of all their labors into their mother's lap. . . . How many British authors have demonstrated, that the present wealth, power and glory of their country are founded on these colonies?"

Dickinson spared no vitriol in attacking the Townshend Acts for stripping colonial assemblies of financial control over judges and governors. "Is it possible," he asked, "to form an idea of slavery more *compleat*, more *miserable*, more *disgraceful*, than that of a people where *justice is administered, government exercized* . . . AT THE EXPENCE OF THE PEOPLE, and yet WITHOUT THE LEAST DEPENDENCE AMONG THEM. . . . If we can find no relief from this infamous situation . . . we may bow down our necks, and with all the stupid serenity of servitude, to any drudgery which our lords and masters shall please to command."

Dickinson warned that the Townshend Acts would make America another Ireland, where British taxes had benefited only British sinecures and pensioners. "Besides the burdens of *pensions* in Ireland," he added, "all the *offices* in that poor kingdom have been . . . bestowed upon strangers. . . . In the same manner shall we unquestionably be treated."[21]

The *Letters from a Farmer in Pennsylvania*, as they would come to be called, provoked deep anger among colonists and equally deep anxiety among loyalists. Newport and Providence joined the Massachusetts boycott, and New York did the same just before the end of the year. Massachusetts governor Bernard called the letters "artfully wrote" and sent "a compleat set" to a friend in Par-

liament with the warning that they had been "universally circulated" and that if they "should receive no refutation . . . [they] will
become a kind of colonial Bill of Rights." On December 5, three
days after his first letter appeared in Philadelphia, Dickinson sent
copies of all twelve to James Otis in Boston and urged that Massachusetts, as the center of colonial trade with England, take the
lead in organizing colonial opposition. "The Liberties of our Common Country appear to me to be at this moment exposed to the
most imminent Danger," he wrote to Otis, "and this Apprehension
has engag'd me to lay my Sentiments before the Public in Letters
of which I send you a Copy. . . . Only one has yet been publish'd
and what there [*sic*] Effect may be, cannot yet be known, but whenever the Cause of American Freedom is to be vindicated, I look
towards the Province of Massachusetts Bay. She must, as she has
hitherto done, first kindle the Sacred Flame, that on such occasions must warm and illuminate the Continent."[22]

The first Dickinson letter appeared in all three Boston newspapers on December 21, and the following day Otis, Hancock,
Sam Adams, and Thomas Cushing petitioned the king to repeal
the Townshend Acts as violations of their "sacred right[s]," as
Englishmen, "of being taxed only by representatives of their own
free election." Sam Adams and James Otis sent a circular letter to
the other North American colonial assemblies urging them to send
similar petitions. Governor Bernard called the letter seditious and
dissolved the General Court in early March of 1768, but it was too
late. In England, the secretary of state for colonial affairs, Lord
Hillsborough, shot off two letters—the first to Governor Bernard
with the king's order that the Massachusetts House "rescind the
resolution which gave birth to the circular letter." Hillsborough
addressed the second letter to all other provincial governors,
instructing them to prevent their assemblies from acting on the
Massachusetts resolution—by dissolving them if necessary.

Both Bernard's and Hillsborough's moves came too late to
thwart the inexorable march of the colonies toward independence.
Indeed, far from slowing the march, Hillsborough's letters spurred
it forward. In Boston, Hancock called for expanding the partial
boycott of British goods into a total boycott. Virginia, New Jersey,

and Connecticut issued their own petitions to the king, with Virginia sending a circular letter to other colonies urging support for the Massachusetts boycott. By the end of the year, Maryland, Pennsylvania, Delaware, New Hampshire, South Carolina, North Carolina, and New York had ignored the admonitions of their royal governors and sent their own petitions to the king.

On March 14 the Boston town meeting overwhelmingly re-elected Hancock as selectman, then named him fire warden because of his work at the previous winter's huge fire. As his role in House affairs expanded, he turned over more responsibilities at the House of Hancock to his trusted aide William Palfrey. The town also appointed Hancock to two other committees—one made up of "patriots . . . to prepare and publish a letter of thanks" to John Dickinson, another to examine town accounts to determine how much Sam Adams had embezzled. The meeting demanded that Sam Adams pay £1,463 of the missing funds in his accounts at the tax collector's office, but he asked for another six-month stay to prepare a full financial statement. After a long debate that tarred Adams with epithets ranging from patriot to pilferer, the town decided to ask the treasurer to stay all action against Adams until Hancock's committee examined town accounts. The tide of events, however, quickly washed away memories of Adams's embezzlement. Although Hancock loaned Adams some of the money to repay the town, and Adams collected additional funds here and there, he never repaid his entire debt.

Indeed, Adams managed to refocus Boston's attention almost immediately after the town meeting by announcing plans for another of his constant demonstrations and parades to celebrate Repeal Day—a "Day of Triumph over Great Britain"—on March 18. The customs commissioners, anticipating tar and feathers, went into hiding, but to their own and the governor's surprise, Sam Adams astonished his followers by announcing, "NO MOBS—NO CONFUSIONS—NO TUMULTS." To ease the mob's disappointment, he added, "We know *WHO* have abus'd us . . . but let not a hair of their scalps be touched: The time is coming, when they shall lick the dust and melt away."[23]

7

"Idol of the Mob"

~~~

(1768-1770)

Aꜰᴛᴇʀ ᴘᴀssᴀɢᴇ of the Townshend Acts, Hancock made it clear that he would not permit English customs commissioners to board his ships. Indeed, he refused even to shake hands or speak with them. Although he was Boston's most eligible bachelor, Boston's social elite who sought to introduce him to unmarried young ladies knew better than to invite any customs commissioners to the same dinner. The net result was that Boston's elite ostracized the customs commissioners, while the mob regularly hanged them in effigy. The commissioners, in turn, blamed Hancock for their miseries and awaited an opportunity to retaliate.

Other merchants and shipowners followed Hancock's example, leaving the commissioners all but powerless to prevent virtually the entire American merchant fleet from landing goods duty free. Indeed, illicit trade so expanded economic activity that the Massachusetts government reduced its war debt to a mere £75,000—a sum it could reduce to zero by selling provincial lands to new settlers. The wealth that illicit foreign trade generated made it all the more imperative for the British government to extract its due in the form of duties. Despite eight commissioners and a small force of agents and clerks, the customs service had seized only six ships in two years—and angry mobs had forced them to release them before trial.

Early in 1768, the commissioners complained to London that they needed troops to enforce the Townshend Acts. "Our Officers were resisted and defeated in almost every Attempt to do their duty . . . we have every reason to expect that we shall find it totally impracticable to enforce the Execution of the Revenue Laws until the Hand of Government is strengthened. At present there is not a ship of war in the Province, nor a company of soldiers nearer than New York, which is two hundred and fifty Miles distant from this place."

On April 8, 1768, three weeks after his reelection as selectman, Hancock's brig *Lydia* tied up at Hancock Wharf with his spring orders from London, which the commissioners suspected included tea, paper, and other dutiable goods. Two customs agents boarded her the following morning. Hancock charged from his office to the wharf, and with a small mob, including the ship's captain, rushed on board and blocked the men's access to the hold. That night one of the agents slipped belowdecks under cover of darkness. Hancock was waiting with about eight or ten men and his uncle's slave Cato, who shone the lantern in the frightened agent's face. Hancock demanded to see the agent's orders and writ of assistance, or search warrant. His orders were undated and he had no writ. Hancock told his men to seize the agent and carry him topside. With the mate and boson suspending the terrified young man by his arms and thighs, Hancock asked him, "Do you want to search the vessel?" He insisted he did not, and they let him go ashore unharmed, with Hancock warning, "You may search the vessel, but shall not tarry below."

Hancock's assault on the British agent was the first physical assault on British authority in the colonies, and overnight it raised him to hero's status in Boston. Although the commissioners appealed to the attorney general of Massachusetts to prosecute Hancock, the attorney general decided that the men who had carried the agent ashore had borne no arms. Moreover, the agent had boarded the vessel illegally, without a writ or the permission of the captain, and when Hancock brought him topside and asked whether he now wanted to search the vessel, the agent himself had said that he did not. The attorney general ruled that "though Mr. Hancock may not have conducted himself so prudently or courteously as might be wished, yet from what appears it is probable that his intention was to keep within the bounds of the law."

It was now Hancock's turn, with Adams and Otis, to laugh at the royalists. Several days later a mob stoned two commissioners while they rowed away from Long Wharf. The commissioners blamed Hancock for the incident, calling him "an idol of the Mob" and adding that "this infatuated man now gives out in public, that if We, the Commrs, are not recalled he will get rid of us before Christmas."[1] Hancock informed the governor he would not attend the governor's election day banquet in Faneuil Hall if any commissioners were present. When the governor rebuffed him, Hancock retaliated by using his authority as selectman to bar the use of Faneuil Hall for the governor's banquet. As Sam Adams and James Otis cheered him on, Hancock was accumulating more enemies than he had ever had—or wanted—in his life. He was a businessman at heart—not a rebel. His eyes and heart searched for accommodation, not confrontation.

On May 4 Boston jubilantly reelected Hancock to the House of Representatives, which in turn elected him to the Governor's Council, or upper house. The governor, however, rejected Hancock, as well as Adams, Otis, and other patriot leaders. Five days later another Hancock ship, a small sloop called *Liberty*, sailed into port at sunset, on May 9. It had come from Madeira, and customs inspectors expected to find a shipload of wine. Because of the darkness they postponed their inspection until morning, by which time they found only twenty-five pipes (casks holding 125 gallons each)—less than one-quarter of the ship's capacity. When questioned by the commissioners, the agents could not explain the curious void and insisted they had seen no wine run ashore during the night.

A month later, after Hancock had unloaded the *Liberty* and reloaded her with cargo bound for England, the *Romney*, a fifty-gun

British man-of-war, sailed into Boston Harbor, commanded by a ruthless captain who thundered to all within earshot, "The town is a blackguard town and ruled by mobs . . . and, by the eternal God, I will make their hearts ache before I leave."[2] And so he did. He sent press gangs swarming ashore to terrorize the waterfront and carry away whatever unlucky young man happened to cross their path.

With the menacing silhouette of the *Romney* to protect them, the commissioners leaped at the chance to avenge Hancock's insults and insolence. One of the customs agents who had inspected the *Liberty* reversed his earlier statement. He said he had been forcibly held aboard the *Liberty* on the night of May 9 and heard the squeal of tackles hoisting goods, but was threatened with loss of life and home if he told what he knew. A senior customs official responded by painting a broad arrow on the *Liberty*'s mast—a signal she was now government property—and on June 10, the captain of the *Romney* sent a detachment of marines to haul the *Liberty* to a mooring beneath the *Romney*'s massive guns. While marines made fast their lines, a mob of about five hundred "sturdy boys & negroes" gathered on the wharf and pelted the marines with paving stones ripped from the streets. A Hancock employee ran up Beacon Hill to tell him what was happening, but Hancock did not want to get involved in the violence.

As the sailors gradually towed the *Liberty* out of range of the missiles, the mob focused its attack on the customs official and his aide, beating them as they ran to their homes, catching one and dragging him through the streets while pelting him with rocks and filth until friends could rescue him. The mob then gathered about the officials' homes and smashed their windows with rocks. Another group at the harbor pulled the customs boat from the water, carted it up to the Common, and set it afire within sight of Hancock's home. The commissioners, meanwhile, fled with their families to the customs house to retrieve government cash, and then rowed away under cover of darkness to the safety of the *Romney* and Castle William. Signs went up on the Liberty Tree urging citizens to attack the commissioners if they should reappear and attempt to collect duties. Governor Bernard prepared to flee and sent an urgent message to Gen. Thomas Gage "to rescue the Government out of the hands of a trained mob." Gage ordered two regiments to march on Boston.

For Samuel Adams, the seizure of the *Liberty* and its cargo was the spark he had awaited to light the flames of outright rebellion against British rule. He called to the growing mob at the Liberty Tree, "If you are Men, behave like Men; let us take up arms immediately and be free and Seize all the King's Officers; we shall have thirty thousand Men to join us from the Country. . . . We will take up arms and spend our last drop of blood."[3] Adams pledged that the English masses would join in the uprising, citing "the great tumults and risings of the people all over England and Ireland . . . the Weavers mob, the Seamens mob, the Tayllors mob, the Coal miners mob, and some say the Clergys mob . . . will unite in one general scene of tumult . . . at the very gates of the palace, and even in the royal presence."[4]

In contrast to Adams, Hancock saw the seizure of the *Liberty* as a serious business loss. Months might pass while his loaded cargo ship lay idle awaiting a resolution of the court case. On Saturday morning, June 11, he sent his lawyers and his friend and fellow Mason Dr. Joseph Warren to negotiate its release. He offered to post a bond to guarantee the ship's availability when the case went to court. Meanwhile, he would be able to send his ship and its cargo to London and carry on his trade. Fearful that the mobs would resume their rioting following the Sunday sabbath, the customs commissioners agreed; Hancock would repossess his ship on Monday morning. In the interests of restoring calm, the commissioners even promised to relent in pressing charges against him for smuggling. Other merchants—as fearful of the possible effects of riots as the commissioners—poured into Hancock's house urging him to accept the settlement, and he did, happily and triumphantly.

Otis and Adams, however, stormed into his house, angrily accusing him of capitulating to the customs commission, the royal governor, and the Townshend Acts—in effect, committing treason against the patriot cause. Adams and Otis seemed less interested in liberty than in power. They longed for war at any cost; reconciliation and peace were alien to their thinking. Although they unfurled the banner of liberty to rally mobs around them, their fight with the royal governor was over political power and personal vengeance for the humiliation of their fathers. Although Hancock normally followed the path of accommodation and reconciliation, there was little opportunity for either with a mob bent on violence against the wealthy merchant class. Numbers favored the Otis-Adams camp. Even if British troops eventually crushed the patriots, the mob would have ample time to destroy the properties of all their perceived enemies. As the wealthiest of the merchants, Hancock would almost certainly have been among those enemies. Rather than risk a potentially dangerous falling-out with the powerful Long Room Club and Boston Caucus, he evidently decided to swallow his financial losses and assume the role of martyr and symbol of patriot resistance. On Sunday evening, Hancock canceled his deal to recover the *Liberty* and threw his lot in with the Sons of Liberty.

Always the shrewd businessman, Hancock began planning ways to preserve his huge mercantile empire and personal wealth in the event the British restored order. He decided to try to seize patriot leadership from the radicals, which would allow him to emerge a wealthy hero in the event of a patriot victory and a wealthy peacemaker if the patriots agreed to surrender to superior British forces. Seizing control of the Whigs would not be difficult. Adams had become a near-rabid streetfighter, whom moderates in the merchant class mistrusted, while Otis had gained a reputation as a "mad dictator," subject to sharp mood swings that provoked "incoherent ravings." One minute he called Boston voters "damned stupid fools," only to court them, the next minute, to join in combat against British "tyranny."[5] If either Otis or Adams faltered, Hancock stood ready to use his wealth to replace one or both.

On June 30 Governor Bernard asked the General Court to rescind its petition to the king for repeal of the Townshend Acts. The Court refused, resolving defiantly "that this House do concur in and adhere to . . . that essential Principle, that no man can be taxed, or bound in Conscience to obey any Law, to which he has not given his Consent in Person, or by his Representative."[6] With Gage's troops on their way, however, the House suddenly moderated the tone of the resolution to read, "That the sole right of imposing taxes on the inhabitants of this his majesty's colony of the Massachusetts Bay, is now and ever has been vested in the house of representatives . . . with the consent of the council, and of his majesty the king of Great Britain, or his governor for the time being."

Much as had Patrick Henry's original inflammatory resolves, however, the offensive resolve went out to newspapers across the colony, and an infuriated governor dissolved the House of Representatives. Hancock wrote to his agent in London, "We have now two regiments, part of a third, and a train of artillery in this town. The report of the troops coming here alarmed the people much . . . the people are quiet and peaceable, and not the least disturbance has taken place. It is a great grief to this people that they are deprived of the benefits of a General Assembly."[7]

On August 1 sixty "Merchants and Traders of the Town of Boston" adopted a sweeping two-part nonimportation agreement. The first part banned imports of tea, paper, glass, and painters' colors, beginning January 1, 1769, "until the acts imposing duties on these articles are repealed." The second part of the agreement was a one-year ban on *all* other products imported from Britain except for ten essentials, including salt, coals, fishhooks and lines, hemp, duck, and shot. In the year that followed, merchant groups in New York, Philadelphia, Connecticut, Delaware, and Rhode Island would adopt similar agreements, although the products and the degree of enforcement would vary. Only New Hampshire and New Jersey merchants refused to act; and of course, Tory merchants in Boston such as the Hutchinsons, Olivers, and Clarkes continued filling their warehouses with British goods. In Virginia the wealthy planter George Washington led the effort for agreement. He wrote to his friend and neighbor George Mason in April 1769: "At a time when our lordly Masters in Great Britain will be

satisfied with nothing less than the deprivation of American freedom, it seems highly necessary that something shou'd be done to
avert the stroke and maintain the freedom that we have derived
from our Ancestors. . . . How far then their attention to our rights
and priviledges is to be awakened or alarmed by Starving their
Treade and manufactures remains to be tryed."[8]

Throughout the summer of 1768, Hancock's captive *Liberty*
bobbed in the water beneath the cruel guns of the British man-of-
war. Merchants and artisans—and even the poor—made the pil-
grimage up the hill to Hancock House to pay homage to Hancock
for his martyrdom. At the Liberty Tree, Otis and Adams kept
the mob's war fever burning with furious calls to arms. If British
troops marched into Boston, Otis raged at the town meeting on
July 14, there was "nothing more to do but to gird the sword to
the Thigh and Shoulder the Musquet. . . . We should one and all
resist even unto Blood. There are your arms," he shouted, and ges-
tured at an armory of four hundred muskets. "When an attempt is
made against your liberties they will be delivered to you."[9] The
meeting ended with Hancock, Adams, and other leaders going off
in a convoy of carriages to petition the governor to recall the General Court. Bernard rejected the appeal, and Adams issued a call to
all the towns in Massachusetts to send delegates to a convention
in Boston on September 22, to discuss "the peace and safety of his
[Majesty's] Subjects in this Province."[10]

Early in August, the trial of John Hancock and the *Liberty* got
under way. John Adams agreed to represent Hancock in both actions. Both cases ended after two weeks, with the charges against
Hancock dropped. In the second case, however, the court ordered
the forfeiture of the *Liberty*. Although the customs commissioners
put her up for sale, there were no buyers, and they decided to arm
her and send her roaming the coast in search of smugglers. A year
later, the *Liberty*'s searches and seizures had so infuriated merchants and shipowners in Newport that they would send a mob to
pierside to burn the ship to her waterline.

On September 22 about seventy delegates, representing nearly
one hundred Massachusetts communities, answered Adams's call

to convention in Boston's Faneuil Hall, but they were less eager than he to take up arms against professional British soldiers. Indeed, they were terrified. The *New Hampshire Gazette* proclaimed, "We are not to act like Rebels. Scorn the Thought—we have a good King and his royal Ear is not wilfully shut against us . . . we are represented as Rebels against the Crown and Dignity— But let us convince him by a dutiful Submission to his Government, and the British Constitution, that we are oppressed, and that we have a Right to Petition him theron."[11] Hatfield, Massachusetts, in the western part of Massachusetts, not only refused to send delegates to the Adams convention; it urged rural Massachusetts to let the Boston mob, which had started the rebellion on its own, fight British troops on its own. After it became evident that most delegates opposed violence, merchant Thomas Cushing, who like Hancock was helping to finance the patriot cause, abandoned Sam Adams and joined the moderates.

Aware of the changing mood, Otis did not even show up for the first three days of the convention, and Hancock darted in and out, pretending that the press of business did not allow him to attend for any length of time. Although Governor Bernard called the convention illegal and warned delegates to return home, he reveled in the political schism and considered inviting Hancock to resume his place in the ruling oligarchy by offering him a seat in the Governor's Council.[12] When, on the fourth day, British men-of-war pulled within sight of the Massachusetts coast, the delegates dashed off an innocuous petition for relief from taxation and military coercion and "rushed out of town like a herd of scalded dogs."[13] That afternoon the governor rejected the petition, and five days later, on October 1, an armada of British naval vessels rode into Boston Harbor with twelve hundred regular, red-coated troops aboard and pulled close enough to shore for Boston to see the grim faces of the force they opposed.

Boston greeted the ships with silence as the commander of the troops, Lt. Col. William Dalrymple, stepped ashore to meet select-men and arrange quartering the troops. All agreed to try to avoid violence. The selectmen suggested quartering the troops at Castle

William, the harbor island, but the colonel rejected it as too small. The colonel agreed not to quarter troops in private homes, but fearing an outbreak of disease and violence if his men remained in tight quarters aboard ship, he insisted that his troops disembark and spend the weekend quartered in Faneuil Hall. The selectmen had no choice but to agree.

One by one the longboats rowed to Long Wharf, discharging redcoats in full battle regalia, each bearing sixteen rounds of ammunition, until two regiments—twelve hundred soldiers for a city with barely fifteen thousand people—stood smartly at attention at the pier. Suddenly a staccato of commands pierced the stillness of the harbor, and "with Drums beating, Fifes playing and Colours flying" they marched in precision up King Street, onto the Common, "as if taking possession of a conquered town."[14] After a drill on the Common to intimidate the Boston mob, they went off to Faneuil Hall for the weekend. Paul Revere, whose anger had been building as he watched the troops land, walked back to his shop at the end of Hancock Wharf to engrave the "insolent parade" on copper.[15] When General Gage arrived from New York, some troops moved to the Common to establish a permanent encampment. Rumors swept through Boston that Gage would declare martial law and send troops into every home to disarm the citizenry and arrest "a number of gentlemen, who have exerted themselves in the cause of their country."[16] Gage's only goal, however, was to restore order in the streets and the smooth functioning of government. By the end of the month he felt confident enough to report "the Appearance of Peace and Quiet in this Place."[17]

To Hancock and the rest of Boston, however, the troops seemed a disease, infecting every nook and cranny of the city. They had turned the green of the Common into a sea of muck, sprouting tents and reeking of campfires, rotting garbage, human and animal wastes, and all other imaginable filth. Despite their promise to leave, troops continued living in Faneuil Hall—and in the Town House, the government building. In the harbor, the fleet commander had anchored his ships along the shore, one behind the other, broadsides facing town with big guns exposed and ready

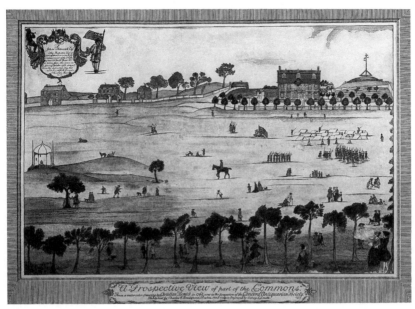

British troops drill on Boston Common in 1768, after landing in Boston to quell the beginning of the American Revolution. Hancock House, the palatial mansion of the patriot John Hancock, stands at the upper right. Engraved by Sidney L. Smith from a watercolor drawing by Christian Remick in 1768. Published by Charles E. Goodspeed, Boston, in 1902. (*Photograph courtesy of the Concord Museum, Concord, Mass.*)

to fire. Backed by armed sailors, customs commissioners boarded every vessel that entered or left the harbor.

On October 13, less than two weeks after the fleet arrived, a New York newspaper published an anonymously written article called "Journal of Transactions in Boston," purportedly chronicling events in Boston. It proved to be the first of a yearlong series that would appear in newspapers across the colonies and in England under the eventual title "Journal of Occurrences." Insisting its report was "strictly fact," the "Journal of Occurrences" described daily, bloodcurdling atrocities of British troops in Boston—their beating small boys and raping young girls, their violations of the sabbath with gunfire, drinking, and gambling. It portrayed the inconsolable grief of an elderly patriot who "the other morning discovered a soldier in bed with a favorite grand daughter."[18] The anonymous author was the consummate propagandist Sam Adams, who used the "Journal" to promote the cause of independence and venerate its heroes. Governor Bernard called the articles a "collection of impudent virulent & Seditious Lies, Perversions of Truth & Misrepresentations." Suspecting Adams as author, he accused him of publishing the articles in New York to prevent Bostonians from disputing their accuracy.

Misrepresentations notwithstanding, the "Journal" would not have succeeded without the arrogance and miscalculations of British political and military leaders. Most refused to believe that anyone fortunate enough to be a British subject would dare or even want to rebel. As Massachusetts chief justice Hutchinson had put it in early October 1768, "I cannot think that, in any colony, people of any consideration have ever been so mad as to think of revolt. Many of the common people have been in a frenzy and talked of dying in defence of their liberties and have spoke and printed what is highly criminal; and too many of rank above the vulgar, and some in *public posts*, have countenanced and encouraged them until they increased so much in their numbers and in their opinion of their importance as to submit to government no further than they thought proper."[19]

Ignoring all appeals from saner minds—at home and abroad—for restraint, the British political and military high commands remained intent on asserting their authority in the most provocative ways. In doing so they fed Adams more fuel than he needed to keep the flames of discontent raging in Boston and everywhere else his "Journal of Occurrences" appeared. On October 29 British troops in Boston abandoned the Common for winter quarters in various public buildings. Hancock and other Bostonians were just beginning to relax in their absence when the troops returned two days later in full force, at a slow march, with drums rolling ominously. In their midst was a young deserter, draped in white, accompanied by a chaplain reading from an open Bible. The regiments halted. A firing squad snapped to the ready, aimed, fired, and marched away, leaving the body and its pale shroud in a pool of blood and mud. As echoes of the fatal round resounded through the silent grove, the drums resumed their eerie roll, while commanders led their regiments on an endless slow march, around and around the corpse, to demonstrate the inevitable fate of deserters.

Adams had no sooner written his description of the grisly scene when, on the evening of November 2, the British once again went out of their way to provoke colonists with an order to the troops to stand ready for possible rioting the next day. The next morning, the marshal of the vice-admiralty court marched up Beacon Hill and arrested John Hancock. Not satisfied with having confiscated the *Liberty*, Governor Bernard had decided to crush Hancock and the Sons of Liberty by filing criminal charges against the merchant for smuggling on the *Liberty*. Bernard believed he could destroy the patriot movement by cutting off its source of funds at the House of Hancock. To avoid imprisonment, Hancock posted a £3,000 bond—an amount equal to the value of the goods the crown said he had smuggled on the *Liberty*. John Adams agreed to defend him.

From the outset, the trial was illegal. Although off-loading a vessel without a true and perfect inventory was grounds for seizure and forfeiture, there was no eyewitness or evidence of such off-loading. Nevertheless, the attorney general of the province charged Hancock with landing one hundred pipes of wine, worth £3,000; and under the law, smugglers were subject to fines equal to triple the value of the goods they smuggled—in this case, £9,000, with one-third to go to the crown, one-third to the governor, and one-third to the informer. To ensure Hancock's subsequent bankruptcy, the attorney asked for penalties adding up to another £100,000 for failing to obey lawful orders of an agent of the crown, encouraging assault on such an agent, and encouraging the illegal imprisonment of the agent. The attorney general made the case as costly as possible for Hancock and everyone he knew, demanding that all Hancock's friends, relatives, business associates, and employees appear in court for hours of endless questioning. He even considered calling Hancock's aging aunt Lydia. One after the other, the witnesses answered the attorney general's questions with expressions of ignorance or lapses of memory. The case dragged on day after day, exhausting the entire town. "I was thoroughly weary and disgusted with the Court, the officers of the Crown, the Cause, and even with the tyrannical Bell that dangled me out of my House every Morning," admitted John Adams.[20] As the trial enervated the rest of Boston, it energized Samuel Adams, whose accounts of the trial in the "Journal of Occurrences" lifted John Hancock to national prominence as a martyred hero for what patriots now universally called "the cause."

At the end of three months, the attorney general had no evidence or eyewitness testimony to substantiate his charges against Hancock, and he was forced to declare, "Our Sovereign Lord the King will prosecute no further hereon." Boston greeted the decision with a mixture of joy and anger—joy at Hancock's acquittal, anger at the mean-spirited governor and attorney general who had put Hancock and the rest of the town through the unnecessarily long and painful trial. Hancock himself sat at ease in his home, luxuriating in the adulation that enveloped Beacon Hill. Letters of praise, encouragement, and congratulations arrived from across the colonies, from Britain, from Europe. Sam Adams had created a new champion of resistance, who to Adams's eventual regret would ultimately displace him in the front ranks of the Revolutionary leadership.

Despite loss of time and money, the trial hardly left Hancock in ruin. At home he had an abundant supply of Madeira—including a hundred pipes that materialized after the arrival of the all but empty *Liberty*. At work, his retail stores were stocked fully and doing well. Sales totaled well over £10,000 in 1768 and seemed certain to top £12,000 the following year, as customers hoarded to hedge against the effects of the boycott. Together with his wholesale trade, Hancock had more than £20,000 in accounts receivable at the end of 1768, including £29 owed by British general Thomas Gage. He remained Boston's largest shipowner, and his banking operations held reserves of more than £20,000 in interest-bearing loans, or more than 20 percent of all the money loaned in Boston. In real estate, his aggressive acquisitions had accumulated tens of thousands of acres in New Hampshire, Connecticut, Massachusetts (including present-day Maine), and in Boston proper. Some properties lay fallow, but others produced an abundant flow of income, from lumber sales from the woodlots, from crop sales by tenant sharecroppers on his farms, and from rents at his stores and residences in town.[21]

Although Hancock had also lost a ship, the *Liberty*, and (not surprisingly) his contract to supply the British military in Nova Scotia, his fleet still numbered five vessels, and while half its previous size, it continued carrying whale oil and potash abroad and imported more than £8,000 worth of goods. Hancock sought to increase the revenues from each ship by converting one part into passenger quarters. He ran advertisements in newspapers on both sides of the Atlantic.

for LONDON

The Ship *Boston Packet*, James Scott, Commander;

A prime Sailor, with good

Accommodation for Passengers, lying at *Hancock's* wharf,

and sails with all convenient Speed.

Freighters or Passengers may apply to

John Hancock Esq: at his store, or the Master on Board.[22]

The fare to London was negotiated with each passenger—in effect, whatever the market would bear for each type of accommodation. On one voyage from Nevis (in the West Indies) to London, the captain charged £27 per passenger, not including costs of food and drink.

On January 1, 1769, Massachusetts merchants imposed a near-total boycott that shut down the flow of all but a handful of British goods into the province. Every colony except New Hampshire followed suit, and by the end of the year, British imports into the colonies would plunge 38 percent, to about £1.34 million, down from £2.2 million in 1768. In Boston, Hancock promoted the boycott tirelessly, even supplying goods on credit to small merchants faced with closing for lack of English merchandise. Some English goods continued to flow to a handful of Tory importers who refused to join the boycott, but Hancock, Adams, and the other patriot leaders rallied consumers to support it, and even Boston's grandest dames—including Hancock's aunt Lydia—refused to drink English tea. Milch cow or not, Hancock was not only buying personal political power; by extending credit to other merchants he was acquiring a stake in so many mercantile establishments that if the patriot conflict with England had ended then, he would have had a monopoly on Massachusetts banking, retailing, and wholesaling.

In February 1769 the events in Massachusetts associated with the *Liberty* had so aroused Parliament that it decided to apply Henry VIII's ancient Treason Act to punish those responsible. Long unused, the act ordered those suspected of treason to be brought to trial in England, regardless of whether the crimes were committed in or out of the realm. Edmund Burke, a champion of reconciliation with the colonies, asked Parliament, "Why are the provisions of the statute of Henry the Eighth to be put in force against the Americans? Because you cannot trust a jury of that country. Sir, that word must carry horror to every feeling mind. If you have not a party among two millions of people, you must either change your plan of government, or renounce your colonies forever."[23] Parliament listened to the great orator—it was impossible not to listen to him—but in the end they did not understand the implications of what he said. Even the face of utter failure did not dissuade Parliament from asserting its outdated authoritarian ways over the colonies. Lord Hillsborough, the British secretary of state for the colonies, argued against any policy changes "which can in any way derogate from the legislative authority of Great Britain over the colonies."[24] Then, acting with the king's authority under Henry VIII's Treason Act, Hillsborough secured a parliamentary resolution ordering Governor Bernard to send "the fullest information that can be obtained, touching all treasons and misprision [concealment] of treason committed within your government since the 30th day of December 1767."[25]

The Treason Resolution produced angry counterresolutions in Massachusetts and nine other colonies. In addition to protesting the Treason Resolution and the Townshend Acts, the Massachu-setts House of Representatives complained about "the establish-ment of a standing army in the colony in time of peace without the consent of the General Assembly."[26] In Boston, all eyes turned toward Beacon Hill, awaiting Hancock's response. He was beset by pressures from every direction—political, business, social, and personal. The first rays of sunlight saw him jump into his coach each morning to ride down to his office; then it was off to the wharf to meet with the captains of his ships, chase down missing cargo, or negotiate new deals. Members of the Boston mob lurked in every shadow. Uniformed soldiers added to the tense, colorful, impenetrable mix of workers, merchants, and thugs that milled about the wharves. His coach could barely jolt a few inches along the crowded waterfront. As the sun climbed to the perpendicular, Hancock stopped at his store for a conference with Palfrey before going to the Merchants Club and then back up to Hancock House for meetings and conferences.

At every stop townsmen queued up for his ear—to whisper rumors or plead for help. At every stop he listened graciously and patiently, but always regally, dressed in his velvet suit, his white lace shirt cuffs—a portrait of the eighteenth-century nobleman, with a gold-headed cane, stepping from his carriage while a liver-ied footman held the door and a second extended an arm to help his lordship into the street to hear the members of his realm.

"It was astonishing with what patience, perseverance, and punc-tuality he attended to business," John Adams wrote of Hancock many years later. "Nor were his talents or attainments inconsider-able. They were far superior to many who have been made more celebrated. He had a great deal of political sagacity and penetration into men."[27]

At the town meeting in March, Hancock garnered the most votes for selectman, and in May his townsmen returned him to the House of Representatives with five hundred of the possible 508 votes. The House of Representatives elected Hancock speaker pro tem and a member of the Governor's Council. Governor Ber-nard was out of town and had named Chief Justice Hutchinson as lieutenant governor; he vetoed Hancock for both posts, and the House replaced Hancock with Dr. Joseph Warren. Like Hancock, Warren was a Harvard graduate. Although he set out to be a schoolmaster, he switched course in 1761 to study medicine and gained fame by developing an unusual method of inoculating smallpox patients. His marriage to the daughter of a wealthy merchant brought him the luxury of dabbling in politics. He joined the Masons and became grand master of the Masonic Grand Lodge, where he formed close ties to John Hancock and other young Masons. Like them he soon fell under the spell of Samuel Adams at the Green Dragon, and passage of the Stamp Act saw him plunge irretrievably into the maelstrom of patriot politics. Less outspoken than Otis, Adams, or Hancock, Warren may have seemed more ineffectual to Hutchinson, when in reality he was at least as dangerous to royal governance as the others.

Under the Massachusetts charter, the governor had to convene the General Court at least once a year, and when they met on May 31 under Speaker Warren, the delegates demanded removal of the troops. After the governor claimed that troop removal was beyond his jurisdiction, the House of Representatives refused to appropriate any funds to billet soldiers or even pay the governor his annual salary. After two weeks of inaction, Bernard ordered the House to move from Boston's charged atmosphere to the quiet of Cambridge, where they could no longer interact with the mobs.

Once at Harvard, Speaker Warren brought all General Court activity to a halt, and after a six-week stalemate, the governor condemned the Court and said he would return to England to "report . . . the State of the Province" to the king. The House called him an "enemy of the colony, and . . . the Nation in general" and petitioned the king to remove Bernard as governor, to which the enraged governor responded by dissolving the Court.[28]

On August 1 Boston steeple bells rang out, flags covered the Liberty Tree, guns fired continuously from Hancock Wharf, and a bonfire blazed from the top of one of the hills as Governor Bernard sailed off to London, leaving Lt. Gov. Thomas Hutchinson, the former merchant and still chief justice, as new governor

MAJOR GENL. JOSEPH WARREN
Slain at the Battle of Bunker's Hill June y 1775

Dr. Joseph Warren, a renowned physician and
close friend of John Hancock, became speaker of
the Massachusetts General Court and later shared
command of the Revolution with Hancock. (*National
Portrait Gallery, Smithsonian Institution*)

ex officio. Two weeks later the Sons of Liberty marched under the
noses of British troops to the Liberty Tree to toast the anniversary
of their founding four years earlier, when they had hung Andrew
Oliver's effigy and attacked his home. That evening Hancock's
coach led a procession of 119 carriages—with Otis at the rear—
across the neck to a tavern in Dorchester, on the mainland, to toast
victory at another of Hancock's elegant dinners.

Their celebration was short lived, however. A week later, the Tory *Boston Chronicle* charged Hancock and other Boston merchants with using a loophole in the nonimportation agreement to continue importing British goods. Focusing on Hancock as the boycott organizer, the newspaper published a manifest from one of Hancock's ships, which showed he had imported a handsome new carriage for himself and expensive table linen—fraudulently listed as canvas—for his aunt. The newspaper pointed out that the boycott did not prevent merchants from importing goods that they had no intention of reselling. Thus they could still import goods intended for their personal use or goods that belonged to others. Newspapers throughout the colonies reprinted the *Chronicle* stories, with Boston merchants, including Hancock, portrayed as liars and charlatans. Newspapers in New Hampshire, Newport, New York, and Philadelphia assailed Hancock.

"The Boston News Writers," said an article in the *Newport Mercury*, "make JOHN HANCOCK Esq. one of the foremost Patriots in Boston and the strictest observer of the agreement for non-importation: he would perhaps shine more conspicuously and be less suspected in this character if he did not keep a number of vessels running to London and back full freighted getting rich by receiving freight and goods made contraband by the Colonies."[29]

Hancock responded immediately in the *New York Journal:* "This is ONCE FOR ALL to certify to whom it may concern, That I have not in one single instance directly or indirectly deviated from said Agreement; and I now publicly defy all Mankind to prove to the CONTRARY."

Despite his denials, the *Chronicle* articles undermined merchant support for nonimportation, and Hancock had to call Boston merchants together to sign an amended nonimportation agreement not to bring in any dutied goods on their vessels, regardless of who would use the goods. He then packed his things and set off in his coach for New York and Philadelphia to shore up support in those towns. In Philadelphia he convinced John Dickinson, the author of the *Letters from a Farmer in Pennsylvania*, to stand by him, and together they managed to restore some merchant support for nonimportation. But the articles substantially weakened the agreement.

The Tory *Chronicle* persisted in its attacks, calling Hancock "Johnny Dupe, Esq., alias the Milch-Cow . . . a good natured young man with long ears—a silly conceited grin on his countenance—a fool's cap on his head—a bandage tied over his eyes—richly dressed and surrounded with a crowd of people, some of whom are stroking his ears, others tickling his nose with straws while the rest are employed in riffling his pockets; all of them with labels out of their mouths bearing these words OUR COMMON FRIEND."[30]

Two days later a mob formed to lynch one of the *Chronicle* editors. Although he escaped unharmed, they found a scapegoat—a suspected informer, whom they promptly "stripped naked, put in a cart where he was first tarred, then feathered and in this condition carried through the principal streets of the town followed by a great concourse of People."[31] The editor sailed for London on the next ship out, leaving his partner to run the business. In the meantime Hancock's ever-present good fortune once again came into play, when a letter arrived from Thomas Longman, London's great bookseller and stationer. Longman was a longtime Hancock supplier and close friend of both Thomas and John Hancock. He asked John to assume power of attorney and collect some £2,000 in long-overdue debts from, of all people, the editors of the *Chronicle*. After sending a disingenuous "anything-for-a-friend" reply, Hancock set out to destroy the publication. With John Adams as attorney, he won a judgment against the newspaper. The sheriff seized the printing shop and its assets; Hancock closed the newspaper, sold the press and everything else in the shop, and sent the proceeds to Longman.

EARLY IN SEPTEMBER 1769, James Otis swaggered provocatively into the British Coffee House, a rendezvous for army and navy officers, and challenged the customs commissioner. The confrontation escalated into a full-scale brawl, from which Otis emerged bloodied, beaten badly, and somewhat incoherent after repeated clubbing about the head and at least one severe cutlass blow. "A number of sticks at once were over Mr. Otis's head—a drawn sword—the cry in the room G——d d——n him, meaning Mr. Otis, knock him down—kill him—kill him."[32]

Otis sued one of the officers and won £2,000 in damages and an apology, but he never recovered from the effects of his head injuries. "He rambles and wanders like a ship without a helm."[33] He had always exhibited some eccentricities, but now he wavered between fits of verbosity and melancholy, and lamented—to Governor Hutchinson, of all people—his responsibility for the violence then plaguing Boston. "I meant well," he told the governor, "but am now convinced I was mistaken. Cursed be the day I was born."[34]

Otis sank deeper and deeper into insanity, giving up his law practice and turning to drink. "He talks so much," reported John Adams, for whom Otis was a hero, friend, and mentor in the law, "and fills it with trash, obsceneness, profaneness, nonsense and distraction. . . . I never saw such an object of admiration, reverence, contempt, and compassion, all at once. I fear, I tremble, I mourn for the man and for his country; many others mourn over him, with tears in their eyes." In February the following year, Otis snapped and began smashing windows at the Town House before he was finally bound hand and foot in a chair and carted away. The Whigs named John Adams to fill his seat in the General Court. As one of the luminaries of the Revolution went into eclipse, a bright new star was ascending.

The Otis brawl combined with Sam Adams's increasingly provocative articles to plunge Boston into near anarchy. Personal feuds and rivalries deteriorated into accusations of Tory collaboration—and inevitably, broken windows, vandalism, and vicious graffiti. In January and February 1770, reports poured into Boston of serious clashes in New York between bayonet-wielding British soldiers and mobs armed with clubs. In Boston fights erupted nightly in the city's many taverns and spilled onto the streets. In every alley, small gangs lay in wait to assault any lone

John Adams

John Adams, the Boston lawyer (and future vice president of the United States) who defended John Hancock in the *Liberty* case and the British soldiers accused of murder in the Boston Massacre. (*Library of Congress*)

redcoat who chanced by. With Otis incapacitated and Hancock busy rallying merchants for nonimportation, Sam Adams roamed the taverns with thugs dressed as Mohawks, spreading anarchy. In London, William Pitt, who had once sided with the colonists, now warned the House of Lords that colonists had carried "their notions of freedom too far . . . [and] will not be subject to the laws of this country."[35]

Boston's children contributed to tension in the streets by pelting redcoats or suspected redcoat sympathizers with snowballs. On February 22, 1770, a small mob assailed a merchant who refused to sign the nonimportation agreement. After he took refuge in his shop, a friend came to his help, and as the mob broke down the door, the friend fired his shotgun at them, wounding a nineteen-year-old and killing eleven-year-old Christopher Seider (variously spelled Snyder and Snider). Seider's death—the first in what would become the American Revolution—inflamed the street mobs. Sam Adams turned the Seider funeral into the largest ever held in America—an enormous mass mourning of a martyr that stretched more than a half mile, with more than four hundred carefully groomed angelic children leading the coffin and two thousand mourners walking behind it. Thirty chariots and chaises followed.

"Mine eyes have never beheld such a funeral," said John Adams. "This Shewes, there are many more Lives to Spend if wanted in the Service of their Country. It Shewes, too that the Faction is not yet expiring—that the Ardor of People is not to be quelled by the Slaughter of one Child and the Wounding of another."[36] The *Boston Gazette* said Seider's death "crieth for Vengeance. . . . Young as he was, he died in his Country's Cause."

Relations between colonists and British troops deteriorated badly. The air filled with a constant staccato of catcalls and cries of "Lobster, hey lobster." Fights erupted between "lobsters" and "Mohawks" on the waterfront—with Sam Adams never far away, always goading his thugs to harass, insult, and provoke violence. General Gage recognized—as John Hancock had recognized from the beginning—his error in ordering troops to Boston:

"The people were as Lawless and Licentious after the Troops arrived as they were before," Gage would write. "The Troops could not act by Military Authority and no Person in Civil Authority would ask their aid. They were there contrary to the wishes of the Council, Assembly, Magistrates and People, and seemed only to offer abuse and Ruin. And the Soldiers were either to suffer ill usage and even assaults upon their Persons till their Lives were in

Danger, or by resisting and defending themselves, to run almost a Certainty of suffering by the Law."[37]

At the beginning of March the king appointed Hutchinson governor, consolidating his authority as chief justice with that of chief executive and, in effect, giving him a tyrant's absolute power. Moreover, as owner of one of Boston's great mercantile empires, he was independently wealthy and therefore immune to legislative sanction to withhold his salary. The king hoped that Hutchinson would rally Boston's merchants to the Tory side. They, like Hancock, were less interested in political independence than in stability and peace in a tax-free climate that would allow them to prosper. In elevating Hutchinson to governor, the king appointed Hutchinson's brother-in-law, the wealthy merchant Andrew Oliver, as lieutenant governor.

Hutchinson and Oliver could not have assumed their new posts at a worse time. "I think I could support myself well enough at first," Hutchinson wrote in dismay to former governor Pownall in London, "but the spirit of Anarchy which prevails in Boston is more than I am able to cope with."[38] From the moment the Seider boy went to his rest, townsmen seldom let a moment pass without provoking fights with soldiers. On March 2 rope maker Samuel Gray, one of Adams's most brawl-hardened Mohawks, sneered at a soldier seeking part-time work that he might clean the rope maker's privy. As onlookers cawed with laughter, the soldier called his comrades and set off a brawl that flashed intermittently for the next three days and nights, with gangs of boys fueling the conflict by continually pelting the redcoats with snowballs.

On the evening of March 5, belligerent bands of laborers and soldiers roamed the streets, only narrowly avoiding conflict until 9 P.M., when a young barber's apprentice provoked a sentry at the customs house on King Street. The sentry knocked the boy down and sent him off screaming for help. A crowd of boys gathered and pelted the sentry with snowballs, all the while shouting, "Kill him, kill him. Knock him down."[39] A crowd of men joined in. Suddenly the town's bells began pealing, and other townsmen rushed from their homes thinking a fire had broken out. Mobs surged through

Royal governor Thomas Hutchinson, the former merchant, whose efforts to quell the Revolution ultimately forced him into exile in Britain. (*Bostonian Society*)

the streets. At Faneuil Hall a man described as tall, wearing a red cloak and white wig, was whipping a crowd of men into a frenzy, while another crowd gathered at the barracks.

By this time, Capt. Thomas Preston, the officer of the day, heard of the sentry's predicament at the customs house and marched six privates and a corporal to the scene, their guns unloaded but bayonets fixed, intent on escorting the sentry into the customs house, away from the mob's missiles and taunts. By the time he reached the sentry's post, small gangs swept in from all directions. The mob swelled and made it impossible for Preston to march away. Volleys of ice, oyster shells, and sticks rained on the troops. Rope maker Samuel Gray, Crispus Attucks (a massive "mulatto fellow," according to later testimony), ship's mate James Caldwell, and Patrick Carr, "a seasoned Irish rioter," pushed their way to the front of the crowd with a group of sailors.[40]

"The multitude was shouting and Huzzaing, and threatening life, the bells ringing, the mob whistling, screaming and rending like an Indian yell, the people from all quarters throwing every species of rubbish they could pick up in the streets"—all the while daring the soldiers to fire. As the missiles rained down, some townsmen lunged at the troops with sticks held as swords, crying "bloody backs," "lobsters," and other epithets.[41] Then Attucks hurled his club at one of the soldiers. It found its mark; the soldier fell; he staggered to his feet and shouted, "Damn you, fire," and fired his own weapon into the crowd. A second soldier fired a hole into Gray's skull, and before his body hit the ground a volley of shots left four others dead and six wounded. Attucks and Caldwell fell at the feet of the beleaguered soldiers. Eight others lay wounded, including Carr and a seventeen-year-old, both of whom later died of their wounds. The other six recovered.[42] Samuel Adams now had the massacre he had sought in order to incite a revolution against British rule. He sent messengers into the country to alert farmers to arm themselves but to await ignition of a bonfire on Beacon Hill as a signal to march on Boston.

"Endeavors had been systematically pursued for months by certain busy characters," wrote John Adams, "to excite quarrels, encounters, and combats . . . in the night between the inhabitants of the lower class and the soldiers . . . to enkindle a mortal hatred between them. I suspected this was the explosion which had been intentionally wrought up by designing men who knew what they were aiming at better than the instruments employed."[43]

For a while, Boston awaited an even greater massacre. Merchants tried as best they could to protect their shops from looters. Appalled by the violence, Hancock remained cloistered in his mansion on Beacon Hill. Messengers from town—his clerks, various followers, and others—bounded up and down Beacon Street with breathless reports of the goings-on below. He was trapped in a war of madmen—each side set on destroying the other. His own survival depended on taking personal control of the patriots, unseating the fanatics who controlled the mobs, and restoring reason to Boston leadership. Regardless of the outcome of the conflict with Britain, reason would have to prevail. Hancock wanted peace in the streets of Boston and a return to normal life.

In the terrifying moments after the shootings, Preston and his men returned to the main guard and readied for an assault by the mob, now rumored to have reached five thousand. The British regiment quartered at the Town House, already seething from months of insults and assaults, moved toward King Street prepared to crush a rebellion. Governor Hutchinson knew that unless he took control immediately, "the whole town would be up in arms and the most bloody scene would follow that had ever been known in America."[44] Hutchinson raced to the Town House, and as the crowd gathered beneath the second-floor balcony, he called on them to return to their homes. "The law shall have its course," he promised. "I will live and die by the law."[45]

Enough of the mob went home to restore a semblance of peace, and Hutchinson, now acting as chief justice of the Massachusetts Superior Court, decided to implement his pledge immediately. The sheriff brought in Captain Preston at 2 A.M. Although he insisted he had never given the order to fire, witnesses claimed he did, and the justices sent Preston to prison at 3 A.M. The next morning more than three thousand people gathered at the Town House as the eight soldiers under Preston's command surrendered, were indicted for murder, and were imprisoned to await trial. The court postponed the trial until autumn to allow a return to calm and improve the chances of finding an impartial jury. Hancock, Adams, Cushing, and another assemblyman met with Hutchinson, Oliver, and the British military commander Colonel Dalrymple at the Town House to try to end the violence. With House speaker Cushing acting as moderator, Hancock warned Oliver that "there were upwards of 4000 Men ready to take Arms

... and many of them of the first Property, Character and Distinction in the Province."[46] Ten thousand more, he said, stood poised, muskets in hand, on the outskirts of Boston, their eyes fixed on Beacon Hill for the signal to march into Boston if British troops did not withdraw from the city.

It was a bluff, of course. Dalrymple and Hutchinson knew it was a bluff, but they agreed with Hancock that the violence had gone on too long and had reached unnecessarily tragic proportions. Dalrymple agreed to withdraw the troops, and a few days later the redcoats retreated to Castle William; and Boston again hailed John Hancock as a hero—this time for negotiating the troop withdrawal. A few weeks later, tensions in Boston eased still further as Dalrymple cut troop strength nearly in half by sending one of the two regiments at Castle William to New Jersey.

Sam Adams, of course, could not reveal his role in provoking the Boston Massacre without incurring merchant outrage—not to mention charges of treason by the governor—so he gritted his teeth and joined in disingenuous praise of Hancock's extraordinary negotiating skills. Fearful of losing control, he rallied the Sons of Liberty, elevated the dead hooligans to near sainthood, and staged a grandiose procession with more than ten thousand mourners to carry them to their graves. Adams encouraged James Bowdoin, a friend from Harvard days, to write (anonymously) an inflammatory pamphlet entitled *A Short Narrative of the Horrid Massacre of Boston,* which called the shootings part of a conspiracy between the army and the customs commission to silence their critics. Although born to mercantile wealth, Bowdoin was a radical who seldom let facts stand in the way of his conclusions. He sent his pamphlet to newspapers across the colonies and in Britain, where it received widespread circulation.

Edes's *Boston Gazette* of March 12 appeared edged in black mourning and charged that British soldiers had provoked the massacre by "parading the Streets with drawn Cutlasses and Bayonets, abusing and wounding Numbers of the Inhabitants."[47] The issue included a provocative and grossly inaccurate drawing by Henry Pelham, the half brother of portrait artist John Singleton Copley. Entitled *Fruits of Arbitrary Power, or The Bloody Massacre in King Street,* Pelham's drawing showed soldiers slaughtering helpless townsmen. Paul Revere made an engraving and sold prints of it, without permission or attribution.[48]

In the days following the massacre, Adams, Cushing, and Josiah Quincy, a lawyer and the youngest son of old Col. Josiah Quincy of Braintree, wrote influential friends in London, including former Massachusetts governor Pownall, "acquainting them with the circumstances & Facts relative to the late horrid Massacre, and asking the continuance of their good services in behalf of this Town and Province." The letter was designed "to prevent any ill impressions from being made upon the minds of his Majesty's Ministers, and Others, of the Town [of Boston]."[49]

Governor Hutchinson tried to restore calm with a public appeal delivered to the General Court. Sam Adams and his followers would have none of it. They packed town meetings with three and four thousand people to shout, hoot, cheer, sing, and do whatever else they could to disrupt proceedings. On March 15 Hutchinson followed the example of his predecessor Governor Bernard and ordered the General Court to meet in mob-free Cambridge—much to the distress of Hancock, who had to leave his home and business again. The Court met intermittently over the next six months, debating the sole issue of whether the governor had the constitutional right to tell the House where to meet. In a surprise split with Samuel Adams, Hancock supported the governor. He sensed a growing alienation of rural representatives from Adams and the Boston radicals for forcing delegates from across the colony to travel into the dirty streets of Boston every time the General Court convened. They welcomed the opportunity to meet in Cambridge, and Hancock joined them. After months of inaction, however, the governor finally ordered the Court adjourned until the following year. Boston's town meeting responded with warnings of "a deep-laid plan of imperial despotism . . . for the extinction of all civil liberty."[50]

Despite efforts to sustain the embers of violence, calmer voices began to prevail, with members of the Suffolk County bar association taking the lead in organizing a force of three hundred lawyers,

Paul Revere's engraving of the Boston Massacre, copied without permission from a drawing by Henry Pelham, the half brother of portrait artist John Singleton Copley. Pelham threatened legal action against Revere for the theft. (*Bostonian Society*)

merchants, and other stable townsmen to stand armed watch and patrol the town to prevent further mob violence. Equipped with musket, bayonet, broadsword, and cartridge box, thirty-five-year-old attorney John Adams volunteered for and took his regular turn on sentry duty outside the Town House.[51] Recalling the Boston Massacre later, he concluded, "On that night the foundation of American independence was laid."[52]

8

"Tea in a Trice"

(1770-1773)

EARLY IN APRIL 1770, Lord North began his career as new prime minister with a political miscalculation that would cost his country the richest gem of its empire. He made a semblance of concession to colonist grievances by asking Parliament to repeal all but one of the Townshend Acts duties, namely the insignificant three-pence-a-pound duty on tea. Aware of its unimportance to the British treasury, he nevertheless insisted on retaining it "as a mark of the supremacy of Parliament, and an efficient declaration of their right to govern the colonies."[1] Although Britain had levied tariffs on tea since 1721, smugglers imported about nine hundred thousand tons of cheap foreign tea duty free each year. The quality did not approach that of East India Company tea, and discriminating Americans continued buying 562,000 tons of dutiable tea a year. Nevertheless, the smuggled tea represented a considerable loss in revenues from unpaid duties.

News of the repeal of the Townshend Acts cheered the rational and calmed the irrational—except for the redoubtable James Otis, who continued acting irrationally and was confined to his home. At the end of May he erupted in uncontrollable rage and began firing guns from his window over the heads of a large and frightened crowd. "His friends were obliged to take him under their care, and he was removed to the country."[2]

As with the Stamp Act's repeal, the official announcement of the Townshend Acts' repeal arrived on one of Hancock's ships. Its loyal master, Capt. James Scott, delivered it straight to Hancock at the town meeting, which again confused Hancock's announcement of good news with his having played a role in generating it. He did nothing to discourage their cheers and, indeed, could display numerous letters of protest he had sent to men of influence in England that may or may not have affected repeal. Boston cast a resounding 511 of the possible 513 votes for Hancock in the May elections for House of Representatives.

Repeal of the Townshend Acts duties convinced American merchants to abandon nonimportation agreements, except for tea. In the end, the boycott cost British merchants £860,000 in American sales, although some partially offset losses with increased sales to Europe.

With the end of nonimportation, trade between England and the colonies returned to normal. Renewed prosperity created jobs for the unemployed and weakened popular support for Sam Adams and the Sons of Liberty. The city also lost its appetite for vengeance against the British soldiers who had languished in prison since the Boston Massacre. Moreover, two outstanding patriot lawyers—John Adams and young Josiah Quincy—had agreed to represent the soldiers. Sam Adams tried to renew public hysteria, but to his dismay the court allowed his cousin John to select a jury of men from outside Boston, who had never lived under redcoat occupation and harbored no animosities toward British troops. Several even had business ties to the British army, and five jurors later became loyalist exiles. Using their challenges in expert fashion, Adams and Quincy prevented the seating of even a single Son of Liberty or Bostonian on the jury. The first trial, *Rex v. Preston*, began on October 24; Robert Treat Paine was appointed prosecutor, with no option to refuse. Although a brilliant lawyer who had graduated from Boston Latin and Harvard, he inherited a case that was laughably weak.

The first prosecution witness admitted he had not been on King Street the night of the tragedy. Other prosecution witnesses agreed that the crowd, not Preston, had shouted, "Fire! Fire!" John Adams and young Quincy quickly dismantled the prosecution's case, presenting thirty-eight witnesses to testify that civilians had plotted to attack the soldiers. In addition they had the deathbed confession of Patrick Carr that the townspeople had been the aggressors and that the soldiers had not fired until attacked by "a motley rabble of saucy boys, negroes and mulattoes, Irish teagues and outlandish jack tars."[3]

At the end of the six-day trial, Judge Peter Oliver, the lieutenant governor's brother, presented the case to the jury and all but assured victory for the defense: "I feel myself deeply affected that this affair turns out so much to the disgrace of every person concerned against him [Preston], and so much to the town in general." The jury immediately acquitted Preston. With Sam Adams's thugs still calling for Preston's neck, the officer sought refuge at Castle William and returned to England, where the crown awarded him a handsome life pension of £200 a year—twice the annual income of a skilled craftsman. The trial of the eight soldiers began a month later, on November 17, and on December 5 the jury acquitted six of them and found two guilty of manslaughter with mitigating circumstances. They were punished in the courtroom by being branded on their thumbs and released. On December 12 the jury dismissed, without leaving their seats, a charge that four customs officials had fired on the mob from the customs house windows. Adams and Quincy proved that the boy who had been the patriots' star witness was a perjurer, coached and bribed by "divers high Whigs."[4]

With his power slipping away, Sam Adams tried to incite resentment against the court and its verdicts in a series of anonymous articles signed "Vindix"[5] in the *Boston Gazette*. Although he portrayed the massacre as a slaughter of innocents by evil tyrants and their bloodthirsty mercenaries, the articles had little effect. The testimony at the soldiers' trials had unmasked Sam Adams as a sinister, power-hungry plotter willing to sacrifice innocent lives and destroy the city, if necessary, to further his designs. The trial fractured Adams's carefully constructed coalition of thugs, laborers, artisans, merchants, lawyers, and Harvard intellectuals. Governor Hutchinson reported to Hillsborough that Massachusetts displayed more "general appearance of Contentment" than at any time since passage of the Stamp Act and that he hoped to build a Tory party as a political sanctuary for merchants and farmers.[6] The mob violence that Adams generated the night of the massacre had turned even those merchants who opposed Tory rule against Adams and the radicals. Given a choice of tyranny by street thugs or the tyranny of higher Tory tariffs, all preferred the latter. Tories not only maintained peace, they paid for merchandise in sterling. With all its faults, the royal government at least represented stability.

Outside Boston, farmers across New England turned against Boston's Whigs for misrepresenting the events leading up to the massacre, and in England the testimony from the Preston trial turned public opinion squarely against the people of Boston. As Parliament debated appropriate punishment for Boston's duplicity, even the colonists' staunchest defenders spoke of Boston as a lawless city of hoodlums and a hotbed of anarchy.

Early in 1771 a family crisis almost shattered John Hancock's hopes for a peaceful and prosperous year. While he had shuttled back and forth to Cambridge tending everybody's business but his own, his incompetent younger brother, Ebenezer, had plunged his hardware store into bankruptcy and incurred so many debts he had to flee to Rhode Island to escape his creditors. To add to his hardships, Ebenezer had married, and his wife was now pregnant. John Hancock rushed to his brother's aid, paid his brother's debts, cleared all outstanding sheriff's warrants, and made it possible for Ebenezer to return to Boston without fear of imprisonment.

"Your affairs are now brought to such a close as that you are at liberty to come abroad; you will Deliver me all the Notes," he wrote to Ebenezer.

In bringing your affairs to a final settlement, and as you must
be Sensible great loss will Accrue to each one of your creditors,
I recommend to you to be particularly Careful & Modest in
your Deportment to Mr Harrison & Mr Willcox [creditors]
who hav been Remarkably Civil & kind in this matter

    and one word more, as you are now coming out afresh into
Life, my serious Advice to you is that you would calmly reflect
on your former Imprudencies & Resolve to quit yourself like a
Man, determined carefully to avoid the Rocks you have hereto-
fore Split upon, Conduct so as the Consequences may Reflect
Honour on yourself & your Connections. And you must think
on what you are to Depend for a Subsistence in Life. Devise
some way for your future Employ, you are Dependent on
your own Industry for your support & that of your family. . . .
Great, you are Sensible, is my Burthen & Loss in these matters
of your's, I shall never throw it in your Teeth but always
Conduct towards you as a Brother, but the Consideration of
that near Connection must by no means prevent your making
out for yourself. You must expect to undergo some hardships,
& it will be for the best, but always Remember that by Dili-
gence & Industry & good Conduct a man will push thro' this
. . . with comfort, but above all let one recommend to you to be
Steadfast & immoveable, always abounding in the Work of the
Lord & then you may be assured that your Labour shall not
be in vain for Time & Eternity

    That God may bless your future Endeavors is the sincerest
wish of

Your affectionate Brother
John Hancock[7]

A few weeks later, John set his brother up in a House of Hancock store and ordered goods from his London agent "for my
brother, whom I am determined to establish in business again in
hopes he may better succeed, and over whom I shall be careful to
keep a watchful eye."[8] Hancock was hoping against hope that Ebenezer would emulate the four other young men John had installed
as managers of his retail stores. All were doing well; two had done

remarkably: William Bant, the young attorney, and William Palfrey, who had been chief clerk and now managed the largest Hancock store, at Faneuil Hall, while overseeing many aspects of the rest of the Hancock business. Hancock trusted Palfrey implicitly, and early in 1771 he sent Palfrey to buy whale oil and fins and travel with the cargo to London to assure the best price and resolve payment problems with London agents.

"Undoubtedly the non-importation plan [for tea] will be much the Subject of Conversation," he warned Palfrey, "& my name perhaps will be frequently & freely us'd[.] On this subject I would desire you to state matters fairly, & with respect to me to represent the truth, & if that prevails I am easy. . . . I recommend to you to be prudent in all you conduct, particularly with regard to America, that you may honour yourself & your country."9

Hancock asked Palfrey to gather political intelligence, and Palfrey replied almost immediately after arriving in London: "Honored Sir, There is at present no probability of a War."10

Two weeks later he sent his patron more news: "The affairs of America are scarcely mention'd here and there is not at present the least prospect of the Duty on Tea being taken off. The N Yorkers and Philadelphians adhere very strictly to their resolution of not importing any of that . . . pernicious article. Not an ounce has been suffered to go on board any of their vessels, while those in the Boston trade take large quantities. . . . I am sorry for the honour of my dear native Country that any opportunity should be given our enemies to triumph over us. Tea is an article we can most assuredly do without, and if we[']re honestly firm in a determination not to import it the Act must infallibly be repealed."

Palfrey could not resist sending Hancock the latest social gossip: "The Duke of Cumberland has another Amour upon his hands with a Merchant's Wife in the City. . . . His Royal Highness meets with much better luck here than with Lady Grosvenor. Mrs. Harrison says he is so fond of the honor of being cuckolded by a Prince that he invites his R.H. to her house, actually puts them to Bed & tucks them up. Such a Nicodemus, she says, never was known."11

Ten days later, Palfrey sent good news: "There is talk of an intention to move for a repeal of the Tea Act, the people in general imagine it will not take effect. But you may rely upon it no additional tax will be laid upon America, nor any attempts to alter the present constitution of our Government."[12]

As distaste increased for the rowdyism of Sam Adams and the Sons of Liberty, Governor Hutchinson sensed an opportunity for reconciliation with John Hancock. The entire merchant community was abandoning Adams and his street thugs, who had sullied Boston's reputation, hurt trade, and given Philadelphia and New York opportunities to surpass Boston as primary trade centers. Hancock's own tolerance for street mobs had also worn thin—along with his inclination to cover the personal and public debts of the profligate Sam Adams.

In the spring a Tory resoundingly defeated Sam Adams—by a two-to-one margin—in the election for Suffolk County registrar of deeds. After Hancock easily won reelection to the General Court, Hutchinson confided, "I was much pressed by many persons well affected in general to consent to the election of Mr. Hancock. They assured me he wished to be separated from Mr. Adams. . . . I have now reason to believe that, before another election, he will alter his conduct so as to justify my acceptance of him."[13] Although the House of Representatives had consistently elected Hancock to serve on the Governor's Council, Hutchinson had exercised his veto just as consistently. In June 1771, however, he assured Hancock he did not bear "any degree of ill-will towards him" and that "it would be a pleasure to consent to his election to the Council." Hancock surprised the governor by refusing the offer, saying he intended to abandon public affairs "to attend to his private business, which . . . had been too much neglected."

Although Hancock did not resign his public posts, Ebenezer's failure had awakened him to the need to pay more attention to his business. He went to fewer town meetings and spent less time at taverns and clubs. The boycott had reduced his stocks to their lowest levels in twenty years, and sales had reflected the reduction by falling to less than £500 in January 1771. He ordered new inventories, and March advertisements brought crowds streaming back into his stores. April sales soared to more than £4,000—the seventh-highest monthly total in House of Hancock history. To everyone's joy, Boston had returned to normal. Aunt Lydia staged lavish banquets again, and at one of these her nephew embarked on his first courtship. " 'Tis said that John Hancock courts Dolly Quincy," wrote one gossip. " 'Tis certain he visits her and has her company in private every evening."[14]

Aunt Lydia had despaired of her nephew's ever getting married. He seemed obsessed with business and politics and spent his idle hours socializing with men of similar interests while ignoring the ladies. Deciding to act on his behalf, she made a point of inviting families with unmarried daughters to regular Hancock House entertainments, including the widower Edmund Quincy and his daughter Dorothy—or Dolly, as her father called her. From Aunt Lydia's point of view a tie with the Quincy family would link the Hancocks to one of America's oldest and grandest, if not wealthiest, names. The first Quincys had arrived in Boston in 1633 and could trace their family to the baron de Quincy, one of the noblemen who forced King John to sign the Magna Carta. Such claims were not uncommon in New England, where almost all families found or invented noble progenitors rather than admit any ties to the villains that probably spawned their lineage. Although Edmund Quincy and his brother Josiah had made fortunes as privateers, Edmund invested his so foolishly that within five years he had to sell his Boston home and his land in Braintree to raise enough money to support his wife and daughters.

Dolly Quincy was born on May 10, 1747, and like most proper New England girls grew up learning the "ornamental arts" to prepare for marriage—reading, writing, arithmetic, sewing, music, and dance. Her mother died in 1769, when she was twenty-two, and Aunt Lydia comforted her and became a confidante. The following summer Aunt Lydia invited Dolly to vacation with her and John, and he promised his aunt he would ask Dolly to marry him. There were good reasons for John's attraction to Dorothy: she was, for her era, a beautiful woman (if perhaps a bit slim at the bust),

Dorothy (Dolly) Quincy, after her marriage to John Hancock.
(*Library of Congress*)

with dark brown hair that she combed back in the latest style, to give her a tall, elegant appearance that matched his own. Despite his evident attraction to her, he nevertheless allowed his summer vacation to end—to Aunt Lydia's deep disappointment—with John and Dolly still unbetrothed when they returned to Boston.

When Hancock returned to Boston, a fleet of twelve warships had anchored in the harbor. Despite its menacing look, the fleet proved a valuable addition to Boston's economy. House of Hancock sales reached nearly £4,000 during the last quarter of the year. Prosperity made rebellion seem absurd to Hancock and other merchants. In December 1771, as the festive Christmas banquet season got under way, Hancock confided to Governor Hutchinson that he would "never again connect himself with the Adamses."[15]

As the new year began, the Whigs faced collapse. In a letter to former governor Bernard in London, Hutchinson all but proclaimed victory: "Dr Church . . . is now on the side of government. Hancock has not been with their [Long Room] club for two months past and seems to have a new set of acquaintances. . . . H[e] will be a great loss to them, as they support themselves with his money." He omitted the news that a court had declared James Otis non compus mentis and appointed his younger brother as guardian.

Hancock's relations with the governor warmed considerably, as did those of Thomas Cushing. Together the two moderates approached Hutchinson about moving the General Court, or Assembly, as it began to be called, back to Boston from Cambridge. They agreed to base their resolution solely on convenience, rather than on constitutional grounds as Sam Adams had done. Even radicals had wearied of Adams's mindless obstructionism in the General Court. One of his closest allies, Dr. Benjamin Church, switched to the Tories and wrote newspaper articles that ridiculed Adams in parodies of patriot songs. The pro-Tory movement spread elsewhere, with conservatives winning elections in New York, Philadelphia, and even in Patrick Henry's Virginia. Samuel Adams raged in the *Gazette* against "the Silence of the other Assemblies of late upon every Subject that concerns the joynt Interest of the Colonies." He asked John Dickinson to write more letters to rouse the people from "dozing upon the Brink of Ruin," but Dickinson declined.

As spring 1772 elections approached, Hutchinson and the resurgent Tories hoped to oust Adams from government and silence his voice. Knowing that he was too incompetent to support himself in normal trade, they believed his removal from political power would extinguish the last embers of rebellion. Although one-third of Boston's voters cast their ballots against him, Adams nevertheless won reelection. Both Hancock and Cushing received nearly 40 percent more votes than Adams, and they teamed up to defeat his radicals in the House by passing a modest request for a return to Boston. In June the governor replied, "It is his Excellency's Pleasure that the Great and General Court or Assembly be Adjourn'd till Tuesday next at Ten the Clock in the Forenoon then to meet at the Court House in Boston."[16] Sam Adams continued disrupting the General Court, as Hancock and other moderates yawned—and finally adjourned.

Under directions from King George to court Hancock's allegiance, Governor Hutchinson bestowed one of the province's highest honors on the thirty-five-year-old merchant: "His Excellency the Captain-General, has been pleased to commission John Hancock, Esq., to be Captain [commander] of the Company of Cadets, with the rank of Colonel." Sam Adams lashed out angrily, scoffing that "it is not in the power of the Governor to give a commission for that company to whom he pleases, as their officers are chosen by themselves. Mr. Hancock was elected by an unanimous vote; and a reluctance at the idea of giving offense to an hundred gentlemen might very well account for the Governor giving the commission to Mr. H., without taking into consideration that most powerful of all other motives, *an instruction*, especially at a time when he vainly hoped he should gain him over."[17]

Technically, Adams was correct. Also called the Independent Corps of Cadets, Hancock's new command was a fraternal gentlemen's militia of eighty men who served as the governor's honor guard, marched at official ceremonies, and spent as much time as possible at the Bunch of Grapes tavern. Hancock had joined the guard, as he had the Masons and the Merchants Club, for informal fellowship with men of similar backgrounds and interests. As Adams stated, the corps did, indeed, elect Hancock, but his election—like Hutchinson's appointment—was a slap at Adams as a recognition of Hancock's leadership of Boston's responsible citizens.

The election and appointment sent Hancock into spasms of ecstasy—a military command to complement his civic and political leadership. For someone who adored the trappings of leadership—and recognized their importance in commanding awe and respect—command of the corps could not have been a more perfect acquisition. He envisioned himself in regimentals with sparkling gold epaulets, atop a white horse, sword at his side. He set to work immediately, passionately, converting his vision into reality. He ordered magnificent new uniforms for the entire corps: scarlet coats with buff lapels, white gaiters with black buttons, and three-cornered beaver hats with brims turned up smartly—one of them bearing a rosette secured by a gilded button. He drew up a small manual of arms and asked his former adversary, the British commander Colonel Dalrymple, to assign a sergeant to drill the cadets in precision marching. A few days later, Boston newspapers carried this advertisement:

> Wanted. Immediately—For his Excellency's Company
> of Cadets.
> Two Fifers that understand playing. Those that are
> masters of musick and are inclined to engage with the Company are desired to apply to Col. John Hancock.[18]

The Corps of Cadets began drilling twice a month in Faneuil Hall and moved onto the Common for compulsory weekly drills on Wednesdays when the weather turned warm. Hancock fined those who missed drills—usually a round of ale at the Bunch of Grapes. It was not long before Colonel Hancock and his Corps of Cadets looked every inch a precision marching team.[19]

Shortly after Hancock took over the Corps of Cadets, rumors circulated that the crown was preparing to confer a title on Hancock, and there is little question that John Hancock's adoration of pomp and life at the highest levels of society would certainly have swayed him, as Lord Hancock, to abandon all ties to Sam Adams and the radicals. Indeed, he would simply have liquidated his estate and sailed to England with Aunt Lydia and retired on a splendid estate near London. But neither King George nor his minions were farsighted (or democratic) enough to consider elevation of commoners to the nobility as a tool to command colonist loyalties. Hutchinson did the next best thing by again inviting Hancock to join the Governor's Council in June 1772, and again Hancock refused. Hutchinson wrote that Hancock's refusal was simply an effort "to prevent a total breach" from the Whigs and "show the people that he had not been seeking after it."[20]

Hancock's refusal, however, probably had nothing to do with either. He had simply grown frustrated with politics and the inability of the General Court to produce practical benefits for Boston. Through the entire previous winter, the only accomplishment of Boston's selectmen was to name a Massacre Day orator to commemorate the March 5 confrontation. His boredom with selectman meetings reduced his attendance dramatically. He decided he could accomplish more on his own—as his uncle had done in restoring and maintaining the Common. He built a bandstand on the Common and organized a band, at his own expense, to give free concerts. He planted a row of trees along the edge of the Common fronting Beacon Street, and installed walkways that crisscrossed the park and allowed strollers to enjoy the green without destroying it. He contributed £7,500—and a new bell—to cover all the costs of rebuilding the crumbling Brattle Square Church. He gave a bell to another church, and a handsome Bible to a third. In March 1772 the town had appointed him chairman of a committee "to consider of the expediency of fixing lamps in this town," and at his request, they ordered three hundred white globes, which used whale oil for illumination and were the most advanced type of street lamps. As a victim of the perennial fires that raged through Boston's narrow streets and alleys, Hancock ordered the latest-model fire engine from England as a gift for the town. To thank their benefactor, the town meeting named the engine Hancock and ordered it housed "at or near Hancock's Wharf and in case of Fire, the Estate of the Donor shall have the preference of its service." More and more, Hancock relished the power he could exert with his wealth—and the immediate, visible changes, all for the better, he could dictate in Boston, without tedious coaxing of ignorant, reluctant officials and political opponents.

Late in July 1772, John Hancock again postponed his be-
trothal and set off with a half dozen friends—none of them patriot
leaders—for a low-key month of male fellowship aboard a chartered luxury sailing vessel, the *Providence Packet*. Together with
their servants and a stock of fine food and wines, they spent a
month sailing up the Massachusetts coast, past Cape Ann, to the
rugged shores of Maine and back. It would be the last extended
period of relaxation of his life.

When he returned to Boston he found that his lavish contributions had made him Boston's most popular political leader. The
Whig majority at the town meeting voted him, rather than Sam
Adams, moderator, or presiding officer. Adams was furious. He
had invented Hancock and the Whigs, and both now ignored him.
He awaited the first misstep by Parliament to reignite mob passions and seize control of Boston politics again. Parliament did not
disappoint him. It enacted a bill making the crown, rather than
colonial legislatures, responsible for paying all judges' salaries,
thus making the courts dependent on the king instead of the colonial legislatures.

Adams converted the new law into a cause célèbre, writing
in the *Gazette*, "Let every Town assemble. Let Associations and
Combinations be everywhere set up to consult and recover our
just Rights." His article caused a furor. Overruling Hancock's and
Cushing's objections, Adams organized a Committee of Correspondence at the town meeting, "to state the Rights of the Colonists and of this Province in particular, as Men as Christians, and
Subjects: to communicate and publish the same to the several
Towns in this Province and to the World."[21] Adams demanded
that the committee encourage other towns and colonial assemblies
to establish similar groups to work in unison to overthrow royal
rule. Recognizing that Adams would use the Committee of Correspondence as a springboard to revolution and power, Hancock,
Cushing, and other moderates objected. Adams had enough votes,
however, to form a twenty-one-man committee that Governor
Hutchinson called the "foulest, subtlest, and most venomous ser-
pent ever issued from the egg of sedition."[22] Hancock, Cushing,

and the other moderates refused to serve on the committee, with Hancock using the press of business as an excuse. Adams, however, did not intend allowing Hancock's money to slip from his grasp, and he cunningly set about repairing the political machine he had organized so carefully at the Long Room Club.

Incredibly, he brought in the demented hero James Otis to chair the committee. Otis had experienced one of his occasional moments of lucidity and Adams convinced his keepers to release him from his straitjacket to return to Boston. Then, with Adams barking orders, the committee agreed to produce documents of "Rights, Liberties and Privileges" for the people of Massachusetts. Three weeks later, the committee presented a seven-thousand-word declaration of the "State of the Rights of Colonists," written by Sam Adams; a "List of *Infringements,* and Violations of those Rights," written by Dr. Joseph Warren; and "A Letter of Correspondence" by Dr. Benjamin Church, of all people, who had apparently abandoned his brief flirtation with the Tories and reespoused the patriots.

"Gentlemen," Church's letter began, "We the Freeholders and other Inhabitants of *Boston . . .* can no longer conceal our impatience under a constant, unremitted, uniform aim to enslave us, or confide in an Administration which threatens us with certain and inevitable destruction."[23]

Governor Hutchinson condemned the documents for inciting rebellion, saying their principles "would be sufficient to justify the colonies in revolting, and forming an independent state."[24] Although Hancock and Cushing also disapproved, the cunning of Sam Adams trapped both into playing roles neither had sought. After the town meeting approved his documents, the moderator would have to sign them or resign. Hancock had little choice but to pen his legendary signature across each near-treasonous document or flee with Aunt Lydia to London as quickly as possible, with as many of his assets as he could salvage. So much of his wealth was real property, however, that he knew he would not be able to leave with enough money to live in his accustomed style in London. So there it was, atop the signatures of Cushing and the other selectmen, printed across the front page of the Adams incitements to rebellion: *JOHN HANCOCK, moderator*. Suddenly, John Hancock was the leader of the American Revolution.

After the town meeting, Edes and Gill at the *Gazette* printed six hundred copies for distribution to selectmen in nearly every town in Massachusetts. All saw John Hancock's name and believed he was leading the rebellion against royal rule in Massachusetts. As Samuel Adams grinned malevolently, Hancock knew he had little choice but to serve as Adams's milch cow or to seize control of the Whigs and sweep Adams aside.

The Adams statement of colonist rights and the circular letter produced a network of Committees of Correspondence throughout Massachusetts, and when the General Court met in January, it declared that Parliament had no authority to tax colonists without their consent. Governor Hutchinson replied, "I know no line that can be drawn between the supreme authority of Parliament and the total independence of the colonies. It is impossible that there should be two independent Legislatures in one and the same state, for although there may be but one head, the King, yet two legislative bodies will make two Governments as distinct as the Kingdoms of England and Scotland before union."[25]

Ironically, John Adams agreed with the royal governor, adding, in his response to the governor's speech, that "it is difficult, if possible, to draw a Line of Distinction between the universal Authority of Parliament over the colonies . . . and no authority at all. . . . If there be no such Line, the Consequence is, Either that the Colonies are Vassals of the Parliament, or, that they are totally independent. As it cannot be supposed to have been the Intentions of the Parties in the Compact that we should be reduced to a State of Vassalage, the Conclusion is, that it was their Sense, that we are thus independent."[26] Thus John Adams's pronouncement to the Massachusetts General Court was, in effect, the first declaration of independence, and Parliament received it as further proof that the time had come to crush the treasonous activities in Massachusetts.

Instead of rallying merchant support in the colonies, the English government persisted in driving them into the rebel camp. Early in 1773, East India Company shares plunged from 280 to

160 pence on the London stock exchange. The Townshend Acts duty on tea had cut American consumption and left the company facing bankruptcy, with 17 million tons of unsold tea spilling out of its warehouses. Although the company asked the government to eliminate the tea duty in North America, Lord North refused, saying the colonists would interpret repeal as a sign of weakness. Instead, Parliament, many of whose most powerful members owned East India Company shares, passed a new law, the Tea Act of 1773, which excused the company from the 20 percent English duties it would normally pay on tea if it reexported the tea to America. The act also created a tea monopoly by letting the company sell tea directly to consumers through exclusive sales agents in the colonies, who would bypass middlemen merchants like John Hancock. With elimination of the 20 percent duty, the East India Company would be able to sell its tea at prices below the cheapest smuggled tea.

The Tea Act would also drive hundreds of colonial merchants and shopkeepers out of business. Tea was America's most popular beverage, a staple that meant survival for most storekeepers and many small merchants—many of them loyal Tories and almost all of them political moderates who opposed rebellion. To compound the government's blunder, the East India Company named as its agents in the most politically volatile province—Massachusetts—the two sons of Governor Hutchinson and Richard Clarke, whose daughter had married one of the Hutchinson boys. Hancock was furious. The Hutchinsons and Clarkes had both ignored colonist nonimportation agreements, and their appointment as East India Company agents convinced him that the Hutchinsons were conspiring to monopolize trade in Massachusetts. Even more infuriating was the Tea Act diversion of colonial duties to subsidize a tea monopoly designed to drive colonist merchants out of business.

With the East India Company about to cut consumer prices on tea, Hancock knew he would gain little public sympathy for merchants if he didn't restore political ties with Sam Adams. The opportunity came almost immediately with the theft of a packet of outrageous letters that Governor Hutchinson and his brother-in-law Lt. Gov. Andrew Oliver had sent to a friend in Parliament years earlier, exposing their true feelings about popular rule. The letters urged "an abridgment of what are called English liberties" in the American colonies and stripping self-government from "the hands of the populace . . . by degrees."[27]

Benjamin Franklin, who was agent in London for Massachusetts as well as Pennsylvania, was first to get hold of the stolen letters and sent them to Thomas Cushing, with instructions not to reproduce or publish them. Cushing passed them on to Sam Adams, who read them to a secret session of the House of Representatives. A committee headed by Hancock concluded that the letters had been "designed to overthrow the [provincial] government and introduce arbitrary rule into the Province."[28] Despite Franklin's admonition, Adams published them and sent copies to the king with a petition asking that Hutchinson and Oliver be removed from office.

The scandal over the Hutchinson-Oliver letters allowed Hancock and Adams to close ranks, but Hancock made it clear that Adams would never recapture merchant support unless he prevented his gangs of thugs from disrupting democratic town meetings and committing acts of violence and vandalism. Knowing his movement would die without the political and financial support of merchants and other stable elements of the growing middle class, Adams agreed.

EARLY IN THE SUMMER, Aunt Lydia grew concerned about John's marital future. She decided to take Dorothy Quincy with her on vacation to the Hancock summer home at Point Shirley, the popular holiday area John had developed on the north shore of Boston Harbor. By then, Edmund Quincy, Dorothy's father, was as eager as Aunt Lydia for a union of the two families. Neither he nor Aunt Lydia could understand why John had not formally proposed to Dolly. Had he done so? Had Dolly refused? Neither parent knew. When John went to Point Shirley with the coach to bring his aunt and Dorothy home to Boston, Edmund Quincy gave John a letter for Dorothy.

"You have the honour of Colonel Handcock's [*sic*] being the bearer," he wrote to his daughter. "I wish him a pleasant journey and a happy meeting with his valuable aunt and you; and that you, with them, may have a safe and comfortable journey home. . . . Colonel Handcock and his associates have had a hard task respecting the G[overnor]'s and Lt.-G[overnor]'s, and other letters, of which you'll see the copies. But I think, notwithstanding, he appears to rise higher, the greater the burthens."[29]

On June 29, the House adjourned, and Hancock was able to take Edmund Quincy's note to Point Shirley, and after a few days of vacation, escort Aunt Lydia and Dorothy Quincy back to Boston. Again, he had not openly asked Dolly for her hand. A month later, he and Aunt Lydia attended the first service in the new Brattle Square Church they had built. The cornerstone bore the name *Hon. John Hancock.* Harvard's trustees also honored their patriot son—and benefactor—by naming him treasurer of the college, a position they hoped would serve to remind him of the college's constant need for financial gifts and bequests. Although overburdened with work, he could hardly refuse the honor, and he took over not only the college's books, but its cash hoard of nearly £15,500 to invest.

Hancock also spent much of the summer untangling his business affairs, which he had badly neglected because of his political activities. Although Palfrey and the others were willing store managers, none had Hancock's merchandising savvy. Without him, sales had barely reached £1,000 during the spring quarter. Anticipating the Tea Act, Hancock stepped up tea imports, and never neglecting his personal taste for luxury, he ordered "100 squares of the best London glass 18 by 11½ for the use of my own House. I pray may be the very best." Nor did he forget his aunt. He bought her "as neat a Mahogany Cabinet as can be made, suitable for a Lady's chamber, rather convenient than Remarkable for any outward Decorations. I have it very neat & respectable as it is for my Aunt, widow of my late Uncle, with whom I now reside, & a Lady for whom I have the highest affection & Esteem."

IN SEPTEMBER the *Gazette* reprinted a series of inflammatory articles against the Tea Act that had appeared in Philadelphia and New York newspapers. The articles argued that the state-supported tea monopoly would drive merchants out of business, encourage establishment of other government monopolies, and eventually destroy free trade. Boston's Whig leaders dusted off the scheme that had prevented implementation of the Stamp Act: they would frighten East India Company agents into resigning, much as they had forced stamp distributors to do in 1765. On October 21 the Massachusetts Bay Committee called on other colonies in the Intercolonial Committee of Correspondence to prevent East India Company tea from landing in America. Five days later the *Gazette* printed a handbill from Philadelphia that threatened the lives of "the Commissioners appointed by the East India Company for the sale of tea in America" unless they resigned.[30] On November 3 Sam Adams, John Hancock, Dr. Joseph Warren, and other selectmen and patriot leaders led more than five hundred Sons of Liberty to the Liberty Tree and demanded the resignation of the Hutchinsons and Clarke as tea agents. They refused, and two days later Hancock chaired a town meeting that declared them "*Daringly Affrontive* to the Town."[31] In London, meanwhile, a few captains, including James Scott, the loyal captain of John Hancock's ship *Hayley*, refused to load their vessels with tea bound for America, but the East India Company quickly bribed its way onto other vessels, and by the end of October, seventeen hundred chests sailed off to America on other ships.

On November 18 the Sons of Liberty gathered at the Liberty Tree and again demanded that the tea agents resign. Again they refused. On Saturday, November 27, the *Dartmouth*, the first of four ships bound for Boston, anchored outside the harbor, and the next day, as it glided to the wharf, Sam Adams and a group of his street thugs dressed as Mohawks prevented it from tying up.

On Monday morning posters appeared throughout the town: "Friends, Brethren, Countrymen! That worst of Plagues, the detestable Tea shipped for this Port by the East India Company, is now arrived in this Harbor. The Hour of Destruction or Manly Opposition to the Machinations of Tyranny stares you in the face. Every Friend to his Country, to Himself and Posterity, is now Called to Meet at Faneuil Hall at 9 o'clock this Day (at which time the Bells will begin to ring) to make a United and Successful Resistance to this last, worst, and most Destructive Measure of Administration."[32]

As predicted, bells across the city pealed at nine. What began as a crowd of several hundred swelled to nearly five thousand, and organizers moved the meeting from Faneuil Hall to the more spacious Old South Meeting House. The governor ordered Hancock to assemble the Corps of Cadets and disperse the crowd. Hancock refused. Adams called the meeting to order and moved that the tea be shipped back to England, duties unpaid. A radical supporter, Dr. Thomas Young, shouted above the cheers with a call to dump the tea overboard. After Adams restored order, the meeting rejected the Young proposal and unanimously approved the Adams resolution. Adams ordered a watch on the wharf to prevent the *Dartmouth* from tying up and unloading its tea. Hancock jumped onto his horse and led the Corps of Cadets to pierside to guard the tea.

The town meeting resumed the following morning, with word that Hutchinson's sons and Clarke had fled to Castle William. The sheriff read a governor's order to disperse, but the crowd booed, cursed, and jeered until he fled the hall. The meeting voted again to block landing of the tea, and it agreed to send a report of its proceedings to the other colonies and to London. At five the next morning, Hancock sent his aide Palfrey on horseback with copies for New York and Philadelphia. Governor Hutchinson responded to the extraordinary two-day meeting by ordering harbor authorities to bar the tea ships from leaving the harbor until their owners paid duties. He condemned Hancock for joining the rebel camp. "It is in everybody's mouth," he wrote, "that Hancock said at the close of this meeting he would be willing to spend his fortune and life itself in so good a cause."33

The *Dartmouth* remained at anchor for three days before docking at Griffin's Wharf, more than a half mile south of Long Wharf. A few days later the second of the four Boston-bound tea ships tied up beside the *Dartmouth*. One of the two trailing ships sailed into port two days later, but the fourth ship, which carried Boston's precious new street lamps as well as tea, ran aground at Provincetown. Local workers joined the crew in salvaging the three hundred lamps—all undamaged—and fifty-eight chests of tea. As wagons carried the lamps off to Boston, one of the Clarkes sneaked into Provincetown, put the tea aboard a fishing schooner, and brought it safely to Castle William—the only tea that slipped through patriot hands into consumer teapots.

Customs regulations called for seizure of any tea for which duties went unpaid after twenty days. At 10 A.M. on Thursday, December 16, more than five thousand people from Boston and the surrounding area again pushed their way into Old South and demanded that Francis Rotch, part owner of one of the tea ships, order his vessel back to England. Rotch said the British guns at Castle William would not let him pass without paying duties. After sending him to demand safe passage for his ship from the governor, the meeting adjourned until three that afternoon. Hancock, Adams, and the other leaders huddled in conference, deciding on their next move. When the meeting resumed, Rotch was nowhere to be found. Patriot leaders kept the crowd under control with a few rousing, albeit repetitive, speeches. After several hours the crowd tired and the meeting was about to adjourn, when Rotch returned. It was five forty-five, with only a bit of candlelight piercing the winter's eerie evening darkness. Rotch said the governor had rejected Boston's demands and refused to let the ship return to England.

An angry murmur filled the hall. Some in the crowd said they heard Hancock call out, "Let every man do what is right in his own eyes."34 Adams adjourned the meeting with an angry cry,

"This meeting can do no more to save the country."[35] Some called it a prearranged signal for the Mohawks to march to Griffin's Wharf. Others in the hall shouted, "Boston harbor a tea-pot tonight!" or, "Hurrah for Griffin's Wharf!" or, "The Mohawks are come!"[36]

The crowd poured from the meeting house and streamed to Griffin's Wharf. A group of forty to fifty, amateurishly disguised as Indians, with blankets over their heads and coloring on their faces, boarded the *Dartmouth* and the other tea ships. Methodically, skillfully, they lifted the tea chests from the holds with blocks and tackles, carefully split each open with axes, and dumped the tea and splintered chests into the water. They worked steadily until they had dumped all the tea—342 chests in all, valued at £9,659,[37] or $1 million in today's currency[38]—in the harbor, without damaging any other cargo, stores, or materiel. There were no fights, no brutality, no injuries—nothing but calm, orderly, disciplined discharging of tea.

Just who participated in the Tea Party and who witnessed it from shore remains one of the mouthwatering mysteries in American history. Although the notorious Ebenezer Mackintosh of the South End Gang claimed that his "chickens did the job," there is no evidence that any Adams street thugs participated. Hancock had warned Adams sternly that any repetition of the violence, plundering, and wanton destruction of property that had accompanied the Boston Massacre would forever alienate merchants and other moderate Whigs, and Adams was careful to make the Tea Party an orderly affair, conducted by responsible citizens. Whoever they were, they kept their names secret to the grave. The skills of the "war party" point to craftsmen, while the discipline they displayed and the quickness and ease with which they boarded and moved about the ships indicate participation by members of Hancock's Corps of Cadets, who had stood watch the previous night. The *Massachusetts Spy* reported that John Hancock "was the first man that went aboard the vessel, to destroy the tea," but most historians discount the possibility that a man as wealthy and recognizable, not to mention as cautious, as Hancock would

An engraving—largely the product of Nathaniel Currier's imagination in 1846—of the Boston Tea Party. (*Library of Congress*)

have risked arrest, trial, and imprisonment in England, along with a huge lawsuit. Moreover, Hancock's huge gilt-trimmed coach and liveried servants never stood far from their master, and he seldom moved without them. He, too, was beginning to suffer attacks of gout, a congenital disease that affected the men in the Hancock family. It is unlikely that his gout would have allowed him to bound aboard and about a tea ship.

As the Tea Party entered the legends of American history, descriptions, most of them contradictory, continued surfacing for years thereafter. Governor Hutchinson, who was out of town at the time, claimed that most of the crowd at Old South had marched to the wharves and watched while the Mohawks dumped the tea. The *Dartmouth* log of December 16 claims the crowd numbered only about one thousand, including men "dressed and whooping like Indians."[39] One Boston merchant said the meeting at Old South did not end until "the candles were light" and that those who boarded the tea ships were "cloath'd in Blankets with the head muffled, and copper color'd countenances, being each

armed with a hatchet or axe, and pair pistoles . . . before *nine* o'clock
. . . every chest . . . was knock'd to pieces and flung over the sides."[40]

As with all such events, tens of thousands claimed they were at
the meeting at Old South and participated in or witnessed the Tea
Party. All four ships would have sunk under their weight. In
1835, more than sixty years later, one alleged witness produced
a list of fifty-eight participants, including Hancock and Adams;
another claimed to have recognized Hancock "not only by his ruffles" but "by his figure and gait . . . his features . . . and by his voice,
also, for he exchanged . . . an Indian grunt."[41] Years later, a team-
ster claimed he "loaded at John Hancock's warehouse and was
about to leave town when Mr. Hancock requested me to be on
Long Wharf at 2 o'clock P.M. [the very time Hancock and the
others sat in Old South] and informed me what was to be done. I
went accordingly [and] joined the band . . . We mounted the ships
and made *tea* in a trice. This done, I took my team and went home,
as an honest man should."[42] Still another unlikely witness cited
Dr. Joseph Warren and Paul Revere as participants, and a popular
street ballad about the Tea Party, opened with the words

Rally Mohawks! Bring out your axes,
And tell King George we'll pay no taxes
On his foreign tea.

Another verse included the lines

Our Warren's there and bold Revere,
With hands to do and words to cheer,
For Liberty and laws.[43]

On December 17, the day after the Tea Party, Revere did ride
to Philadelphia, spreading news of the Tea Party everywhere—
with dramatic effects. The colonies stopped drinking tea.[44] Patriots in Philadelphia, New York, and Charleston forced East India
Company tea agents to resign. New York governor William Tryon
warned the British Board of Trade that it would require "the Protection of the Point of the Bayonet and Muzzle of the Cannon" to

Paul Revere, the Boston silversmith who warned John Hancock and Samuel Adams that the British troops were on their way to Lexington with orders to arrest the two patriots. (*Library of Congress*)

land tea in New York.[45] A newspaper reported that "a vast number of the inhabitants, including most of the principal lawyers, merchants, landowners, masters of ships and mechanics" joined the "Sons of Liberty of New York" and pledged to turn back tea ships. Outside Philadelphia, a crowd of eight thousand greeted the ship *Polly*, carrying 697 chests of tea as it prepared to sail up the Delaware on Christmas Day. It put about and sailed out to sea.

In all his breathless rides and many descriptions of the Tea Party, Paul Revere never said he participated in dumping tea into

Boston Harbor, and indeed, there is not a shred of evidence to show who did or did not participate. The sheriff arrested a barber named Eckley but released him for lack of evidence. John Adams, who had been in court in Plymouth for a week and rode back into Boston the morning after the Tea Party, said he did not know any Tea Party participants. As he rode into town, he saw splintered tea chests and huge clots of tea leaves covering the water as far as his eyes could see. They washed ashore along a fifty-mile stretch of coastline as well as on the offshore islands.

"This," he entered in his diary when he reached his home, "is the most magnificent Movement of all. There is a dignity, a Majesty, a Sublimity in this last Effort of the Patriots I greatly admire. . . . This Destruction of the Tea is so bold, so daring, so firm, intrepid & inflexible, and it must have so important Consequences and so lasting, that I cannot but consider it as an Epocha in History."

Three days later, on December 21, John Hancock wrote to his London agent:

> We have been much agitated in consequence of the arrival of Tea Ships by the East India Company, and after every effort was made to Induce the consignees to return it from whence it came & all proving ineffectual, in a very few Hours the whole of the tea on Board . . . was thrown into the salt water. The particulars I must refer you to Capt. Scott for indeed I am not acquainted with them myself, so as to give a Detail. Philadelphia & [New] York are Determined the Tea shall not land. I enclose you an extract of a letter I Rec'd from Phila., by which you will see the spirit of that people. No one circumstance could possibly have taken place more effectively to unite the Colonies than this manouvre of the Tea. . . . I determine if my Oyle gets up tomorrow my Brigt *Lydia* shall depart in six days. I shall recommend her to be sold.[46]

Hancock shipped all his stocks of tea back to England at his own expense.

9

High Treason

(1774-1775)

On January 22, 1774, the *London Chronicle* published a long, grisly account of the Boston Tea Party—an exaggerated portrait of a city in open rebellion against the crown. Though profitable for the *Chronicle*, the report would prove incredibly costly to Britain, for it so infuriated Parliament, the king, and his cabinet that they began a sequence of actions and reactions that would determine "the fate of a great empire."[1] Unfortunately, England's leaders miscalculated the depth of the growing enmity for Britain in the colonies, and they focused their efforts on crushing Boston and bringing its popular rebel chiefs to the gallows. Boston, however, prepared to act just as forcefully to throw off the yoke of British rule.

Two weeks after the *Chronicle* article appeared, England's attorney general formally charged John Hancock, Samuel Adams, Dr. Joseph Warren, and Dr. Benjamin Church with "the Crime of High Treason" and "high misdemeanours." He ordered them brought to justice either "by prosecuting Them for their Treason" in Massachusetts or by "transmitting them hither to be tried in some County in England."[2] News of the arrest orders arrived in

Massachusetts several weeks before the documents themselves. Sam Adams responded by demanding impeachment of provincial chief justice Andrew Oliver for accepting a salary from King George. The Massachusetts House voted overwhelmingly to impeach, ninety-two to eight, but before the trial could begin, Governor Hutchinson adjourned the General Court. No longer certain how to respond, the Boston town meeting turned to John Hancock, inviting him to address them as Massacre Day orator on March 5.

Massacre Day fell on a Saturday—market day—and the crowds were larger than expected. Everyone loved good oratory. It was a principal form of entertainment. Market crowds and the curious joined patriots from Boston and outlying areas flocking to Faneuil Hall to hear the merchant king. The huge crowd forced organizers to move the meeting to Old South Meeting House. Still, they filled every pew, every inch of space along the aisles, in the galleries and stairways, and even the outer hall. Hancock's coach arrived, and dressed as always in princely scarlet velvet, he made his way to the great pulpit, climbed the stairs to the rostrum, and waited for silence.

"He looked every inch an aristocrat," according to one observer, "from his dress and powdered wig to his smart pumps of grained leather . . . sturdily built . . . dashing good looks. . . . His dark eyes were penetrating, his mouth was firm, his chin determined."[3] Another called Hancock's facial expression "beautiful, manly, expressive." His delivery could excite audiences to "the highest pitch of phrenzy" or "sooth them into tears."[4] On Massacre Day 1774, Hancock did both as he delivered the most important speech of his life, in effect seizing the leadership of the American Revolution in Massachusetts. He began humbly, almost inaudibly:

> Men, brethren, fathers and fellow-countrymen; The attentive gravity, the venerable appearance of this crowded audience; the dignity which I behold in the countenances of so many in this great assembly; the solemnity of the occasion upon which we have met together, joined to a consideration of the part I am to take in the important business of this day, fill me with an awe

hitherto unknown; and heighten the sense which I have ever had, of my unworthiness to fill this sacred desk; but allured by the call of some of my respected fellow-citizens, with whose request it is always my greatest pleasure to comply, I almost forgot my want of ability to perform what they required.... I pray, that my sincere attachment to the interest of my country, and hearty detestation of every design formed against her liberties, may be admired as some form of apology for my appearance in this place.

Hancock lifted his voice a bit. "I have always, from my earliest youth . . . considered it as the indispensable duty of every member of society . . . as a faithful subject of the state, to use his utmost endeavors . . . [to] oppose every traitorous plot which its enemies may devise for its destruction. . . ."

His voice grew still stronger. "I glory in publicly avowing my eternal enmity to tyranny. Is the present system, which the British administration have adopted for the government of the colonies, a righteous government? or is it tyranny?"

"Tyranny!" the audience cried out in response.

"Tell me, ye bloody butchers!" he thundered. "Ye dark designing knaves, ye murderers, parricides! how dare you tread upon the earth, which has drank the blood of the slaughtered innocents, shed by your wicked hands? How dare you breathe the air which wafted to the ear of heaven, the groans of those who fell a sacrifice to your accursed ambition?"

The crowd was his to command. Referring to the Tea Party, he charged that if Boston had not acted, "we soon should have found our trade in the hands of foreigners, and taxes imposed on every thing which we consumed." He demanded "total disuse of tea in this country . . . [to] free ourselves from those unmannerly pillagers who impudently tell us that they are licensed by an act of the British parliament to thrust their dirty hands into the pockets of every American." He called on all patriots to arm themselves and prepare to "fight for [your] houses, lands, wives, children . . . [your] liberty and [your] God" so that "those noxious vermin will be swept forever from the streets of Boston."

He then delivered the two most significant elements of his speech. First he urged Massachusetts towns to organize militias and "be ready to take the field whenever danger calls." Then he issued America's first call for "a general union among us . . . and our sister colonies" into an independent nation. "Much has been done by the committees of correspondence . . . for uniting the inhabitants of the whole continent," he continued,

> but permit me here to suggest a general congress of deputies, from the several houses of assembly, on the continent, as the most effectual method of establishing such a union. . . .
>
> I conjure you by all that is dear, by all that is honorable, by all that is sacred, not only that ye pray, but that you act; that, if necessary, ye fight, and even die, for the prosperity of our Jerusalem. . . . I thank God, that America abounds in men who are superior to all temptation, whom nothing can divert from a steady pursuit of the interest of their country . . . their revered names, in all succeeding times, shall grace the annals of America. From them, let us, my friends, take example; from them, let us catch the divine enthusiasm; and feel, each for himself, the God-like pleasure of . . . delivering the oppressed from the iron grasp of tyranny.[5]

He finished with a passage from the Bible that left the immense crowd spellbound. As he descended the pulpit and shook hands with Sam Adams and other patriot leaders, murmurs grew into applause, then erupted into cheers that swelled into a sustained roar as he made his way back to his coach to return to Hancock House. Old Bishop Hancock could not have stirred a congregation more than his grandson had just done. He had captured the hearts and minds of Boston's patriot movement and become the undeniable ruler of Massachusetts. John Adams called the oration "an elegant, a pathetic [that is, moving] and a spirited performance. A vast crowd, rainy eyes, etc. The composition, the pronunciation, the action—all exceeded the expectations of everybody. They exceeded even mine, which were very considerable. Many of the sentiments . . . came from him with a singular dignity and grace."[6]

In London, an angry Parliament passed the first so-called Coercive Act to punish Boston and crush its rebellious spirit. Under the Port Bill the navy would shut Boston Harbor on June 1, 1774, until the city repaid both the East India Company for its Tea Party losses and the British government for the duties it would have collected on the tea. Except for military supplies and essential food and fuel, the law banned loading and unloading of all ships until "peace and obedience to the laws shall be . . . restored in the said town of Boston, that the trade of Great Britain may safely be carried on there and his Majesty's customs duly collected."[7] To ensure enforcement, the government replaced Thomas Hutchinson as governor with Gen. Thomas Gage, commander in chief of all British forces in North America, and ordered the transfer of four regiments from England and Ireland to Boston. Gage was "to repel force and violence by every means within his reach."[8] Hutchinson, whom Sam Adams called "that damned arch traitor,"[9] was granted leave in England, with the understanding that he would return as governor "as soon as General Gage should be judged no longer necessary."[10]

With only a few days left before the British shut the harbor, Hancock closed the House of Hancock and set to work clearing his good name and his credit in England, where he still owed £11,000. He filled his remaining ships with merchandise and sent them to his London agent on consignment—ships and all—for resale, with all proceeds to be used to clear his debts. The agent realized £13,000. With no remaining debts, Hancock's loyal captain James Scott refused to sell his ship. "I hope you won't give up your navigation," he pleaded in a letter to Hancock. "I am determined never to leave you while you please to employ me."[11]

On May 13, Gage arrived at Castle William with instructions to move the General Court from Boston to Salem and prosecute Hancock, Adams, and the rest of the patriot leaders for treason. Peter Oliver, who had succeeded his brother Andrew as chief justice, warned Gage that "the Times are not favorable for Prosecutions," and rather than provoke more riots, Gage deferred action. Four days later, Gage sailed from Castle William to Boston to assume his office—just as a town meeting was about to meet to protest the Port Bill. Hancock ordered the Corps of Cadets to escort the new governor to the Town House for his induction into office and from there to Province House, where, in a stunning act of public insolence, Hancock failed to order the cadets to salute the governor as he passed between their lines to his official residence.

The town meeting then acted on Hancock's Massacre Day proposal and invited other colonies to join a "Solemn League and Covenant" to end all business dealings with Britain and stop consumption of British imports after October 1. Paul Revere rode out again to distribute the request to other cities and sound the warning that the Port Bill, "though made immediately upon us, is doubtless design'd for every other Colony. . . . Now therefore is the Time, when ALL should be united in opposition to this violation of the Liberties of ALL . . . It is not the Rights of Boston only, but of ALL AMERICA which are now struck at. Not the Merchants only but the Farmer, and every order of Men who inhabit this noble Continent."[12]

Ten days later, more than one hundred loyalists signed a farewell to Hutchinson, deploring the losses to the East India Company and pledging "to bear our share of those damages" in exchange for repeal of the Port Bill.[13]

Far from considering repeal, however, vengeful parliamentary leaders prepared two more Coercive Acts. The first gave British colonial officials the right to be tried in England instead of the colonies for capital crimes committed while collecting duties or quelling riots in America. Sam Adams called it the "Murderers' Act." The far harsher Massachusetts Government Act annulled the Massachusetts charter and colonial self-government. It gave the king sole power to appoint and dismiss the Council, the attorney general, all judges, justices of the peace, and sheriffs. The act limited town meetings to one a year, and then only with the governor's permission.

Patriots along the Atlantic coast rallied to support Massachusetts by forming militias, and all the colonies but Georgia answered

Hancock's call to meet at an intercolonial congress in September. On June 1 Gage closed Boston Harbor to all trade except food and fuel, and he imposed virtual martial law on the city. Even ferries to Charleston and Cambridge ceased operations. The following day Parliament passed still another Coercive Act that permitted quartering British troops in private homes. Somehow Hancock got word to Capt. James Scott in London to fill the last remaining Hancock ship with gunpowder and smuggle it to Salem.

On June 7 Gage convened the General Court in Salem, but instead of following Gage's agenda, the House of Representatives barred the doors, pledged unanimous support for Boston, and appointed five delegates to go to Philadelphia to the Continental Congress the following September: Thomas Cushing, James Bowdoin, Robert Treat Paine, and Sam and John Adams—three merchants, a bankrupt brewer, and a lawyer. Calculating the probable outcome in Philadelphia, Hancock chose to remain in Boston, where in the absence of Sam Adams and other patriot leaders, he could consolidate his own power in Massachusetts as leader of the Sons of Liberty, moderator of the town meeting, and speaker of the House of Representatives. It was a brilliant political decision.

When Hancock got home to Beacon Hill, Gage sent him a message dismissing him as colonel of the Corps of Cadets for failing to command them to salute on the day of the governor's arrival at Province House. To the governor's astonishment, the entire company resigned. "The Governor appeared to be much agitated as the Committee came upon him quite sudden [and] unexpectedly," said William Palfrey, Hancock's chief clerk. "Had he known our intention he would have prevented it by disbanding us before we would put it in execution. This we foresaw but were determined to be before hand with him and I was highly pleased to find that we had out Generaled the General."[14]

After a few weeks the port closure created food shortages that sent prices soaring beyond the reach of the poor and unemployed. On June 28, however, a flock of more than two hundred sheep arrived in Boston from Windham, Connecticut, with a letter: "This Town is very sensible of the obligations we, and with us, all

British America, are under to the Town of Boston who . . . are the generous defenders of our common rights and liberties."[15] On the same day, Groton, Connecticut, sent forty bushels of rye and corn, followed by more than one hundred sheep and some cattle a few weeks later. During the summer a dozen more Connecticut towns sent similar gifts, and over the months that followed towns and cities throughout the colonies sent hundreds of sheep and thousands of bushels of grain and produce to feed the people of Boston.

Although the trade embargo had left thousands out of work, Sam Adams formed a Committee of Ways and Means to organize public works and a Committee on Donations to collect money to pay for them. Unemployed men went to work repairing the town's pavements, operating the brickyard, digging a town well, and building a new town wharf. The committee set up looms for weavers to make clothes and a distribution center for wool, flax, cotton, leather, and other materials for producing clothes. Tensions nevertheless remained high, with soldiers nervously patrolling every street. Even the sound of church bells signaling a fire sent soldiers running for cover.

Before the Boston delegation could leave for Philadelphia, James Bowdoin fell ill. Although the others pleaded with Hancock to fill his place, Hancock refused, insisting that Boston needed at least one leader at home to command patriot forces and represent the city at a forthcoming provincial congress. Hancock hosted a farewell dinner for the four remaining delegates, and the following morning they gathered at Cushing's mansion. In full view of British troops, they boarded Cushing's coach and four—its two drivers conspicuously armed—and trotted off on the six-day trip to Philadelphia.

Gage reacted immediately to what he saw as an implicit threat of revolution by sending troops to Cambridge and Charlestown to seize the provincial militia's arms and ammunition. They found none. The patriots had anticipated his move and rolled the Charlestown cannons to secret hiding places. Fearing attack, Gage began fortifying Boston Neck, the narrow strip of land connecting Boston to the mainland.

"The flames of sedition had spread universally throughout the country," Gage wrote to the king's counselor Lord Dartmouth, "with daily publications of determined Resolutions not to obey the late Acts of Parliament. The Country People are exercizing in Arms in this Province, Connecticut and Rhode Island and getting Magazines of Arms and Ammunition . . . and such Artillery as they can procure. . . . Sedition flows copiously from the Pulpits." Gage reported that jurors refused to serve in royal courts and that scattered mobs were roaming the countryside assaulting suspected Tories. In the face of near anarchy, customs officials at other ports had fled to the safety of Boston, and he, too, feared for his safety if he left the protection of his troops.[16]

On September 5, fifty-six delegates from all the colonies except Georgia assembled, for the first time in colonial history, as the Continental Congress, in Carpenter's Hall, Philadelphia. All but seven were or had been members of their own colonial assemblies, and nine were speakers or former speakers. All except Sam Adams ranged from relatively wealthy to incredibly so. There were five Northern farmers, seven Southern planters, thirty lawyers, and fourteen businessmen, of whom eleven were merchants, one a builder, one a miller, and another a wharf owner. By unanimous vote they elected Peyton Randolph president. He was a Virginia lawyer and head of his colony's seven-man delegation, which included three other lawyers, among them Patrick Henry, and three planters—Benjamin Harrison, Richard Henry Lee, and George Washington. Like the Northern merchants, the wealthy Southern planters had boycotted British imports to try to force repeal of duties. Washington summed up his motive for joining the boycott succinctly and honestly: "They have no right to put their hands in my pockets."[17] Washington, of course, had some of the deepest pockets in America, with eight thousand acres of tobacco and wheat at Mount Vernon, about one hundred slaves to work the acreage, a cloth manufactury, a fishing operation, a lumbering firm, a frontier farm, and title to about sixty thousand acres of wilderness in western Virginia and the Ohio country.

As the merchants, landowners, and lawyers presented their pompous speeches and petitions in Philadelphia, Boston prepared for rebellion, with the Tory *Evening Post* listing Hancock, Sam Adams, Bowdoin, and Cushing as "the authors . . . of all the misfortunes brought upon the province." The newspaper demanded of "you soldiers—the instant rebellion happens—that you will put the above persons to the sword, destroy their houses, and plunder their effects. It is just that they should be the first victims to the evils they brought upon us."[18]

On September 20 Captain Scott arrived safely in Salem Port with the shipload of gunpowder and, with patriot ammunition at the ready, Hancock ordered carpenters who were building barracks for new contingents of British troops to walk off their jobs. Gage demanded that Hancock order the men back to work. Hancock responded angrily that food shortages had made the men too hungry to work and that Gage was responsible for having "taken every possible measure to distress us."[19] Gage agreed to allow goods to be shipped to and from points within the harbor if the men went back to work, but Hancock refused, suspecting that Gage would close the harbor once the barracks were finished. Gage had to send to Halifax for carpenters to build the barracks.

Three weeks later 250 delegates from across Massachusetts met in Concord at the First Provincial Congress, which in effect represented a coup d'état that overthrew royal rule and created the first independent government in America. It assumed all powers to rule the province, collect taxes, buy supplies, and raise a militia. The congress elected Hancock president, in effect making him governor of Massachusetts, with far-reaching powers across the province. He immediately sent Paul Revere to the Continental Congress in Philadelphia with news that Massachusetts had established America's first autonomous government.

After three days at Concord, the Provincial Congress moved to Cambridge, and after a few days there it moved again, continually changing locations every few days to prevent Gage from interfering in its deliberations. After two months it agreed on a broad program of military preparedness. It authorized the Committee of Safety to organize a corps of "minute men" to "hold themselves in readiness [for battle] on the shortest notice." It agreed to provide each militiaman with "an effective fire arm, bayonet, pouch, knapsack, thirty rounds of cartridges and balls."[20] The Provincial Congress also ordered immediate procurement of twenty pieces of field artillery, carriages for twelve battering cannon, four mortars, twenty tons of grape and round shot, ten tons of bombshells, five tons of lead balls, one thousand barrels of powder, five thousand arms and bayonets, and seventy-five thousand flints. Total costs came to almost £21,000. To raise the money, Hancock ordered provincial tax collectors to turn over their receipts to a congressional receiver general instead of the royal provincial treasurer. Those collectors who did not flee to British camps did so willingly rather than risk patriot tar and feathers, but the taxes they collected fell far short of the cost of arming the militia. Whenever he had to, Hancock solicited whatever resources he could from other merchants and used his own money to cover the difference.

Just as the Provincial Congress had achieved unity on military issues, a bitter debate ensued over a motion that "while we are attempting to preserve ourselves from slavery, . . . we also take into consideration the state and circumstances of negro slaves in this province."[21] The motion was a response to a circular letter from Massachusetts slaves that referred to "the efforts made by the Legislature of this province in their last sessions to free themselves from *Slavery*," and went on to state: "[We] cannot but expect your House will . . . take our deplorable case into serious consideration, and give us that ample relief, which, *as men*, we have a natural right to."[22] It was signed by Peter Bestes, Sambo Freeman, Felix Holbrook, and Chester Joie, all of them slaves.

The irony of Whig slave owners protesting duties as a form of enslavement had undermined support of liberal thinkers in England and America for the colonist cause. As Samuel Johnson put it, "How is it that we hear the loudest yelps for liberty among the drivers of negroes?"[23] The First Provincial Congress of Massachusetts nevertheless rejected outright the motion to consider the slave issue.

In mid-October the Continental Congress in Philadelphia declared unconstitutional thirteen parliamentary acts dating back to 1763. Calling the Coercive Acts cruel and unjust, it passed ten resolutions defining colonist rights, including individual rights to "life, liberty and property" and exclusive jurisdiction of elected provincial assemblies over taxation and internal legislation. The provinces pledged to stop importing British goods, to end the slave trade, end consumption of British products and foreign luxury products, and end all exports to Britain, Ireland, and the British West Indies. Congress also established the first union of American colonies by forming the Continental Association. With establishment of that association, John Adams later argued, "the revolution was complete, in the minds of the people, and the Union of the colonies, before the war commenced."[24]

After forming the Continental Association, Congress issued a proclamation to the king and the British and American peoples, reasserting the rights of colonists to govern themselves. Delegates agreed to reconvene on May 10, 1775, if Britain did not redress American grievances before then. In effect, the Congress rejected all authority of the British Parliament and declared the provinces independent, with only the British king retaining any sovereignty.

When Samuel Adams and the other Massachusetts delegates returned to Boston, they found that in their absence, John Hancock had gathered the reins of power in the new patriot government in his hands—especially the powerful Committee of Safety. The Provincial Congress was still hopping from town to town, with Gage unable to act against it without scattering his troops across the face of eastern Massachusetts and diluting his strength in Boston. At the beginning of November, Hancock usurped the royal governor's prerogative of issuing the annual Thanksgiving Day proclamation in Massachusetts. He omitted the king's name from the document for the first time in colonial history. Two weeks later, Hancock and the Provincial Congress called for twelve thousand volunteer minutemen "who shall equip and hold themselves in readiness to march at the shortest notice." Before it adjourned in December, the Provincial Congress elected Hancock to replace Bowdoin as delegate to the Second Continental Congress, the following May. Sensing the historic import of the Second Congress, Hancock accepted, adjourned the Provincial Congress until February 1, 1775, and returned to Boston.

Tory colonists and British soldiers were pouring into Boston from outlying areas, where patriots had put them in fear of their lives. In Boston it was their turn to bully patriots who stood in their way, and Hancock's political prominence combined with his wealth to put him in great personal danger. Rumors circulated that Hancock and Adams were to be arrested, tried, and hanged. Other rumors insisted that British officers planned to assassinate Hancock, Adams, and Warren, but an officer vigorously denied the charges: "It would, indeed, have been a pity for them to make their exit in that way, as I hope we shall have the pleasure of seeing them do it by the hands of the hangman."[25]

Early in March 1775, British troops tarred and feathered a patriot farmer and paraded him through town in a cart, while the regimental band played and the troops sang a tune that was new to Boston:

Yankee Doodle came to town
For to buy a firelock;
We will tar and feather him,
And so we will John Hancock.[26]

Harvard's president picked that day to demand an accounting of college funds from Hancock. Hopping as he had from town to town with the Provincial Congress, Hancock had failed to pay faculty salaries since the beginning of the academic year. He apologized and promised to meet with the president in Cambridge later in the month. He failed to appear, however, after his Beacon Hill property came under attack by British troops.

"Colonel Hancock's elegant home . . . was attacked by a group of officers who, with their swords, cut and hacked the fence before his house in a most scandalous manner," merchant John Andrews wrote to his brother-in-law. Two days later, "four sergeants and as

many men were sent to insult John Hancock under pretense of seeing if his stables would do for barracks." Andrews said that when
Hancock protested, the soldiers sneered and taunted the merchant,
saying "his house, stablers, etc., would soon be theirs, and then
they would do as they pleased." Hancock raged at General Gage,
who rather than ignite an incendiary situation, sent "one of his
aides-de-camp to the officer of the guard at the bottom of the
Common to seize any officer or private who should molest Colonel
Hancock or any inhabitant in their lawful calling." Gage issued an
abject apology and promised to "redress him . . . if he was in any
ways insulted again,"[27] but Hancock now recognized that he and
his family were in great danger.

On March 22 he left Boston for Concord, twenty miles away,
where the Provincial Congress reconvened out of reach of Gage's
forces. Hancock's Committee of Safety began purchasing medi-
cines, canteens, "and all kinds of stores, sufficient for an army of
fifteen thousand to take the field."[28] Some delegates worried that
they had given Hancock and his committee too many war-making
powers. They voted to restrict his authority to call out the militia
until "the Army under command of General Gage, or any part
thereof to the Number of Five Hundred, shall march out of the
Town of Boston, with Artillery and Baggage."[29]

With Hancock's duties as chairman of the Committee of Safety
requiring all his time, he yielded the presidency of the Provincial
Congress to Dr. Joseph Warren. Three days later, Hancock wrote
a love letter of sorts—one of the few that have survived. Dorothy
Quincy had obviously not appreciated him at their last meeting.

My Dear Dolly.
    I am necessitated to abide here to add my mite towards
compleating Business of the utmost importance for a Determination of the Congress on Monday, which prevents me the
pleasure of seeing you so early as I expected; our Remaining
here will promote the rising of Congress sooner, which I
Acquiesce in, & shall return as soon as possible, when I shall
be with you & I hope not be *saucy*. . . . Remember your promise;
I am vastly engaged. . . . My dear Girl, I must close as the room

where I am writing is full of Committee Men, I can only add
that no Person on Earth can be possess'd of greater affection &
regard for anyone, than I have for the Lady to whom I address
this, & be fully convinc'd that no Distance of Time or place can
ever Erase the Impressions made & the determinations I have
formed being forever yours, in that Confidence & Expectation
I close with the addition, of,

> My Dear Dolly
> Yours, for ever
> in every respect

He added his famous signature, complete with the flourish beneath it.[30]

The following day Hancock's coach carried him at a gallop
back to Boston, where he ordered the theft of the provincial militia's four mounted cannon from the British. Two each were in the
New and Old Gun Houses, by the school at the bottom of the
Common. While the sergeant usually on guard was at roll call,
patriots entered a side door of the Old Gun House, removed the
cannon barrels from their carriages, and hid them in a large chest
in the school next door. British soldiers who searched the school
ignored the chest, which the schoolmaster calmly used as a rest for
his lame foot while listening to students recite their lessons. As the
soldiers searched the school in vain, the patriots stole the two
other cannon from the New Gun House and acquired the first
artillery of the American army. They named the first two cannon
Hancock and Adams.[31]

On April 2 Hancock returned to the Provincial Congress at
Concord before leaving with the other Massachusetts delegates
for the Second Continental Congress, in Philadelphia. Harvard's
president sent word to Hancock demanding the return of college
account books, securities, and cash. Hancock answered angrily:
"Mr. Hancock presents his compliments to the Reverend President and the other gentlemen ... and acquaints them that he has at
heart the interest of the college as much as any one and will pursue
it. He is much surprised and astonished at the contents of the
President's letter ... *which he very seriously resents.*" Hancock then

guaranteed that the college would not "suffer any detriment," and he went back to the business of planning a revolution.[32]

Recognizing the dangers of leaving his family in Boston, Hancock arranged for Aunt Lydia and Dolly to follow him to Lexington—with enough furnishings and furniture for comfort during a potentially long stay away from home. At the same time, he wrote to Dolly's father, Edmund Quincy, to flee Boston with his servants. "I am not at liberty to say what I know, but pray . . . remove immediately from Boston. . . . But pray do not make my Name known abroad as to this advice. I hope to see my D[ea]r Aunt & Dolly at Lexington. I shall be utterly against their returning to Town. Things will very soon be serious." In a postscript Hancock added, "Pray tell Dr. Cooper [pastor at Brattle Square Church] I think as all his friends do here that he aught instantly to Remove out of Town."[33]

Aunt Lydia and Dolly left Boston immediately, joining a stream of other panic-stricken families. Hancock's younger brother, Ebenezer, terrified that his family name would get him hanged, disguised himself as a fisherman and fled with other fisherfolk. "The inhabitants of Boston are on the move," wrote James Warren to his wife from Concord on April 6. No relation to Dr. Joseph Warren, James Warren was a merchant, farmer, and radical patriot from Plymouth, who had married James Otis's sister Mercy, a talented writer who had contributed propaganda to the *Gazette* during the Stamp Act crisis and wrote several plays that satirized British officials. "H and A go no more into that garrison," Warren continued. "The female connections of the first come out early this morning, and measures are taken relative to those of the last."[34] The "female connections," of course, were Aunt Lydia and Dorothy Quincy. Together with John Hancock and Sam Adams, they went to nearby Lexington to stay with Hancock's cousins at the parsonage where John had lived as a child with his grandfather, Bishop John Hancock. After the Bishop's death, the Reverend Jonas Clarke had become Congregational minister in Lexington and married Lucy Bowes, the Bishop's granddaughter.

Hancock-Clarke House, Lexington, Massachusetts, the manse of the Congregational church and home of the Reverend John Hancock, the patriot's grandfather and "Bishop" of Lexington. It was here that John Hancock fled with his family and with Samuel Adams after British troops occupied Boston and placed a price on his head. (*Lexington Historical Society*)

Unfortunately, Lucy Bowes Clarke's brother William Bowes was a Tory who had invested money with Hancock's bank. When he saw John flee the city, he got a sheriff's order and seized goods worth £3,000 from Hancock's store and £350 worth of Madeira wine from Hancock's cellar to compensate him for his lost investment.

The Hancocks had not moved to Lexington a moment too soon. A week later, on April 14, General Gage received the official documents from the king "to arrest the principal actors and abettors in the Provincial Congress,"[35] and with additional troops on their way, Gage made plans to turn the trade war into an armed conflict.

Gage had planted enough spies in the patriot camp to learn where the patriots had hidden their arsenal at Concord and that Hancock and Adams had fled to Lexington. He ordered a two-stage assault, with the main force to march to Concord to destroy the patriot arsenal while a detachment stopped in Lexington to capture the traitors Hancock and Adams. But the patriots had spies of their own, along with so-called vigilance committees in almost every hamlet. In Boston, Dr. Joseph Warren had organized thirty craftsmen like Revere, who moved about with their apprentices, plying their trades—and gathering intelligence on British troop movements. They learned that someone in the patriot camp had alerted Gage to the secret arsenal at Concord and the whereabouts of Hancock and Sam Adams.

"We frequently took turns, two and two, to watch the soldiers patrolling the streets all night," Revere wrote; "the boats belonging to the transports were all launched and carried under the sterns of the men-of-war. . . . On Tuesday evening . . . a number of soldiers were marching towards the bottom of the Common. About 10 o'clock, Dr Warren sent in great haste for me and begged that I would immediately set off for Lexington, where Messrs. Hancock and Adams were, and acquaint them of the movements and that it was thought they were the objects."[36]

Gage dispatched small bands of soldiers to intercept patriot spies on the Lexington and Concord road, but there were too few soldiers and too many patriots. Warren sent two of them—Revere and William Dawes—by different routes to warn Hancock and Adams. Revere set off on his famous midnight ride on Tuesday, April 18. Two friends rowed him across the Charles River to Charlestown, where he picked up a horse and rode toward Lexington, stopping at Medford to awaken the captain of the minutemen. "I alarmed almost every house till I got to Lexington. I found Messrs. Hancock and Adams at the Reverend Mr. Clark[e]'s. I told them my errand and inquired for Mr. Dawes. They said he had not been there. . . . [After] about half an hour Mr Dawes came. We refreshed ourselves and set off for Concord to secure the stores."[37]

Revere gave Hancock and Adams a letter from Warren "stating that a large body of British troops . . . were on their march to Lexington."[38] "Mr. Hancock gave the alarm immediately," Dorothy Quincy Hancock later recalled, "and the Lexington bell was rung all night; and before light about 150 men were collected. Mr. H. was all night cleaning his gun and sword and putting his accouterments in order, and was determined to go out to the plain by the meetinghouse . . . to fight with the men . . . and it was with very great difficulty that he was dissuaded from it by Mr. Clark[e] and Mr. Adams, the latter clapping him on the shoulder, said to him, 'that is not our business; we belong to the cabinet.' It was not till break of day that Mr. H. could be persuaded that it was improper for him to expose himself against such a powerful force . . . that the enemy would indeed triumph if they could get him and Mr. Adams in their power."[39]

Revere and Dawes, meanwhile, rode off to warn Concord, joined by Dr. Samuel Prescott. On the way, a British patrol surprised them, but Prescott escaped and got through to Concord. The troops captured Revere, brought him back to Lexington, and released him.

The following day after nightfall, a force of seven hundred redcoats began their march to Concord with orders "to seize and destroy . . . Military Stores." Gage ordered the commander to "take care that the Soldiers do not plunder the Inhabitants, or hurt private property."[40] He sent "a small party on Horseback" to ride ahead "to stop all advice of your March getting to Concord before you," but, of course, Revere, Dawes, and Prescott had already alerted the entire countryside.

After much discussion, Hancock and Adams road away to safety at dawn, leaving Aunt Lydia and Dolly to face the British. In fact, they were far safer in the parsonage with the minister's family than they would have been with the fugitives. Except for a British round shot that whizzed by her head as she watched the action on the green, Aunt Lydia was unharmed, as was Dolly, who helped care for two wounded minutemen.

Years later, Elizabeth Clarke, the minister's daughter, described the scene: "Oh! I now can see from this window . . . in my mind just as plain—all the British troops marching off the common . . . how Aunt [was] crying and wringing her hands and helping Mother dress the children. Dolly going round with Father to hide money,

watches, and anything down in the potatoes and up [in the] garret.
. . . And in the afternoon, Father, Mother, with me and the baby,
went to the meeting-house. There was the eight men that was
killed . . . all in boxes made of four large boards nailed up, and,
after Pa had prayed, they were put into two horse carts and took
into the graveyard."[41]

The following day, patriot messengers galloped off in all
directions with copies of a dispatch from the Massachusetts Committee of Safety:

> Watertown, Wednesday Morning near 10 o'clock
>
> To all the Friends of American Liberty. Be it known that
> the Morning before Break of Day a Brigade consisting of
> about 1000 or 1200 Men landed at Phips' Farm at Cambridge
> & marched to Lexington, where they found a Company of our
> Colony Militia in Arms, upon which they fir'd without any
> Provocation & killed 6 Men and wounded 4 others; by an
> Express from Boston this Moment we find another Brigade
> are now upon the March from Boston, supposed to be about
> 1000. . . . [42]

10

President of Congress

(1775-1776)

HANCOCK'S LIGHTWEIGHT PHAETON had just raced off the Lexington-Concord road when he and Samuel Adams heard the shots behind them in Lexington. The shots did not last long. As the British approached Lexington, militia captain John Parker positioned the minutemen in two lines on the green, one behind the other. They ranged in age from sixteen to sixty-five—almost half the town's population—and included eight pairs of fathers and sons who stood side by side to face the dreaded redcoats.

Maj. John Pitcairn led the advance guard of some seven hundred troops of the crack British field artillery into town, convinced that "one active campaign, a smart action, and burning two or three of their towns, will set everything to rights."[1] Pitcairn ordered the patriots to lay down their arms and surrender, but Parker ordered them to hold their ground. When Pitcairn saw a few of the minutemen break ranks and run for cover behind nearby stone walls, he commanded his men to move against the minutemen. Amidst the confusion and shouting that followed, someone fired the "shot heard round the world."[2] No two accounts agree on the details of the engagement, and like so many events leading up to the Revolutionary War, the number who claimed to have been eyewitnesses far exceeded the actual number of people at the scene. Although the Massachusetts Provincial Congress heard many American testimonials, only a handful of British accounts remain, including this written report by Pitcairn to General Gage:

> I gave directions to the Troops to move forward, but on no account to Fire, or even attempt it without orders; when I arrived at the end of the Village, I observed drawn upon a Green near 200 of the Rebels; and when I came within about One Hundred Yards of them, they began to File off toward some stone Walls on our Right Flank—the Light Infantry observing this, ran after them—I instantly called to the Soldiers not to Fire, but to surround and disarm them, and after several repetitions of those positive Orders to the men, not to Fire &c, some of the Rebels who had jumped over the Wall, Fired Four or Five Shott at the Soldiers, which wounded a man of the Tenth, and my Horse was wounded in two places from some quarter or other and at the same time several Shott were fired from a Meeting House on our Left—upon this, without any order or Regularity, the Light Infantry began a scattered Fire and continued in that situation for some little time, contrary to the repeated orders of both me and the officers that were present.
>
> Your most obedt humble Servant,
John Pitcairn[3]

When the firing ceased, eight minutemen, including Parker, lay dead and ten lay wounded. Although Parker only suffered a musket ball wound in the initial skirmish, a British soldier subsequently ran him through with a bayonet. The minutemen managed to wound only one British soldier and Pitcairn's horse, but they had ignited a revolution that would send the world's greatest empire into irreversible decline.

As the smoke of gunshot drifted across the silent wood, the British troops rode off to Concord, and Dr. Benjamin Church, the Whig leader, tended the wounded but ran out of medical supplies and rode off to Boston to find more.

While the British force searched in vain for the patriot arms at Concord, minutemen attacked a platoon the British had posted to guard Concord's North Bridge. Realizing the patriots had removed most of the arsenal, the British commander ordered his force to return to Lexington. On the way they met a growing rain of sniper fire. Minuteman ranks had swelled into the thousands. Musket barrels materialized behind every tree, every boulder, every stone wall. Facing annihilation unless they returned to Boston, they abandoned plans to search for Hancock and Adams and stepped up their pace to double time. Although Gen. Lord Hugh Percy met them in Lexington with one thousand more troops, the minuteman force had grown to four thousand. They came from every direction, with town after town—Watertown, Roxbury, Needham, Danvers, and others—sending one hundred, two hundred, or whatever number it could muster to join their fellow countrymen. Had there been a supreme commander to organize the growing force and plan the attack, the colonists would have wiped out the British force. Their relentless, albeit uncoordinated, assault nevertheless left seventy-three British soldiers dead, 174 wounded, and twenty-six missing before the expedition reached cover at Charlestown and could board their boats to Boston, across the bay. The patriots suffered forty-nine killed, forty-two wounded, and five missing. The humiliated British troops wreaked revenge in every town, looting and burning houses, bayoneting anyone who stood in their way, civilian or military. But in the end Thomas Hancock's warning twenty years earlier had come back to haunt them: British "parade ground tactics" were impotent in the harsh American landscape.

After the British debacle on the retreat from Concord, Lord Percy, who several weeks before Lexington had scoffed at colonists as "cowards—frightened out of their wits . . . whenever we appear," admitted, "Whosoever looks upon them as an irregular mob, will find himself much mistaken. They have men amongst them who know very well what they are about, having been employed as Rangers against the Indians & Canadians, & this country being much covered with wood, and hill, is very advantageous for their method of fighting. . . . For my part, I never believed, I confess that they would have attacked the King's troops, or have the perseverance I found in them yesterday."[4]

The patriot propaganda machine sent riders like Revere with word of victory throughout the colonies, along with reports of alleged British atrocities. Besides accusing the British of setting fire to homes, shops, and barns in Lexington, the patriots claimed the British "pillaged almost every House they passed by, breaking and destroying Doors, Windows, Glasses, etc. and carrying off Cloathing and other valuable effects. It appeared to be their Design to burn and destroy all before them. . . . But the savage Barbarity exercised upon the Bodies of our Brethren who fell, is almost incredible; Not contented with shooting down the unarmed, aged and infirm, they disregarded the Cries of the wounded, killing them without Mercy; and mangling their Bodies in the most shocking Manner."[5] The propaganda had its desired effect, inflaming passions and provoking hundreds, at first, and then thousands upon thousands of colonists from farms and villages and cities to gather their arms and rally to the side of the minuteman force outside Boston.

The British countered with reports that patriot soldiers "scalped and otherwise ill-treated one or two of the men who were either killed or wounded." Another British report claimed that "the Rebels . . . scalped & cut off the ears of some of the wounded men who fell into their hands." And the sister of a Boston customs officer wrote a friend in England that British soldiers had "found two or three of their people Lying in the Agonies of Death, scalp'd & their Noses and ears cut off & Eyes bored out."[6] As for who fired first, both sides tried to sway public opinion in England and America. The patriots were careful to obtain depositions that the British fired first.

HANCOCK AND ADAMS had taken refuge at Woburn, less than five miles northeast of Lexington, off the Concord road. After learning of the British retreat, Hancock rode northwest through treacherous woodlands to Billerica, about ten miles north of Concord, and sent for his aunt and fiancée—reminding Lydia to "bring the fine salmon" that had awaited them for dinner the day the British showed up. When the ladies arrived, Dolly announced that she planned to return to Boston the following morning to see to the safety of her father, Edmund Quincy. "No, madam," replied the tired, exasperated colonel. "You shall not return as long as there is a British bayonet in Boston."

"Recollect, Mr. Hancock," Dolly snapped back, "I am not under your control yet. I *shall* go to my father's."[7] Dolly had tired of the lonely hours with Aunt Lydia while John roamed the countryside with the Provincial Congress. Only Aunt Lydia's persuasion managed to keep her from going to Boston—along with Hancock's word that he had already written to Quincy to leave Boston and that he might well be on his way, in which case any venture by Dolly into Boston would be at cross-purposes.

Hancock and his aunt agreed that, while he went to Philadelphia, the safest, most comfortable place for the ladies would be the spacious home of Thaddeus Burr, an old family friend and business associate, a staunch patriot and political leader in Fairfield, Connecticut. With Aunt Lydia and Dolly following, Hancock and Adams left for Worcester, Massachusetts, the next morning to rendezvous with John Adams, Thomas Cushing, and Robert Treat Paine. Sam Adams was not dressed to attend an intercolonial congress. His clothes—always the coarse cloth of workingmen—were soiled and torn. Despite Adams's angry protests, Hancock bought him a new suit, wig, shoes, and silk hose, and gave him some pocket money.

Cushing and Paine arrived the next day with a military escort and breathless reports of seventy thousand minutemen on the march to lay siege to Boston. In addition, Connecticut's Benedict Arnold was raising a force in western Massachusetts to try to capture the huge cache of British artillery and military supplies at Fort Ticonderoga on Lake Champlain. Volunteers by the thousands were pouring into Cambridge from everywhere in New England. Although patriot leader Dr. Benjamin Church had been captured in Boston, General Gage issued a proclamation permitting inhabitants, including Church, to evacuate the city with all their belongings, except weapons.

On April 28, Hancock, Sam Adams, Cushing, and Paine set off for Philadelphia. John Adams caught up with them in Hartford, Connecticut, where on April 29 they met with Gov. Jonathan Trumbull, another Harvard graduate and former merchant—and the only royal governor in America to support the patriots. After the British defeat at Concord and on the retreat to Boston, civil government in other colonies had disintegrated, with every royal governor except Trumbull fleeing to the safety of the nearest British military enclave.

From Hartford, Hancock took his ladies to the Burr home in Fairfield before continuing along the dusty, rutted road to New York. Hancock described the welcome that awaited them there:

> New York, Sabbath Even'g, May 7, 1775.
>
> My Dear Dolly:
>
> I arrived well, tho' Fatigued ... and then set out in the Procession for New York, the Carriage of your humble servant of course being the first in the Procession. When we Arriv'd within three Miles of the City, we were Met by the Grenadier Company and Regiment of the City Militia under Arms, Gentlemen in Carriages and on Horseback, and many Thousand of Persons on Foot, the Roads fill'd with people and the greatest Cloud of Dust I ever saw. In this Scituation we Entered the City, and passing thro' the Principal Streets of New York amidst the Acclamations of Thousands ... the Numbers of Spectators increas'd to perhaps Seven Thousand or more ... no Person could possibly be more notic'd than myself.
>
> The Grenadier Company of the City is to Continue under Arms during our stay here, and we have a guard of them Night and Day at our Doors. This is a sad mortification for the Tories. ...
>
> Tomorrow morning propose to Cross the Ferry. We are to have a large Guard in several Boats and a Number of the City

Gentlemen will attend us over. I can't think they will Dare attack us.

I beg you will write me. Do acquaint me every Circumstance. Relative to that Dear Aunt of Mine; write Lengthy and often. . . . My best Respects to Mr. and Mrs. Burr. My poor Face and Eyes are in a most shocking scituation, burnt up and much swell'd and a little painfull. I don't know how to manage with it.

Is your Father out [of Boston] safely? As soon as you know, do acquaint me, and send me the letters, and I will then write him. Pray let me hear from you by every Post. God bless you my D[ea]r Girl, and believe me most Sincerely,

Yours most Affectionately,
John Hancock[8]

Hancock did not exaggerate New York's welcome. His exploits in the Massachusetts rebellion had reached mythic proportions. Thousands turned out to cheer. As church bells pealed incessantly and bands played, hundreds of mounted militiamen with swords drawn joined a battalion of eight hundred infantrymen in leading the Hancock carriage through the city to Wall Street and down to Fraunces Tavern. New York merchants hosted a dinner that was the most elegant that either of the Adamses had ever seen.

For reasons that remain unclear, some friction developed between Hancock and Sam Adams. Perhaps Adams resented the attention the merchants paid Hancock, or he may have harbored lingering resentment over Hancock's insistence on his getting new clothes for Congress. Whatever the reason, Sam Adams spread the lie that during their ride through the city, cheering citizens tried to detach the horses from the carriage and pull it through the streets themselves. Adams claimed Hancock saw it as a compliment and beamed approval, while he, Adams, objected angrily. "If you wish to be gratified with so humiliating a spectacle," he shouted above the roar, "I will get out and walk, for I will not countenance an act by which my fellow citizens shall degrade themselves into beasts."

But Hancock's description to Dolly of the same incident differed sharply: "Persons appearing with proper Harnesses insisted on Taking out my Horses and Dragging me into and through the City, a Circumstance I would not have had Taken place upon any consideration, not being fond of such Parade. . . . I was obliged to apply to the Leading Gentlemen in the procession to intercede with them not to Carry their Designs into Execution; as it was very disagreeable to me. They were at last prevail'd upon and I proceeded." Hancock would face defamation by Adams and his followers the rest of his life. But as in this case, Adams never slandered Hancock to his face where he risked refutation.

Hancock was not well at the end of the journey. The effects of sun, wind, and dust left his face red and his eyes swollen. John Adams reported that Hancock's eyes were so sore and inflamed he could hardly read.

The following morning, New York delegates joined those from Massachusetts and Connecticut at the North [Hudson] River ferry to begin the trip to Philadelphia. Huge military and civilian groups hailed them on both sides of the river and at every city, town, and crossing—at Newark, Elizabethtown, Woodbridge, New Brunswick, Trenton, Princeton. . . . At Princeton, Scottish minister John Witherspoon,[9] president of the College of New Jersey, joined cheering marchers behind the delegates' carriages. To ensure the safety of the procession, each city's militia escorted the travelers to the succeeding city.

On the morning of May 10, the huge procession reached Philadelphia, led by an escort of two to three hundred mounted militiamen with swords drawn. Philadelphia was larger than Boston, with a population of about twenty-five thousand squeezed into an area twenty-five blocks long but only twelve blocks wide. Squalid slums covered the western part of the city, but the area around the State House boasted wide, tree-lined streets, with brick walkways lit by whale oil lamps. Again, church bells pealed and crowds roared—somewhat to the envy of delegates from other colonies, who were waiting impatiently for the Second Continental Congress to convene. But even they agreed that Hancock, more than anyone else there, had made enormous sacrifices for the patriot cause and deserved public acclaim. He had lost his sloop *Liberty*, had spent at least £100,000 of his own money on arms and ammunition, and risked the rest of his fortune on the success of the Revolution. If arrested on the king's warrant, he faced trial on charges of treason, with the possible loss of both his honor and his life. Even as Hancock arrived in Philadelphia, British general Henry Clinton was comfortably ensconced in Hancock House on Beacon Hill, drinking his fill of fine Madeira wine from Hancock's prized cellar.

The raucous procession notwithstanding, the Second Continental Congress convened on May 10 at the Pennsylvania State House. Hancock was one of several important new faces—another being the venerable Benjamin Franklin.

From the beginning, Congress had little opportunity for quiet reflection. Outside the State House windows, twenty-eight Philadelphia infantry companies drilled twice a day, to the incessant squeal of fifes and the roll of drums. Inside, regional antagonisms delayed the most basic organizational proceedings. The Southern provinces had long-standing disputes with the New England colonies over territorial claims in the West. Moreover, the South, which had no intention of arming its slave majority, had far smaller militias than the North, and some Southern delegates feared that the huge Massachusetts militia might take advantage of a colonist victory by replacing rule by Britain with rule by New England.

Although delegates reelected Virginia's Peyton Randolph president, North-South frictions surfaced when Randolph returned home abruptly after only two weeks. None of the delegates had any ambition to replace him as moderator of the increasingly bitter, almost intractable North-South disputes. Without Georgia, Congress was evenly divided between North and South, with the North consisting of New York, New Jersey, and the four New England colonies, while the South encompassed Pennsylvania and all the other colonies.

John Adams and George Washington, however, stepped forward with a solution. They had developed one of the few collegial relationships that crossed the North-South barrier. Physically they were an incongruous pair. Washington was the most visible delegate: at six feet, four inches, he towered over most of the others.

Benjamin Franklin, the great scholar, who joined
John Hancock as a first-time delegate at the Continental Congress during its second session. A delegate from Pennsylvania, Franklin later signed the
Declaration of Independence. (*Library of Congress*)

Although forty-three, he was fit and strong. In contrast, the forty-
year-old Adams was one of the least-imposing delegates. As his
wife conceded, he was "short, thick and fat."[10] Although some delegates considered Washington aloof and unfriendly, Adams found
"something charming . . . in [his] conduct" and he admired Washington's willingness to risk his enormous fortune by supporting
the rebellion.[11]

WASHINGTON.

George Washington, a Virginia delegate to the Continental Congress but not a signatory of the Declaration of Independence. To the consternation of John Hancock, the Congress named Washington commander in chief of the Continental Army, instead of Hancock. He is seen here in his general's uniform in 1785. (*Library of Congress*)

As Northerners accused Southerners of slighting them in the presidential selection process, Adams and his new friend Washington acted to ease tensions, and they convinced Benjamin Harrison, another Virginia planter, to support them. With Washington and Harrison's support, John Adams nominated John Hancock for the presidency—not just because of his personal sacrifices but, as Adams accurately stated, because of his years of experience as moderator at Boston town meetings, in the Massachusetts

House of Representatives, and most recently at the Massachusetts Provincial Congress. In all three, he had often reconciled Tories with Whigs, radicals with conservatives, and rural interests with urban interests. Congress elected John Hancock unanimously. He considered his election as president of Congress the greatest honor of his life. Amidst "general acclamation," the Southerner Benjamin Harrison led the Northerner Hancock to the chair and proclaimed, "We will show Great Britain how much we value her proscriptions."[12]

In addition to the North-South divisions in Congress, Hancock faced a second, three-way political divide between radicals, moderates, and conservatives, whose membership had little to do with geography. Congressional radicals, led by Sam Adams, demanded nothing less than independence. Philadelphia's John Dickinson, whose *Letters from a Farmer in Pennsylvania* had brought him international renown, led the conservatives. They sought nothing more than a redress of grievances and a return to the normalcy of pre–Stamp Act days. The moderates found a voice to define their amorphous goals in another new delegate, who arrived late and took his seat just as Hancock took over the presidency of Congress. Thirty-two-year-old Virginia legislator Thomas Jefferson had written a widely circulated essay, *A Summary View of the Rights of British America*. Although Jefferson accepted the king's sovereignty in America, he insisted that provincial legislatures held all authority in the colonies, including taxation, and that "British parliament has no right to exercise authority over us."

As moderator, Hancock had to remain impartial. Although his neutral stance incurred the growing enmity of Sam Adams, he won the respect of all other delegates. He was the perfect president, with some appeal to all factions but favoritism for none. He understood everyone's point of view. His experience as moderator and legislator appealed to moderates; his wealth, business position, and education appealed to conservatives; and his defiance of British authority in Boston appealed to radicals. And what appealed to all was his vast experience directing a large organization, namely the House of Hancock.

Thomas Jefferson, a Virginia delegate at the second session of the Continental Congress. Although he was principal author and signatory of the Declaration of Independence, he originally favored retaining George III as sovereign of the new nation. (*Library of Congress*)

His broad appeal cannot be overstated for a body made up not of united states, but of twelve separate and independent colonies—Georgia remained absent—with no ties to one another. Indeed, they had seldom communicated with one another until a year earlier, and their leaders had never met face-to-face as a group until six months earlier. They were independent in every respect and in some cases almost at war with one another. Massachusetts, Virginia, and

Connecticut all claimed lands surrounding the southern tongue of Lake Michigan in the Northwest Territory above the Ohio River; Massachusetts claimed all the territory in western New York along Lakes Ontario and Erie; New York, Massachusetts, and New Hampshire all claimed what later became Vermont; and the Carolinas and Virginia (and Georgia) were at one another's throats over lands west of their borders. In Congress, however, all were equals, with only one vote to cast—although each could send as many delegates as it chose. For the first month, Hancock tried to pick men from these disparate delegations to work together in committees and to keep the larger body intact, focused, and moving forward in pursuit of an agenda. Along the way, he had to prevent defections, soothe injured feelings, and calm any anger over perceived slights or oversights.

"Such a vast Multitude of Objects, civil, political, commercial and military, press and crowd upon us so fast that We know not what to do first," said John Adams about the opening days of the Continental Congress. "Our unwieldy Body moves very slow. We shall do something in Time."[13]

Despite the overwhelming press of congressional affairs, Hancock wrote to Dolly and Aunt Lydia almost daily and even found time to shower them with gifts—all with no response except for short thank-you notes acknowledging receipt. By early June, he despaired for news from home as a relief from the constant press of business. "I am almost prevailed upon to think that my letters to my aunt and you are not read," Hancock wrote angrily, "for I cannot obtain a reply. I have asked [a] million questions and not an answer to one. . . . I really take it extremely unkind. Pray, my dear[,] use not so much ceremony and reservedness. Why can't you use freedom in writing? Be not afraid of me. I want long letters."[14]

On June 2 Dr. Benjamin Church arrived from Boston with a letter from Dr. Joseph Warren, the new president of the Massachusetts Provincial Congress, urging the Continental Congress to assume control of the disorganized intercolonial army laying siege to Boston and appoint a commander in chief.

"The army now collecting from different colonies is for the general defence," Warren wrote. "The sword should, in all free States, be subservient to the civil powers . . . we tremble at having an Army (although consisting of our own countrymen) established here without a civil power to provide for and control them. . . . We would beg leave to suggest to your consideration the propriety of your taking the regulation and general direction of it."[15] In a letter to Samuel Adams, Warren warned, "The continent must strengthen and support with all its weight the civil authority here; otherwise our soldiery will lose the ideas of right and wrong, and will plunder, instead of protecting the inhabitants."[16] A week later, John Adams proposed and the Continental Congress agreed to make the patriot forces besieging Boston a national Continental Army, and it appropriated £6,000 for supplies.

Two days later, Gen. Thomas Gage imposed martial law in Boston and declared all Americans in arms and those siding with them to be rebels and traitors. To avoid unnecessary bloodshed, however, he issued a general amnesty in Massachusetts—to all but two men: John Hancock and Samuel Adams.

"In this exigency of complicated calamities," Gage wrote in the amnesty, "I avail myself of the last effort . . . to spare the effusion of blood; to offer . . . in His Majesty's name . . . his most gracious pardon to all persons who shall forthwith lay down their arms and return to their duties of peaceable subjects; excepting only . . . Samuel Adams and John Hancock, whose offenses are of too flagitious a nature to admit of any other consideration than that of condign punishment."[17] The amnesty made it official: Hancock and Adams were now fugitives from justice, wanted by the British government for treason and subject to arrest on sight for treason—with all but certain death to follow. Gage offered a reward of £500 each for their capture.

Meanwhile, Congress had resolved to raise six companies of riflemen in Pennsylvania, Maryland, and Virginia to march to New England, and Hancock appointed a five-man committee to draft rules for the administration of the army and to name a commanding general. With each delegation eager to name a worthy patriot from its state, the committee decided to give the top position to the most qualified man they could find and to create a dozen subsidiary positions—for four major generals and eight brigadier generals—to give each colony a general. When it became clear that few delegates had any military experience, New Englanders won nine of the subsidiary posts. As for commander in chief, Hancock adored his gold-braided colonel's uniform and believed sincerely that his service on the Boston Common with the Corps of Cadets had made him an incomparable military leader and the logical choice as commander in chief. He all but grinned as he recognized his Massachusetts colleague John Adams to nominate the commander in chief of the Continental Army.

When John Adams rose, however, he had a different perspective from Hancock's. Adams had mingled discreetly among the delegates for several days—Southerners as well as Northerners—listening to and trying to understand every view and sentiment. There was little doubt that delegates from middle and Southern colonies harbored "a Jealousy against a New England Army under the Command of a New England General."[18] Connecticut delegate Eliphalet Dyer suggested that selection of a non–New Englander "removes all jealousies, more firmly Cements the Southern to the Northern, and takes away the fear of the former lest an Enterprising eastern New England Genll. proving Successful, might with his Victorious Army give law to the Southern or Western Gentry."

It was evident to all that George Washington had the most "Skill and Experience as an Officer" of any candidate.[19] He had commanded the Virginia militia for nearly five years during the French and Indian War, gaining an intimate knowledge of appropriate wilderness battle tactics. On June 10, John Adams stood to propose Washington as commander in chief of the Continental Army. His interminable preamble, however, wearied all but President Hancock, who beamed approvingly with the certainty that he would hear his name called when Adams reached the end of his speech. "I had no hesitation to declare," John Adams later wrote, "that I had but one gentleman in mind for that important command, and that was a gentleman from Virginia who was among us and very well known to all of us, a gentleman, whose skill and experience as an officer, whose independent fortune, great talents, and excellent universal character, would command the approbation of all the colonies better than any other person in the Union."

When Adams pronounced the name George Washington, Hancock's face fell. "Mortification and resentment were expressed as forcibly as his face could exhibit them," according to John Adams. Sam Adams, still piqued at having to share political power with Hancock in Boston, sprang up to second the Washington nomination—a move that did not "soften the President's physiognomy."[20] Hancock was furious and broke completely with Sam Adams, whose outspoken radicalism had already alienated Northern moderates and most of the Southerners. Hancock had developed increasingly warm friendships with Southerners, who like him were wealthy, well educated, cultured men who appreciated fine clothes, foods, wines, and other luxuries. Ever bitter about Hancock's wealth and good fortune, Sam Adams tried to undermine Hancock's reputation in Philadelphia, calling him, alternatively, "an oriental prince," "King Hancock," and a victim of "Southern manners and the parade of courtly living."[21]

The Adams attacks only convinced Dickinson, John Jay of New York, and all the other "aristocrats" in Congress that New England was a land of "Goths and Vandals." Hancock responded by keeping Sam Adams off committees, while investing his own office with all the trappings of a sovereign nation's chief executive. As he had done at the House of Hancock, he dressed magnificently, traveled in an "elegant chariot"—again, Sam Adams's bitter description—attended by four liveried servants mounted on richly ornamented horses, escorted by fifty horsemen, half ahead and half trailing, their swords drawn. Sam Adams muttered bitterly about Hancock's "unrepublican ostentation,"[22] but Hancock was, after all, spending his own money, and in his mind he was honoring the office he held. As the bitterness grew between the two, John Adams, whose dislike for Hancock reached back to their childhood in Braintree, drew closer to his cousin and Hancock's other political enemies.

Although New Englanders argued that a New England army required a New Englander to lead them, John Adams and other moderates convinced the delegates to vote unanimously for Washington. Washington accepted the post but refused the $500 monthly salary, asking only that Congress pay all his expenses. A week later, Hancock wrote to Dr. Joseph Warren in Watertown, Massachusetts, where the Third Provincial Congress had convened. His letter bore no trace of disappointment: "The Congress here have appointed George Washington, Esq., General and Commander-in-Chief, of the Continental Army. His commission is made out, and I shall sign it tomorrow. He is a gentleman you will all like. I submit to you the propriety of providing a suitable place for his residence and the mode of his reception . . . such as to do . . . the Commander-in-Chief great honor."[23]

As Hancock penned his inimitable signature, however, Warren already lay dead on the field of battle at Breed's Hill, on the Charlestown peninsula, opposite Boston. Like Boston, Charlestown sat on a near island across the bay, connected to the mainland by a narrow neck (see Map, page 213). Two hills dominated the peninsula—Bunker Hill (then called Bunker's Hill), near the neck, and the far smaller Breed's Hill, near the water, overlooking Boston. Warren had gone to Bunker Hill to warn the commander of ammunition shortages and then joined the troops at a makeshift fortification on Breed's Hill. At dawn on June 17, British warships all but surrounded the head of land and fired relentlessly on Breed's Hill. When the tide ebbed, an assault force of twenty-four hundred landed and charged up the hill, only to be repelled by a sixteen-hundred-man patriot force. Again they charged; again they fell back. With the third charge, however, the patriots ran out of powder and fell back to Bunker Hill. The British seized Breed's Hill, then quickly overran Bunker Hill. Somehow the madman James Otis managed to flee his brother's home with a rifle, charge up Bunker Hill through a hail of British shot, and emerge unharmed. Patriot soldiers finally subdued him and carried him to safety. One hundred other patriots died, however. One of them was Dr. Joseph Warren. The British wounded 267 and took thirty

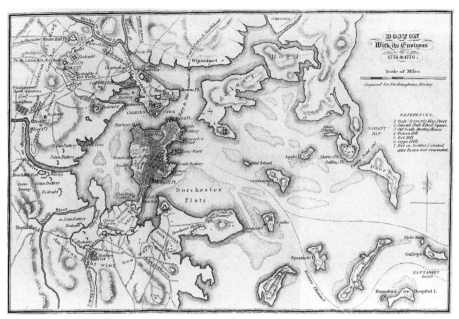

Boston, its harbor and environs, 1775. Charlestown is across the water, with Breed's Hill on the right extremity and Bunker Hill a bit north, near Charlestown Neck. (*Bostonian Society*)

prisoners. But the British paid a heavy price for their victory, with more than a thousand casualties—most of them officers. Never before had Britain suffered so many casualties in a single day's battle.

On July 3 George Washington arrived in Cambridge and took control of the Continental Army, as colonist troops at Fort Ticonderoga began moving northward to seize points in Canada that might be vital to the security of New York and the New England colonies. Two days later, John Hancock signed a so-called Olive Branch Petition, which John Dickinson had written, reiterating the allegiance of the American people to George III and their sincere hopes for peace. There were many merchants and planters in Congress who were more loath than Hancock to sacrifice their fortunes to the ill-defined, ephemeral concept of "liberty." They

Battle of Bunker Hill, where more than a thousand patriots perished, including Dr. Joseph Warren, the Revolutionary War leader and close friend of John Hancock. The dying Warren is portrayed here in an engraving by Gotthard von Muller, after the painting by John Trumbull. (*National Portrait Gallery, Smithsonian Institution*)

pleaded with the king to order an end to hostilities to permit reconciliation. The following day, however, Hancock signed another Dickinson resolution, a "Declaration of the Causes and Necessities of Taking Up Arms." It reasserted colonist willingness to die rather than submit to enslavement by the British Parliament.

By July 10 the enormous workload was taking a toll on John Hancock. He was deeply depressed by Warren's death—the first death of a close friend. He had first met Warren when they joined the Masons together in 1761. The failure of Aunt Lydia and Dolly to write him also hurt, as did the sting of Sam Adams's daily insults and the sheer agony of settling sectarian disputes between colleagues he admired and preventing new ones from breaking out. Hancock decided he might better serve his country as a soldier and wrote to George Washington: "I must beg the favor that you will reserve some berth for me in such department as you may judge proper; for I am determined to act under you, if it be to take a fire-lock and join the ranks as a volunteer."[24]

Although spawned, possibly, by melancholy, it was one of the most selfless gestures of patriotism Hancock had ever displayed. Historians offer no logical explanation for Washington's curious reply:

> I am particular to acknowledge that part of your favor of the 10th instant wherein you do me the honor of determining to join the army under my command. I need certainly to make no professions of the pleasure I shall have in seeing you. At the same time I have to regret, that so little is in my power to offer to Colonel Hancock's merits, and worth his acceptance. I shall be happy in every opportunity to show the regard and esteem with which
>
> I am, Sir, your most obedient and very humble servant.[25]

The most logical explanation of Washington's response is that many other illustrious Americans had besieged him with offers to serve. Even fat little John Adams was considering such service. Above all else Washington was a superb leader, and he recognized the need, first, to appoint the most skilled military leaders he could find to command his forces and, second, not to allow politics to enter into his military decisions. Moreover, it is likely that, not knowing Hancock personally, he considered Hancock's offer a pro forma gesture of loyalty and responded in kind.

Hancock accepted Washington's reply with grace and resumed his work as president with vigor, showing enormous skill in restoring calm during heated debates that boiled over into irrationality amidst swarms of flies and searing summer heat. While Sam Adams alienated Congress, Hancock won widespread personal respect. Indeed, as George Washington was writing his rejection of Hancock's offer to serve, Benjamin Harrison, Washington's good friend from Virginia, was writing to the commander in chief to report the goings-on in Congress. "Our President," Harrison wrote, "is . . . Noble, Disinterested and Generous to a very great Degree."[26]

In the days that followed, Hancock steered Congress toward consideration of practical matters, such as raising money and troops for the Continental Army and establishing basic governmental institutions. Congress authorized the printing and distribution of £2 million in bills of credit—which, however necessary, had virtually no value at home or abroad. Each of the colonies was also printing its own, equally worthless certificates. To prevent the Revolution from stalling, Hancock and other men of great wealth in Congress made huge loans from their own personal sterling reserves to purchase essential supplies. In late July, Congress appointed commissioners to negotiate treaties of peace with Indian tribes and established a Post Office Department with Benjamin Franklin as postmaster general. Congress also appointed Dr. Benjamin Church director and chief physician of the first army hospital, at the central Continental Army headquarters in Cambridge. Hancock ordered his former aide William Palfrey, who had joined the Massachusetts minutemen, transferred to the Continental Army as paymaster general.

Hancock gave Washington his full, unequivocal, and unquestioning support, approving all commissions immediately of men Washington proposed as officers. Washington wrote of his gratitude, saying he was "much honored by the confidence [Hancock] reposed in him . . . and shall endeavor to select such persons as are best qualified to fill these important posts." Hancock acted in other ways, writing continually to colonial assemblies to rally support for the Continental Army, asking each for more troops, weapons, ammunition, and money.

"Let us . . . exert every Nerve," he wrote to his own Massachusetts assembly, "to distinguish ourselves. I entreat you to quicken your Preparations, and to stimulate the good people of our Government."[27] To the New Jersey assembly he wrote of

the indispensable Necessity of sending forth all the Troops that can possibly be collected, to strengthen both the Army in New York, and that on this side of Canada. I do therefore, once more, in the Name, and by the Authority of Congress, beseech and request you,—as you regard the Liberties of your Country, and the Happiness of Posterity; and as you stand engaged in the most solemn Ties of Honour to support the Common Cause—to strain every Nerve to send forward your Militia . . . the Critical Period has arrived, that will seal the Fate, not only of ourselves, but of Posterity. Whether they shall arise the generous Heirs of Freedom, or the dastardly Slaves of imperious Task-Masters, it is now in your Power to determine.[28]

Before the end of summer, Hancock wrote to every colonial assembly. He coaxed the Philadelphia Committee of Safety to contribute nine quarter casks of powder, and he raised $500,000 for troop salaries, which he personally delivered to Washington at Cambridge after the Congress adjourned for five weeks on August 1.

Unlike his trip to Philadelphia, the trip back left Hancock alone in his own coach, his mind fixed on two goals. One was to marry Dolly and bring her back to Philadelphia when Congress reconvened in September. He was fed up with living alone, with no one to care for his home and his personal needs. His second goal was to remove Sam Adams from the political picture—both national and regional. Hancock and Cushing were the financiers of the Massachusetts Whigs—they controlled the purse strings—and Hancock believed he could force Adams out of the picture and take control of the party himself. The radical wing of the Massachusetts Whigs was shrinking. Dr. Joseph Warren was dead; Dr. Benjamin Church seemed immersed in tending the wounded—and a new mistress. At the national level, Thomas Cushing and Robert Treat Paine had already deserted Sam Adams by supporting Dickinson's Olive Branch Petition. At the Continental Congress, only Sam's cousin John Adams still associated with him; in Boston, Adams could count only on James Warren and Elbridge Gerry for support. Warren and Gerry, however, had already had a falling-out, with Warren accusing Gerry of a "want of faith and ardor" for the patriot cause. The son of a Marblehead shipmaster and fish merchant, Gerry was a relative newcomer to politics and the patriots. A graduate of Harvard, he worked in his father's business and did not win election to the General Court until 1772, when he succumbed entirely to Sam Adams's spell.

After Congress recessed, Hancock went to Fairfield, Connecticut, to make arrangements to marry Dorothy Quincy. Although Dorothy was less than enthusiastic, she agreed on August 28 as a wedding day, and Hancock set off for Cambridge, where he delivered the $500,000 payroll to Washington on August 11. They conferred for many hours over Washington's administrative problems in feeding, clothing, and lodging the huge force laying siege to Boston. There was, of course, no way for Hancock to get into Boston to determine the condition of his vast holdings. He knew that the British had seized all his properties and assets other than the considerable cash and silver cache he and Aunt Lydia had taken with them when they fled the city. But his income from trade and rental properties had stopped and there was no way of collecting from his enormous list of debtors.

On August 23 King George III proclaimed the American colonies in open rebellion. The following day, thirty-eight-year-old John Hancock returned to Fairfield, Connecticut, and four days later he married Dorothy Quincy, ten years his junior, in a quiet, dispassionate ceremony. The next day the Hancocks left Aunt Lydia in Fairfield and rode away to Philadelphia, where Congress was to reconvene on September 5. With the cost of the war draining every resource, New York and the other towns through which the Hancocks passed could not afford the pomp and ceremony that had greeted him on his visit the previous spring. The *New York Gazette* ran a brief report of his marriage, implying—intentionally or not—that Dolly had married Hancock for his money.

The Hancocks reached Philadelphia for the scheduled opening of Congress and took lodgings in a crowded boardinghouse with most of the other Massachusetts delegates, including John Adams. "The lady sends her compliments and good wishes," John Adams would write to Abigail after visiting the Hancocks sometime later. "Among a hundred men, almost, at this house, she lives and behaves with modest decency, dignity and discretion, I assure you.

Her behavior is easy and genteel. She avoids talking upon politics. In large and mixed companies she is totally silent, as a lady ought to be. But," Adams was quick to add, "whether her eyes are so penetrating, and her attention so quick to the words, looks gestures sentiments &c of the company as yours would be, saucy as you are in this way, I won't say."[29] After seeing the Hancocks together, Adams vowed never to return to Philadelphia again without his own Abigail and their son John Quincy.

When Congress reconvened, a delegation from Georgia asked to be seated with the other twelve delegations. All thirteen colonies now sat together in convention for the first time. Hancock had no sooner called the delegates to order than Sam Adams's venomous tongue began wagging in his direction. Peyton Randolph, whom Hancock had replaced as president, had returned to Philadelphia as a member of the Virginia delegation. Adams argued that Hancock had been elected as a temporary replacement and that Congress should remove him and return Randolph to the presidency. Sam Adams had the support of his cousin John Adams, still the country boy who had never outgrown his petty envy of the good fortune of his young neighbor when they were boys. "Mr. Randolph, our former President, is here," he wrote to James Warren, "and sits very humbly in his seat while our new one continues in the chair without seeming to feel the impropriety."[30]

The two Adamses, however, won no support from Congress. Indeed, all but the Adamses strongly supported Hancock as president—precisely for the objectivity he brought to the position and his ability to impose total fairness on all sides in every debate. It was an impossibly exhausting task few others could have handled. The controversy Sam Adams tried to create came to a humiliating end for him on October 22, when Peyton Randolph died.

The initial sessions of Congress were packed with paperwork—officers' commissions for Washington's Continental Army and the piece-by-piece construction from scratch of a continental government. The paperwork put an enormous burden of work on Hancock's shoulders. Delegates simply voted each piece of paper up or down, but it was Hancock who had to supervise the printing of documents and sign them all. It was he who had to supervise the acquisition, collection, and shipment of money, arms, and ammunition that Congress approved for transfer to the army. Congress legislated, but President Hancock executed. It was an enormous, exhausting task that took its toll on his health—and on Dolly, who shared part of his burden by "packing up commissions to be sent off for the officers appointed by Congress.

"It was not till some months after this," Dolly recalled, "that Mr. Hancock kept a clerk, though all the business of Congress was done by the President. [I] was for months engaged with [my] scissors in trimming off the rough edges of the bills of credit issued by the Congress and signed by the President, and packing them up in saddle bags to be sent off to various quarters for the use of the army."[31]

In effect, Hancock's desk was the central command post for the entire Continental Army, with Hancock himself serving as liaison between the various commanders, General Washington, and Congress. Washington and the other field commanders showered Hancock with requests for additional troops and ammunition, and it was up to him to shift elements of both from battleground to battleground as needed. Each shift, however, required the approval of Congress and of Washington, the commander in chief, before Hancock could put in motion the wide range of complicated movements of men, materiel, and money. Congress had eased part of his burden by approving his request for the appointment of his aide William Palfrey as paymaster general. Other than himself, Hancock trusted no one more than Palfrey to handle the kinds of sums involved in everyday transactions. "I transmit herewith," Hancock would write routinely to Palfrey, "four Hundred Thousand Dollars for the Use of the Troops in New York and Massachusetts Bay, which you will please apply accordingly. . . . The money is contained in six boxes, five large ones, and one of a smaller size."[32]

Palfrey not only relieved Hancock of the task of issuing payments, he also served as another pair of eyes and ears for the president. The Southern and Northern delegates were at each other's throats. Benjamin Harrison called New Englanders (all but his

friend Hancock) Turks trying to rule their empire. Palfrey confirmed the widespread Southern antipathy for the North. He
quoted some Southern leaders as saying, "Boston aimed at nothing
less than the sovereignty of the whole continent."[33] John Adams
led the New England attack against the South, saying, "The dons,
the bashaws, the grandees, the sachems, the nabobs, call them by
what name you please, sigh, groan, fret, and sometimes stamp and
foam and curse, but all in vain."

In addition to North-South controversies, all the old small
colony/large colony controversies flared up, along with bitter inter-
colony conflicts over land. Connecticut renewed its claim to lands
in Pennsylvania; New York and New Hampshire each claimed
Vermont, which in turn wanted independence from both as a separate state. Hancock stood amidst these rival factions day after
exhausting day, coaxing each of the delegates to lay aside his differences and focus on the common enemies and issues facing all.
He wrote dozens of letters a day, hurriedly, in a scrawl that belied
his magnificent signature, with seldom any time to reflect on his
grammar or spelling.

"Sir," he wrote to Rhode Island's lieutenant governor and
commander of the militia.

> The Congress having received certain intelligence of the sailing
> of two north Country built Brigs . . . from England on the 11th
> of August last loaded with 6000 stand [? MS illegible] of arms
> and a large quantity of powder and other stores for Quebec
> without a convoy: and it being of importance if possible to
> intercept them, I am directed by Congress to desire you with
> all possible expedition to dispatch the armed vessels of the
> Colony of Rhode Island on this service that the vessels you
> dispatch be supplied with a sufficient number of men, stores
> and particularly with oars: That you give the command[er] or
> commanders such instructions as are necessary and also proper
> encouragement to the marines & seamen that shall be sent on
> this enterprise, which instructions so are to be delivered to the
> commander or commanders sealed up with orders not to open
> the same until out of sight of land on account of secrecy . . .

a large quantity of brass and ordinance military stores & provision are sending out to Boston . . . seize all ammunition, clothing or other stores for the use of the American army

For the encouragement of the men employed in this service, I am ordered to inform you that the Congress has resolved that the Master, Officer and Seamen shall be entitled to one half of the value of the prizes by them taken, the wages they receive from the Colony notwithstanding.[34]

Later he dashed off another, more urgent letter to Rhode Island stating that the

City and Colony of New York are in great Distress for want of Powder, and Information having been received that some Powder had lately arriv'd in your Colony, I am Directed by the Congress to Apply to you and Request you immediately to Send to the Committee of Safety of New York One Ton of Powder for the Defence of that City and Colony.

I am so busy engag'd in the Business of Congress that I have not Time to Add, but that I am with much Esteem,

Hon Sir,
Your most Obed Servt
John Hancock Presidt[35]

Hancock kept Washington apprised of every move. "I yesterday morning Rec'd an Express from General Lee," a typical letter read, "requesting an augmentation of Troops[.] Congress immediately directed one Battalion of Minute Men from New Jersey in addition to Lord Sterling's Battalion, & one Battalion of Associators from this City to proceed to New York & be under the Command of General Lee, the latter Commanded by Col. Dickinson who very cheerfully step'd forth, & both Battalions will immediately march. . . . [rest of MS missing]"[36]

In early October, George Washington informed Hancock that Dr. Benjamin Church, the radical Whig who had shared quarters with Hancock at Harvard, had been arrested as a Tory spy. It was he who had divulged minuteman plans to Gen. Thomas Gage over the past year. Contrary to his claim, he had not been arrested in

Boston after the battle of Lexington, but had gone straight to Gage's headquarters to report minuteman activities. After assuming administration of the army hospital in Cambridge, Church had shown a remarkable ability to slip in and out of Boston—always, of course, returning with medical supplies. During the summer he had sent his mistress with a coded message to one of Gage's aides, but she asked someone else, who turned out to be a patriot, to run the errand for her. The patriot reported her, and she was arrested and confessed. The Massachusetts Provincial Congress, perhaps out of consideration for the past services of their longtime colleague, sent Church to jail in Norwich, Connecticut, where he remained until the end of the Revolution, "debarred the use of pen, ink and paper." After the war he sailed to exile in the West Indies, but the ship never arrived and he was never heard from again.

On October 3 Congress appointed Hancock to head a Marine Committee to build a navy. On his own, George Washington had already started organizing a ragtag fleet of armed fishing vessels to harass the British. He also ordered construction of four ships with ten guns each and recruited two battalions of marines to man them. In December, however, Congress decided to build a proper navy, ordering construction of thirteen men-of-war, five with thirty-two guns, five with twenty-eight, and three with twenty-four. Hancock was the most experienced shipbuilder and operator in Congress, and delegates put him in charge. At the same time it invited privateers into the war by declaring all British ships fair game for capture by any American vessel.

On November 9 Arthur Lee, the agent for Congress in London, sent word that George III had shattered all hopes for reconciliation by refusing even to receive, let alone read, the Dickinson Olive Branch Petition. Lee, the younger brother of Virginia delegate Richard Henry Lee, reported meeting Lord Dartmouth, the king's counselor, who "informed us that 'no answer would be given' by the king to the petition. Upon this answer, I expressed to Ld Dartmouth my sorrow that his Majesty had been advised to a measure which would occasion so much bloodshed. To this his Lordship answered that if he thought it would be the cause of

GEORGE III. KING of GREAT BRITAIN
AND IRELAND.

From an Original Picture in the

Royal Academy.

King George III. His refusal even to read John Dickinson's Olive Branch Petition left delegates at the Constitutional Convention no choice but to issue and sign the Declaration of Independence, thus ending all chance of the English king retaining sovereignty over the richest jewel of the English empire. (*Library of Congress*)

shedding one drop of blood, he would never have concurred in it; but that he could not be of opinion that it would be attendant with such consequence. My Lord, I replied, as sure as we exist, this answer will cause much blood being shed in America & of most dreadful consequences. We then took our leave. Persuaded as I was that the determination of the King & his Ministers had been long fixed for using forces."[37]

At the end of November, Hancock authorized a congressional Committee of Correspondence to court "our friends" in France and Spain. A month later French agent Julien Achard de Bonvouloir came to Philadelphia with unofficial guarantees of safety for American ships in French harbors, along with the promise of clandestine material support for the Continental Army.

As what had seemed a year of hope approached its end, a torrent of disheartening news flowed across Hancock's desk. Gen. William Alexander, Lord Stirling, commander of the New Jersey militia and one of the few English noblemen to join the patriots, reported a strong Tory counterrevolution under way in New Jersey.

"The Tories . . . assume fresh courage and talk vary daringly," said Stirling, who was a direct descendant of the founder of Nova Scotia.[38] "I was yesterday evening informed of a combination carrying on for opposing the measures of the Congress . . . about 4000 men and that they have had a supply of ammunition from on board the *Asia* man-of-war. On this foundation the Committee [of safety] have applied to me for a party of men to seize the two most active of the gang in this country, and I hope to surprise them tomorrow evening."[39]

Shortly thereafter, Virginia's royal governor declared martial law and recruited a loyalist force that included a regiment of slaves whom he promised freedom for deserting their masters to fight the patriots. Hancock described the slave recruitments to Gen. Philip Schuyler, commander of the army in Canada, as "the horrid attempts of the Southern governors to excite domestic insurrections."[40]

Topping all the bad news was the crushing defeat in Quebec and rumors that New York was about to withdraw from the United Colonies. "We have had this day received," Hancock wrote to Thomas Cushing, "disagreeable accounts from Canada; poor [Brig. Gen. Richard] Montgomery and several officers killed, [Benedict] Arnold wounded, etc. . . . I fear for the defection of New York. The spring will open before we are ready."[41]

As the year ended, President Hancock abandoned his usual neutral stance to support a congressional resolution empowering George Washington to attack Boston. "It is true," he told Congress, "nearly all of the property I have in the world is in houses and other real estate in the town of Boston, but if the expulsion of the British army from it—and the liberties of our country—require their being burnt to ashes, issue the order for that purpose immediately."[42] Opponents argued that the attack would convert the rebellion into all-out war and end all chances for reconciliation, but a majority approved the measure, and Hancock was able to write to Washington that the resolution "passed after a most serious debate in a committee of the whole House, and the execution referred to you. And may God crown your attempt with success. I most heartily wish it, though individually I may be the greatest sufferer."[43]

11

Founding Father

(1776)

As Hancock continued undermining Sam Adams's influence at the Second Continental Congress in Philadelphia, Adams retaliated by rallying Massachusetts radicals against reelection of Hancock and his ally Thomas Cushing as delegates to the Continental Congress. The radicals managed to oust Cushing and replace him with the radical Adams protégé Elbridge Gerry, but Hancock was too popular in Massachusetts to unseat. The legislature not only returned him to Congress in January 1776; it appointed him commander in chief and first major general of the Massachusetts militia, a position that sent Hancock into raptures of joy. Later, when he received the actual commission, he pledged to "put the Militia upon a respectable footing" as soon as he returned from Philadelphia.[1]

Although disappointed by Cushing's defeat, General Hancock realized immediately—as did Cushing—that the two could work more effectively to wrest control of Massachusetts from Sam Adams and the radicals with Cushing acting as Hancock's ally on the scene in Massachusetts.

"I shall look on you," Hancock wrote to Cushing, "as a stated friendly correspondent. I make offers of sincere attachment to you and wish for a return of yours; and you may rely on every service in my power and that I am totally undisguised. . . . I will give you everything from hence . . . and, pray, write me every occurrence with you."

Hancock enclosed "a pamphlet, which makes much talk here, said to be wrote by an English gentleman resident here by the name of Paine; and I believe him the author. I send it for your and friends' amusement."[2] The pamphlet was one of the first of one hundred thousand copies of the Englishman Tom Paine's explosive essay *Common Sense,* which destroyed the argument that the colonies could retain the English king as sovereign and win autonomy from Parliament.

"It is unreasonable to suppose," Paine wrote, "that France or Spain will give us any kind of assistance, if we mean only to make use of that assistance for the purpose of repairing the breach, and strengthening the connection between Britain and America; because, those powers would be sufferers by the consequences. . . . Under our present denominations of British subjects, we can neither be received nor heard abroad; the custom of all courts is against us, and will be so, until by an independence we take rank with other nations."

Cushing replied immediately to Hancock's letter with a pledge of allegiance. Calling Hancock "a gentleman of an amiable, humane, generous and benevolent disposition," Cushing wrote that he was "sincerely obliged to you for your kind offers of . . . friendship. . . . Soon after I arrived here, I found you as well as myself, had been placed in a disagreeable light and measures taken to hurt our influence. . . . I shall leave no stone unturned to serve you here. . . . It is true, I am informed, some few . . . have endeavored by their little, low, dirty, and sly insinuating arts and machinations to destroy my influence among the new members of the House."[3]

Although defeated in his reelection bid for Congress, Cushing remained on the Council of the General Court, and Hancock immediately shored up Cushing's political strength by appointing him to the powerful post of continental naval agent in Massachusetts, which gave him authority to award lucrative contracts for construction of naval vessels. On Hancock's orders, Cushing awarded contracts to build two costly new frigates, one with thirty-two guns, the other with twenty-four. As commander of the Massachusetts militia, Hancock was eager that the Massachusetts ships be first in the new navy to go to sea and that they be the most beautiful.

"I most earnestly entreat and beg of you," he wrote Cushing, "that you exert every nerve in forwarding our two ships. . . . In short, spare no expense . . . for, *inter nos,* some *here* who are not very friendly to you and I begin publicly to say that the Massachusetts ships will be the last finished."[4] Reverting to character as head of a great merchant house, Hancock ordered his friend to "set every wheel in motion . . . let the heads and Galleries for the ships be neatly Carv'd and Executed . . . by all means let ours be as good, handsome, strong, and as easily Completed as any that are building here or in any of the other Colonies; for your reputation and mine are at stake, and there are not wanting those who are fond of prejudging both."[5]

As Cushing prepared to win the hearts and bellies of Massachusetts with rich shipbuilding contracts, Hancock was winning the minds of congressional moderates. Congress had tired of the constant bickering with Sam Adams and his snarling New England radicals, who seemed more intent on winning a war of words than the war of independence. Hancock acted to isolate the radicals by appointing a new chairman when Congress convened as a committee of the whole. Instead of renaming the radical Rhode Island governor Samuel Ward, Hancock used his prerogative as president to appoint a political ally and friend of Washington, Virginia's Benjamin Harrison. New England delegates were furious and, as a body, stopped talking to Hancock—and he to them. He considered them obstructionists and replaced them with moderates on key committees whenever he could.

In addition to using his power of appointment, Hancock also won congressional support by his judicious dissemination of news from the various fronts. All field commanders reported to Washington and Hancock, and Washington reported to Congress through

Hancock. As he had in Boston, Hancock was careful to be the bearer of only good news, while letting aides disseminate bad news in bits and pieces to individual delegates.

Early in March 1776, patriot general Henry Knox moved forty-three cannon and sixteen mortars captured at Ticonderoga into commanding positions on Dorchester Heights. The positions overlooked Boston, the British fort on Castle William, and the British fleet in Boston Harbor. By then, nearly twelve hundred loyalists—men, women, and children—had crowded into Boston to seek the protection of British forces. They included two hundred merchants, four hundred farmers, and hundreds of civilian British officials. With patriot cannon looming above, British commander Gen. William Howe, who had replaced Thomas Gage, had no choice but to flee Boston or allow patriot shells to slaughter thousands of British troops and loyal civilians. He began an immediate evacuation by sea, and the civilians in his protection joined a stream of eighty-five thousand other loyalists who chose Canadian exile over disloyalty to the king.

As Howe evacuated Boston, Hancock was able to report that General Alexander, Lord Stirling, had crushed the Tory counter-revolution in nearby New Jersey and arrested its leader. It was with some reluctance that Hancock announced that the man under arrest was royal governor William Franklin, the illegitimate son of Benjamin Franklin. "I thought it most prudent to secure him and bring him to this place," General Alexander wrote Hancock from Elizabethtown. "I have provided good, genteel, private lodgings for him . . . where I intend he shall remain until I have directions from Congress what to do with him."[6] After discreet discussions with Benjamin Franklin, Hancock ordered William Franklin imprisoned in Litchfield, Connecticut, where he remained for two years before being exchanged for patriot prisoners. He eventually went into exile in England.

As spring approached, Hancock received wonderful news from Washington: "It is with great pleasure I inform you that, on Sunday last, the 17th March, 1776, about 9 o'clock in the forenoon, the Ministerial army evacuated the town of Boston and that the forces of the United Colonies are now in actual possession thereof. . . . The town, although it has suffered greatly, is not in so bad a state as I expected to find it; and I have a particular pleasure in being able to inform you, Sir, that your house has received no damage worth mentioning. Your furniture is in tolerable order, and the family pictures are all left entire and untouched. Captain Cazneau takes charge of the whole until he shall receive further orders from you."[7]

Hancock's house had, indeed, escaped much of the looting that other mansions suffered—primarily because its occupant, British general Henry Clinton, was a career officer who prided himself on gentlemanly conduct. A few days after receiving Washington's letter, Hancock received a detailed report from Capt. Isaac Cazneau, one of his loyal former ship captains, who had taken it upon himself to try to save the house after the Hancocks had left for Lexington:

The mansion house was thought by most people a place devoted to destruction; [it] has escaped a scouring in more than one sense. The best furniture I put into the chamber back of the great chamber, and kept the key till about three weeks before General Clinton left the house; then was sent for, and they demanded to search for papers. . . . When we came to open the door, the key would not open. . . . On this he seemed much displeased and said would break it open. . . . He kept the key and wished me good morning, which I took as a signal to depart. . . .

A few days before he left the house he sent for me and desired I would look about and see if anything was wanting. I told him the great settee was not in the house and desired he would see [it] returned, which he did. The backgammon table in the library was wanting, but none knew anything of it. He desired one of the captains to purchase one as good and send it up, but I never saw it yet. The china and glassware was found out, unpacked, and put into the great room. I was sent for, and Mr. Clinton was very angry that I did not acquaint him 'twas secreted. . . . Said I had not used him well. If his servants had been dishonest it might been sold and given suspicion that 'twas done by his orders. He put it into the back chamber with the other things and . . . gave me the key.[8]

Although the British had spared his house, they caused Hancock a total of £4,732 in damages on Beacon Hill and elsewhere in Boston, according to a comprehensive inventory taken by William Bant, the lawyer-shopkeeper who had taken over management of Hancock's business affairs from William Palfrey. "Sundries destroyed at, & carried away from the House" included

1 Butt & 1 Pipe of choice Vinegar ....25..0..0

6 Puncheons Cyder ....28..16..0

20 bushells Charcoal 20/, 172 Chaldron Sea Coal @ £10 ....16..0..0

6 Musketts given in to Gen. Gage by his Arbitrary
    Order @80/ ....24..0..0

Delph Glass & China Ware broke while the House was
    occupied by the officers ....3..0..0

Rent of the House one Year ....133..6..8

Bant also listed one year's rent of £100 for a house Hancock owned on Queen Street, £50 for damages to a house on Sudbury Street, £500 for a "House in Ann Street pull'd down and destroyed," and £300 for a house in west Boston that received similar treatment. He charged the British £35 for "fences around the Garden & Pasture belonging to this place, all destroyed." The British had used Hancock's coach house and stable as hospitals and burned all the fences as firewood. A fire on Hancock Wharf had caused more than £1,700 worth of damage and burned out a number of stores. The British had stolen three anchors and other materials worth £115 and "17 Bolts of English Duck" worth £136. Other charges included

To a Briggs foresail, foretopsail, and a Sloop's trisail
    all in good Order, not much worn ....50..0..

a Sett of topmast Shrouds ....6..0..

a 9 Inch Cable 120 fathom long . . . almost new . . . . .64..0..

20 Loaves of double refined Sugar . . . . .14..0..

Elsewhere, Bant found that British soldiers who had lived in seven small brick apartment buildings had left them so damaged they had to be rebuilt, at an estimated cost of £275.[9] Finally:

To 100 hogsheads of Salt, which these Scoundrells threw
  into the Dock, out of one of the Stores on this Wharff ..180..0..0

To a large Scow, destroyed by the Soldiers . . . . .26..13..4

To damage done the new Ship that lies at the Wharff,
  Her Stern part is cut almost through, several Beams
  saw'd off, all the Timber heads Split and other damage
  done to her Cabbin &c. &c. &c . . . . .300..0..0

a sett of Masts Yards Sparrs, Tops Caps &c. all carried off . . .30 . . .

On the whole, however, Hancock was fortunate. Indeed, the town's fine homes that survived the occupation did so only because high-ranking British officers had commandeered them as their own. But the British troops looted virtually every other house in Boston and left a trail of destruction in every area of town. They chopped down most of the trees—including the Liberty Tree—and many wood buildings for firewood. Old North Meeting House was gone, and Old South stripped of its pews. They reacted viciously whenever they saw the name of their enemy Hancock inscribed on a building. "The town in general is shockingly defaced, especially the places of public worship," Cazneau wrote. "Your name on the cornerstone of Dr. Cooper's [Brattle Square] church is mangled out with an axe."[10]

In contrast, the patriot Committee of Safety acted swiftly to protect the homes and furnishings of loyalists who had fled to the protection of the British army. The Provincial Congress appointed each town guardian of abandoned estates and ordered selectmen to take loyalist property into their personal care, "make the best improvement thereof in their power," "keep an account of all the rents and profits arising from the same," and be accountable for them to the Provincial Congress.[11]

Early in April, Dolly told John she was pregnant, and they made plans to go to the Burr home in Connecticut and bring Aunt Lydia to Philadelphia to help manage the Hancock home. The press of congressional business prevented them from leaving, and on April 15, his sixty-two-year-old aunt suffered a stroke. Ten days later she died, leaving Dolly as devastated as John. She had been a devoted surrogate mother to them both. She left the bulk of her estate to her nephew. Her will freed her slaves and provided each with a small sum. She left about £5,000 to various friends and relatives and gave a large brick house to the Brattle Square Church as a parsonage. John inherited £4,000 in cash and her vast real estate holdings—properties in Boston and scattered land throughout New England. Dolly's older, unmarried sister, Katherine Quincy, came to Philadelphia to help care for the house during Dolly's pregnancy.

Hancock and Dolly moved into a suite of rooms where they resumed their Beacon Hill–style entertaining and quickly made theirs the most sought-after salon in Philadelphia. Although time, circumstances, and tight quarters limited the size and number of the entertainments, Dolly's exquisite taste—largely acquired from John's aunt Lydia—made many delegates lust for invitations to her small formal dinners. Hancock continued to dress, speak, and behave like the consummate aristocrat. He preferred the company of men with similar tastes and backgrounds. Wealthy, cultured political moderates such as John Dickinson and Robert Morris, a Philadelphia merchant and financier, were among his most frequent guests. As before, he distanced himself from the coarse Samuel Adams, who had a knack of disparaging and insulting all those who disagreed with him.

In the spring of 1776 Congress declared commercial independence from England with a resolution to ignore all British trade laws and trade freely with every nation except Britain. Congress and the provincial legislatures soon realized, however, that commercial independence from Britain, coupled with political independence from Parliament, added up to nothing less than complete independence. It became senseless to wage all-out war against the king's armies, only to reestablish ties to the king in the event of victory. One by one the legislature of each colony instructed its delegates in Congress to vote for total independence. On April 12 North Carolina had resolved "that the delegates for this colony in the Continental Congress be impowered to concur with the delegates of the other Colonies in declaring Independency."[12] Virginia followed suit on May 15, and step by step, Congress moved in that direction, authorizing more privateers to attack British ships, embargoing trade to Britain and the British West Indies, opening ports to all foreign shipping except Britain's, and voting to disarm all loyalists. Congress also sent Connecticut delegate Silas Deane to Paris to buy supplies and ask the French government to recognize American independence and agree to a commercial and military alliance.

On May 1, 1776, Massachusetts enacted a test act that required every male over sixteen to declare "to God and the world" that the "war, resistance and opposition in which the United states are now engaged against the fleets and armies of Great Britain, is, on the part of the said colonies, just and necessary." The act banned all assistance to British forces, and stripped the governors of Harvard College of their salaries "if any . . . shall refuse to sign the declaration aforesaid."[13] Within a year, all thirteen provincial governments would pass similar test acts.

On June 7 John Hancock recognized Richard Henry Lee, Washington's neighbor planter from Virginia, who proposed "that these United Colonies are, and of right ought to be, free and independent states; that they are absolved from all allegiance to the British Crown and that all political connection between them and the State of Great Britain is, and ought to be, totally dissolved." Lee called on the colonies to form an American confederation and to take "measures for forming Alliances."[14] He moved that Congress prepare a plan of confederation "for the respective colonies for their consideration and approbation." John Adams seconded the resolution. Moderates who hoped for reconciliation with the crown argued tenaciously against the Lee resolution, and after four days, Hancock put it to a vote. The vote was too close—seven colonies to five, with one absent—to permit passage without shattering the fragile union. The middle colonies—especially Franklin's Pennsylvania—still favored reconciliation and dominion status, with autonomy from Parliament but with a titular British sovereign. "It was argued that the people of the Middle Colonies . . . were not yet ripe for bidding Adieu to British connection but that they were fast ripening."[15] Congress postponed action for three weeks, with supporters of complete independence hoping to win unanimous approval and conservatives hoping to win enough votes to defeat it. Hancock then appointed Thomas Jefferson, Benjamin Franklin, John Adams, Roger Sherman, and Robert R. Livingston to use Lee's resolution as a basis for a declaration of independence. The name of Samuel Adams, one of the original champions of independence, was conspicuously absent, along with that of Patrick Henry.

Before the committee started its work, Hancock learned that Boston had failed to reelect him to the Massachusetts House of Representatives, and with Adams radicals in control, the House in turn refused to return Hancock to the Council. The news hurt him deeply. As Samuel Adams gloated, Hancock grew convinced that Adams had wreaked his vengeance and destroyed Hancock's political career. He saw little hope of remaining in Congress after his term ended at the end of the year, and he now looked to a future in the military, as commander of the Massachusetts militia, although his formal commission had yet to arrive—six months after his appointment.

"Do send me my commission as major-general, that I may appear in character," he pleaded in a letter to Thomas Cushing that went on to describe his disappointment in the election results. "I find I am left out of both House and Council. I can't help it, they have a Right to do as they please. I think I do not merit such Treatment but my exertions [and] my life are [and] shall be at their service."[16]

His burden of work, however, soon took his mind off Boston politics. Often he remained at his desk at the State House six days a week, reading and writing from first morning light until late at night, when his eyes teared from fatigue and flickering candle-light. Congressional committees began their deliberations at seven; Congress convened at ten and sat until five, except for a short luncheon break. Delegates then went to supper before returning for a resumption of committee meetings, which often continued until ten. Although he hired a clerk at his own expense, the work was overwhelming. He had to preside over every session of Congress and participate in the committees to which he had been assigned in his role as a delegate. He had to sign every document that Congress issued and originate much of its correspondence. He apprised the leaders of each colony of troop movements by its sister colonies and forwarded all intelligence of enemy movements. He had hardly finished presiding over the long and tiring debate on the Lee resolution when he penned a note to the speaker of the New Jersey assembly warning that General Howe planned to attack New York within ten days. The New York militia needed New Jersey reinforcements "with all dispatch. . . . The important day is at hand that will decide not only the fate of . . . New York, but, in all probability, the whole continent."[17] Then he wrote to the General Court of Massachusetts for additional help. The Continental Army had been "reduced by sickness," and without help, he warned, it would be "obliged to flee before an enemy of vastly superior force . . . we see the British army reinforced under Lord Howe and ready to strike a blow which may be attended with the most foul consequences if not timely resisted. . . . The intelligence received this day from General Washington points out the absolute, the indispensable, necessity of sending forward all the troops that can possibly be collected to strengthen . . . the army in New York."[18]

As he worked on matters that would decide the fate of nations, petty matters invariably interrupted him. An Indian chief walked into the State House, sent by his tribe to adopt the president and confer the name Karonduaan, or Great Tree. Then his younger brother, Ebenezer, who had bankrupted three businesses, asked for a better-paying job in the army. John saw an opportunity to help both his brother and his friend Palfrey, the overworked paymaster general:

Philadelphia June 19th 1776

Dear Brother

I have the pleasure to Acquaint you that the Congress have been pleased to appoint you Deputy Pay Master General to the Continental Troops in the Eastern Department, with a Salary of Fifty Dollars a Month, which I hope will prove agreeable to you, and I most earnestly Recommend to you a very close and strict attention to the Business of your office. The Department to which your office extends, takes in the Colony of Massachusetts, New Hampshire, Rhode Island, & Connict, the Continental Troops in all those places fall under your care.

I inclose you Several Resolves of Congress respecting your office, which I must direct that you closely adhere to and you are to obey all orders from General Washington, or the Commander in Chief for the time being in the Eastern Department. You will apply to the Commanding Officer at Boston for a Centinel to be placed at the Door of your office by night & Day. Be careful to make your monthly returns regularly to me. By next post I shall transmit the Pay list.

Inclosed you have your Commission. I wish you happy, and am

Your hum Servt

[In margin] The 150,000 Dollars mention'd in the Resolve is on its way . . . to you. Send me a Rect for the money.

With the Howe attack on New York a foregone conclusion, Congress asked Hancock to summon Washington to determine how he planned to respond. Hancock complied, adding a personal invitation to the commander in chief: "I request that you will . . . honor me and your lady's company at my house, where I have a bed at your service . . . and where every endeavor of mine and Mrs. Hancock's shall be exerted to make your abode agreeable." He described his lodgings as "a noble house in an airy open place in Arch Street corner of Arch and Fourth Streets."[19] Washington replied on May 20 but did not respond to Hancock's invitation. Hancock reiterated "the very great pleasure it would afford Mrs. Hancock and myself to have the happiness of accommodating you during your stay in this city as the house I live in is large and roomy, it will be entirely in your power to live in that manner you should wish.... Mrs. Washington may be as retired as she pleases while under inoculation, and Mrs. Hancock will esteem it an honor to have Mrs. Washington inoculated in her house."[20]

Despite Hancock's warmest entreaties, Washington inexplicably declined the invitation. Rumors persisted that John Adams had warned Washington that Hancock's aristocratic entertainments might provoke dissent and desertions among troops suffering deprivations in the field. Hancock, however, was puzzled and hurt by Washington's refusal, and when Washington prepared to return to New York, Hancock failed to deliver a congressional message of good wishes personally. Some historians claim it was a display of characteristic pettiness; but the origins of such interpretations usually can be found in the acid ink of Hancock's enemies, the Adamses and Warrens, who refused to admit that Hancock was a sick man.

"I am extremely sorry," Hancock wrote to Washington, "it is not in my power to wait on you in person to execute the commands of Congress but, being deprived of that pleasure by a severe fit of the gout, I am . . . taking this method to acquaint you that the Congress have directed me . . . to make the thanks of that body to you for the unmerited attention you have paid to your important trust." Hancock wished Washington "success equal to your merit and the righteousness of our cause."[21] On the day following Washington's visit, Hancock sent a circular letter to the assemblies in seven states to rally their support for the commander in chief, thus belying the argument that he bore ill will toward Washington.

"Our affairs are hastening fast to a crisis," Hancock wrote,

and the approaching campaign will, in all probability, determine forever the fate of America. Such is the unrelenting spirit which possesses the Tyrant of Britain and his Parliament that they have left no measure unessayed that had a tendency to accomplish our destruction. . . . Should the Canadians and Indians take up arms against us (which there is too much reason to fear), we shall then have the whole force of that country to contend with. . . . Our continental troops alone are unable to stem the torrent . . . The militia of the United Colonies . . . are called upon to say whether they will live slaves or die free men. . . . The cause is certainly a glorious one. . . . On your exertions . . . the salvation of America now evidently depends. . . . Quicken your preparations and stimulate the good people of your government—and there is no danger, not withstanding the mighty armament with which we are threatened, but you will be able to lead them to victor, to liberty, and to happiness.[22]

On June 28 the committee appointed to write a declaration of independence presented a draft, written largely by Thomas Jefferson, with some changes by Franklin and John Adams. After three days of debate over form and content, Congress approved, by a vote of twelve to none, "The Unanimous Declaration of the Thirteen United States of America"[23] that "these United Colonies are, and of Right ought to be Free and Independent States; that they are Absolved from all Allegiance to the British Crown, and that all political connection between them and the State of Great Britain, is and ought to be totally dissolved."[24] It was two in the afternoon, July 4, 1776. Only New York's delegates had abstained, pending approval of their colonial legislature.

Congress adjourned for the day, ordering Hancock to authenticate and sign the corrected document and send printed copies to the army and the colonial legislatures for approval. After he received a corrected copy, he sat at his desk before an empty chamber and affixed his famous signature and flourish to the historic parchment. By his side stood Secretary of Congress Charles Thomson, a Pennsylvania delegate from Philadelphia and the only man to see and hear Pres. John Hancock declare the United States of America an independent nation.

There are many stories and paintings of the signing. Few stories are accurate, including the aging Thomas Jefferson's foggy recollection in 1819 that all delegates except John Dickinson were present. Only one-fourth of the delegates even set foot in Congress that day, and the copies of the Declaration that came off the press the following day—some still exist—bore but one signature: *John Hancock*. Nor is there evidence to support the various statements attributed to Hancock as he signed the document: "There, I guess King George will be able to read that"[25] or, "There! John Bull can read my name without spectacles and may now double his reward of £500 for my head. That is my defiance."[26] What is true is that during the month that followed, his signature was the only one on the document, and it constituted tangible evidence of treason that would have cost him his life if he had been captured. Had Britain won the war, John Hancock would have been a mere footnote in history. As it was, he became a founding father. He was thirty-nine when he signed the Declaration of Independence; its primary author, Thomas Jefferson, was only thirty-three. Neither were fathers.

12

President of the United States

(1776-1777)

THE MORNING AFTER John Hancock signed the Declaration of
Independence, he resumed his routine, workaday functions and
ordered copies of the document printed for posting to each of the
state legislatures and to General Washington. He asked Washington to proclaim it to the troops "in the way you shall think most
proper."[1] On July 8, the Declaration of Independence was published and proclaimed publicly in front of the State House in
Philadelphia. The crowd exploded with excitement. "The battalion
paraded the common," according to John Adams. "The bells rung
all day and almost all night. Even the chimers chimed away."[2] In
New York, crowds tore down the statue of George III, while other
cities fired thirteen blasts from their cannon, one for each of the
former colonies. New York's celebration was short lived, however.
General William Howe, who had replaced the ineffectual General
Gage as British commander in chief, had just landed ten thousand
troops unopposed on Long Island, just east of the city, reinforced
by a strong fleet and 150 transports.

Hancock renewed his call to other states for help. Howe was
"ready to strike a blow which may be attended with the most fatal
consequences if not timely resisted," Hancock pleaded. He reiter-

ated the "absolute, indispensable, necessity of sending forward all the troops that can possibly be collected to strengthen both the army in New York and that on this side of Canada."[3] Earlier, he had written to Maryland, "The Congress have this day received intelligence which renders it absolutely necessary that the greatest exertions should be made to save our country from being desolated by the hand of tyranny. General Howe having taken possession of Staten Island, and the Jerseys being drained of their militia for the defense of New York, I am directed by Congress to request you will proceed immediately to embody your militia for the establishment of a flying camp and march them with all possible expedition to the city of Philadelphia."[4] Hancock wrote volumes of letters—all in quill pen, usually late into the night. He knew that the success of the Revolution depended on his powers of persuasion, because Congress had no power to enforce his requests. He could only hope his letters would succeed, then extinguish his candle, step out of the deserted State House, and shuffle off exhausted through the silent streets to his home to rest.

On July 12 the committee headed by John Dickinson presented Congress with the "Articles of Confederation and Perpetual Union" and set off a storm of debate that would rage continually for more than a year. At the heart of the debate was which, if any, powers each of the sovereign states—independent nations, in effect—would cede to a central government in the interest of forming a union. Only occasionally did delegates put aside their differences, as on August 2, when they signed "engrossed," or corrected, hand-copied texts of the Declaration of Independence to send to each of the state legislatures for changes they might want to make. As other delegates added their names to the treasonous document, Benjamin Franklin is said to have quipped, "We must be unanimous; there is no pulling different ways; we must all hang together."[5] The last delegate did not sign until January 1777, and even then, Congress kept the names secret to protect signers from charges of treason as long as possible.

Hancock sent the signed document to the printer and left the Pennsylvania State House elated—as much by the signing as he

The Signing of the Declaration of Independence, July 4, 1776. Perhaps the most famous painting in early American art, this epic painting by George Washington's aide de camp John Trumbull (1756–1843) hangs in the Capitol in Washington, D.C. Started in 1796, the work is the product of the artist's imagination. Using a floor plan, provided by Thomas Jefferson, of the Assembly Room where Congress met, Trumbull portrayed all signers, including those not present. The majority of faces were added over a period of twenty-four years from pencil sketches or oil studies. Only John Hancock, the president of Congress, seated at the right, actually signed the document on July 4, 1776, and the only witness was Pennsylvania delegate Charles Thomson, the secretary of Congress, the tall solitary figure to Hancock's right. In this symbolic painting, however, Hancock faces the five members of the committee assigned to write the document: from left to right, John Adams of Massachusetts, Roger Sherman of Connecticut, Robert R. Livingston of New York, Thomas Jefferson of Virginia, and Benjamin Franklin of Pennsylvania. Other significant figures in the painting include John Dickinson, author of the *Letters from a Farmer in Pennsylvania* and the Olive Branch Petition to King George. Dickinson is the middle figure in the threesome standing to Hancock's right. Benjamin Harrison, the Virginia planter who was both Washington's and Hancock's good friend, is seated alone in the extreme left foreground. Seated in the foreground over Harrison's left shoulder are, in succession, Richard Henry Lee of Virginia, Samuel Adams of Massachusetts, and George Clinton of New York, the state's future governor. The stout delegate seated slightly apart from Clinton, to his left, is Benjamin Rush, the famous Philadelphia physician, and the stout man to Rush's left is Massachusetts delegate Elbridge Gerry. Robert Treat Paine, the other Massachusetts delegate, is seated to Gerry's immediate left. Trumbull painted three versions. One hangs in the Art Gallery at Yale University, Trumbull's alma mater, and the other at the Athenaeum in his hometown of Hartford, Connecticut. (*Photo courtesy of the Library of Congress. Key to delegate identities from the Yale Art Gallery*)

was by the news from Thomas Cushing in Boston of the launching of the two Massachusetts frigates. Although Rhode Island had launched its new ships first, Hancock was assuaged by Cushing's having named the larger of the two vessels, with its thirty-two guns, the *Hancock*. The smaller ship bore the name *Boston*. Hancock ordered that the *Hancock* be made "ready for sea immediately." At the same time, Hancock ordered John Paul Jones to "proceed immediately on a cruise against our enemies"[6] aboard the new *Providence*. In building the ships, Cushing had ordered Hancock Wharf refurbished, and Hancock, who received no pay for his service in Congress, assured himself some steady income by making it the official wharf for naval affairs in Boston.

Late in August, Howe's force on Long Island swelled to more than fifty thousand troops, including about nine thousand German mercenaries. He assaulted Brooklyn Heights, wiping out almost one-third of the American force of five thousand and capturing the American commanders Gens. John Sullivan and William Alexander, Lord Stirling. Washington managed to escape with his forces to Manhattan. In an effort to arrange an exchange of prisoners, Hancock sent his trusted aide William Palfrey to meet General Howe. Palfrey sent Hancock this report:

> Sir
>
> Agreeable to your direction, I went yesterday with a Flag of truce on board the Eagle, in company with Mr. Nat Tracey of Newburyport who was empowered by the Council of Massachusetts Bay to negotiate an Exchange of the Prisoners taken in the Yankee Hero. We were treated with the utmost politeness and Civility by Lord [General William] Howe, with whom we had a Conference of near two hours. . . . He spoke with the highest respect of General Washington . . . and of his earnest desire that a reconciliation might take place. . . .

Palfrey said that Howe agreed

> to open an Account with Gen'l Washington, and, if agreeable to him would immediately send all Prisoners in his possession, and leave it with General Washington to return him an equal number. . . .

When we parted he desir'd his Compliments to General
Washington. . . .

Lord Howe appears to be upwards of fifty years of age,
is tall & well made, dressed plain. In his manner and address,
much like Governor Hutchinson. I wish he may not be possessed of Hutchinson's art and duplicity, as he seems very open
and candid. Upon the whole he appears to be calculated by his
ease & politeness to engage the affections. A Person of this
disposition is the most dangerous enemy we can encounter—
and we ought to keep a very strict Guard to prevent being
deceiv'd by plausible appearances. . . . [7]

On September 6, General Howe sent his prisoner General Sullivan to Congress to propose an informal peace conference on
Staten Island, just south of New York City. King George had
appointed Howe and his brother Admiral Richard Howe peace
commissioners, with powers to pardon and protect all Americans
who reaffirmed their allegiance to the king, but with no powers to
deal with colonial assemblies. Congress sent Benjamin Franklin,
John Adams, and Edward Rutledge, of South Carolina, but they
turned around and returned to Philadelphia after Admiral Howe
demanded a revocation of the Declaration of Independence as a
precondition to all negotiations. On September 12 Washington
evacuated lower Manhattan rather than risk entrapment on the
southern end of the island, and three days later Gen. William
Howe's forces occupied New York City, but were repulsed when
they tried storming Washington's forces in Harlem Heights, in the
northern part of Manhattan. Also hampering Howe's advance was
a huge fire that destroyed three hundred buildings in New York
City on September 21. The fire did not interfere with the hanging
of Nathan Hale the following day—the first patriot to die for treason to the crown. A lieutenant in the Connecticut militia, the
twenty-one-year-old schoolmaster from Yale College had volunteered to undertake a reconnaissance mission behind enemy lines.
British troops captured him in civilian clothes and brought him
to Howe, who ordered the young man hanged. His last words,

"I only regret that I have but one life to lose for my country," made him a martyr of American independence.

A few days later Congress sent Benjamin Franklin to Paris to join Silas Deane and present the French government with a three-part treaty establishing "a firm inviolable & UNIVERSAL PEACE AND A TRUE AND SINCERE FRIENDSHIP BETWEEN THE MOST SERENE AND MIGHTY PRINCE Louis the sixteenth, the most Christian King, his heirs and successors and the united States of America."[8]

The proposed treaty would establish commercial and military ties that permitted Americans to trade natural resources for arms. At the same time, "the most Christian king shall endeavour by all the means in his power to protect and defend all the vessels belonging to the subjects, people or inhabitants of the said united States" and the United States would promise to reciprocate. France also would agree "to find, apprehend and punish" pirates and return all vessels and goods to the United States and obtain reparations. The king would promise to defend U.S. citizens and their vessels "against all attacks, assaults, violences, depredations or plunderings by or from the king or emperor of Morocco or Fez and every other prince state and power on the coast of Barbary in Africa." The United States would agree not to help Britain if Britain declared war against France.

To calm American fears of French expansion, France would agree not to invade "nor under any pretense to possess Labrador, New Britain, Nova Scotia, Acadia, Canada, Florida nor any of the countries, cities or towns on the continental of North America, nor any of the islands of Newfoundland, Cape Breton, St. John, Anticosh, nor any other island lying near to the said continent in the seas or in any gulf, bay or river." Each side would agree not to fish in the other's waters.

Shortly after Franklin left for France, the British destroyed a makeshift American flotilla on Lake Champlain and sent Benedict Arnold's forces fleeing northward. Meanwhile, Howe's forces outflanked Washington's positions in northern Manhattan. In less than a month the British captured the entire area north of New York City, taking three thousand American troops prisoner with Gen. Charles Lee. With British troops in pursuit, Washington and his remaining forces fled across the Hudson River, southward through New Jersey into Pennsylvania.

In early December Howe's troops approached Philadelphia, intent on capturing or killing the political leaders of the Revolution. For once, Congress halted its incessant bickering over the Articles of Confederation and agreed to flee to Baltimore. Before leaving, Congress responded to reports of bitter rivalries between American military commanders by vesting Washington with dictatorial powers to govern and direct all military operations.

Initially, Hancock opposed the move to Baltimore—for two reasons. First, it was far from certain that the British would succeed in capturing Philadelphia. For Congress to flee prematurely, he believed, would signal a lack of courage to American troops. The second, more personal reason for his reluctance to leave Philadelphia was the difficulties the move would pose for his wife, Dolly. Sometime in November, she had given birth to a girl, whom they named, after John's aunt, Lydia Henchman Hancock.[9] So, along with Robert Morris, whom Congress appointed to conduct congressional business in their absence, Hancock stubbornly refused, at first, to budge from Philadelphia. When British troops were within twenty miles of the city, however, he recognized the recklessness of a man wanted for treason remaining in Philadelphia with a newborn infant and a wife enfeebled by childbirth. A few days later they navigated the deep ruts and mud on the road to Baltimore.

Baltimore was a thriving seaport and shipbuilding center, but with the exception of a handful of mansions, a city of vermin-infested waterfront shanties, with few rooms, let alone suites or homes, available for rent to members of Congress. Delegates described the city as "the dirtiest place" they ever saw.[10] A prominent merchant with whom Hancock had engaged in triangular trade invited Hancock's family to his home until they could find their own. When they did, it was a small, shabby £25-a-month house in a poor section of town, where Dolly dared not walk. "I have got to housekeeping," Hancock wrote in January 1777 to his friend Robert Morris back in Philadelphia, "but really my friend, in a very poor house.... I have only two rooms below, and one of them I am obliged to let my servants occupy."[11]

Two days after the Hancocks moved into their little house, thieves broke in and stole trunks of linens, books, papers, and money. To make matters worse, a Harvard tutor arrived with instructions from the board of trustees to retrieve the college records and securities that Hancock had taken. The British had requisitioned the college buildings as barracks the previous year and the college had closed down. With Howe's evacuation of Boston, the college was trying to reopen but had no funds and faced financial ruin unless Hancock returned the securities and cash in his possession. Hancock gave the tutor all the records and securities he could find, and later sent Harvard an accounting that showed his having returned securities worth £16,443, for a £1,000 profit, or slightly more than 6 percent, over four years.

In early December 1776 the Massachusetts General Court had reelected Hancock to a second term as a delegate to the Continental Congress, allowing him to remain president of the United States for at least another year. Before the year ended, Howe sent his forces back to winter quarters in New York but posted garrisons at Trenton, Princeton, Bordentown, Perth Amboy, New Brunswick, and other towns in New Jersey. Washington took advantage of the situation, crossed the Delaware, and caught the Hessian garrison in Trenton by surprise. After an hour of sporadic fighting, the garrison surrendered. Howe reinforced his remaining garrisons, but three days later Washington drove British forces out of Princeton and back up to New Brunswick, clearing western and southern New Jersey of British occupation. The Washington victories sent morale soaring among the uncomfortably lodged congressional delegates. Less than two weeks later, on January 12, 1777, John Hancock was forty years old, and on January 31 he received the final copies of the Declaration of Independence—all signed by all delegates—to forward to each of the states for ratification by their legislatures. For the first time all the world would know the identity of those who had committed treason against King George III.

As president of the United States, Hancock enclosed a letter with each copy, which said in part: "As there is not a more distinguished event in the history of America than the Declaration of her Independence—nor any that, in all probability, will so much excite the attention of future ages,—it is highly proper that the memory of that transaction, together with the causes that gave rise to it, should be preserved in the most careful manner that can be devised . . . that it may henceforth form a part of the archives of your state and remain a lasting testimony of your approbation of that necessary and important measure."[12]

By the middle of February, the gloom of their dismal lodgings and the Baltimore winter made the Hancocks—and indeed, most other congressional delegates—long for home. It was impossible to get anything done in Baltimore. Only Hancock's mediative skills managed to win congressional agreement to send more agents chasing after European military and financial aid. Franklin's commission was expanded to include Spain as well as France, and other agents went to Austria, Prussia, and Tuscany, which was an independent grand duchy. In addition to recruiting military support, the agents recruited officers to convert America's ragtag collection of woodsmen into a well-trained, efficient fighting force. The first to arrive was the highly successful twenty-year-old Frenchman Marie-Joseph, marquis de Lafayette, whom Washington commissioned a major general after he volunteered to serve without pay. Other volunteers included the German Baron Johann de Kalb; the Polish engineer Thaddeus Kosciuszko, who was to become colonel of engineers; and the Prussian Baron Friedrich Wilhelm von Steuben, whom Washington appointed inspector general and head of training for the Continental Army.

Communications in Baltimore were slow, however, and Congress had no place to work. Everyone was uncomfortable, irritable, and increasingly bitter about the continuing debate over the

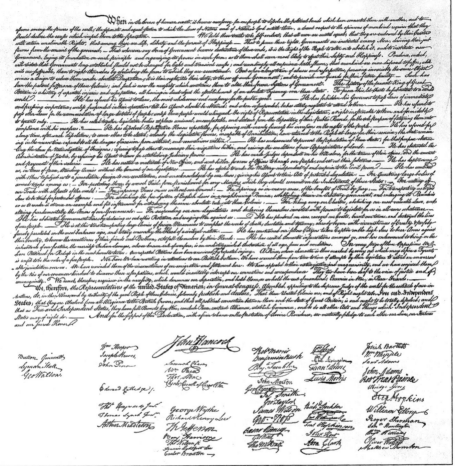

Engrossed (corrected) hand copy of the Declaration of Independence, issued in early 1777. The original document of July 4, 1776, bore but one signature—that of John Hancock—for more than a month. (*Library of Congress*)

Articles of Confederation. As successful as he had been in steering the Declaration of Independence through Congress, Hancock seemed helpless to move the Articles toward resolution. All the intercolonial enmities resurfaced, with South Carolina's Edward Rutledge and Virginia's Benjamin Harrison accusing the Adamses and all the New Englanders except Hancock of attempting to domineer the proceedings. Some accused the Northerners of plotting to use Congress as an instrument to dominate the new nation. And of course, state boundaries remained a constant source of dispute. A few delegates walked out—some because of disgust, others to return home to run for governor of their state.

Hancock decided to take his family home to Boston. All but the New Englanders expressed dismay. Many depended on Hancock's mediative skills as the last shreds of the fragile tissue that held Congress together.

"I am much concerned," said one congressman, "though his great fatigue and long attendance entitle him to some relaxation. How we shall do without him I know not, for we have never yet put a chairman on a committee of the whole House that could, in any measure, fill his place. He has not only dignity and impartiality, which are the great requisites of a president of such a body; but has alertness, attention, readiness to conceive of any motion and its tendency and of every alteration proposed in the course of the debate, which greatly tends to facilitate and expedite business."[13]

Although Dolly wanted to postpone departure with the baby until the weather turned warmer, Hancock hoped to leave in April, before the May elections, when the Massachusetts legislature would plan a new state government. John Adams could not resist commenting in a letter to his wife that despite Dolly's preference for a May departure, "Mr. Hancock was determined upon April. Perhaps the choice of a Governor may come in May. What aspiring little creatures we are. How subtle, sagacious, and judicious this passion is! How clearly it sees its object, how constantly it pursues it, and what wise plans it devises for obtaining it."[14]

On February 17, Congress voted to return to Philadelphia and reconvene on March 5. Hancock immediately wrote to Robert

Morris to send "four good covered wagons, with four good horses and a sober driver each to . . . convey down to Philadelphia the public papers, etc." He asked Morris to help Hancock's clerk "procure a suitable house, well furnished, for me. . . . I hope soon to join you at the Oyster Club."[15] On February 20, Hancock's merchant friend in Baltimore hosted a grand farewell dinner for the Hancocks and Katherine Quincy, but a week later, after all the other delegates had left for Philadelphia, the wagons Hancock had ordered had not yet arrived—probably because the army had commandeered most horses. Hancock was quick to show his pique. "My dear friend," he wrote to Morris, "you have reduced me to a most distressed situation. . . . What I shall do I know not. I can't get away here. Congress is adjourned to Philadelphia, and I must be there on Wednesday next . . . I cannot remove my papers and . . . am obliged to leave my whole family behind. For God's sake, hurry the wagons along." Hancock said he would leave his clerk behind with the congressional papers to await the wagons and "set off on Saturday alone, to my great mortification, and hope to meet the wagons on the road."[16]

Hancock packed as many essentials as he could in his own coach and left for Philadelphia on March 3, arriving at God's Graces, a Maryland village that no longer exists. He arrived in time for midday dinner at an apparently upscale inn, where he met the governor. "Through much bad road I arrived here at 1 o'clock in good order," he wrote to Dolly. "Dinner is coming. I have just taken up the vinegar bottle. Poor stuff . . . 1/2 after 2. I have got up from dinner and standing at the window. Dinner served up. Boiled beef, roast turkey, ham roast beef, greens salad, gooseberry and apple tarts, cheese, apples, etc.; Baltimore punch, wine, etc. . . .

"P. S.—The turkey was so tough I broke out one of my teeth."[17]

The remainder of his trip was no smoother. The roads were bad and ice floes blocked a ferry crossing at the Susquehanna River, on the Maryland-Pennsylvania line. He settled into a private room at the nearby inn, only to have the innkeeper ask him to cede it to a married couple. The president of the United States spent the night in the ground-floor common room with other single men.[18]

During the second night, one of his servants "treated me very ill. He drank a deal of my wine in the wagon; broke and lost several bottles; dropped out my trunk, which was luckily found; and was brought to the tavern drunk and put to bed. I shall turn him adrift at Philadelphia," he wrote to Dolly. "God bless you. Take care of yourself. There is wine in the closet. When that is gone get more. Live reputably. Keep up the part of a family."[19] The following morning an exasperated Hancock set out on horseback for Philadelphia. He arrived on March 7, but without a quorum, Congress could not reconvene. He was desperately lonely without his wife and baby and spent more than an hour writing a letter to his "Dear Dear Dolly," describing his every movement since his return. "I spend my evenings at home, snuff my candles with a pair of scissors.... I shall make out as well as I can, but I assure you, my Dear Soul I long to have you here & I know you will be as expeditious as you can. When I part from you again it must be a vary extraordinary occasion...."

"My Dear Dolly," he concluded, "I am yours forever." He signed the letter with his famous signature, *John Hancock*.

The following day, with still no quorum at Congress, he wrote an even longer letter, admitting he remained "quite lonesome. I am up to the eyes in papers. Joe comes in with a plate of minced veal. ... I shall take the plate in one hand, the knife in the other, without cloth or any comfort, and eat a little and then to writing, for I have not room on the table to put a plate." He bemoaned his "doleful, lonesome life," and added, "Supper is over—no relish, nor shall I till I have you here ... I shall have fires made and everything ready for your reception."[20]

Dolly's arrival with the baby reinvigorated Hancock. He plunged into his work with new enthusiasm, and they postponed plans for returning to Boston. Congress reconvened on March 12, and as debates droned on through spring, Hancock struggled to find the funds to buy supplies and pay troops. Paymaster General William Palfrey was desperate for money, pleading with Hancock that "the chest is again exhausted ... I beg you will hurry on the money with all possible speed. There is no doing without it."[21]

France had sent a clandestine trickle of money and supplies but feared England would declare war if the flow became too evident. Meanwhile, Congress kept printing worthless continental dollars and letters of credit—the total was approaching $200 million. The states printed an equal aggregate of worthless paper of their own, which together with the continentals had plunged the nation into an economic depression. Printed money bought next to nothing; barter was the only certain means of procuring one's daily bread other than baking it oneself.

In May, Thomas Cushing engineered John Hancock's reelection to the Massachusetts General Court, but in early June the frigate *Hancock* had the questionable honor of being the first ship in the American navy to lose an encounter with the British. Hancock's other frigate, the *Boston*, managed to escape, but the British captured the *Hancock* and renamed her the *Iris*.[22] A week later Congress resolved that the flag of the United States be "thirteen stripes alternate red and white, that the Union be thirteen stars, white in a blue field."[23]

As summer heat enveloped the middle states, the Hancocks put off their return to Massachusetts until Congress adjourned for its summer recess. In July, however, an armada of more than 250 ships sailed into Chesapeake Bay, with a force of twenty-three thousand troops intent on capturing the American capital. Hancock sent Dolly, her sister, and the baby racing off to the safety of New England. A few weeks later, their daughter died.

A month later the British landed at the northern end of Chesapeake Bay and began their march to Philadelphia. Washington threw up a force of 10,500 men at Brandywine Creek, but the British swept through undeterred, decimating the patriots and forcing Congress to flee to Lancaster, sixty miles to the west. A week later Howe's forces took Philadelphia, and Congress fled farther, to the tiny village of York. Washington and his generals counterattacked sporadically, but each assault ended indecisively until October 3, when the British routed the Americans at Germantown, just north

of Philadelphia, while another British force captured Fort Mer-
cer, south of Philadelphia on the Delaware River. By the end of
November, Howe would clear the entire Delaware River basin of
patriot forces and free it for unimpeded navigation by British
convoys. In mid-December, Washington's forces would limp into
their dismal winter encampment at Valley Forge, while Howe settled comfortably in the American capital city.

York was simply too small for Congress to conduct effective
business. Delegates began leaving even before the Congress held
its first session, and Hancock, exhausted by overwork and incessant moves from city to city, decided to return home to Boston.
The loss of his daughter had depressed him, and Dolly's infuriating unwillingness or inability to write left him disconsolate. On
October 15 he asked Congress for a leave of absence, and Congress
granted him until January 1, 1778. It named Henry Laurens, a
South Carolina merchant and planter from Charleston, as president pro tem. Hancock informed Washington of his plans:

"It is now above two years since I have had the honor of presiding in Congress, and I should esteem myself happy to . . . render
further service to my country in that department. But the decline
of health occasioned by so long and unremitting application to the
duties of my office, both in Congress and out of Congress, joined
to the situation of my own private affairs, has at length taught me
to think of retiring for two or three months. . . . I flatter myself my
conduct . . . will meet with your approbation. The politeness and
attention I have experienced from you . . . will always be a source
of the most pleasant satisfaction to me."[24] Hancock asked Washington for an escort of light horse, not only to protect him from
Tory attack, but also to demonstrate publicly the importance of
and respect due the office of the presidency.

The following day he wrote a bitter letter to his wife saying he
planned to leave York in eight days and that she should order
their carriage driver to prepare the light carriage and four horses
"to proceed on to Hartford or Fairfield, as I shall hereafter direct,
to meet me on the road. If my old black horses are not able to per-

form the journey he must hire two." Hancock scolded Dolly for her persistent failure to write.

"Not a single word have I heard from you . . . I must submit & will only say that I expected oftener to have been the object of your attention. This is my sixth letter to you." In no uncertain terms he told her, "[I] must desire that you will take a seat in the carriage and meet me on the road . . . I have desired Mr. Bant to accompany you . . . and when we meet he can take my sulkey and I return with you in the carriage to town." As he finished his long letter, however, he could not hide his deep affection for his wife. "I long to see you," he confessed. "I have much to say, which I leave to a cheerful evening with you in person. God bless you, my dear Dolly."[25]

Not long after he had sent his melancholy letter to Dolly, Hancock exulted as he told Congress that British general John Burgoyne's entire army—nearly six thousand men—had laid down their arms at Saratoga and surrendered to patriot general Horatio Gates. Under the Convention of Saratoga of October 17, Burgoyne had agreed to march his men to Boston, sail to England, and never again serve in the war against America. The Northern campaign had all but ended; the Americans had won. It was the great victory Congress had awaited as assurance of eventual independence from England. The Americans now controlled much of New York and New England, along with most of the South.

A few days later, Hancock received a gracious letter from George Washington: "It gives me real pain to learn that the declining state of your health . . . oblige[s] you to relinquish a station . . . which you have so long filled with acknowledged propriety. Motives, as well of a personal as of a general concern, make me regret the necessity that compels you to retire and to wish your absence from office may be of as short a duration as possible." Despite the devastating defeats Washington had suffered over the previous five weeks, Washington sent an escort of "Cornet[26] Buckmer and twelve dragoons" and an apology for its "being so small . . . but the severe duty the horse have been obliged to perform for a long time past has rendered many of them unfit for service."[27]

Before leaving York, Hancock scored one of his greatest triumphs as a mediator by guiding Congress to a resolution of its fifteen-month-long debate over the Articles of Confederation. His imminent departure evidently forced delegates to recognize how important his mediative skills had been in holding Congress together. Without him, many delegates would have deserted and shattered the unity essential to effective prosecution of the war. In his absence they would need a contract to bind them together. As fragile and imperfect as they were, the Articles provided an amorphous political formula for pursuing the war of independence in concert.

The Articles created a new, central government with but one branch—a unicameral legislature, or Congress, where each state had but one vote, regardless of size or population. Although the states agreed to perpetual union, they gave the Congress no powers to assure that union. It could regulate foreign affairs, make peace or war, negotiate treaties, and maintain an army and navy. It could also coin money, establish a postal service, and manage Indian affairs. But the Articles also included restrictions that, in effect, annulled each of these powers. Congress could not tax or obtain funds of its own without unanimous approval of the states, and it could not pass laws, although it could request each state do so. The Articles left everyone angry and disgruntled. In trying to please every one, Congress had emasculated the Articles and, in the end, pleased no one; but delegates had no choice but to ratify the document or be left with no government, and most of them agreed that an imperfect union was better than no union at all. On October 29 Hancock stood before about twenty delegates to say farewell, in a simple, emotional statement that lasted slightly more than two minutes:

Gentlemen: Friday last compleated two years and five months since you did me the honor of electing me to fill this chair. As I could never flatter myself your choice proceeded from any idea of my abilities, but rather from a partial opinion of my attachment to the liberties of America, I felt myself under the strongest obligation to discharge the duties of office.... I think

I shall be forgiven, if I say, I have spared no pains, expence, or labour to gratify your wishes and to accomplish the views of Congress.

My health being much impaired, I find some relaxation absolutely necessary, after such constant application. . . . But I cannot take my departure, Gentlemen, without expressing my thanks for the civility and politeness I have experienced from you. It is impossible to mention this, without a heartfelt pleasure.

If in the course of so long a period, as I have had the honour to fill this chair, any expressions may have dropped from me, that may have given the least offence to any member, as it was not intentional, so I hope this candor will pass it over.

May every happiness, Gentlemen, attend you, both as members of this house & as individuals and I pray heaven, that unanimity & perseverance may go hand in hand in this house, and that everything, which may tend to distract or divide your councils be forever banished.[28]

No sooner had Hancock left the house than the venomous tongue of Sam Adams began to "distract and divide" Congress—over, of all things, a motion "that the thanks of Congress be presented to John Hancock, Esq for the unremitted attention and steady impartiality which he has manifested in the discharge of the various duties of his office as president." He had, after all, served with no pay, had advanced at least $1,392 to the continental treasury, and had not, unlike all other delegates, been reimbursed for household expenses, of $3,248. Knowing the condition of the treasury, he simply had not asked for it.

Samuel Adams cackled that the principle of thanking a president for simply fulfilling his obligations was "unprecedented, impolitick, dangerous." A pawn of Samuel Adams then moved "to resolve, as the opinion of this Congress, that it is improper to thank any president for the discharge of the duties of that office." The vote was a tie, and without a majority, the resolution failed to pass. Delegates from only ten states were present when the resolution to thank Hancock finally came to a vote. Six states voted yes—Connecticut, New York, New Jersey, Virginia, North Carolina, and South Carolina. Pennsylvania, New Hampshire, Rhode Island,

and Massachusetts voted no.[29] Discretion dictated Hancock's absence during the debate, but Sam Adams made certain not to let Hancock savor his victory. He penned a vitriolic letter to James Warren with all the arguments against thanking the president—and he sent a copy to Hancock before the president left for home.

Before leaving, Hancock had written a farewell note to Paymaster General William Palfrey, the young man for whom he had done so much:

> Dear Palfrey
>
> I have only time to bid you Farewell; immediately on Return of this Express, I shall set out for Boston, I have notified Congress. . . . I am wore down, however I . . . have Executed the Business of Congress with Dispatch & Fidelity. This much I may say & add that the prospect of Gain did not influence me; I have expended my own money & in that case had a Right to drink wine if I pleas'd. . . . God Bless you & believe me,
>
> Your Real Friend
> John Hancock[30]

Within a few days of Hancock's departure, the two Adamses realized that in their absence, Hancock would seize control of Massachusetts government and destroy the radical wing of the Whig party they had built—along with all their chances of ever governing their state. They packed hurriedly and raced off in their carriage to catch Hancock, but they were too late. By the time they reached Massachusetts, Hancock had seized the reins of political power and assured his place as what Samuel Adams called the "American King."[31]

13

A Model Major General

(1777-1780)

Hancock arrived in Boston to a hero's welcome—a king's welcome. "His Excellency John Hancock," wrote the *Independent Chronicle*, "arrived here under the escort of light dragoons. . . . His arrival was made known by the ringing of bells, the discharge of thirteen cannon . . . on the Common, the cannon from the fortress on the hill, and the ships in the harbor. The independent and light infantry companies paid him their military salutes. He received the compliments of gentlemen of all orders, and recent indication was given of the sense the public has of his important services to the American cause."

In contrast, no one even noticed the Adamses when they got to Massachusetts a few days later. John went to North Braintree and Samuel rode into Boston, but the *Chronicle* spent barely a line of ink in recognition of their coming. Both were bitter. John Adams planted rumors that Hancock had failed to pay innkeepers on his way from York to Boston.

"The taverners, all along, are complaining of the guard of light horse which attended Mr. H. They did not pay, and the taverners were obliged to go after them to demand their dues. The expense, which is supposed to be the country's, is unpopular. The Tories laugh at the tavern-keepers, who have often turned them out of their houses for abusing Mr. H. They now scoff at them for being imposed upon by their king, as they call him. Vanity is always mean; vanity is never rich enough to be generous."[1]

Hancock ignored the Adamses—with good reason. Dolly was pregnant and needed his attention. Moreover, he was exhausted from his work and the long trip home. He needed rest. He was aging prematurely—the result of excessively long hours, a huge burden of responsibilities, and genetic predisposition. Some earlier biographers maintain his love of fine foods and wines contributed to his deterioration, but there is no medical evidence to substantiate such statements. He was simply exhausted.

"I have gone through many difficulties on the road," he wrote to Dolly on the way home from York, "but . . . the remembrance of these difficulties will vanish when I have the happiness of seeing you. I am still obliged to have my foot wrapped up in baize [a warm woolen fabric used by men who complained of gout] but I brave all these things. I shall get along as fast as I can but, having a party of eight horse with me and a wagon, I do not travel as fast as I otherwise should."

After a few days' rest, Hancock began seeing to his Beacon Hill estate. He repaired the damage to fences around his home and the Common. He ordered construction of a new wing to the house, for a large, elegant banquet hall that would become, in effect, his court. Boston soon learned who stood in favor or disfavor. At Hancock Wharf he found that his manager, William Bant, had collected £1,500, or about 15 percent of outstanding House of Hancock debts. The war and the accompanying economic depression had made the rest uncollectable. The last sale in the Hancock store had been recorded in March 1775. Bant had also sold Hancock's last two ships for £1,000, and Captain Scott had sold the last ship in London. Hancock Wharf was still busy, and most of the stores he rented were still in business, although sales had slowed. All House of Hancock stores and its other operations had closed forever, and John Hancock would have to depend on interest from his bonds—about £13,000 a year—and income from the wharf, from store and building rents, and from his real estate to support himself and his family.

With some order restored in his personal affairs, Hancock began shoring up his political power. As other states had done, Massachusetts would soon form a new government and elect a governor, and Hancock fully intended assuming that office. He drove continuously about the city in his carriage, viewing the devastation wrought by the British troops. The trees and fences were gone—all used for firewood—and huge piles of timbers lay where thriving stores and warehouses had stood only two years earlier. The streets seemed empty. Almost all the Tories had fled to Canada or Britain, and many frightened patriots had moved to the country. With one-third of the population missing, Boston was now a small, somewhat subdued city of about ten thousand. Hancock stepped from his carriage at almost every corner to talk with poor and rich alike. Wherever and whenever he could afford to do so, he ordered repairs of homes and shops at his expense. In response to a need "for providing the poor ... aged [and] infirm persons in the Almshouse who are improvided with Wood [and] Clothing,"[2] he bought 150 cords of wood for distribution to the poor. Hancock went out of his way to help widows and orphans. He was generous to his friends as well, helping support the children of Dr. Joseph Warren, who had fallen at Bunker Hill, and lending money to others.

"President Hancock," wrote a captured German officer in Boston awaiting deportation, "is so frank and condescending to the lowest that one would think he was talking to a brother or a relative. He visits the coffee-houses of Boston, where are congregated the poorest of the inhabitants—men who get their living by bringing wood and vegetables into the city. Indeed, he who desires to advance in popularity must understand the art of making himself popular. In no country does wealth and birth count for so little as in this; and yet one can maintain the position given him by fate without being in the least familiar with the lowest."[3]

In early December 1777 the Boston town meeting all but ignored the Adamses by reelecting the generous John Hancock to the Continental Congress and asking him to serve as town meeting moderator, after voting its official thanks for his gift of firewood. Immediately thereafter, Congress removed John Adams from the Massachusetts political arena by naming him to replace Silas Deane as envoy in Paris. Although Sam Adams continued sniping, the people of Boston adored Hancock. The owners of a privateer expressed their adoration by presenting Hancock with a prize their ship had captured—an "elegant coach . . . as a token of respect for that gentleman which has so nobly distinguished himself in the present contest with Great Britain."[4]

He immediately put the vehicle in service as his official carriage. It was an ornate yellow chariot that sparkled like gold in sunlight. It drew gasps of awe and admiring applause—and of course, poison-tipped barbs of criticism from his radical critics, who usually disguised their identities with pseudonyms to avoid public outrage. "John Hancock of Boston appears in public," wrote one anonymous critic in suspiciously familiar phrases, "with all the state and pageantry of an Oriental prince. He rides in an elegant chariot, which was taken in a prize to the *Civil Usage* pirate vessel and by the owners presented to him. He is attended by four servants dressed in superb livery, mounted on fine horses richly caparisoned; and escorted by fifty horsemen [his Corps of Cadets] with drawn sabers—the one half of whom precede, and the other follow, his carriage."[5]

It was Hancock, however, who had the chairman's gavel in his hand at town meetings, and he used his access to the latest news to enhance his popularity. It was he who brought news that Congress had approved the Articles of Confederation, and it was he who led Boston's New Year's celebration with news that France had recognized American independence. At the beginning of 1778, Hancock sensed approaching victory over the radicals. John Adams would soon be out of the country, and Sam Adams was about to return to the Continental Congress in York, Pennsylvania. Only James Warren remained, albeit in the powerful post of speaker of the state House of Representatives. Hancock decided to risk postponing his own return to Congress to reclaim his seat in the Massachu-

James Warren, a would-be leader of the American Revolution who avoided military action and spent much of his time criticizing John Hancock's aristocratic trappings. (*Museum of Fine Arts, Boston*)

setts House of Representatives and test his strength. Although he did not win reelection by many votes, he found his support as strong in the House as it was in the Boston town meeting. In what amounted to a humiliating rebuke for Warren, the House honored Hancock by temporarily removing Warren from the speaker's chair and seating Hancock while it voted to approve the Articles of Confederation.

A few weeks later, as John Adams prepared to sail for France, the House resolved to pay Hancock £2,335.15 for his services and expenses as their delegate in the Continental Congress, dating from the day he had left Worcester, April 26, 1775, to the day he returned to Boston, November 19, 1777. The amount was twice what the Continental Congress would eventually pay him. Two days later Hancock stood at Hancock Wharf to bid John Adams an official farewell as he sailed off to France—ironically, on the twenty-four-gun frigate *Boston,* one of the two warships that Hancock and Thomas Cushing had built for the navy. Earlier that month, France and the United States had signed treaties of friendship, commerce, and military assistance. France agreed to guarantee "the liberty Sovereignty and independence" of the United States if France and England engaged in war. In the event of such a war, the treaty divided the unconquered territories in the Americas: it gave the United States the right to conquer Canada and Bermuda and France the right to conquer the British West Indies. In March, with Adams still at sea, French king Louis XVI received Franklin, Deane, and Arthur Lee, the younger brother of Virginia congressman Richard Henry Lee, and he officially recognized the United States as an independent nation. Franklin was to stay on in France as America's first ambassador. (Congress would approve the treaties in May, and in June an Anglo-French naval engagement would provoke an official declaration of war between England and France, assuring the United States of a powerful military ally.)

With only James Warren standing in his way, John Hancock began his campaign to win control of Massachusetts government. During the winter of 1778 the General Court drew up a state constitution. Everyone agreed on the need for an elected chief executive, but the western farm areas wanted to limit his powers. Moreover, they wanted every village to have one representative in the legislature, while populated eastern areas favored proportional representation. Hancock purposely avoided favoring either side on thorny constitutional issues, but sent his two close allies Thomas Cushing and Cushing's friend John Pickering, a conservative from Salem, to reach out to western farmers—the only easterners to do so. Although voters rejected the first version of the state constitution, Hancock emerged stronger than ever by building a political bridge between his moderate eastern bloc and the western farmers. As spring began, Hancock wrote to the Continental Congress asking for an extension of his already overextended leave as president. He said he needed to remain with his wife during the remaining weeks of her pregnancy.

As the Hancocks awaited the birth of their baby, the coalition he had built won control of the Massachusetts House of Representatives, unseating James Warren and putting Hancock's ally John Pickering in the speaker's chair. The crestfallen Warren wrote to his mentor Sam Adams: "Your Curiosity will lead you to Enquire how my Town came to leave me out, and how the Interest I used to have in the House vanished and sunk. . . . The versatility and Caprice of Mankind . . . have had their effects, but they would not do alone. Envy and the Ambition of some people has aided them, and the policy or rather what you will Call the Cunning of a party here, who have set up an Idol they are determined to worship. . . . the plan is to sacrifice you and me to the shrine of their idol."[6]

On May 21, 1778, Dolly gave birth to John Hancock's first son. Three days later, the minister at the Brattle Square Church, which John Hancock and his aunt Lydia had paid to rebuild, baptized the baby John George Washington Hancock, the fourth John Hancock born in America—and the first born American rather than British.

After the baby's birth, Hancock longed to return to Congress. Momentous events were taking place, and he wanted to participate. The British had sued for peace, and Hancock already envisioned penning his florid signature on the historic peace treaty. A parliamentary peace commission was on its way to Philadelphia with powers to negotiate with Congress and suspend all acts passed since 1763. Parliament had completely reversed itself. As an inducement to the colonies to remain a part of Britain, it had repealed the Tea Act and the Coercive Acts and pledged never again to impose any taxes on the American colonies. Hancock wanted to participate in the negotiations between Congress and Parliament. In any case, there was little more he could do in Massachusetts until a new General Court worked out another constitution. He knew that Cushing and Pickering would represent his interests well, and by distancing himself from the constitutional debate, he believed, he could present himself to the people of Massachusetts as a candidate of all the people rather than of a particular faction.

Writing to Sam Adams, an embittered James Warren described Hancock's farewell to the House of Representatives: "General Hancock . . . took pompous leave of the House by going up and shaking hands with the speaker, etc., after moving for leave to return soon if his health would not admit of his tarrying long. I suppose a cavalcade will attend him, subscriptions for that purpose having been circulated for a week. I believe he will go tomorrow. You will provide for his reception as you see fit."[7]

On June 3, Hancock left for York, Pennsylvania, with a new delegate, Dr. Samuel Holten, who had been elected to replace John Adams. As Warren predicted and as Holten noted in his diary, "A large number of gentlemen, with their servants and carriages, accompanied us to Watertown, where an elegant dinner was provided"—along with toasts, firing of guns, and cheers from the townsfolk.[8]

After two weeks of bad roads, Hancock and Holten arrived in York. No cheers or church bells greeted them, and Henry Laurens had converted his presidency pro tempore to a permanent presidency. Laurens was now the second president of the United States, and Hancock quietly took his seat in the Massachusetts delegation. To his pleasant surprise he found that even the members from Massachusetts had tired of Sam Adams's insulting diatribes against the "asses and slaves" in Congress.

Hancock had arrived too late to participate in negotiations with the British Parliament. Congress had firmly asserted that the only terms it would consider were a complete withdrawal of British troops from the territories of the thirteen former colonies and recognition of United States independence. The British refused and abandoned the talks.

With Laurens as president, Hancock had little to do in York, and he found life there intolerably dull—made all the more so by Dolly's continuing failure to write. "I wrote you Two Letters the

Day before yesterday, & this is my Seventh Letter, and not one word have I heard from you. . . . I can by no means, in justice to myself continue long under such disagreeable circumstances," he wrote to Dolly. "The mode is so very different from what I have been always accustomed to that to continue long would prejudice my health exceedingly. . . . This moment the post arrived, and, to my very great surprise and disappointment, not a single line from Boston. I am much disposed to resent . . . those from whom I have . . . a right to expect different conduct. . . . I shall write no more till I hear from you."[9]

Even as Hancock penned his letter to Dolly, British troops were evacuating Philadelphia and withdrawing to New York in anticipation of attack by a French fleet carrying a force led by General Lafayette. With the British on the run, Congress eagerly voted to adjourn and reconvene in the nation's capital. Although Hancock had decided to return to Boston, he postponed his departure to participate in final approval of the Articles of Confederation. All the states had ratified the Articles, and Congress wanted to sign them and create the new nation at the same site where it had issued the Declaration of Independence.

Congress reconvened in Philadelphia on July 2, 1778, in time for the fireworks and street parades for the second anniversary of the Declaration of Independence. Hancock celebrated with delegates and friends at an elegant banquet at the City Tavern, with entertainment by an orchestra of "Clarinets, Hautboys, French hornsmen, Violins, and Bass Viols." On the head table sat "a large baked Pudding, in the centre of which was a planted Staff on which was displayed a crimson Flag, in the midst of which was this emblematic device: An Eye denoting Providence, a label in which was inscribed an appeal to heaven; a man with a drawn sword in one hand and in the other the Declaration of Independence, and at his feet a scroll inscribed 'The Declaratory acts.'"[10]

Four days later Congress and the rest of Philadelphia erupted in more celebration as the French fleet under command of the renowned comte d'Estaing, lieutenant general of the French navy, appeared in Delaware Bay, south of Philadelphia. Aboard the flagship was Conrad-Alexandre Gérard, the world's first ambassador to the United States. After Gérard disembarked, d'Estaing sailed northward for a direct assault on one or the other of the last two British bastions in the North, in New York and in Newport, Rhode Island.

Hancock led a congressional delegation that greeted the French *ministre plénipotentiaire*, and the following day, July 9, 1778, he joined delegates from eight states, including Massachusetts, in signing the Articles of Confederation that created a new American nation. He then left for Boston to assume command of the Massachusetts militia and join the last assault against the British.

Two days after he left, d'Estaing's fleet arrived off the northern New Jersey coast, at the entrance of New York Bay, but his deep-draught ships could not navigate the sandbars, and he changed course to join a combined assault with American forces on the three-thousand-man British garrison at Newport, Rhode Island. Continental Army general John Sullivan had devised a plan for d'Estaing to land four thousand marines by sea on the southwest part of the island of Rhode Island. Meanwhile patriot forces—Hancock's six-thousand-man Massachusetts militia and Sullivan's four thousand Continental Army soldiers—were to attack by land from the northeast, trapping the British garrison in a deadly vise. It was to be a quick campaign, and indeed would have to be. Most of Hancock's militia were farmers who had enlisted for only fifteen days so that they could return to their fields to harvest their crops.

Hancock arrived in Boston on July 16 and prepared to lead his men into battle—believing he would actually know what to do when he got there. For Hancock, preparation for battle meant proper dress and bearing, as well as proper arms, and it took him three weeks to organize his wardrobe and trunks. While other commanders gathered in Rhode Island to discuss strategy, Hancock supervised his servants as they packed and repacked his trunks, arranging his formal parade dress and battle dress one way, then another. He needed enough fresh clothes to last while aides galloped home to clean his dirty clothes and return them before he exhausted the fresh ones. On the evening of August 7 he was ready for war, having filled six carriages with clothes, bedding, tents, and other essentials, including an ample stock of Madeira and French wines.

The following morning Maj. Gen. John Hancock mounted his horse before his troops on the Common. It was one of the most exhilarating moments of his life. He sat poised on his coal black charger, his helmet plumes whipping in the breeze, sparks of light flashing off his golden epaulets and buttons. With trusting eyes trained on his every move, the Corps of Cadets and the rest of the militia awaited his orders, prepared to shed their blood in battle. At last he raised his sword and commanded the force to advance. Led by its fifers, the cadets, in splendid military dress, escorted Hancock's carriages out of town ahead of a long line of oddly dressed farmers, who staggered behind shouldering their hunting muskets haphazardly.

"What a noble example of heroism, as well as patriotism does this conduct exhibit!" James Warren commented. "We want a Homer or a Virgil to celebrate it!" [11]

Hancock rode into camp on the mainland northeast of Newport the following afternoon—a day late for the planned assault—with no idea of the battle plans. Bypassing all ceremony, an angry General Sullivan summarily ordered Hancock to await orders from Gen. Nathanael Greene, Sullivan's chief aide. Eighty-six flat-bottomed boats lined the shore to take them across the Seakonnet (now Sakonnet) River onto the island of Rhode Island. Without opposition, the Americans crossed the river and marched southward to within eyesight of the British fortifications at Newport, which were under the command of Brig. Gen. Sir Robert Pigot, the victor at Bunker Hill. Expecting d'Estaing to land Lafayette's forces at any moment, Sullivan's army opened fire. Hancock was ecstatic at the sounds of the cannon.

"We yesterday morning opened one battery on the enemy," he wrote to Dolly. "They cannonaded the whole day, with no other loss to us but one man killed and two wounded. As soon as the fog clears away this morning we shall open another battery. We have a strong report the French fleet is seen off [Newport]. If they arrive, our business will soon be over, and hope we shall soon enter New Port."[12]

But the fog did not clear away, and the French fleet never landed its forces. As d'Estaing was about to sail into Narragansett Bay, twenty-five ships materialized on the horizon to the rear, under the command of British admiral Lord Richard Howe, General Howe's brother, and threatened to bottle up the French fleet in the bay. With Lafayette's troops still aboard, d'Estaing put about and set out to sea to engage the British. Before either fleet could assume a decisive position, a gale blew up, reached hurricane proportions, and scattered them about for the next two days, dismasting d'Estaing's flagship and two other French ships.

On shore, the hurricane howled through the American troop encampments. The Americans were defenseless as the British fired away from atop their ramparts. Hancock's dreams of glories were bathed in mud, amidst "scenes of blood and carnage." His nightly slumbers were "short and uncertain," and he complained to Dolly that her messenger

> arrived with the things, but you forgot to send any gaiters or black cloth short boots. Pray send them by any person. I had yesterday a bad turn of the Head Ache but am much better this morning. I rejoice to find that our little Boy is much better. God grant he may speedily recover. My Dear, do you not intend to give me a Line, what prevents, I beg & I am very serious that you would turn your thoughts toward one in that way, I long to hear from you. . . . My Love to all in the Family as if nam'd & pray Mrs. Brackett & Sally to take the utmost care of our little John. Remember me to all friends. I hope soon to be with you
>
> God bless you my Dear, I am with unsurpassed love, Yours for ever, John Hancock[13]

The envelope was addressed simply, "To Mrs. Hancock, near the Common, Boston."

As the storm subsided, the French fleet had yet to land any troops, and three hundred Massachusetts militiamen whose fifteen-day enlistments had expired left—"notwithstanding all my desires and entreaties." Despite appeals to d'Estaing from Hancock and Sullivan—and even General Lafayette—French admiral d'Estaing remained too concerned for the safety of his men and ships to risk entrapment in Narragansett Bay. D'Estaing, the consummate French aristocrat, had a bitter exchange with Sullivan, who was a coarse, self-educated lawyer from the New Hampshire wilderness. The two developed so deep a personal animosity that d'Estaing announced he would sail his fleet back to France and urge King Louis to end French support for the American Revolution.

As the French sails dropped below the horizon, all but a thousand of Hancock's untrained militia fled in terror, leaving the American force too depleted to engage the British. The desertions left Hancock a general with no army, and on August 26 he conceded defeat and left for Boston. He recognized he was not a soldier. He had not devised a single strategy or originated a single order; he had done little but strut and plume himself and utter ineffectual bluster to prevent his men from losing confidence in his leadership.

"When he got to Rhode Island," wrote James Warren's close friend Stephen Higginson, a former Salem merchant and shipowner-turned-privateer,

> he took an eligible situation for his quarters—he appeared on the parade *en militaire*—he sallied out often for air and exercise and he sometimes approached so near the enemy, under the idea of reconnoitering, as to distinguish by the aid of a good perspective that the British flag was still flying at some miles distant. Martial musick and military movements alone delighted; and never was the fire of military ambition so conspicuous in any man's countenance and conduct. . . . But this flame was of short duration . . . the departure of the fleet, the roar of the cannon as they passed the lines of the enemy, and the smell of powder . . . was too much for our hero to support. He resolved to return home

... he fancied that the fleet had gone to Boston and could not refit in his absence.[14]

James Warren, for once, had to keep his mouth shut. After the General Court appointed him a major general, he pleaded illness and refused even to go to the Rhode Island campaign. Nor was Higginson at the battle. He was simply another Sam Adams radical who continually assailed Hancock throughout his political career—never letting facts or truth stand in the way of his accusations and hatred. The *New York Gazette* published a parody of "Yankee Doodle" that lampooned the Newport campaign and included this verse:

In dread array their tatter'd crew,
Advanced with colours spread Sir,
Their fifes play'd Yankee Doodle do,
King Hancock at their Head Sir.[15]

Hancock was as aware as anyone—more so, perhaps—that he had not been an outstanding leader at Rhode Island, but he had not fared worse than many other inexperienced military leaders during the Revolutionary War. In fact, it was the refusal of the French to land their forces as planned—not Hancock's incompetence—that provoked wholesale desertions of militiamen. Censure for the defeat, he insisted in a letter to Jeremiah Powell, president of the upper house of the General Court,

must not fall upon us. . . . the expedition was undertaken in full confidence that the fleet and troops would co-operate with us. . . . I am exceedingly mortified . . . and could almost wish I had not been here to undergo such feelings, which I scarce before experienced.

I write this particular to you in full confidence that it will by no means be suffered to go into the newspapers. Any persons you may be pleased to show the letter to I have no objection, nor do I regard how publicly it is talked of, for the failure must center with the [French] fleet. But I beg that my name not be annexed to these particulars in the paper.[16]

Two days after Hancock left Rhode Island, Sullivan withdrew the remaining patriot force—his original four thousand, and one thousand remaining Massachusetts militiamen—under cover of night, while the French fleet sailed to Boston Harbor for refitting before returning to France.

The Newport disaster all but shattered tenuous Franco-American relations. Sullivan was furious at d'Estaing, calling him a royalist deserter; d'Estaing was equally furious at Sullivan for devising a plan that had almost subjected the French fleet and thousands of French troops to mass destruction and slaughter in an indefensible bay. He considered the patriots incompetent, amateur soldiers. As an admiral, a professional commander, and a nobleman, he refused to take instructions from a commoner. Like many members of Louis XVI's court, d'Estaing had mixed feelings about the American Revolution. Although eager to crush France's traditional enemy, Great Britain, he saw the American Revolution as a mob assault on monarchic institutions and feared—correctly, as it turned out—that it might provoke revolutions in France and other European monarchies.

Boston rejected Hancock's critics and welcomed him back as a hero. He responded accordingly, gathering his Corps of Cadets about him and riding through the city before a cheering, adulatory crowd that soon marched alongside—all to the utter dismay of James Warren.

"General Hancock returned last evening," Warren wrote to Samuel Adams. "It is reported and believed, I suppose, that he is come to order back the French squadron. If it was reported he came to arrest the Course of Nature, or reverse the decrees of Providence, there are enough to believe that practicable."[17]

With his public posture reinforced, Hancock ignored his critics and began what he considered a task essential to patriot victory in the war: restoring and cementing military relations with the French. He now knew from firsthand experience that the amateur soldiers of the patriot armies were no match for British professionals. The assault on Newport had failed because relations with the French had failed, and he realized the Revolution itself would fail without wholehearted French cooperation and support.

Memories of the French and Indian War had not faded in Massachusetts, however. Boston still hated the French and everything to do with Roman Catholicism. Boston parents disciplined their children with terrifying tales of black-robed French priests and their savage Indian friends carrying off bad little boys and girls into the forest. Twice in his lifetime Hancock had seen colonists march off to war against the French. Indeed, the House of Hancock had been built on a foundation of profits from war materiel his uncle Thomas provided British forces fighting the French. So, when d'Estaing's fleet—a dozen ships in all—put into Boston harbor for refitting, Boston's shipfitters, even the unemployed, claimed they had too much work and that refitting the French ships could take months or even years. They reinforced their assertions by assaulting any French sailor who dared step ashore.

When Hancock had been president of Congress, however, he had supported the French alliance, and he now acted to strengthen it. He urged Washington to thank d'Estaing for his abortive efforts at Newport and to keep Sullivan out of contact with the French. Aware of Sullivan's abrasive conduct toward d'Estaing, Congress passed a resolution that, in the face of the gale and superior British force, d'Estaing had "behaved as a brave and wise officer." Meanwhile, Hancock rode down to Boston Harbor in his resplendent chariot to invite d'Estaing and Lafayette to a formal dinner at Hancock House. Dressed in purple velvet as brilliantly as any French aristocrat, he was piped aboard the admiral's flagship and personally delivered the invitations. They were accepted.

He sent his chariot to bring d'Estaing and Lafayette to Beacon Hill to dinner in the glittering new banquet hall. A servant stood behind each chair to serve guests individually. The settings displayed the finest china, crystal, and silver, and Hancock's cellar provided the finest French wines the comte had ever savored. On entering Hancock House, Lafayette immediately noticed a portrait of George Washington that Hancock had ordered painted in Philadelphia. A deep admirer of Washington, he asked Hancock whether he had a copy. Hancock did, indeed, have one ready to present—as a token of friendship to Admiral d'Estaing, Lafayette's senior. After an awkward moment, Hancock promised another copy for Lafayette and presented the copy to d'Estaing as planned. The admiral was deeply moved. Lafayette said he had never seen "a man so glad to possess a sweetheart's picture as the admiral was to have this one of Washington." D'Estaing fired a royal salute as the portrait was hoisted aboard his flagship, and he hung it above the mantel in his cabin and framed it with laurel wreaths.

In the days that followed, Hancock interceded with ship-fitters, and as they began refitting the French fleet, Hancock and Dolly refitted Franco-American friendships and reinforced French loyalty to America's War of Independence. Night after night they held lavish dinner parties for French officers, with virtually every officer in the fleet getting his turn to breakfast, dine, or sup at Hancock House. Costs of a single evening often reached £300—more than twice the costs of tuition for a four-year education at Harvard College. Hancock's servants killed, plucked, dressed, and cooked an average of three turkeys a day to feed the guests. His gardener kept a flock of 150 turkeys in the barn. As accidental breakage depleted the supply of china, Hancock ordered pewter plates as replacements. One day Hancock invited thirty officers for breakfast, "but the Count brought up almost all the officers of his fleet, midshipmen included," Dolly Hancock later recalled.

> Mr H. sent word for her [Mrs. H.] to get breakfast for 120 more, and she was obliged to prepare it as they were coming in to the house. They spread twelve pounds of butter on to bread, and sent to the guard on the common to milk all the cows and bring her the milk. She sent to all the neighbors for cake. . . . The Frenchmen . . . ate voraciously, and one of them drank seventeen cups of tea at the table.
>
> The midshipmen . . . made sad destruction with the fruit in the garden. The Count d'Estaing, however, politely said he would make it up to her, and told her she must come down to the fleet, and bring all her friends with her; and true enough she did . . . for she went down and carried a party of five hundred.

They were all transported in the boats of the fleet and stayed all day. The Count . . . asked her to pull a string to fire a gun, which, half frightened to death, she did, and found she had given a signal for a *feu de joie* to the fleet, the whole bunch of which immediately commenced firing, and they were all enveloped in smoke and stunned with the noise. Such a noise she never heard before, nor wishes to again.[18]

Late in September, Hancock sponsored a sumptuous reception at Faneuil Hall for the admiral and his officers to meet about five hundred of the leading citizens of Boston and surrounding communities. With Hancock presiding, thirteen-gun salutes accompanied successive toasts to the United States and the king of France. It was the finest affair ever held on American soil, according to Abigail Adams, and showed Hancock at his best, in his element—not as a soldier but as an aristocrat entertaining aristocrats in the most aristocratic manner. "Comte d'Estaing," Abigail Adams wrote to her husband, John, "has been exceedingly polite to me . . . I have been more desirous to take notice of them, as . . . they have been neglected in the town of Boston."[19] Even Warren was impressed and begrudgingly acknowledged Hancock's achievement in saving the alliance. "The disposition that at first appeared to cause an odium on the Count and to discredit our new allies," he admitted in a letter to Sam Adams, "seems to have entirely subsided and has been succeeded by the most perfect good humor . . . General Hancock has made the most magnificent entertainments for the Count and his officers, both at his own and the public houses."[20]

Hancock's reception established strong social bonds between Boston's propertied class and the French officers. As they were invited into more homes, they quickly integrated into Boston society and pledged to support America's Revolution. There were ugly incidents along the waterfront, of course—brawls and the like. A French officer was slain trying to intercede in one fight. But Boston was, after all, a seaport, and such melees were the normal consequence of every visit by ships from other ports. Of far greater consequence than the waterfront melees were the riches the

French landed on shore. Indeed, the huge French fleet brought Boston the most prosperity since the outbreak of the war. The French bought foodstuffs for their crews, timber for their vessels, and a wide range of other products, from clothing and paper to whalebone combs and souvenirs—and they paid for it with silver and gold.

At the end of October d'Estaing and his fleet prepared to leave, and Hancock sponsored a grand ball in the Concert Hall he had built, inviting more than two hundred leading citizens. Warren and other Sam Adams radicals refused to attend, scorning the affair as wasteful extravagance at a time when Congress could no longer afford to pay its troops. Hancock paid for the evening with his own funds, believing he was underwriting the success of the Revolution and investing in the future of the nation. Indeed, as d'Estaing prepared to sail, he gave Hancock his personal pledge—in public—that the French fleet would never again fail the Americans.

After Hancock's great accomplishment, an aging Boston Whig sought to mend the split in his party by writing to Samuel Adams in Philadelphia. "I most sincerely value you as my friend, but as much as I value you my country lies nearer my heart, and I greatly fear the differences now subsisting between you and your once friend Mr. H. may greatly hurt her interest. . . . Permit me my Friend to attempt . . . a Restoration of Friendship between two who once were dear to each other." Adams angrily rejected the proposal and demanded that Hancock ask forgiveness, adding that "it is not in my power to serve him. *He* is above it."[21]

Before the end of the year, British military operations shifted to the South, and on December 29 they captured Savannah, Georgia. Although winter skirmishes in the South proved destructive to patriot armies, the losses were indecisive in the overall war, and they gave the war-weary Northeast a respite. As Boston began rebuilding its homes, Hancock received a plea from exiled Tory Bostonians in Halifax, whose number had swelled to fifteen hundred. They asked to be allowed to return to Boston rather than face permanent exile in England. Among them was a Church of

England minister whose congregation, he said, was "Loth to quit this Shore and will be Loth, where there is a glimmering of hope of returning to their beloved abode in Peace and credit."[22] Bostonians had mixed feelings about the loyalists. Although some protested their return "from political principals," others argued that "the wealth they will bring will more than counter-balance the detriment."[23] Hancock had little sympathy, and presented his answer to the legislature:

> *Resolved*—that the Inhabitants of this Town will exert themselves to the utmost in supporting the Civil Magistrate in the execution of this Law, that those professed enemies to our Rights and Liberties, the first fomenters of our present Troubles, who have left this Country and aided the British Tyrant in his worse than savage measures, to deprive Americans of everything that ought to be held dear and sacred by any People, may not return and enjoy in common, the fruits of what our immortal Patriots, have toil'd and bled to procure us, and in some future time to be again base and cursed Instruments of British Seducers, in involving a happy People in confusion and bloodshed, in order to realize the reward, and private advantages held out to such Traitors by the enemies of America.[24]

On May 1, 1779, the Massachusetts legislature responded by confiscating the properties of every Tory who did "withdraw himself from the jurisdiction of the [Massachusetts] government, and thereby deprive it of the benefit of his personal services," and fled behind British lines for protection. The act was in keeping with a recommendation by the Continental Congress that the states appropriate the property of residents who had "forfeited the right to protection." Massachusetts issued a blacklist of almost four hundred loyalists whose estates were confiscated and who would be arrested and deported if ever again they set foot in Massachusetts. The other states published similar lists, while eight states exiled their prominent Tories and four disenfranchised all loyalists. Almost all the states expelled loyalists from public offices, barred them from the professions, and forced them to pay double or triple taxes. The Massachusetts blacklist included the great and the small: former governors and wig makers, wealthy merchants and mariners, distillers and shopkeepers, lawyers, doctors, and laborers. On the list were former governor Thomas Hutchinson and his two sons, former governor Francis Bernard and his family, the Olivers, Hancock's former partner William Apthorp and his family, and the former patriot turned traitor, Dr. Benjamin Church. The property of such persons was to "escheat, enure, and accrue to the sole use and benefit of the government and people of this state."

For Thomas Hutchinson, blacklisting proved a heavy blow. From the time of his arrival in England five years earlier, he had been homesick for his native Boston and had never despaired of returning to "lay his bones in New England."

"I assure you," he wrote to a friend in New England, "I had rather die in a little country farm house in New England than in the best Nobleman's seat in Old England; and have therefore given no ear to any proposal of settling here." There were many others in London who felt as he—so many, in fact, that they formed the New England Club, which dined weekly at London's Adelphi. Although loyal to the king and, indeed, sustained in England by a court grant, Hutchinson had continually advised reconciliation. A Harvard graduate, he spent his life in exile writing about his homeland, and his three-volume *History of the Colony of Massachusetts* became and remains a classic. A year almost to the day after Massachusetts blacklisted him, he died and was buried in Croyden, England, far from his native home. By then the state had seized his magnificent Boston mansion and the homes of both his sons.[25]

In the summer of 1779, American forces drove the British out of the areas surrounding New York City, bottling them up largely on Manhattan Island. In the West, the Americans defeated a combined loyalist-Indian force that had been marauding frontier settlements in Pennsylvania and New York. On August 15 Congress set forth its minimum demands for peace with Britain: independence, certain minimum boundaries, complete British evacuation of U.S. territories, and free navigation of the Mississippi.

On September 1 about three hundred delegates to the Massachusetts Constitutional Convention met in Cambridge, with

Boston's James Bowdoin, an ally of Sam Adams, elected president. To everyone's surprise, Hancock not only declined to serve on the committee to draft the new constitution, he made no objection when the convention asked Sam Adams and John Adams—who had returned home from France on temporary leave—to serve on the committee. Ultimately John Adams drew up the entire document, while Hancock purposely remained in the background, where no one could accuse him of shaping the executive branch he planned to lead. In the meantime he simply worked on building essential political friendships that would be far more important in assuring his election as governor than any words in the constitution.

When French ships called again, Hancock resumed his role as official host, writing to his brother-in-law Henry Quincy, who lived in Braintree, for help in finding "chickens, geese, hams, Partridges, mutton etc. that will save my reputation in a dinner . . . and by all means some butter . . . good Mellons or Peaches or any good fruit. . . . Can I get a good Turkey? . . . I dine on board the French Frigate tomorrow."[26]

While Massachusetts delegates debated state constitutional issues, Hancock spent a restful autumn and winter at home with Dolly, enjoying their son, John, who was now walking, babbling happily, and beginning to reach and grab at the precious bric-a-brac that lay about the house.

In December, he won reelection to Congress and election as "captain of the castle," which made him commander of the fortifications on Castle Island, the former Castle William. (Boston and other American cities had already started discarding royal names.) The task brought him into conflict with Paul Revere, Hancock's tenant and the man who had warned him of the British threat at Lexington. By then an artillery colonel on the island, Revere had allowed the fortifications to deteriorate, and when Revere returned from a disastrous expedition against the British to Maine, Hancock ordered him confined to his house and replaced him with a new artillery commander.

In March 1780, the convention approved the state constitution that John Adams had drawn up and sent it off to 290 towns across the state for approval. It reflected conservative eastern preferences for a powerful governor, with far-reaching unilateral appointive rights. Unlike most other state constitutions, it gave the governor veto powers over legislation, subject to override by a two-thirds majority of the legislature. The only rein on his power was an annual election, which would give voters frequent opportunity to discharge him if they disapproved of his service. The constitution also mandated strict separation of powers between legislative, judicial, and executive branches of government—again giving the governor an advantage over the other branches with his veto powers over legislation, and powers of pardon that could override certain judicial decisions.

Although it contained a bill of rights of sorts, it required all towns to maintain a Congregational Church and pay "for the institution of the public worship of GOD, and for the support and maintenance of public Protestant [read, Congregational] teachers of piety, religion and morality." It required all elected officials "to be of the Christian religion." Although it did not expressly prevent Roman Catholics from seeking elective office, it required all officeholders to take an oath "that no foreign Prince, Person, Prelate, State or Potentate"—that is, the pope—had any influence over them. The so-called bill of rights sections guaranteed free elections, protection against unreasonable search and seizure, trial by jury, freedom of the press, the right to assemble, the right to keep and bear arms, and free, though not unrestrained, public speech. (Most towns, including Boston, had strict laws against public blasphemy and profanity.) The declaration also listed among the "natural, essential, and unalienable rights" of mankind "the right of enjoying and defending their lives and liberties; that of acquiring, possessing, and protecting property."

The constitution also imposed property ownership qualifications, ranging from £60 to £300, to hold various levels of elected office. In a slap at farmers, it established proportional representation in the legislature, which favored the highly populated eastern towns over sparsely populated rural communities in the west. The constitution renewed state support of Harvard College, and it urged future legislatures to provide grants to schools for "the Encouragement of Literature" and diffusion of "wisdom and knowledge, as well as virtue." In mid-June, eastern urban voters overwhelmed western farm opposition and ratified the Massachusetts constitution.

Hancock was pleased with the document, knowing he could not be accused of having given the office he sought such sweeping powers. His only serious opponent for the governorship, James Bowdoin, had helped John Adams define the governor's powers. Bowdoin was a wealthy Boston merchant ten years older than Hancock. Like Hancock, he had graduated from Harvard and had inherited his business and his fortune, and after falling under the spell of Samuel Adams, he joined the Revolution to protect that fortune. Unlike Hancock, he had developed little political independence and showed little concern for the ordinary citizen.

On September 4 John Hancock won a stunning victory over sixteen other candidates, with eleven thousand votes out of a possible 12,281. Voters humiliated the Sam Adams radicals by giving James Bowdoin an embarrassing 888 votes. Fifteen independent candidates divided the other votes. Robert Treat Paine, a signer of the Declaration of Independence, won election as attorney general. The coalition Hancock had built proved all-powerful, capturing a large majority of votes from every economic level, occupation, and region. His title was governor, but under the vast powers that his enemies had written into the new constitution and the virtual independence that the Articles of Confederation conferred on each state, John Hancock assumed office as virtual monarch. James Warren mourned the results and warned Samuel Adams that the overwhelming vote would "render their idol [Hancock] . . . uncontrollable" and reduce the influence of those who "don't worship devoutly . . . very small, and you and I may have none at all."[27]

Nor could John Adams avoid venting his dismay at Hancock's election victory: "John Hancock! A man without head and without heart—the mere shadow of a man!—and yet a Governor of old Massachusetts."[28]

14

His Excellency the Governor

(1780-1785)

ON OCTOBER 25, 1780, at noon, John Hancock rode in his golden chariot amidst the cheers of the adoring crowd and the tolling church bells to his inauguration as first governor of the commonwealth of Massachusetts. He wore a crimson velvet jacket with gold trim and gold buttons and an embroidered white vest. His magnificently dressed Corps of Cadets, swords drawn, rode smartly, fifty in front and fifty behind, to the State House, where the General Court dissolved itself and a new constitutionally determined legislature took its place. Hancock's friend Thomas Cushing administered the oath in his capacity as president of the Senate, the newly named upper house of the General Court. As the cheers subsided, Hancock delivered a humble, one-minute inaugural speech that lacked all his usual fire. He pledged, simply, "to devote my whole Time and Services . . . in my Country's Cause to the utter Exclusion of all private Benefits, even to the end of the War, and being ever ready to obey the Call of My Country, I venture to offer myself. . . . I shall endeavor strictly to adhere to the Laws of the Constitution, and regularly punctually attend to the Duties of the Department in which my Country has been pleased to place me."

After his little statement, the secretary of the assembly stepped out onto the balcony overlooking the expectant crowd and introduced "His Excellency John Hancock, Esquire, Governor of the Commonwealth of Massachusetts." As roars of joy erupted, cannon fired thirteen-gun salutes from Fort Hill, Castle Island, and aboard the ships in the harbor. Hancock and his entourage then went to the Brattle Square Church for prayers of thanks and a short sermon, after which they began a celebration at Faneuil Hall that lasted until dawn the following day—much to the annoyance of Sam Adams, of course, who railed that Hancock was surrounding himself with "the Pomp and retinue of an Eastern Prince" not "consistent with sober republican principle. . . . Why should this new era be introduced with entertainments expensive and tending to dissipate the minds of the people . . . [and] promote superfluity of dress and ornament when it is as much as they can bear to support the expense of clothing a naked army. Will vanity and levity be the stability of government?"[1] James Warren echoed his master's complaints, charging that Hancock had infected Boston with "a plague of feasts and entertainments" that were "more suitable to effeminacy and ridiculous manners of Asiatic slavery, than the hardy and sober manners of a New-England republic."[2] Despite the disapproval of Adams and Warren, war-weary Boston continued celebrating peace with a "round of balls and glittering entertainments" long after Hancock himself had tired and gone to bed in his mansion on Beacon Hill.

At the time Hancock was elected governor, no candidate had won a majority in the race for lieutenant governor, and the election was subsequently thrown into the General Court. The Court's first choice was James Bowdoin, but he refused to serve under Hancock. The next choice was Hancock's good friend and close political ally Thomas Cushing, who gladly accepted, thus ensuring Hancock's absolute control of the executive branch of state government.

On October 31 Governor Hancock delivered his first address to the legislature—the progenitor of the traditional "state of the state" address that every governor now delivers annually.

Although he began in what now seem predictable words, at the time he uttered them no nation in the world allowed its people to elect its chief executive, and no people in the world had ever heard their chief executive address them as masters of their own government. Although Massachusetts was not the first state to ratify its own constitution, Hancock's words were a preamble to liberty and self-government in America and, just as important, in the world. It was a signal moment in history.

"Gentlemen of the Senate and Gentlemen of the House of Representatives," he began.

> With a sincere and warm heart I congratulate you and my country on the singular favor of heaven in the peaceable & auspicious settlement of our [state] Government upon a [state] Constitution framed by the Wisdom & sanctified by the solemn choice of the people who are to live under it. May the Supreme Ruler of the World be pleased to establish and perpetuate the new foundations of Liberty and Glory!
>
> Finding myself placed at the head of this Commonwealth by the free suffrages of citizens, which I most sensibly feel the distinction they have conferred upon me in this Election, I am at a loss to express the sentiments of Gratitude which it has impressed me: in addition to my natural affection for them, and the obligations they have laid upon me, I have now a new and irresistible motive ever to consider their happiness as my greatest interest and their freedom my highest honor.
>
> Deeply impressed with a sense of the important Duties to which my Country now calls me, while I obey the call, I most ardently wish myself adequate to those duties, but can only promise in concurrence with you Gentlemen, a faithful & unremitting attention to them, supported as I am by the advice & assistance of the Council, happily provided by the Constitution, to whose judgment I shall always pay the greatest respect, and on whose wisdom and integrity I shall ever rely. May unanimity among the several branches of this new Government consolidate its force, and establish such measures as shall most effectually advance the Interest and Reputation of the Commonwealth. This can never be done, but by strict adherence to every point to

the principles of our excellent Constitution, which on my own
part I engage most sacredly to preserve.

After concluding his preamble, Hancock addressed the practical aspects of government with a presentation of "the weighty
business that lies before you." With independence from British
rule came independence from British laws—in effect, an absence of
all law until each state enacted its own body of laws. Independence,
left unmodified, meant anarchy unless the legislature acted swiftly,
and Hancock proposed a practical, no-nonsense agenda. First came
defense. He urged the state to contribute men, arms, ammunition,
and money to Washington's Continental Army; to provide for a
larger state militia to protect the western borders of Massachusetts and a naval militia to protect her coastline and ports from
British assaults. He made an impassioned plea to improve the
state's common, or public, schools, which the war had left in ruins.
Calling education a bulwark of democracy, he asked the legislature to increase teacher salaries and revive the Massachusetts Bay
Colony law of 1647 requiring every town to teach *all* its children—
including servants'[3]—to read, write, and calculate. The law also
required towns of fifty or more families to provide a common, or
public, school and employ teachers to give every child an elementary school education.

"Our wise and magnanimous ancestors," Hancock declared,
"were very careful and liberal in the establishment of institutions
for this purpose, among which the University in Cambridge, and
grammar schools in the several towns, were believed highly
important. Every necessary attention, I trust, will be paid to the
former; and I cannot but earnestly recommend to your inquiry the
reason the latter is so much neglected in the State. The public
schools and our University at Cambridge have been no small support to the cause of liberty." (The legislature would respond by
mandating public school education in towns of two hundred or
more families, instead of the fifty families Hancock had requested.)

The governor asked the state to provide relief for widows and
orphans and to pass laws "for the suppression of idleness, dissipa-

tion, extravagance and all those vices that are peculiarly inimical to Free Republics." Inasmuch as Massachusetts retained Congregationalism as the official state religion, Hancock asked the legislature to pass a law requiring "due observation of the Lord's Day." (The legislature would respond by outlawing all vices and imposing fines of ten shillings to anyone who failed to attend church for three consecutive months.)

Hancock indirectly reminded the legislature of how Parliament had abused its powers and warned that "the separation which the [state] Constitution has made between the Legislative and Judicial powers, and that just degree of Independence it has given to the latter, is one of the surest guards to the PERSONS, PROPERTY, and LIBERTIES of the subjects of this Commonwealth, and accordingly you are, I am thoroughly persuaded, heartily disposed to support this INDEPENDENCE, the honor and vigor of the SUPREME JUDICIAL DEPARTMENT in its whole constitutional extent."

He concluded by establishing a precedent that continues at the national and state levels to this day, of the chief executive periodically proposing legislation for the advice and consent of the legislature. At the time it was a generous gesture from the chief executive of what was not just a sovereign state but, under the tissue-thin Articles of Confederation, virtually a sovereign nation. "In such measures as I have now mentioned and in every other tending to promote the public welfare," Hancock declared to the legislature, "you may always depend on my cheerful concurrence with you, and giving every dispatch in my power to the public business. And I shall from time to time seasonably communicate to you such information & proposals of business as may be proper to lay before you." He ended with a prayer: "May Heaven assist us to set out well, to brighten the auspices of our Constitution, to render it still more loved & admired by the Citizens of the Commonwealth & to recommend it to the whole world, by a wise and impartial, a firm & vigorous administration of it."

A few days after Hancock delivered his address to the General Court, William Bant, who had overseen Hancock's business affairs, died; and a month later, William Palfrey, whom Bant had replaced at the House of Hancock, sailed to France as the new American consul in Paris. Before leaving, he wrote to the man who had lifted him from a clerk's position to responsibility for a huge commercial enterprise and then high rank in the American government:

Sir

You have doubtless heard before this that Congress have done me the honour to appoint me their Consul General & Commercial Agent in France, for which place I shall embark in three or four days in a new ship of 16 guns.

It is a particular mortification that I am obliged to leave America without first visiting my family & native town & partaking with my country men in the joy so generally diffused on account of your Excellency's promotion to the chief seat of Government there, under a Constitution which you have so long & so ably laboured to establish. I feel it though at a distance & most sincerely congratulate you & my country upon the event adding my warmest wishes that your administration may be attended with satisfaction to yourself & happiness to the people over whom you are placed. I should be wanting in gratitude to your excellency did I not acknowledge the obligations I am under to you of a private nature, and assure you that I have at no time been unmindful of them. If providence preserves my health & smiles upon my honest endeavours, I hope I shall soon be able to make you ample compensation as far as interest is concerned without distressing my family. . . .

But there are obligations of another nature which I shall never be able to return. Your kindness to me through a long connexion & acquaintance, but above all your attention to my family in my absence has made me a bankrupt indeed, although I see no prospect of paying, am still desirous of increasing the debt.

Mrs. Palfrey will stand in need of every attention of her friends to make my absence supportable and I beg leave to solicit a continuance of your favours.

Palfrey said he would give his wife the choice of whether to risk the voyage to France with their two sons in wartime, and he then

Governor and Mrs. John Hancock at Hancock House,
from a portrait by Edward Savage. (*Corcoran Gallery of Art*)

paid his "respects to Mrs. Hancock, with a kiss to your dear little boy[.]

"Be pleased in my name to bid your Sunday evening with Adieu."[4]

Palfrey's ship disappeared at sea and he was lost. Hancock supported his widow and her two sons, and paid for a Harvard education for both boys.

Such generosity was possible because Hancock remained a wealthy man, despite having spent a large part of his fortune during the Revolutionary War. He received a salary of £1,000 a year as governor, and many times that amount in rents from his many buildings in the city, his stores on Hancock Wharf—the second-largest in Boston Harbor—and from wharfage fees. He also earned interest on £13,000 in bonds and considerable income from the sale of logs and land from his thousands of acres in Connecticut, New Hampshire, Maine, and Massachusetts.

Thus, Hancock paid for all his lavish entertainments with his own money, and despite Samuel Adams's criticisms, they not only served to provide him with personal joy and relaxation; they became an important tool in international diplomacy. Many foreign diplomats arrived in the United States at Boston Harbor, which remained America's most important port, and it was Gov. John Hancock, as head of a virtually independent state, who welcomed them officially and seduced them into becoming champions of American independence and approving loans of arms, ammunition, and money by their governments for the Revolutionary War.

After taking office, John Hancock faced two major tasks as leader of his commonwealth: to help the union win the War of Independence and to pay for the victory. In response to Washington's request for more men, he approved conscription of 4,240 more men for the Continental Army and imposed a mandatory three-year term of service, instead of allowing conscripts to select the length of time they wanted to serve.

Paying for the war, however, was far more complex than finding recruits to fight it—especially during an economic depression. Many of the unemployed stood ready to pick up guns, but neither the states nor the Congress in Philadelphia had enough money to pay them or buy their weapons, ammunition, and supplies. By 1781 Massachusetts was £11 million in debt and had to raise £940,000 more to pay for the war. The state had already contributed more men, money, and resources than any other state and had the highest taxes in the nation—poll taxes, sales taxes on liquor and consumer goods, import duties, and property taxes. All had their harshest effects on the poor and middle class, with farmers paying one-third of their income in taxes. Making matters worse for farmers, many of their fields were "farmed out" by overplanting, and barren of nutrients. With no knowledge of land conservation, farmers produced and earned less, while paying ever higher taxes.

Adding still more economic misery was the collapse in the value of paper money. Congress had printed $241 million in continental dollars, and the states had collectively printed nearly $210 million in thirteen different types of state currencies, whose values ranged from about one-third face value in-state to next to nothing out of state. The value of continentals, which Congress hoped would serve as universally acceptable currency, fell to a hundredth of their face value. A paper dollar bought only a penny's worth of goods, and the phrase "not worth a continental" entered everyday speech. Sam Adams complained to all who would listen that he had spent $2,000 in continentals to buy a $20 suit of clothes.

The high property taxes, the decline in farm production, and the drop in the purchasing power of paper currency combined to drive farmers into debt. Some sold their lands at whatever price they could get; others simply gathered up whatever possessions and livestock they could and fled before the sheriff appeared to haul them to jail for nonpayment of debts. Land speculators—many of them sitting in the legislature in Boston raising taxes—snapped up lands at bargain prices and made fortunes reselling them to gullible immigrants who expected the barren farms to yield a bounty of riches.

In 1781 farmer outrage exploded into rioting in the western part of Massachusetts. Hancock could easily have used his powers to establish tyranny, but he limited the use of those powers to maintain public order—and nothing more. He had little choice but to order those who incited riots sent to jail, but instead of repeating the errors of parliamentary leaders, he restored peace to Massachusetts farmlands by forbidding the jailing of farmers too poor to pay taxes. They would never be able to pay taxes sitting in jail, he said, instead of working their fields.

His sympathy for beleaguered farmers grew fervent after overzealous tax collectors seized more than two thousand acres of his own wilderness holdings in New Hampshire for nonpayment of property taxes. They had no obligation to notify him out of state—New Hampshire was, in effect, in a separate nation—and he had failed to manage his properties as he had when the House of Hancock had employees to visit all properties periodically and attend to such matters. Moreover, he risked further losses if he failed to pay overdue taxes on other properties. With most of his cash tied up in other investments, he hired a professional debt collector to demand immediate repayment of debts for purchases from Hancock retail stores before the battle of Lexington. One letter went to Hancock's bitter political enemy James Warren, who obsequiously asked Hancock to forgive the interest on the debt. As usual, the generous Hancock agreed—only to have Warren respond with only partial payment. The bill collector sent an angry rejoinder: "The Governor thinks this Balance ought to have been Immediately paid him, as it has been done for years back and has not availed himself of any Consideration for your use of it." The debt collector also dunned James Otis, who was still drifting in and out of insanity in Andover, Massachusetts. He was struck and killed by a bolt of lightning before ever repaying Hancock.

By the end of August 1781, a combined army of nine thousand American troops and nearly eight thousand French troops lay siege to the encampment of British commander Lord Cornwallis at Yorktown, Virginia. On October 19 the British force of almost eight thousand men laid down their arms, all but ending any hope for British victory in America. Washington marched his army north and surrounded New York City, the last British bastion in the United States. Traveling with him was his close friend French general Lafayette, whom he dispatched to Boston to carry the news of the Yorktown victory to Governor Hancock. Boston erupted in jubilation, with bonfires on the hilltops and bells pealing all day and all night. Hancock hosted a gala feast on Beacon Hill for Lafayette, his old acquaintance from the battle of Newport.

In December, Governor Hancock traveled to Cambridge to invest the Reverend Joseph Willard as the new president of Harvard, which remained a public college, with the governor as ex officio head of the board of overseers. He delivered his twelve-minute speech in the perfect Latin he had learned as an undergraduate, saying in part, "*Alma mater nostra* . . . Our alma mater in some degree gave birth to that most recent revolution which is renowned throughout the entire world and she nourished that which has been born. She has taught her sons the nature of liberty and its price, she has taught them by what means to defend liberty and how to form a civil constitution relying upon principles that are pure and more free." After handing Willard the seal, charter, keys, insignia, and other symbols of office, Hancock declared, "Reverend Sir, according to custom I declare and openly proclaim to this most notable assembly, that having been duly chosen, appointed and installed, you are the president of Harvard University."[5]

In January 1782 Hancock stood before the General Court and officially proclaimed victory over the British at Yorktown. "With particular pleasure," he declared, "I embrace this opportunity to congratulate you on the important & glorious success which it has pleased heaven to crown the arms of these United States & those of our illustrious Ally in the reduction of York, & the surrender of Lord Cornwallis & his whole Army . . . an event that gives new lustre to the name of General Washington."

Two months later Lord North resigned as British prime minister, and his successor, Lord Rockingham, pledged to begin peace negotiations. In June, Benjamin Franklin, John Jay, and John Adams would begin preliminary peace negotiations in Paris with the British. Washington remained suspicious of the British, however, and wrote to Hancock for help in gathering military intelligence:

Newburgh May 8, 1782
Sir

As the plan of my Campaign must depend entirely on the means that are put into your hands, of which I have scarce a confidential knowledge at this time, and on the number of Enemy at their different posts; I shall be obliged to your Excellency (as the communication between Boston & Halifax is open to Flags which frequently pass) for the most accurate account you can obtain covertly of the Enemy's numbers at Halifax and its dependencies—Strength of their Works, temper of the Inhabitants and such other intelligence as may be usefull in a Military point of View and the same of Nova Scotia— I want if possible to have the whole before me at one time, that I may point my operations to such objects as I have means to accomplish[.]

Your compliance which I request and as soon as is convenient and you will very much oblige

Sir

Your Excellency's

Most obedient and

Most humble servant

G. Washington

Although Washington would not have to go to war again, the end of the fighting did not end America's financial troubles. Congress and the states remained deeply in debt. Congress asked the states to approve a 5 percent duty on imports. In the absence of foreign trade during the war, Americans had relied on local craftsmen to fill their needs for cloth, leather, iron, and similar items. With the end of the war, cheaper, better-quality imported goods began flooding the market and putting Americans out of work. Congress hoped that a tax on imports would not only provide income for the government but help American craftsmen compete and encourage growth of American manufacturing.

A champion of state sovereignty, Hancock feared that Congress, like Parliament, might eventually use taxation as a weapon of tyranny, and he urged the General Court to reject the new tax. Rather than see imports restricted and foreign commerce hurt, he joined merchants who called for a ban on British ships. The ban would force all imports and exports onto American vessels, thus expanding the shipbuilding industry and the merchant fleet and putting thousands back to work in both industries. The General Court rejected his proposal and passed the 5 percent impost that Congress had requested. Hancock refused to sign the bill, but rather than alienate the General Court by vetoing it within the five days allowed under the constitution, he allowed it to become law without his signature. His tactic was a clever political move that held together his coalition of moderates on both sides of the tax issue. He had not broken ranks with either group. As he had in 1781, he easily won reelection to the governorship in the May elections.

As spring turned to summer, Hancock's health deteriorated and he began muttering about retirement. He had "the appearance of advanced age, though only forty-five," according to William Sullivan, a friend of Hancock and a political ally in the Massachusetts House of Representatives. "He had been reportedly and severely afflicted with the gout. . . . Mr. Hancock was nearly six feet in stature and of slender person, stooping a little and apparently enfeebled with disease. His manners were very gracious, of the old style of dignified complaisance." Sullivan had called on Hancock at noon and was surprised to find the governor still not dressed. "He wore a blue damask gown lined with silk; a white stock; a white satin, embroidered waistcoat; black satin small clothes; white silk stockings, and red morocco slippers."[6]

Hancock spent as much of the summer as possible with his wife and four-year-old son, Johnny, at their summer home, on Point Shirley—which he had developed into a popular summer playground for Boston's aristocrats, across the harbor from Boston. His health did not improve, however. In the fall, a friend noted, "He has not been able to hold a pen."[7] Hancock remained bedridden for days at a time—congenital gout often felled its victims with intense joint pains and swellings for a week or more. Fortunately, there was little need for him at either the General Court or the governor's office. Boston was busy rebuilding and replanting. When he was able, he rode about town in his coach, stopping to talk to all, encouraging their work, lending his own money when appropriate, and even paying for some projects, such as the planting of trees on the Common. The town began building bridges across the Charles and other waterways to speed the flow of commerce.

On November 30, 1782, Adams, Franklin, Jay, and Henry Laurens signed the preliminary articles of peace in which Britain recognized U.S. independence and agreed to end the fighting and evacuate land and sea forces "with all convenient speed." The citizens of both countries were to settle their debts with each other, and Congress was to "earnestly recommend" to the legislatures of the states restoration of all loyalist rights and properties. The articles established the St. Croix River in Maine, the St. Lawrence–Atlantic watershed, and the forty-fifth parallel through the Great Lakes as boundaries between the United States and Canada, and they gave American fishermen and whalers the right to fish in their traditional grounds off Newfoundland and Nova Scotia and to dry and cure their catch on unsettled shores. France and Spain signed the articles early the following year, and Britain proclaimed a cessation of hostilities on February 4, 1783. On April 15 Congress ratified the provisional articles of peace and also proclaimed a cessation of hostilities. Ten days later, seven thousand loyalists sailed from New York for Britain—the last of nearly one hundred thousand whom the test acts had forced either to repudiate the king or to leave. When the loyalists arrived in Britain, the government there provided food and clothing to the needy, five hundred acres of land to the head of every household, and three hundred acres to every single man, along with building materials and tools. Loyalists in exile submitted claims against the American states to the British government, and an impartial commission eventually awarded them nearly £400,000, with about 10 percent of the total coming from Massachusetts, thus adding still more to its debt and tax burden.

On June 13 most of Washington's Continental Army disbanded. Within a few days hundreds of angry soldiers marched into Philadelphia to protest the worthless certificates Congress had issued to pay for their service. As the mob grew, Congress fled and did not stop running until its members reached the safety of Princeton, New Jersey.

The worthless paper dollars Congress continued printing were provoking outrage everywhere. At the end of 1782 farmers had renewed their protests in Massachusetts. In the western part of the state farmers stopped paying property taxes. Instead of rioting, however, they organized conventions to demand tax repeal and an end to property confiscation and jailing for nonpayment of debts. In Boston, craftsmen, mechanics, and manufacturers marched in protest against imports and demanded higher tariffs to protect their jobs. Soldiers, too, were in the streets, demanding overdue back pay and protesting payments in worthless continentals.

To add to the crises he faced at home, Hancock also faced a conflict with Southern states that demanded the capture and return of runaway slaves who had fled to Massachusetts. When Hancock refused, South Carolina took him to court, but the Massachusetts courts supported him and freed all blacks in Massachusetts jails awaiting return to the South. As he solved one crisis, however, another crisis invariably arose. At a meeting of Harvard College overseers in May 1783, the Reverend William Gordon, who turned out to be a political supporter of Sam Adams, charged that Hancock still owed the college £1,054 in interest on the cash and securities he had held in his custody while attending the Continental Congress. Gordon demanded that the college take legal action. As one of Harvard's most generous donors and ex officio chairman of overseers, the governor all but exploded with rage. He said his accounting showed that he had returned all funds and securities with interest. Moreover, if the wartime interest was less than that obtained in peacetime, Harvard should simply absorb that difference—the way every American, including himself, had absorbed losses in the cause of the Revolution. He not only threatened to end his gifts to Harvard; he threatened to remove the Palfrey boys he was putting through Harvard and send them to Yale. The trustees obsequiously backed away from Gordon's threat of legal action, and fearful that, as governor, Hancock would cut government funding, they tried to placate the angry patriot by inviting him to have his portrait "drawn at the expense of the Corporation and placed in the philosophy chamber by that of his honorable uncle." He angrily snubbed their request but never let his personal anger interfere with his obligations as governor to provide financial support for what was then the state's only public college.

"However illiberal the Treatment I have met with from some of the former and present Governors of the College has been," he wrote to Harvard president Willard, "it shall never operate in my mind to the Prejudice of the University at Cambridge. I most sincerely wish its enlargement; the present appearance of those Buildings is very disagreeable for want of a reputable Inclosure. . . . I wish to remedy this inconvenience." He asked Willard "to erect a Respectable Fence around these Buildings . . . & upon your . . . Transmitting to me the Bill of its amount, it shall meet with immediate payment."[8]

Personal relations between Governor Hancock and Harvard president Willard would improve substantially in the years that followed, as Willard later acknowledged: "President Willard returns his most respectful compliments to his Excellency the Governor, with his best thanks for his very generous and acceptable present of Madeira and a quarter cask of Sherry wine and two large loaves of sugar. The President wishes it was in his power more fully to express his feelings of gratitude to the Governor for his munificence and kindness."[9] Willard's feelings of gratitude did not, apparently have any effect on the college treasurer, who kept dunning Hancock for the rest of his life for the disputed interest from the Revolutionary War. His estate eventually settled the account for about £800, but the shortsighted treatment of a great benefactor cost Harvard a substantial bequest from one of its most generous alumni.

Early in December 1783, the last British troops evacuated New York, and General Washington and New York governor George Clinton returned to New York City. On December 4 Washington said farewell to his officers at Fraunces Tavern and began a triumphal procession to Annapolis, where the Continental Congress was meeting and where he resigned his commission to "take leave of all the employments of public life"[10] and return to his Mount Vernon plantation. In anticipation of Washington's retirement, General Hancock had written to his commander in chief: "After such services, which consecrate your name to all posterity, with what home-felt satisfaction must your future days be blest! Heaven crown them with every favor! May you long live, my dear General, and long have the joy to see the increasing splendor and prosperity of a rising nation, aided by your counsels and defended by your sword! Indulge me the pleasure to believe that I have a place in your recollection and still honor and make me happy in your friendship."[11]

With the war ended, Hancock, too, longed for retirement from public service. The conflicts he faced had sapped his strength. The people he served demanded tax relief, while the state and nation he served demanded higher taxes to pay their debts. He now understood the dilemma the British government had faced trying to meet the costs of the French and Indian War. It was more than he was able—or wanted—to handle. He wanted to spend time with his wife and five-and-a-half-year-old son, Johnny. Moreover, English merchants were reestablishing trade with the United States, and Hancock thought about rebuilding part of his business to provide a future for his son. With the Hutchinsons, the Olivers, and other Tory merchants gone, there would be little serious competition for a merchant of his experience.

"I have, for the past ten years, devoted myself to the concern of the public," he wrote to his loyal former captain James Scott in London.

> I have not the vanity to think that I have been of very extensive service in our late unhappy contest, but one thing I can truly boast: I set out upon honest principles and strictly adhered to them to the close of the contest, and this I defy malice to controvert. I have lost many thousand sterling but, thank God, my country is saved and, by the smile of Heaven, I am a free and independent man. And now, my friend, I can pleasantly congratulate you on the return of peace, which gives a countenance to retire from public life and enjoy the sweets of calm domestic retirement and pursue business for my own amusement. . . . I am determined, in the course of this month, to resign my command of this Commonwealth and return to private life after the many

fatigues I have gone through. I leave the government under the public conviction that a much better man may be my successor.[12]

Hancock told Scott he was sending to London the debt collector who had worked so successfully for him in Boston, to collect prewar debts, and he gave Scott power of attorney to approach a London agent about a trading arrangement with Hancock. If Scott succeeded, he was to buy and command one ship to initiate the House of Hancock's tentative resumption of trade. As he sat at his desk writing, his merchant's blood began flowing again, and he found himself ordering a new "stone yellow" coach "to be lined with crimson velvet. Captain Scott will find inclosed Mr. Hancock's arms, and the motto subjoined" to be affixed to the doors. It was Uncle Thomas's motto, *Nul Plaisir Sans Peine*. Once he ordered the coach, he could not stop himself from adding to the splendor of his mansion. He ordered "six dozen very best pewter plat[e]s . . . oval or long dishes for Saturday's salt fish. You know how it used to be. My crest is to be engraved in each dish and plate." He ordered new furniture—"twelve stuff-back chairs" and matching sofa, because the old was "much worn and Mr. Hancock's son will want it."

In December he told the General Court of his plans to retire before the end of the year, but on Christmas Eve, with no explanation, he just as suddenly announced that he had changed his mind and would finish his term. His friend Lt. Gov. Cushing convinced him that a midterm resignation—"quitting"—would damage his public persona and his place in history. James Warren could not resist commenting, "His character is neither stained with ridicule or contempt—a privilege peculiar to himself."

As spring elections approached in 1784, however, Hancock showed no intent to retire, although ill health forced him to remain home more and cede many duties to Lieutenant Governor Cushing. Cushing was not up to the task, however. The economy was continuing to decline, and as state debts soared, the government was able to collect only about one-fifth of all property taxes due. One town sent in a plea to forgo tax collection because all its men had died in the war, leaving it with a population of widows and orphans with barely enough income to feed themselves. The state had no choice but to increase duties on imports, hoping that high tariffs—some as high as 25 percent—would discourage purchases of foreign goods and encourage domestic manufacturing. An article in Boston's *Independent Chronicle* tried to discourage trade with Britain, warning that "10,000 suits of clothes have this day arrived from Halifax; 10,000 more are hourly expected. Your trade is dead, your mechanics are beggars. Then rouze in the moment. Awake or be forever lost."[13]

To calm the growing furor over the return of loyalists, Hancock coaxed the legislature to repeal all previous acts against loyalists in favor of a new law limiting the ban on reentry to those who had borne arms against the United States or had been identified as traitors. All others might return by obtaining an annually renewable license from the governor.

Although he had no strength to campaign actively, Hancock easily won reelection as governor in the spring of 1784. He remained Boston's hero, and few voters did not believe that the state would almost certainly collapse without him at the helm. Although confined to Hancock House much of the time, he still knew how to entertain! When General Lafayette arrived for a visit, Hancock staged a huge civic welcome, complete with pealing church bells, cannon salutes, and a spectacular banquet for five hundred guests at Faneuil Hall.

Even in a wheelchair, Hancock continued to prove himself one of the nation's formidable mediators by ending the long-standing border dispute with New York. He quelled an incipient farmers' rebellion in western Massachusetts by demanding that the General Court end the requirement that property taxes be paid in specie. A poor harvest had left farmers with little enough to feed their families, let alone pay property taxes. Moreover, creditors—mostly speculators from Boston—were swarming like vultures, taking advantage of the bad times. They filed thousands of lawsuits—two thousand in Worcester County alone—against debt-laden farmers, sending many to jail, where they were helpless to protect their properties from court seizure and resale to speculators. Although the practice infuriated Hancock, he had no authority to overrule the courts.

The following winter, a coalition of Puritans launched a state-wide campaign to halt the decline in public morals by closing private drinking clubs. In Boston a new type of club had opened, adding dancing and card playing to the usual drinking. Called the Sans Souci ("without care"), it drew the immediate blistering fire of the Puritan reformers. "Sans Souci, Alias Free and Easy: Or An Evening's Peep Into A Polite Circle," raged the *Massachusetts Centinal* headline in January 1785—"An Entire New Entertainment in Three Acts." The article warned sternly, "We are prostituting all our glory as a people for new modes of pleasure ruinous in their expenses, injurious to virtue, and totally detrimental to the well being of society."[14] Sam Adams could not resist any opportunity to make Hancock's life miserable, and he eagerly joined the assault. "Why," he asked Boston in the *Centinal,* "do you thus suffer all the intemperances of Great Britain to be fostered in our bosom, in all their vile luxuriance?"[15] His old friends among the Masons at the Green Dragon ridiculed Adams as a dictator of morals, addicted to rabble-rousing and "reckless intrigues of disappointed ambition." Adams responded by citing John Calvin: "I know by their roaring I have hit them right."

The Sans Souci controversy proved one too many for the ailing Hancock. He decided to resign—a decision made all the easier after a particularly painful attack of gout while riding home in his carriage one evening. Servants had to carry him into the mansion, lay him on the sofa, and carefully cut the clothes off his swollen joints before they could carry him up to bed. On January 29, 1785, he sent his message of resignation to the General Court: "Sensible of my infirm state of health and of my incapacity to render that service and give that attention to the concerns of the public that is expected from a person in my station, justice to the public and myself loudly call on me not to prejudice the community but rather to promote its benefit; to effect which, I am obliged Gentlemen, to inform you . . . that I must at present give up all attention to public business, and pursue the means of regaining my health. Under these circumstance, I must request to be indulged with a resignation of the Chair."[16]

In the spring elections James Bowdoin, the Sam Adams candidate, ran on the issue of moral decay and the Sans Souci controversy. He defeated acting governor Thomas Cushing by a two-to-one margin. Samuel Adams could not contain his joy at what he considered his first political victory over his archnemesis. He wrote to his cousin John Adams, whom Congress had appointed the nation's first ambassador to London: "You will have heard of the Change in our chief Magistrate, I confess it is what I have long wished for. Our new Governor has issued his Proclamation for the Encouragement of Piety, Virtue, Education and Manners and for the Suppression of Vice. This with the good Example of a first Magistrate and others may *perhaps* restore our Virtue."[17] To his chagrin, however, Sam Adams himself lost to Cushing in the election for lieutenant governor. But his defeat could not dampen his joy and that of James Warren that John Hancock's political career had apparently ended at last.

15

Hancock! Hancock!
Even to the End

(1785-1793)

AFTER RESIGNING as governor in January 1785, John Hancock spent the next few months recuperating at home, occasionally dabbling in business but mostly enjoying his delightful son, Johnny, who was approaching his seventh birthday. Hancock read continually to the boy—from the Bible, of course, but also from Shakespeare, which he recited with a pompous rhetorical gusto reminiscent of his Harvard days. And he rewarded the boy's enthusiastic responses with bits of maple sugar or Chinese rock candy. Hancock limited business activities to passive real estate investments with syndicates that formed and dissolved like clouds and registered profits through arbitrage based on fluctuating values of paper money and silver. He gave up his fantasy of rebuilding the House of Hancock, however; his debt collector had created such ill will among London agents that they rejected Captain Scott's overtures to resume trading.

As spring's warmth soothed his aching joints, Hancock began venturing in public again in his golden coach, surrounded by his ever-present Corps of Cadets and their gleaming swords. His appearances so cheered Boston and the General Court that, to the absolute consternation of his political enemies, they reelected him to Congress and gave new life to his political career. James Warren accused Hancock of having feigned his gout for political reasons—to avoid confronting the hard decisions in Massachusetts—but recovering in time to win election to the Continental Congress. Warren predicted that Hancock would once again seek to be president of Congress but would wrap his foot in gauze and use his gout as an excuse to resign if he failed. "If everybody loves him as I do," said Warren, "they would save him that trouble and excuse him without the expense of a single piece of baize."[1]

The Reverend William Gordon, the Harvard overseer who had threatened to sue Hancock, wrote to John Adams in London, supporting Warren's contention: "Politicians conjecture [Hancock] is laying out for the President's chair . . . and that, if chosen during absence, he will answer to appearances; but that, if not chosen, illness real or feigned will prevent it."[2] In a particularly sinister attack, Gordon also warned Adams that once in the president's seat in Congress, Hancock would keep Adams in London indefinitely to prevent his return to state and national politics.

With no quorum in Congress, Hancock remained in Massachusetts throughout the summer, sitting in the sun with Dolly and his son at their family summer home, in Point Shirley. On November 23 a quorum of seven states convened in New York and reelected John Hancock to the presidency of the Congress of the United States. Congress was in a sad state, however. Its influence had so deteriorated it could barely lure enough delegates for a quorum, and the states routinely ignored almost all its recommendations. Some delegates believed that Hancock's skills in mediation could rebuild the collegiality and the relative unity and concord that had prevailed under his first presidency. Congress needed a leader of national stature to rally the states to pay the nation's war debts, and a majority of delegates believed Hancock was that man.

Hancock, too, believed he could restore order in Congress. After his reelection to the presidency, he wrote to Rufus King, a

Massachusetts delegate who was secretary of Congress, that he was "exceedingly honored" by his reelection and looked forward to leaving for New York within a few days. He asked King to find a suitably luxurious house, adding that he could not live in New York "without Mrs. Hancock," because "I have scarcely yet recovered from a late severe fit of the gout so as to have the free use of my hands."[3] King, a Harvard lawyer and close ally of Governor Bowdoin, replied with a deference that belied his political antagonism for the former governor. "The house is good and, although the furniture is not such as it should be, it will be within your direction, at the public charge, to make such dispositions and amendments as may be convenient. The servants, carriages, horses, etc., of the late President are retained and wait your coming. The carriage is very ordinary."[4]

By the beginning of January 1786, Hancock's legs had swelled so that he could not dress, let alone walk or get into his carriage for the long ride to New York, and he had to postpone his return to Congress. After months of further postponements and apologies, Hancock finally resigned the presidency of the United States on June 6, 1786. He was simply in too much pain to travel to New York and resume the duties of his office.

As Hancock rested on Beacon Hill, the Massachusetts countryside beyond Boston erupted in rebellion. Court-ordered jailing of farmers for nonpayment of debts had reached intolerable levels. The courts were confiscating thousands of farms and other assets and reselling them to speculators—many of them delegates in the General Court. In effect, the courts acted as agents of both creditors and speculators, by seizing debtor assets and then reselling them at a fraction of their worth. Some rural towns voted not to pay taxes; others simply burned their tax bills. In August fifty rural towns organized a convention in western Massachusetts, and after three days of angry speeches, more than five hundred armed men—former minutemen—marched to Northampton to prevent the court from sitting and ordering more farms seized. Led by farmer Daniel Shays, who had been a captain at Lexington, Bunker Hill, Ticonderoga, and Saratoga, the farmers marched to Worcester a few days later and forced the court there to flee. The rebellion spread eastward. Courts from Great Barrington in the west to Concord all fled before the arms of the former minutemen. Protesters on both sides of the issue demanded the ouster of Gov. James Bowdoin and the return of John Hancock. U.S. Secretary of War Henry Knox, a former general and adviser to Washington during the Revolutionary War, warned that armed mobs in Concord were preparing to march on Boston. On September 26 Shays marched his force to the Supreme Court in Springfield. Governor Bowdoin, the former merchant, sent the forty-four-hundred-man state militia to confront Shays, and after a bloodless standoff, both sides agreed to withdraw after the court agreed to adjourn. With almost all the state's courts in recess and tax collectors too frightened to appear in public, the flow of funds to the state treasury dried up, and the governor seemed powerless to end the economic and social anarchy.

In January 1787, Shays's forces were running out of ammunition, and he led a desperate assault on the Springfield arsenal with a force of twelve hundred. Gen. Benjamin Lincoln, who had helped defeat Burgoyne at Saratoga, routed the farmers. Although Shays fled to New Hampshire, Lincoln captured the other leaders of the rebellion and sentenced them to death for treason, with Samuel Adams, of all people, leading the applause. The man who had faced arrest and execution for rebellion against oppressive British taxation now demanded death for those rebelling against oppressive taxation by his own government. Looking back on Shays's Rebellion, Adams later declared, "The man who dares to rebel against the laws of a republic ought to suffer death."[5]

ON JANUARY 27, two weeks after John Hancock had celebrated his fiftieth birthday, his nine-year-old son, Johnny, took a terrible fall ice-skating and hit his head. He was carried home to Hancock House and died. On February 1 Hancock's coach carried the little coffin to its grave, while "the worthy gentleman and his amiable lady, in great affliction, followed in another coach" as Johnny's schoolmates walked behind. The boy's death devastated the Hancocks, who had twice lost an only child. After long days of prayer and mourning they began making vague plans to leave Boston on extended visits to friends in New York and Philadelphia, where they hoped to put their loss behind them.

IN MARCH the General Court responded to public pressure and offered limited pardons to all participants in Shays's Rebellion except Shays and two other leaders. Lt. Gov. Thomas Cushing appeared at Hancock House on behalf of the state's moderate political leaders to plead with Hancock to return to the governorship and restore calm to Massachusetts. Hancock was still too devastated by the loss of little Johnny to consider anything but escape from Beacon Hill and Boston.

"The obtainment of health is now my pursuit," he wrote to Secretary of War Knox in New York. "Journeying is much recommended to me; and, as my situation is totally deranged by the untimely death of my dear and promising boy, I have no affectionate object to promise myself the enjoyment of what I leave." He said he was "only waiting the roads to be good to set out with Mrs. Hancock . . . to New York and Philadelphia." He asked Knox to "engage lodgings in an airy Place as . . . will be suitable for Mrs. Hancock and myself and three servants. I wish for a decent place [with] two parlors; an handsome, well furnished chamber for us, and decent rooms for my servants, for they lodge and eat at home as well as I do myself."[6]

The Massachusetts public, however, would not let Hancock abandon them. They blamed Governor Bowdoin for the high taxes that had forced farmers into debt, while his merchant friends profited and his militia slaughtered American citizens demanding just redress. On April 2 voters turned Bowdoin and his friends out of office and returned a reluctant John Hancock to the governorship by a two-to-one margin. Hancock never set foot out of his Beacon Hill home. Even Hancock's bitter enemy James Warren conceded that the state might be better off. "I do not regret the change so much as I once should, though I am sorry for it," he admitted to John Adams. "If I used to despise the administration of H., I am disappointed in that of B."7 '

Some Bowdoin supporters seemed to agree. "Our elections are settled and generally to my satisfaction," said Charles Gore, one of Bowdoin's staunchest friends. "That Mr. Hancock is chief magistrate will at least tend to the peace of Massachusetts."8 After reelecting Hancock to restore order in the state, Massachusetts elected delegates to a convention in Philadelphia to restore order in the nation by revising the Articles of Confederation and creating a stronger central government.

Early in June, Governor Hancock displayed his deep compassion for the common man. To restore peace in the state, the aristocrat from Beacon Hill obtained full pardons from the General Court for all participants in Shays's Rebellion, and he put through legislation that prevented creditors from seizing clothing, household goods, or tools of trade as security for debt. He condemned the self-defeating custom of preventing men from earning their livelihoods by seizing their clothing and tools and jailing them for nonpayment of debts.

Hancock again incurred the inevitable wrath of Sam Adams. Once the farmers' champion, Adams now demanded nothing less than death for the leaders of Shays's Rebellion—much as Parliament had demanded his death for participating in the Boston Tea Party. Other radical Whigs echoed his call for retribution. Even twenty-year-old John Quincy Adams, already mesmerized by his old cousin Samuel, railed against Hancock for allowing men to "commit treason and murder with impunity."9

Hancock's policy, however, sought reconciliation and restoration of calm. To reduce the need for high taxes, he cut government spending wherever he could, reducing his own salary by £300 and contributing the savings to the state treasury. He also eliminated sinecures, including that of captain of the castle, the titular command of Castle Island that added £450 a year to the lieutenant governor's meager salary. Again Hancock drew criticism from his enemies, who never let the public good temper their attacks on the one man who, because of his wealth, could act without favoritism. John Quincy Adams charged that Hancock, with his "peculiar talent of pleasing the multitude . . . [is] offering to make a present to the public of £300. But I consider this a pernicious precedent. . . . For if one man gives up £300[,] another, fishing equally for popularity, may give more, and the chair of government may finally be offered to the lowest bidder."[10]

After cutting the budget, Hancock ignored his pain and traveled across the state to restore trust in government among farmers. As farmers cheered Hancock, the dwindling number of Sam Adams's followers—radicals now turned archconservative—railed at the governor and other moderates for freeing the "dregs and scum of mankind" after Shays's Rebellion.

On September 17, 1787, the Constitutional Convention in Philadelphia approved a new Constitution to replace the Articles of Confederation and create a new, stronger central government, with a bicameral legislature instead of the unicameral Continental Congress. The states would have proportionate representation in the lower house and equal representation—two votes each—in the upper house, or Senate. Congress would have powers to regulate foreign *and* interstate commerce, impose and collect taxes, borrow money, coin money, and organize military forces. The Constitution created coequal executive and judiciary branches, with the president to serve for four years and form a cabinet to execute laws. In effect, the Constitution gave the central government powers that the states had been unable to exercise successfully on their own.

For those who had fought the Revolution for local control, the Constitution seemed a return to control by a powerful, distant central government and a threat to state sovereignty. Three delegates, including Salem's Elbridge Gerry, an acolyte of Sam Adams and James Warren, moved to censure the Constitutional Convention for exceeding its authority. On September 20, Congress nonetheless resolved to send the Constitution to special state ratification conventions. The Constitution changed the political mix in each state, with those favoring ratification congregating in a "federalist" camp, while opponents grouped as "antifederalists." Both camps harbored strange bedfellows. Boston was overwhelmingly federalist, with most merchants, mechanics, and artisans favoring a stronger federal government because of the state government's disastrous handling of its debts and the farmer rebellions. In a meeting at the Green Dragon tavern, silversmith Paul Revere drafted a resolution adopted by mechanics offering their "warmest wish and prayer" for ratification.

The rest of Massachusetts, however, divided on the issue of ratification. Farmers did not like any government—federal or state—interfering in their affairs, and they opposed ratification. Elbridge Gerry returned to Boston hell-bent against the Constitution. "Beware! Beware!" he wrote in the *Massachusetts Centinel;* "you are forging chains for yourself and your children—your liberties are at stake." His mentor Sam Adams opposed ratification, but a former member of the Adams caucus, ex-governor James Bowdoin, became a champion of the new Constitution.

Governor Hancock refused to take a public stand, although privately he leaned slightly against ratification. While recognizing the need for stronger central-government controls over trade and mutual defense, he deplored the lack of a bill of rights—an objection that echoed through many state assemblies. The General Court set January 9, 1788, as the date for the Massachusetts ratifying convention to begin deliberations. Hancock, Samuel Adams, Warren, Bowdoin, Rufus King, and Gerry were among Boston's twelve delegates. It took a week for the 360 delegates to find a large enough hall with adequate acoustics, and when deliberations finally began, Hancock was nowhere to be seen; an attack of gout had made it impossible for him to attend.

"Hancock is still confined, or rather he has not yet taken his seat," commented federalist Rufus King a week after the convention had opened. "As soon as the majority is exhibited on either side I think his health will suffice him to be abroad."[11]

Facing long and bitter debates, the convention nevertheless elected Hancock president because of his mediation skills. The Adams-Warren-Gerry coalition led the charge against ratification, and with support from farm communities, they quickly built a majority of about 192 votes. Bowdoin and King led the federalists but were badly outnumbered, with only 144 delegates. To keep track of the debate, Hancock asked both camps to brief him each day at Hancock House. His own opinion shifted back and forth. As head of a sovereign state he did not want to see his own powers or those of his state reduced. On the other hand, a host of internal and external threats threatened to shatter the Union, and the Articles of Confederation gave Congress no power to defend it. Pennsylvania and Connecticut had actually gone to war over claims by Connecticut settlers in northwestern Pennsylvania; New York City had barred New Jersey farmers from landing produce from across the North (now Hudson) River; Pennsylvania, Delaware, Maryland, and Virginia were at swords' points over fishing and trade rights in Chesapeake Bay; and almost every state had conflicting claims over Western territories. Externally, the Spanish in Florida were sending Indian raiders to attack farmers in Georgia, and Spanish troops were poised for a full-scale invasion; and the British, who had yet to withdraw from their western outposts, continued to present a threat from the north, along the New England frontier.

Gradually, Hancock concluded the United States would not survive as a nation unless the states ratified the new Constitution. Delaware, Pennsylvania, New Jersey, and Georgia had already ratified, but the rest of the states would not do so without Massachusetts, which had started the War of Independence. The fate of the United States now depended on him and him alone. With Sam Adams and the antifederalists in the majority at the Massachusetts convention, only Hancock had the influence to sway enough delegates to support the Constitution.

On Thursday afternoon, January 31, 1788, his servants carried a pain-wracked Hancock "wrapped in his flannels" from his coach into the meeting hall. According to Elbridge Gerry, Hancock "took the chair of the Convention, and a scene ensued more on the character of a dramatic presentation than of serious and important business. . . . In a speech wise and plausible enough . . . the governor . . . announced the anxiety of his mind, his doubts, his wishes, his conciliatory plans."[12]

Hancock's speech was perhaps the crowning achievement of his life. It resolved all the bitter conflicts of the convention by recommending nine so-called Conciliatory Amendments—essentially the articles that would later evolve into the Bill of Rights. Most significantly, the first Conciliatory Amendment—eventually translated into the Tenth Amendment in the Bill of Rights—insisted "that it be explicitly declared that all powers not expressly delegated to Congress, are reserved to the States, to be by them exercised."[13]

"That a general system of government is indispensably necessary to save our country from ruin," Hancock proclaimed, "is agreed upon all sides. That the one now to be decided has its defects, all agree; but when we consider the variety of interests and the different habits of men it is intended for, it would be very singular to have an entire union of sentiment respecting it. Were the people of the United States to delegate the powers proposed . . . to men who were not dependent on them frequently for elections . . . the task of delegating authority would be vastly more difficult; but as the matter now stands, the powers reserved by the people render them secure, and until they themselves become corrupt, they will always have upright and able rulers."

Then, in one of the most dramatic moments in the history of Massachusetts, if not the nation, John Hancock declared, "I give my assent to the Constitution, in full confidence that the amendments proposed will soon become a part of the system. These amendments being in no wise local, but calculated to give security and ease alike to all the States, I think that all will agree to them."

Hancock then reached out to the convention and the people of Massachusetts, asking them to unite. Regardless of the outcome of the vote, he said,

> there can be no triumph on the one side, or chagrin on the other. Should there be a great division, every good man, every one who loves his country . . . will sincerely lament the want of unanimity. . . . The people of this Commonwealth are a people of great light, of great intelligence in public business. They know that we have none of us an interest separate from theirs; that it must be our happiness to conduce to theirs; and that we must all rise or fall together. They will never, therefore, forsake the first principle of society, that of being governed by the voice of the majority; and should it be that the proposed form of government

should be rejected, they will zealously attempt another. Should it, by the vote now to be taken, be ratified, they will quietly acquiesce, and where they see a want of perfection in it, endeavor in a constitutional way to have it amended.

Hancock looked out at every delegate—merchant, lawyer, doctor, artisan, shopkeeper, mechanic, and farmer—to impress them all with the import of the historic moment they shared. "The question before you is such as no nation on earth, without the limits of America, has ever had the privilege of deciding upon. As the Supreme Ruler of the Universe has seen fit to bestow upon us this glorious opportunity, let us decide upon it, appealing to him for the rectitude of our intentions, and in humble confidence that he will yet continue to bless and save our country."[14]

Once again John Hancock scored a remarkable, historic triumph, but Samuel Adams, still bathed in bitterness, could not allow the ailing governor his moment of glory. Just as a calm serenity and even joy had blanketed the delegates, Adams shot to his feet with demands for more amendments to the Constitution to further protect individual liberties. A mood of consternation and rancor once again engulfed the convention. Even his friends now assailed Adams for destroying the spirit of near unanimity that Hancock had created by his dramatic emergence from his sickbed. With the sixty-six-year-old Adams firing motion after motion for additional amendments, the ensuing debates postponed ratification for a week and cut the number of votes in favor of ratification. On February 7 an exhausted Adams finally ceded, and the convention ratified the Constitution unconditionally, by a vote of 187 to 168. It then voted to recommend Hancock's nine Conciliatory Amendments to the Congress. They were the last two votes cast by Hancock's loyal political ally Lt. Gov. Thomas Cushing. He died three weeks later, on February 28. Sam Adams, meanwhile, so alienated the federalists that they defeated his bid for reelection to Congress.

Back in his sickbed on Beacon Hill, Hancock had little influence on the selection of a lieutenant governor to finish Cushing's term, and the now powerful federalists in the General Court elected Gen. Benjamin Lincoln, a man of modest means, who had crushed

Shays's Rebellion. Lincoln asked Hancock to restore the £450 stipend normally accorded the lieutenant governor as captain of the castle, the sinecure Hancock had eliminated to cut state spending. Hancock refused—and added one more name to the list of his bitter enemies.

The following month, a popular referendum in neighboring Rhode Island rejected the U.S. Constitution, but the rejection made little difference. The Massachusetts vote had assured ratification, and in June, New Hampshire became the ninth and decisive state to approve the Constitution and provide the necessary two-thirds majority for its adoption. One by one the remaining states would fall into line, although Rhode Island did not ratify until two years later. In September Congress met to lay the groundwork for forming a new government. It set January 7, 1789, as the date for the presidential elections and March 4 for the First Congress of the United States to convene in New York. On October 10, 1788, the Continental Congress conducted its last official business.

Hancock's enemies tried to demean his brilliant speech at the Massachusetts convention, saying he had acted out of sinister motives. One historian even hints that Boston federalists had promised, in exchange for his support for ratification, to support Hancock for the presidency of the United States if Virginia failed to nominate George Washington. But Hancock could hardly walk, let alone travel about the nation. In any case, the people of Massachusetts were having none if it, and across the state they once again hailed Hancock as a national hero in words and song, adding these lyrics to the ever-popular "Yankee Doodle":

> *Then Squire Hancock like a man,*
> *Who dearly loves the nation,*
> *By a conciliatory plan,*
> *Prevented much vexation.*
>   *Yankee doodle, keep it up,*
>   *Yankee doodle dandy,*
>   *Mind the music and the step,*
>   *And with the girls be handy.*

He made a woundy Fed'ral speech,
With sense and elocution,
And then the 'Vention did beseech
T'adopt the Constitution.

The French journalist Jacques-Pierre Brissot de Warville, who would later die at the guillotine in his own nation's revolution, agreed with the popular assessment. "You know the great sacrifices he made in the Revolution," de Warville wrote after visiting Hancock on a tour of the United States in 1788, "and the boldness with which he declared himself at the beginning of the insurrection. The same spirit of patriotism animates him still. A great generosity, united to a vast ambition, forms his character; he has the virtues and the address of popularism; that is to say, that without effort he shows himself the equal and friend of all."[15]

Hancock's stature as a "friend of all" was never more evident than during the previous winter at the beginning of 1788, when the owners of a vessel in Boston Harbor lured three African-Americans on board and carried them to the French West Indies to be sold into slavery. The infuriated governor demanded that the French consul in Boston obtain their immediate release or face an embargo on French imports. The three men arrived back in Boston shortly thereafter.

From his bed in Hancock House, Hancock exacted retribution from his political foes in the spring of that year, when the people of Massachusetts reelected him to the governorship, crushing his opposition by a three-to-one majority—17,841 to 4,516. Gen. Benjamin Lincoln, whom Hancock loathed by then, ran for election as lieutenant governor. Rather than allow his return to office, Hancock somehow—under circumstances that remain unclear—healed the breach between himself and his old nemesis Samuel Adams and convinced the sixty-seven-year-old rebel to run for the office. Some historians speculate that, with his defeat by federalists in his race for Congress, reconciliation with Hancock and the lieutenant governorship represented Adams's last hope for political influence in Massachusetts and the new republic he had fought so hard to create. There is some evidence, too, that even Sam Adams had to admit, albeit reluctantly, that Hancock had been a remarkable governor, mediating disputes and bringing opposing interests together for the greater good of rebuilding Boston and postwar Massachusetts. Rather than battle the inevitable and lose all political influence, Adams did an about-face and made a public reconciliation with his bitter foe. "I am far from being an enemy to that gentleman," Adams would later explain to his wife, "though he has been prevailed upon to mark me as such. I have so much friendship for him as to wish with all my heart that . . . he is able to hold the reins of government with honor. . . . I am disposed to think that my fellow-citizens had upright views in giving him their suffrages . . . his will prove a happy choice."[16] Adams ran and won election as Hancock's lieutenant governor and did not utter a word of protest to an editorial assertion that "John is the first of the tribe, and Samuel is second."[17]

Hancock succeeded brilliantly in restoring the city's former luster and making it, without question, the most beautiful city in the New World. By July 1789, *Massachusetts Magazine* would describe the "enchanting view" of Boston and the surrounding area from Hancock's summer house across the harbor—"the Colleges—the bridges over Charles and Mystic River . . . the cultivated highlands of Brooklyne and the rugged blue hills of Milton and Braintree . . . cultivated villas—verdant hills—smiling hills, and laughing vales . . . upon the east those various islands which are interspersed in the harbor, from Castle William to the lighthouse. . . . This seat is scarcely surpassed by any in the Union."

But above all, Boston was at last a city at peace, and almost all Bostonians—even the old agitator Samuel Adams—gave John Hancock credit for the city's peace and its prosperity.

On June 17, 1788, Ambassador John Adams arrived at the entrance of Boston Harbor, having resigned his embassy in London after nearly a decade abroad. Always ready to seek reconciliation with political foes, Hancock sent a gracious note of welcome to the pilot at the lighthouse to convey to Adams. As Adams's ship sailed into port, cannons fired a salute from Castle Island and Boston's church bells tolled their welcome. Hancock's golden coach

View of Boston, 1789, from Breed's Hill, Charlestown, after John Hancock had led and helped finance its recovery from the war and turned it into America's most beautiful city. (*Bostonian Society*)

stood at dockside to carry the Adams family and servants to Hancock House on Beacon Hill, where Hancock greeted Adams with the wish that "you tarry till you have fixed your place of abode."

That summer John Hancock's health improved and he took his long-postponed holiday with Dolly—not to New York and Philadelphia as originally planned, but to Portsmouth, New Hampshire, where they gradually worked their way down the coast back to Boston. Friendly newspapers interpreted the trip as Hancock's opening bid for the vice presidency—a post many had been urging on him, to balance the Southern influence in the federal government if Virginia's George Washington became president. Early in the year, the *New Hampshire Gazette* had suggested, "Should the new Constitution be adopted, George Washington will undoubtedly be President and Governor Hancock Vice-President of the Union."[18] A Philadelphia supporter wrote, "We drink some excellent wine to Massachusetts patriots. Hancock is the deity for Vice-President."[19]

Aware of Hancock's illness, however, most Massachusetts newspapers seemed to lean toward John Adams, who had just returned to the United States after performing exquisitely at the Paris peace conference and as America's first ambassador to Great Britain. Although some devoted supporters campaigned for Hancock, there is no documentary evidence to support claims that he actively sought national office. John Adams, however, apparently took the efforts of Hancock's supporters more seriously than Hancock himself and wrote an anxious letter to Mercy Otis Warren, James Warren's wife, that Hancock was "ambitious of being President or Vice-President" and that "I stood in the way."

Another Hancock political enemy had a clearer view of the political landscape. "Governor Hancock and Mr. John Adams are considered as the candidates for that office [the vice presidency]," Gen. Benjamin Lincoln wrote to George Washington. "The latter [Adams] will be the man; for I cannot believe that the Governor would, under his present state of health, leave this government, even if he should be elected second in the new one."[20]

Voters throughout the colonies were all too aware of Hancock's physical distress. "Mr. John Adams will probably have all the voters of our State for the Vice-President's chair," predicted Dr. Benjamin Rush, the great Philadelphia physician and Hancock friend who had signed the Declaration of Independence. "Mr. Hancock['s] frequent indispositions *alone* will preclude him from that mark of respect from Pennsylvania."[21] In January 1789 the Revolutionary War general Henry Jackson, a staunch admirer of Hancock, wrote that Hancock "has not been out of his chamber . . . and is now confined to his bed with the gout." Three weeks later, he wrote that "Mr. Hancock remains very sick."[22] The severity of Hancock's illness was evident in the shaky autograph that had replaced his once-bold signature.[23]

Americans gave Hancock four electoral votes in the nation's first presidential election. None came from Massachusetts. He finished fifth among eleven candidates. After the elections, antifederalist Gov. George Clinton of New York approached Hancock to call a new constitutional convention to reduce federal powers, but Hancock rejected the proposal as "dangerous to the Union."[24] To celebrate John Adams's election, Hancock sent the Roxbury light cavalry to escort Adams from his farm to Hancock House, where the governor staged his usual lavish entertainment for members of the General Court and city officials to honor America's first vice president. Samuel Adams, for once, attended a Hancock-sponsored celebration, but General Lincoln, James Warren and his wife, and other Hancock foes refused to attend. They had no hesitation, however, to smother the new vice president with requests for sinecures. Some, like Robert Treat Paine, sought judgeships; others, consular positions overseas or even ambassadorships. Some were willing to settle for appointments as navy officers, and General Lincoln said he'd take whatever was available. By making his request public, Lincoln set off a deluge of requests from everyone who had ever known or met John Adams, including distant relatives. The new vice president had little choice but to reject all the requests. Americans, he said, must "make it a rule never to become dependent on public employment for subsistence." Let them "have a trade, a profession, a farm, a shop, something whereby [they] can honestly live."[25]

Hancock won reelection as Massachusetts governor in the spring of 1789, with Samuel Adams, by now a staunch ally, at his side as lieutenant governor. As Hancock's health deteriorated, Adams assumed an increasing number of public functions. When Pres. George Washington visited Boston on his triumphal procession through the Northern United States in the fall of 1789, Hancock sent troops to escort him across the state to Cambridge and Boston. In addition to military and civilian escorts, Hancock sent six servants to wait on the president personally, and he invited him and his aides to dine with the Hancocks at Hancock House that evening and remain overnight.

To avoid alienating Boston's highly charged political factions, Washington refused the invitation to stay at the governor's mansion, saying he had declined all such invitations to private homes and had slept in public houses during his entire journey. He did, however, "accept your Excellency's polite invitation to take an informal dinner with you."[26]

Hancock was too ill to meet Washington at Cambridge, and Samuel Adams went to lead him and Vice Pres. John Adams along the route into Boston, behind the Corps of Cadets, a marching band, and a long line of dignitaries. Delirium greeted the president as his stunning white horse strutted to a great arch the town had built at the State House. The model of an eagle perched on top, and a dedication stretched across: *To the Man Who Unites All Hearts.* Adams escorted Washington to the balcony overlooking the square where, nineteen years earlier, an angry mob had provoked the Boston Massacre.

Washington was apparently miffed at Hancock's failure to appear, even interpreting it as a test to establish protocol between the governor of a state and the president of the United States, and who should pay his respects first and where. "Under a full persuasion that he would have waited on me so soon as I should have arrived," Washington wrote in his notebook, "I excused myself upon his not doing it. . . . Dined at my lodgings, where the Vice-President favored me with his company."[27]

Told of the president's mood, Hancock sent Washington a note of apology the following morning and, in effect, pledged obeisance, thus permanently establishing the protocol between governors and the United States president for the rest of the nation. "The Governor's best respects to the President. If at home and at leisure, the Governor will do himself the honor to pay his respects in half an hour. This would have been done much sooner had his health, in any degree, permitted. He now hazards everything, as it respects his health, for the desirable purpose."[28]

Washington responded coldly: "The President of the United States presents his best respects to the Governor and has the honor to inform him that he shall be at home till 2 o'clock. The President needs not express the pleasure it will give him to see the Governor; but, at the same time, he most earnestly begs that the Governor will not hazard his health on the occasion."[29]

Hancock's servants carried him into his coach, his legs wrapped in layer upon layer of red flannel to try to ease his pain. They drove him to Washington's lodgings and carried him into the president's room, where, according to Washington, Hancock admitted it would have been a violation of proper protocol for a president to appear at the governor's quarters first. Stunned at Hancock's condition—he had not seen him since the Continental Congress in Philadelphia—Washington listened sympathetically as Hancock "assured me that indisposition alone prevented his doing it yesterday and that he was still indisposed; but as it had been suggested that he expected to *receive* the visit from the President, which he knew was improper, he was resolved . . . to pay his compliments today."[30]

The incident became a cause célèbre in Massachusetts political circles and the Massachusetts press for months thereafter, with Hancock's enemies saying he intentionally snubbed the president to exhibit the supremacy of the state over the federal government. Federalists insisted the president had acted correctly in snubbing the governor until the state leader demonstrated his fealty to the president. There is documentary evidence to indicate that Washington considered the incident a threat to the dignity and authority of his office, but there is also enough evidence to show that illness alone provoked Hancock's admitted faux pas. He was too strong a supporter of the Union ever to have purposely undermined the president's position. What his political enemies refused to recognize is that the man was desperately ill. As his nephew Edmund Quincy noted, when others came to dine at Beacon Hill, Hancock "did not sit at meals with his guests but dined at a small table by himself in a wheel-chair, his legs swathed in flannel. He was a martyr to the gout."[31]

He remained a martyr to his disease until his death, rarely appearing in General Court, and then only to make his most essential policy statements. He relied more and more on Samuel Adams and his aides to handle the reins of government, although he remained a vigorous, active policy maker, and in 1790 he appointed state attorney general Robert Treat Paine, a fellow signer of the Declaration of Independence, to the state Supreme Court.

Late in January 1791 he took a firm stand on the explosive issue of paper certificates—the equivalent of government bonds.

Congress and the states had issued millions of dollars in paper certificates to cover back pay and pensions for Revolutionary War
soldiers, but they had lost 50 to 100 percent of their face value.
During the economic depression that followed the war, veterans
had often sold their certificates at huge discounts to get enough
cash to clothe and feed their families, to buy seed to plant their
fields or tools to ply their trades. Speculators snapped up the
certificates at the lowest possible prices, gambling that the government would eventually redeem them at face value. Many speculators were themselves legislators and government officials who
stood to profit by enacting redemption legislation. A minority of
American leaders, including Noah Webster and John Hancock,
called for repaying the original certificate holders—the former
soldiers—the full face value in silver to let them buy back the certificates they sold to speculators at whatever prices speculators
had paid for them, plus interest. Speculator purchases would thus
have been treated as simple loans, entitled to legitimate interest
but not to the huge profits they had counted on.

"The original holders of Securities issued by this Government,"
Hancock told the General Court, "have received great injury, &
greater still will accrue to them unless, from your proceedings, it
shall be made evident to the world that the interest of the residue
of our debt will be provided for . . . & that a punctual annual Payment may be relied upon."

Despite his isolation on Beacon Hill, the people of Massachusetts returned him to the governor's office in the 1791 spring
elections. James Bowdoin offered only token opposition. Hancock
returned to the legislature in June to report on the state of the
state—a report that explained his continuing popularity among
voters: "I am happy to be able to assure you of the prevalence of
tranquillity throughout our Republick. Industry, Peace & good
order are continued: & Public Felicity every where enjoyed, the
intercourse of the Citizens of Town & Country is continued in
their usual satisfaction & advantage: And we have reason to hope
that under a mild & regular government, we shall continue to
enjoy the inestimable blessings of Peace, Liberty & Safety."

Even from his wheelchair, Hancock remained exceptionally responsive to public concerns, complaining that state courts "make so frequent calls for Juries" in major cities that jury duty interfered with the ability of many tradesmen to earn their living. Hancock said there was "a necessity to revise the Laws made upon this subject, & to shorten the time" required for jury service. Still fearful of incursions by British forces from the north, he said it was "of the highest consequence that the People, with their own Arms, should be able to defend themselves against all invasions of a Foreign Enemy . . . to effect this, they should be universally instructed in the use of Arms. A well disciplined Militia is the only Military force compatible with the People's liberty; & ought to be their main dependence for repelling attacks from a Foreign Enemy."

Despite his personal conflict with Harvard, he called on the legislature to increase its financial support of what still remained a public college and the state's only institution of higher education:

> The attention of the Citizens of the Commonwealth to the Education of the rising generation afford a most pleasing prospect of the future support of those principles for which the Patriots of our Country have nobly contended, & in maintenance of which so many of our Fellow Citizens have fallen in the Field . . . the maintenance of . . . a Republic form of Government . . . depends altogether upon light & knowledge, being universally disseminated in the body of the People. . . . The University of Cambridge was founded by our wise & patriotic Ancestors for this purpose; on the support of this depends all the other literary Institutions of the Commonwealth . . . unless some exertions are immediately made by you Gentlemen for its support, the light of our Country will begin to fade & its glory will be seen in its decline.[32]

Turning to taxes, Hancock came down strongly against lotteries as "a very unequal tax upon the People at large; the indigent & embarrassed part of the Community being in such schemes generally the greatest adventurers."

In July Hancock traveled to Cambridge for the 155th anniversary of the founding of Harvard College. He told the incoming class that the college "stands among the highest marks of the Wisdom and Patriotism of our Ancestors. . . . It is with you, young Gentlemen, who have your residence within Harvard's Walls, to add lustre to the brightness of your Country or to check her progress in glory with an interval of darkness."[33] From commencement exercises he traveled with Dolly to Newport and from there, westward along the coast to visit their old friends the Burrs, in Fairfield, Connecticut, where Aunt Lydia was buried. He arranged for a headstone to be placed at her grave.

When they returned to Boston, chilly autumn winds sent Hancock back to his bed in Hancock House, a martyr to gout once more. As Hancock's unremitting pain dragged on through the winter months, old Samuel Adams allowed his outdated Puritan morality to embroil both himself and the ailing governor in an unnecessarily bitter public controversy over, of all things, theater presentations. Adams urged Hancock to order the arrest of a troupe of traveling actors, under a 1750 law banning theatrical performances. The troupe had rented a stable the previous summer and converted it into a theater for performances disguised as "moral lectures." As long as the public seemed unconcerned, Hancock had ignored the troupe.

In November, Samuel Adams attended a performance himself and raced up Beacon Hill to demand that Hancock enforce the law. Although Hancock protested, he had little choice but to order the troupe's arrest for having committed an "open insult on the law and the Government of the Commonwealth." On December 5 the Suffolk County sheriff and his deputies broke into the theater during a performance and literally brought the house down, timber by timber, carrying off the distraught actors and the stable owner to jail. A Suffolk County grand jury refused to indict them, and at a subsequent town meeting, 75 percent demanded repeal of the act of 1750, calling it a remnant of "Feudal Tyranny" and "an encroachment of the natural Theatrical rights and the Rights of Man." They hooted Sam Adams from the hall when he tried to argue. Although he disagreed with Adams's views and had told him so privately, Hancock remained loyal to his lieutenant governor and threw the question to the General Court to decide the following year.

IN DECEMBER 1791 the Bill of Rights, incorporating John Hancock's Conciliatory Amendments, became a part of the U.S. Constitution, and in the spring of 1792 the public once again returned Hancock to office—this time unopposed. They prayed he would live to govern them forever.

> *Great Hancock's worth thro' every distant clime*
> *Shall be resounded to the latest time;*
> *Millions shall bless the day that they were born,*
> *When God-like Hancock did these States adorn....*
>
> *Seraphs his brows around with laurels grace;*
> *At God's Right Hand he'll take the sacred place;*
> *For deeds so generous and deserved renown*
> *Thy worth, Oh, Hancock, claims a Heavenly crown.*[34]

Hancock's state-of-the-state message to the General Court requested additional money for teacher salaries, for public schools of all levels, and as usual, for Harvard College, "the principal source of the Learning & Intelligence possessed by this Community." He demanded revision of the state's divorce laws, which gave the state legislature sole power to dissolve marriages—by special resolution. In July Hancock returned to Harvard for the fourth time to give a commencement speech.

"The Universities of Europe have paid great attention to the sons of Harvard," he said, "and the great and good men of our own state have ever considered the interest and honour of the Government as inseparably connected with that of this Seminary. They who love their country's happiness, will cherish this source of Science. They who delight in national liberty, will here culture the plant. And they, who feel a zeal for true natural glory, will make this University the object of their highest attention."[35] Student and graduate recitations followed Hancock's address, after which the university conferred degrees of doctor of laws on three of its own—John Hancock, Samuel Adams, and Massachusetts Supreme Court justice Francis Dana—and on Secretary of the Treasury Alexander Hamilton, who had graduated from King's College (now Columbia) in New York.

In November a smallpox epidemic sent Bostonians fleeing to the country. The General Court moved to Concord, and it was here that Hancock asked it to decide on "continuance or the repeal" of the act of 1750 "to prevent Stage-Plays, & other Theatrical Entertainments." (The legislature would repeal the law at the end of the year, and construction would begin on Boston's first legitimate theater in February 1793, on Long Lane.) After devoting half his speech to the question of theaters, he asked the legislature to create a state bank. In January 1793 he asked the General Court to strengthen laws against usury, but called for an end to punishments of "cropping and branding, as well as that of the Public Whipping Post," which he called "an indignity to human nature," and he suggested that "a sentence to hard labor will perhaps have a more salutary effect than mutilating or lacerating the human body." He also called for an end to capital punishment for burglary, saying, "Degrees of guilt demand degrees of Punishment in order to maintain the equity of the Government."[36] Hancock asked the legislature to subsidize expansion of agricultural settlements in the wilderness and to subsidize such private manufacturing industries as cotton and glass.

On September 18, 1793, John Hancock appeared before the General Court for the last time. His strength did not permit him to stand or even read his message, which he asked the secretary to deliver while he watched. It did not lack the fervor of his previous speeches. He devoted the entire address to a lawsuit in federal court that William Vassall, a Jamaican, had filed against Massachusetts for seizing his property under the confiscatory laws against loyalists. The federal court had ordered a marshal to serve Governor Hancock with a subpoena to appear in the suit. Hancock returned the subpoena unanswered, arguing that the federal courts had no jurisdiction over suits against the state by a foreigner. "No mention is made in the Acts of Congress of the suability of a State, nor is there any process against a state provided for in the Laws of the United States," Hancock declared, and he asked the legislature to petition Congress for legislation barring federal courts from interfering in lawsuits against the state by foreigners or citizens of other states. "Massachusetts is, and of right ought to be, a FREE, SOVEREIGN, and INDEPENDENT State!" echoed an article (which he may well have written, under a pseudonym) in the *National Gazette* of Philadelphia. (His petition eventually led to passage of the Eleventh Amendment to the Constitution: "The Judicial power of the United States shall not be construed to extend to any suit in law or equity, commenced or prosecuted against one of the United States by Citizens of another State, or by Citizens or Subjects of any Foreign State.")[37]

John Hancock would not live to see his constitutional handiwork, however. After the secretary of the General Court had read his speech about the Vassall case, Hancock himself, his hands trembling, his voice shaking, personally delivered these last, extemporaneous words to the General Court: "I beg the Pardon of the Honorable Legislature, and I rely on your candor, Gentlemen, to give this method of addressing you: I feel the *seeds* of mortality growing fast within me; but I think I have in this case done no more than my duty, as the servant of the people: I never did, and I never will *deceive* them, while I have life and strength to act in their service."[38]

Three weeks later, on Tuesday morning, October 8, 1793, Hancock awoke too weak to move or speak; his breathing was labored. Dolly sent for a doctor, but it was too late. John Hancock died less than an hour later, with Dolly at his bedside. He was fifty-seven. As word spread through the town, according to the *Independent Chronicle,* "the bells in all the public edifices in his town" began "tolling without cessation an hour; and the flags in town, at the Castle, and on the masts of the shipping in the harbor were half-hoisted."[39]

John Hancock lay in state in his beloved Hancock House through the week, as thousands of mourners from the entire state trooped slowly past his bier. Acting governor Samuel Adams declared the day of Hancock's burial a state holiday, and at two in the afternoon on Wednesday, October 16, more than twenty thousand people from Boston and the surrounding towns began a somber procession, four abreast, to deliver their governor to his grave. It was classic John Hancock: all the pomp and ceremony he treasured; the largest, most glorious, most sumptuous funeral procession America had ever seen—as usual, paid in full by Hancock himself, or at least his estate. Every military unit in Boston and the nearby towns, on foot and horseback, swords drawn, marched from the Common, half-time, to the funereal roll of the drums. The state's most important officials followed. Acting governor Samuel Adams—in his Revolutionary War tie wig, his cocked hat, buckled shoes, and ever-shabby flannel knee breeches—led members of the Council, who served as pallbearers. An artillery guard of honor followed, with the cannon Hancock draped in black. It was one of the four cannon that the patriots had stolen from the British arsenal by the Common at the beginning of the war—the first field artillery in the hands of the minutemen. Behind the Hancock came twenty-one carriages, with Dolly's luxurious coach in the lead. Vice Pres. John Adams followed with members of Congress, judges, members of the General Court, Harvard's president, overseers, and faculty, and Boston's selectmen. Only the mournful drumrolls and cannon booms broke the silence of Boston, as the hourlong procession took John Hancock to his grave beside his uncle Thomas at the Old Granary Burying Ground. Minuteman rifles sounded thirteen times, for the Union that Hancock helped create.

"The sorrow which now oppresses the public," said the *Independent Chronicle,*

> ought not to be increased by the force of eloquence, or heightened by the strain of imagination: But the public good, the rights of civil society, and the claims of patriotism, call for truth on the present melancholy occasion. The copious showers of tears that are shed, the awful solemnities of a funeral procession, and all the sublime tokens of respect, which are paid at the exit

of a patriot, are wisely improved, to call forth and to support, the principles of public virtue; and to establish the freedom and happiness of the community.

HANCOCK IS DEAD

He lived in the smiles of his Fellow-Citizens; and his urn is washed with the tears of a whole people, flowing from a native force, deep sorrow, lively gratitude, and sincere affection.[40]

Epilogue

SAMUEL ADAMS didn't make it to the burial ground. The march was too much for the old man. He began to stagger as the cortege passed the State House, and was helped to his home. In January he opened the next session of the General Court with this tribute: "It having pleased the Supreme Being, since your last meeting, in his holy Providence to remove from this transitory life our late excellent Governor Hancock, the multitude of his surviving fellow-citizens, who have often given strong testimonials of their approbation of his important services, while they drop a tear, may certainly profit by the recollection of his virtuous and patriotic example."

With lukewarm backing from Hancock devotees, Sam Adams won election as Massachusetts governor in his own right in the spring of 1794, but Boston was less than confidant in the old revolutionary's ability to govern. John Quincy Adams commented prophetically that Samuel Adams "may do less harm than some others, but he will certainly never do any good."[1]

Within months of his taking office, Boston mobs rioted again, with pro-French Jacobins aping the French Revolution and demanding the heads—and riches—of federalists, who they claimed were advocating "kingly government" under George Washington and John Adams. Although he was too old to take to the streets, Sam Adams felt the embers of revolution rekindling in his old belly, and in a move that ended a lifelong friendship with his younger cousin John, he publicly embraced the Jacobins, even calling members of the General Court "Citizen" instead of "Mister" and demanding that he be addressed as Citizen Adams. John Adams accused his cousin of having "cast the doctrines of the American Revolution into the sewer of French Jacobinism."[2]

With Sam Adams unwilling and his attorney general unable to halt terror in the streets, Boston citizens organized a force of their own to quell the riots, and in 1796 they crushed Sam Adams's bid to serve as a presidential elector. Boston wanted no more of Sam Adams and his riots and revolutions. They wanted to get on with the business of living—in peace. To everyone's relief, he announced he would not seek reelection to the governorship in 1797, and with few friends left to wish him well, he retired from office, a broken man. He spent the rest of his life shuffling aimlessly about his home, "a grief and distress to his family," according to John Adams, "a weeping, helpless object of compassion." Sam Adams died in Boston on October 3, 1803, at the age of eighty-one. His staunch friend James Warren died in 1806, at eighty-two.

His younger cousin John Adams served two terms as vice president under George Washington and won the presidency himself in 1796. He lost his bid for reelection in 1800 to Thomas Jefferson. A decade later, wearing the calluses of four years of public administration and perhaps viewing the Revolution through a lens of nostalgia, John Adams reevaluated his lifelong antagonist John Hancock: "I could melt into tears when I hear his name. . . . If benevolence, charity, generosity were ever personified in North America, they were in John Hancock. What shall I say of his education? His literary acquisitions? . . . His military, civil and political services? His sufferings and sacrifices?"[3] And five years later, he added, "I can say with truth that I profoundly admired him and more profoundly loved him."[4] John Adams died at the age of ninety-one, on July 4, 1826, only a few hours after Thomas Jefferson, with whom he had helped draft and had signed the Declaration of Independence.

The other signers of the Declaration of Independence from Massachusetts, Robert Treat Paine and Elbridge Gerry, both died in 1814. Paine retired from the Massachusetts Supreme Court in 1804 because of deafness and was eighty-three when he died. Gerry won election as governor of Massachusetts in 1810 and

1811, and as U.S. vice president in the second administration of Pres. James Madison, in 1813. He died in office a year later at the age of seventy.

John Hancock died intestate, leaving his wife, his brother-in-law Richard Perkins (his sister, Mary, had died), and his irresponsible brother, Ebenezer, to squabble over a relatively small estate. Hancock had spent most of his fortune financing the Revolution, rebuilding Boston, and establishing state institutions and charities—never, of course, neglecting the costly luxuries that were an integral part of his own and his wife's comforts and pleasures. The Revolution alone had absorbed about £100,000 of his resources for arms and ammunition. The court named Dolly the administrator of his estate, which amounted to less than £40,000. Dolly inherited Hancock House and the grounds on Beacon Hill, appraised at £5,000, and Hancock Wharf and all its buildings, worth about £7,000. She sold the pasture behind Hancock House to the town of Boston for £4,000, as a site for a new State House (now the west wing of that building). The rest of the estate was not divided up until 1797, but some of the legal disputes—largely over title to various tracts of land—continued for more than a century, into the early 1900s. Hancock's two nephews—Ebenezer's sons—tried to trade on their uncle's name by claiming they had inherited the House of Hancock. Like Ebenezer, they had little success and eventually limited their business to buying and selling cotton and tobacco.

Three years after John Hancock's death, on the twenty-first anniversary of his marriage, Dolly Hancock married Hancock's loyal ship captain James Scott, by then a widower, in the Brattle Square Church that Hancock and his aunt Lydia had built.[5] They lived in Portsmouth, New Hampshire, until Scott's death, in 1809. Dolly returned to Hancock House and lived there alone until 1816, when she sold the mansion and moved to a smaller house on Federal Street. She remained there until her death, in 1830, at the age of eighty-three.

In 1859 the Massachusetts Senate offered $100,000 for Hancock House, which it hoped to preserve as a memorial. For unknown reasons they never consummated the purchase, and in

1863 two Boston merchants bought the property and tore the mansion down.

Although the legislature had named a county in Maine[6] for him, John Hancock lay in an unmarked grave in Boston for more than a century after his death. On February 3, 1894, more than one hundred years after he died, the Massachusetts legislature passed a resolution appropriating "a sum not exceeding three thousand dollars . . . for the purpose of erecting a suitable memorial over the grave of Gov. John Hancock in the Granary Burying-ground in Boston."[7] At the dedication of the monument on September 10, 1896, a great-grandniece, Mary Elizabeth Wood, charged that even George III would not have been guilty of ignoring John Hancock for so long. As she unveiled the stone monument, she declared, "Shabby Commonwealth!!"

Notes

Abbreviations

BPL	Boston Public Library
DAB	*Dictionary of American Biography*, second edition
DNB	*Dictionary of National Biography*
EAE	*Encyclopedia of American Education*
EB	*Encyclopaedia Britannica*
HL	Houghton Library, Harvard University
MA	Massachusetts State Archives
MHS	Massachusetts Historical Society
NEHGS	New England Historical and Genealogical Society
NYHS	New-York Historical Society
NYPL	New York Public Library

Introduction

1. Ferling, 126.

2. John Hancock had no ties to the John Hancock Mutual Life Insurance Company (now John Hancock Financial Services, Inc.). Founded in Boston in 1862, the company chose the Hancock name for a variety of reasons: aside from his importance as a founding father, he was the first governor of Massachusetts, a great Boston philanthropist (who helped rebuild Boston after the ravages of the Revolutionary War), and an insurer of sorts, who personally underwrote the losses of ordinary citizens in natural disasters and in the perennial fires that swept through the city's narrow streets and alleys.

3. Frederick Wagner, *Patriot's Choice: The Story of John Hancock* (New York: Dodd, Mead & Company, 1964), 31.

4. William Sullivan, *Familiar Letters on Public Characters and Public Events* . . . (Boston, 1834).

5. Fowler, 245.

6. Brandes, 200.

7. John Adams to William Tudor, in Allan, ix.

8. James Truslow Adams, "Portrait of an Empty Barrel," *Harper's Magazine* CLXI (1930): 431–32; in Allan, ix.

Chapter 1. *The Boy on Beacon Hill*

1. The name Hancock—literally, "Hans of the cock"—suggests the family's rural origins, perhaps in the Calvinist Lowlands or Germany.

2. William B. Sprague, *Annals of the American Pulpit* (New York, 1857), 239; cited in Allan, 2.

3. Clifford Shipton, "The New England Clergy of the Glacial Age," Colonial Society of Massachusetts *Publications* 32:47–48.

4. John Hancock, "A Sermon Preached at the Ordination of Mr. John Hancock," in William Pattee, *A History of Old Braintree and Quincy with a Sketch of Randolph and Holbrook* (Quincy, 1875), 217–18.

5. Ibid.

6. Koch and Peden, 9.

7. John Adams to William Tudor, June 1, 1817, in Adams, X: 260–61.

8. *EAE*, "Dame School."

9. The Bishop's manse in Lexington, where John Hancock spent part of his childhood, still stands. Called the Hancock-Clarke House, it is a national monument. The Reverend Jonas Clarke succeeded the Bishop as pastor in Lexington.

10. Sears, 13.

11. Attributed to John Hancock's wife in S. A. Drake, *Our Colonial Homes* (Boston, 1894), 4; cited in Baxter, 69.

12. Thomas Hancock to Francis Wilks, June 24, 1737, NEHGS.

13. Thomas Hancock to Francis Wilks, December 20, 1736, NEHGS.

14. Sears, 17. As with several other quotations cited in Sears, I found no original source to corroborate this remark by Thomas Hancock; and Sears provided no bibliography or references. However, there is no reason to doubt Sears's scholarship or the authenticity of his work, which has been recognized as a masterpiece and, for its time, a definitive biography and source (albeit secondary) of information about the Revolutionary War. Thomas Hancock, John Hancock, and their contemporaries produced thousands of letters and notes that are at times bound in letter books at various libraries and historical institutions, or simply scattered about, mixed with other documents in places as far away as the archives of the French Ministry of Foreign Affairs in Paris. Rather than question the authenticity of the

extremely limited number of quotations I've borrowed from Sears, I'd prefer to say that I just never found them elsewhere and may well have overlooked them as I pored through the tens of thousands of pages I read in researching this volume. In any case, I have used only those that I believe ring true and that, based on my own knowledge of each character, reveal much about the man in a few, pithy words.

15. Ibid.

16. Allan, 30–31.

17. Sears, 17. (See also Pattee, *History*, in note 4 above.)

18. Opened on April 13, 1635, the Boston Public Latin School was the first school founded in the British colonies in America and remains today the second-oldest secondary school in America, after the Collegiate School, in New York City, which was founded when that city was Nieuw Amsterdam, a Dutch colony.

19. Some historians suggest that Boston Public Latin did not teach handwriting, spelling, arithmetic, and other elementary subjects, and that the students, including John Hancock, spent an hour each day after Latin School ended at a writing school run by Albiah Holbrook. See Fowler, 21.

20. Arthur W. Brayley, *Schools and Schoolboys of Old Boston* (Boston, 1894), 17.

21. By the end of his life, Thomas Hancock had acquired all the land now bounded by Beacon, Joy, Mount Vernon, and Bowdoin Streets.

22. Hutchinson, II:197–98.

Chapter 2. *The Merchant King*

1. "Indenture of Thomas Hancock," Bostonian Society *Publications* XII: 99–101.

2. Baxter, 7.

3. Ibid., 9.

4. *Boston News-Letter*, May 6, 1736, BPL.

5. Ibid., July 16, 1764.

6. Ibid., 24.

7. Ibid., 22.

8. Ibid., 20.

9. Here are the figures from a ledger sheet dated September 6, 1754, for the outbound leg of a traditional round trip by one of Hancock's ships:

	Cost	Sale price
Cod: 185 cwt. 3 st 6 lb @ 10/-	£92.18.-	
24 hogsheads, and packing @ 8/-	9.12.-	
	£102.10.-	£186. 7. 5

	Cost		Sale price
Mackerel: 164 barrels @ 13/6	110.14.-	@ 25/- to 30/-	215.10.-
Apples: 12 " " 5/4	3.4.-		11.3
Shingles: 28,250 " 10/8		@ 15/-	18. -. -
Hogsheads hoops: 2,000	[MS. torn]	@ 6/-	12. -. -
Staves: 1,000 & other timber		@ 4/-	4. -. -
	£239.16. 3		£436. 8. 8

The ledger sheet for the return leg produced a total of £354.1.3, for sixteen hogsheads of rum (£218.12.6); 115 ⅓ pounds of indigo (£28.17.6); and ten hogsheads, one barrel of molasses (£70.8.3)—plus £36.3.6 for the hogsheads themselves. From the gross profits for the two legs, Hancock had to deduct the captain's commission of 2.5 percent on purchases and 5 percent on sales, along with seamen's *total* wages of £32.5.10 ½ for the two months, seventeen days, they spent on board the ship at sea or in foreign ports. A third leg would have added another 50 percent to the total gross profits, without a commensurate increase in costs, especially if the third leg were a short one between two European ports. MHS.

10. Anne Hutchinson (1591–1643) was born in Lincolnshire, England, the daughter of a clergyman. She married and moved to Massachusetts Bay with her husband in 1634, where she began preaching salvation by individual communication with God, without regard to church or state laws. In 1637 she was tried for and convicted of "traducing the ministers and their ministry" and banished from the Massachusetts Bay Colony. She moved to Rhode Island and then to Long Island, New York, where she was massacred by Indians.

11. *EB,* "War of Jenkins Ear."

12. T. Hancock to Christopher Kilby, June ,1740, MHS.

13. Allan, 155.

14. T. Hancock to Capt. John Rous, December 24, 1741, HL.

15. T. Hancock to J. Maplesdon, November, 1739, MHS.

16. T. Hancock to Christopher Kilby, September 10, 1748, and February 15 and November 11, 1749, in Allan, 34–35; cited from American Antiquarian Society MS. Notes and Sources of H. A. Phillips.

17. *Deponite libros:* "Put down the books."

18. Henry F. Jenks, *Catalogue of the Boston Public Latin School* (Boston, 1886), 6.

Chapter 3. *The Merchant Prince*

1. John Langdon Sable, *Biographical Sketches of Those Who Attended Harvard College* (Boston: 1873–   ), 13:380–97.

2. R.O. and G.D., *New England's First Fruits* (1643), in *EAE.* The authors are unknown.

3. Ibid., "Harvard College."

4. The award of a master's degree was a routine honor that did not require any campus presence or classroom attendance and was available to any Harvard alumnus who paid the appropriate fee and presented a dissertation on any topic he chose at least three years after receiving his bachelor's degree. *EAE,* ibid.

5. Koch and Peden, 22.

6. Born in Boston, Winthrop was a descendant of John Winthrop (1588–1649), the first governor of the Massachusetts Bay Colony, and graduated from Harvard in 1732. His friend Benjamin Franklin, then agent for Pennsylvania in London, read Winthrop's paper on his observations of Halley's comet to the Royal Society in London. In 1771 the University of Edinburgh awarded Winthrop an honorary doctorate, and two years later he was awarded the first honorary doctorate in Harvard's history. *Webster's American Biographies.*

7. Sears, 42–43.

8. Koch and Peden, 18.

9. In 1767, thirteen years after Hancock graduated from Harvard, Holyoke did away with the tutoring system and replaced the tutors with specialists in each subject, making Harvard the world's first college to adopt the modern system of university education.

10. Morison, 115.

11. JH to Mary Hancock, May 1, 1754, in Sears, 42–43.

12. John Adams to William Tudor, June 1, 1817, in Adams, X:259.

13. Anne R. Cunningham, ed., *John Rowe: Letters and Diary* (Boston, 1903), 25–26, 116–17.

14. The church was torn down in 1869, and Brattle Square disappeared. It lay somewhere beyond the bottom of Tremont Street, past King (now State) Street, under the present-day Government Center near Congress Street. Bostonian Society.

15. The first, or original, Hundred Years War between England and France lasted from 1337 to 1453, although periodic fighting can be traced back to the twelfth century. Like the first, the second included many periods of extended, albeit fragile, truce, and the length of the conflict spanned far more than a century, with the first English attacks in the colonies dating back to 1614, when Capt. Samuel Argall's British forces wiped out French settlements on either side of the Bay of Fundy. *EB,* "Hundred Years' War," "Argall, Sir Samuel," and "Acadia."

16. Many of the Acadians whom the British dropped ashore in the South wandered toward French-speaking Louisiana, where the word "Acadian" was corrupted into "Cajun."

17. T. Hancock to Christopher Kilby, June 12, 1755, in Baxter, 132.

18. T. Hancock to Kilby, May 21, 1760, MHS.

19. T. Hancock to Kilby as letter of introduction for JH in London, May 23, 1760, MHS.

20. *Boston News-Letter,* June 5, 1760, BPL.

21. T. Hancock to JH, June 14, 1760, MHS.

22. T. Hancock to JH, July 5, 1760, citing disconnected bits and pieces of the following (*Hamlet* I, iii):

> The wind sits in the shoulder of your sail,
> And you are stay'd for. There; my blessing with thee!
> And these few precepts in the memory
> See thou character. Give thy thoughts no tongue,
> Nor any unproportion'd thought his act.
> Be thou familiar but by no means vulgar.
> Those friends thou hast, and their adoption tried,
> Grapple them to thy soul with hoops of steel;
> But do not dull thy palm with entertainment
> Of each new-hatch'd, unfledged comrade. Beware
> Of entrance to a quarrel, but being in,
> Bear't that th' opposèd may beware of thee.
> Give every man thine ear, but few thy voice;
> Take each man's censure, but reserve thy judgement.
> Costly thy habit as thy purse can buy,
> But not express'd in fancy; rich, not gaudy;
> For the apparel oft proclaims the man,
> And they in France of the best rank and station
> Are of all most select and generous chief in that.
> Neither a borrower nor a lender be;
> For loan oft loses both itself and friend,
> And borrowing dulls the edge of husbandry.
> This above all: to thine own self be true,
> And it must follow, as the night the day,
> Thou canst not then be false to any man.
> Farewell: my blessing season this in thee!

23. Ibid.

24. Baxter, 148.

25. JH to Ebenezer Hancock, August 30, 1760, HL.

26. Baxter, 148.

27. JH to Ebenezer Hancock, December 27, 1760, HL.

28. John E. Alden, "John Mein: Scourge of Patriots," Colonial Society of Massachusetts *Publications* XXXIV (1943): 596.

29. JH to T. Hancock, January 14, 1761, MHS.

30. JH to Daniel Perkins, March 2, 1761, MHS.

31. T. Hancock to JH, May 23, 1761, Letter Books, MHS.

32. JH to T. Hancock, July 11, 1761, MHS.

33. Jonathan Barnard to T. Hancock, July 14, 1761, in American Antiquarian Society *Proceedings,* n.s., XII (1899): 53; cited in Allan, 71.

34. Hancock may have claimed that he had attended the coronation of George III, who had then received him at court and presented him with a snuffbox bearing the king's likeness. A biography, *Ten Chapters in the Life of John Hancock,* published in 1857 by Clarence Burrage, secretary of the Bostonian Society, mentions the alleged claim. It would have been impossible, however, for Hancock to attend the coronation in London on September 22 and arrive in Boston on October 3.

35. Baxter, 144.

36. Ibid., 142.

37. David Barber to T. Hancock, April 24, 1762, MHS.

38. Notation, March 18, 1762, T. Hancock Letter Book, MHS.

39. Notation, August 2, 1762, ibid.

40. T. Hancock to Jonathan Barnard, January 1, 1763, MHS.

41. T. Hancock to Barnard, June 7, 1763, MHS.

42. Margaret H. Mascarene to John Mascarene, January 30, 1764, in Samuel A. Eliot, *History of Cambridge;* cited in Allan, 77.

43. JH to Barnard & Harrison, August 17, 1764, MHS.

Chapter 4. Of Stamps and Taxes

1. Will of Thomas Hancock, August 10, 1764, BPL.

2. Sears, 89.

3. JH to Hill, Lemar, and Bissett, November 12, 1767, MHS.

4. Sears, 91.

5. J. Adams to William Tudor, June 1, 1817, in Adams, X:259–60.

6. *Boston News-Letter,* January 3, 1765, BPL.

7. Fisher, 20.

8. JH to Barnard & Harrison, January 21, 1765, MHS.

9. JH to Barnard & Harrison, February 7, 1765, MHS.

10. Reverend Francis Thackeray, *A History of the Right Honorable William Pitt, Earl of Chatham* (London, 1827), II:31.

11. Knollenberg, *Origin,* 142.

12. Baxter, 226.

13. JH to Barnard & Co., June 23, 1764, MHS.

14. Gipson, 67.

15. *Boston Gazette,* April 4, 1763, BPL.

16. Hutchinson, I:86–88.

17. To this day members of Parliament do not necessarily live in the boroughs they represent, and in the eighteenth century, many came from

so-called "rotten boroughs," inhabited by fewer than 50 people, and pocket boroughs inhabited by a single noble family. As William Pitt charged in his demand for electoral reforms, "The house [of Commons] is not the representative of the people of Great Britain, but of nominal boroughs, ruined towns, noble families, wealthy individuals, and foreign potentates." J. Holland Rose, *The Life of William Pitt* (1911), I:107 n.

18. Soame Jenyns, in Brandes, 45.

19. Morris, 73–75.

20. T. Hancock to Christopher Kilby, August 4, 1755, MHS.

21. Benjamin Franklin, *The Interest of Great Britain Considered* (London, 1740); cited in Knollenberg, *Origin,* 89.

22. Johnson to Board of Trade, August 20, 1762, in Knollenberg, *Origin,* 89–90.

23. JH to Bernard & Harrison, April 5, 1765, MHS.

24. "Proceedings of the House of Commons concerning the resolution and the bill February 7 and 13, 1765," *Journals of the House of Commons,* XXX: 98–101.

25. Jackson Garth (agent for South Carolina) to South Carolina Committee of Correspondence, February 8, 1765, in Knollenberg, *Origin,* 207.

26. JH to Jackson Garth, May 13, 1765, in Knollenberg, *Origin,* 207.

Chapter 5. "Mad Rant and Porterly Reviling"

1. JH to Jonathan Barnard, April 18, May 21, and October 14, 1765, MHS.

2. Adams, II:238.

3. *Boston Evening Post,* February 14, 1763, BPL.

4. Ibid., March 28, 1763.

5. The original English Whigs derived their name from the Scottish Whiggamores, who opposed the court party in the mid-1600s. A British political group that sought to limit royal authority and expand parliamentary powers adopted the name around 1688. See *Oxford English Dictionary.*

6. *Boston Evening Post,* February 14, 1763, BPL.

7. *Maryland Gazette,* July 4, 1765.

8. Gipson, 87 n.

9. Adams, IV:6.

10. Hutchinson, II:117–18.

11. Proceedings of the House of Representatives, June 6, 1765, MA.

12. Governor Bernard to Board of Trade, August 15, 1765, in Gipson, 88.

13. *Boston Gazette,* April 4, 1763, BPL.

14. "Attack on Andrew Oliver of Massachusetts," Governor Bernard to Lord Halifax, August 15 and 16, 1765, Bernard Papers; cited in Knollenberg, *Origin,* 211.

15. Governor Bernard to Board of Trade, August 15, 1765, in Gipson, 991.

16. *Boston Evening Post,* February 14, 1763, BPL.

17. Cushing, II:201.

18. Fowler, 58–59.

19. Governor Bernard to Board of Trade, August 31, 1765, in Gipson, 93.

20. Ibid.

21. Governor Bernard to Board of Trade, August 31, 1765, in Miller, *Adams,* 68.

22. Ibid.

23. JH to Jonathan Barnard, April 5, 1765, MHS.

24. Ferling, 44.

25. Adams, II:259–61.

26. Ibid., X:260.

27. Baxter, 258.

28. JH to Jonathan Barnard, September 11, 1765, as cited in Baxter, 258.

29. Gipson, 100.

30. Ibid.

31. Francis Bernard to Thomas Pownall, November 5, 1765, Bernard Papers, HL.

32. JH to Jonathan Barnard, October 14, 1765, MHS.

33. JH to Barnard, December, 1765, MHS.

34. JH to Barnard, January 18, 1766, MHS.

35. *Pennsylvania Gazette,* February 27, 1766.

36. George Washington to Francis Dandridge, September 20, 1765, in John C. Fitzpatrick, ed., *The Diaries of George Washington, 1748–1799* (1925), II:426; cited in Knollenberg, *Origin,* 218.

Chapter 6. *A Hero by Circumstance*

1. Francis Bernard to Thomas Pownall, November 6, 1765, in Miller, *Adams,* 69.

2. Decades after both men had died, and nearly six decades after the Union Feast, Hancock's widow, only nineteen at the time of the Union Feast and living in Braintree, claimed that Hancock had organized the dinner—an impossibility, because he neither knew the thugs who led each gang, nor would he have deigned, or dared, approach them in their neighborhoods in his

liveried coach and four, with its silver-and-ivory coat of arms. Nevertheless, she insisted that he had spent the equivalent of $1,000 to pay for the Union Feast and that it marked his first burst of oratory as a Revolutionary leader. "He addressed them at table in an eloquent speech," she told an interviewer, "and invoked them, for their countrys [*sic*] sake, to lay aside their animosity, and fully impressed upon them the necessity of their united efforts to the success of the cause in which they were engaged. There is nothing more conducive to domestic unity than a sense of external danger. With the existence of this the whole audience now became fully impressed, and shook hands before they parted, and pledged their united exertions to break the chains with which they were manacled. The happiest results attended this meeting." Sumner, "Reminiscences."

3. Hutchinson correspondence, Bernard Papers; cited in Miller, *Adams*, 70.

4. JH to Barnard & Harrison, December 21, 1765, MHS.

5. Brandes, 53.

6. Grenville to House of Commons, December 17, 1765, in Knollenberg, *Origin*, 16.

7. Morris, 75.

8. English merchants' circular letter, February 28, 1766, MHS *Proceedings* 55 (1922).

9. Customs commissioners to lords of the treasury, March 28, 1766, in Public Record Office, London; cited in Baxter, 260.

10. Adams, II:259–61.

11. *Massachusetts Gazette Extraordinary*, May 22, 1766, BPL.

12. Ibid.

13. Wells, I:124.

14. *Pennsylvania Gazette*, November 27 and December 11, 1766 (with datelines, respectively, of September 20 and September 30).

15. Hutchinson, II:277.

16. Ibid.

17. Adams, II:179.

18. The name Tory originally referred to dispossessed seventeenth-century Irish outlaws. In the eighteenth and early nineteenth centuries it was applied to members of a British political group that (at first) supported the Roman Catholic Stuarts, but gradually broadened their doctrine to encompass support for royal authority—that is, the established order—over Parliament and the people.

19. *Boston Evening Post*, June 9, 1766, BPL.

20. JH to William Reeve, September 3, 1767, NEHGS.

21. For the complete text of Dickinson's *Letters from a Farmer in Pennsylvania*, see Paul Leicester Ford, ed., *The Writings of John Dickinson* (1895), 307–406.

22. John Dickinson to James Otis, December 5, 1767, MHS.

23. *Boston Gazette*, March 14, 1768, BPL.

Chapter 7. "Idol of the Mob"

1. Customs commissioners to lords of the treasury, May 12, 1768, in Knollenberg, *Growth*, 56.

2. Wells, I:186.

3. Miller, *Adams*, 144–45.

4. *Boston Gazette*, August 4, 1768, BPL.

5. *Boston Evening Post*, June 9, 1767, BPL.

6. *Boston Gazette*, July 3, 1769, BPL.

7. JH to George Haley, June 1768, in Allan, 113.

8. Washington to Mason, April 5, 1769, in Knollenberg, *Growth*, 59.

9. Miller, *Adams*, 144; Sears, 114.

10. Miller, *Adams*, 153.

11. *New Hampshire Gazette*, n.d.; cited ibid., 155.

12. Allan, 113.

13. Hutchinson, II:333.

14. Francis Bernard to Lord Hillsborough, October 1, 1768, and Dalrymple to Thomas Gage, October 2, 1768, in Colonial Office Documents; cited in Zobel, 181.

15. Fisher, 22.

16. *Boston Gazette*, October 26, 1768, BPL.

17. Gage to Hillsborough, October 26, 1768, in Gipson, 191.

18. *Boston Evening Post*, July 24 and 31, 1769, BPL.

19. Hutchinson to Thomas Whately, October 4, 1768, in Allan, 114.

20. Lyman H. Butterfield, ed., *Diary and Autobiography of John Adams* (Cambridge, Mass.: Harvard University Press, 1961), III:306; cited in Fowler, 100.

21. Baxter, 269–75.

22. *Massachusetts Gazette*, March 2, 1769, BPL.

23. For Burke's entire speech and the ensuing debate, see Sir H. Cavendish, ed., *Debates in the House of Commons During the Thirteenth Parliament of Great Britain, 1768-1771* (London, 1841–43), I:191–225.

24. Ibid.

25. Hillsborough to Bernard, February 20, 1769, cited in Zobel, 100.

26. Knollenberg, *Growth*, 69.

27. Adams, II:259.

28. *Journals of the House, 1768–69* (Boston, 1976), 45:197–98; cited in Fowler, 105.

29. *Newport Mercury*, September 4, 1769, BPL.

30. *Boston Chronicle*, October 26, 1769, BPL.

31. Ibid., October 30, 1769.
32. *Boston Gazette*, September 25, 1769, BPL.
33. Adams, II:226.
34. Hutchinson to Bernard, November 27, 1769, Bernard Papers.
35. Gipson, 197.
36. Adams, I:349–50.
37. Gage to Lord Hillsborough, April 10, 1770, in Zobel, 181.
38. Brandes, 83.
39. Zobel 189–294 and 346–56 cover these events in detail.
40. Ibid.
41. Ibid.
42. Ibid.
43. Adams, II:229–30.
44. Zobel, 202.
45. Ibid., 203.
46. *New York Public Advertiser*, April 28, 1770, NYPL.
47. *Boston Gazette*, March 12, 1770, BPL.
48. Pelham sent Revere an angry letter accusing the silversmith of printing the Pelham drawing without permission and depriving the artist of his just revenues "as truly as if you had plundered me on the public highway." They eventually settled their differences. Fisher, 23 n.
49. Committee to Pownall, March 12, 1770, in *Gentleman's Magazine* (London), April 1770.
50. *Boston Gazette*, May 21, 1770, BPL.
51. Zobel, 210.
52. Adams, VIII:384.

Chapter 8. "Tea in a Trice"

1. Gipson, 198.
2. Adams, I:348–49.
3. Ferling, 70.
4. Ibid., 188.
5. *Boston Gazette*, December 10, 1770–January 28, 1771, BPL.
6. Miller, *Adams*, 235–36.
7. JH to Ebenezer Hancock, January 11, 1771, BPL.
8. JH to Haley & Hopkins, 1771 (month omitted), in Allan, 122–23.
9. JH to William Palfrey, January 1, 1771, HL.
10. William Palfrey to JH, February 4, 1771, HL.
11. Palfrey to JH, February 15, 1771, HL.
12. Palfrey to JH, February 26, 1771, HL.
13. Hutchinson to person unknown, June 5, 1771, in Allan, 123–24.

14. Samuel Salisbury to Stephen Salisbury, March 19, 1771, in Allan, 159.

15. Hutchinson to Thomas Gage, December 1, 1771, in Allan, 125.

16. *Journals of the House of Representatives of Massachusetts, 1772* (Boston), 15.

17. Allan, 125.

18. *Boston Gazette,* May 12, 1772, BPL.

19. *Boston Weekly Newsletter,* May 27, 1773, BPL.

20. Hutchinson to Lord Hillsborough, June 15, 1772, in Allan, 127.

21. Boston Town Records, 93; cited in Fowler, 148.

22. Ibid.

23. Boston Town Records, 95–108, includes the complete text of "the State of the Rights of Colonists" and Church's "Letter of Correspondence"; cited in Fowler, 149.

24. Hutchinson, II:364–69.

25. *Boston Gazette,* January 11, 1773, BPL.

26. Adams, II:310–14.

27. Thomas Hutchinson to Thomas Whately, October 4, 1768, and January 20, 1769, in Fowler, 131.

28. Sears, 128–29.

29. Edmund Quincy to Dorothy Quincy, June 18, 1773, in Allan, 160.

30. Gipson, 219.

31. Fowler, 158.

32. Allan, 136.

33. Hutchinson to person unknown, December 3, 1773, in Allan, 138.

34. Allan, 139.

35. Attributed to Adams by Francis Rotch, part owner of the *Dartmouth,* in Knollenberg, *Growth,* 100.

36. Labaree, 141.

37. Valuation determined by the East India Company, in Knollenberg, *Growth,* 100.

38. Ferling, 92.

39. Knollenberg, *Growth,* 99–100.

40. Ibid., 100.

41. Allan, 140–41.

42. T. Maxwell, in Allan, 141.

43. Fisher, 25–26.

44. The Boston Tea Party and the hatred it engendered for all things English ended the consumption of tea as the primary beverage in the colonies and, later, the United States. Ironically, England itself produced no tea.

45. Tryon to Lord Dartmouth, January 3, 1774, in Gipson, 221.

46. JH to Jonathan Barnard, December 21, 1773, MHS.

Chapter 9. High Treason

1. *Rivington's New York Gazetteer,* May 12, 1774, NYPL.

2. Cabinet minutes, February 4, 1774, in Knollenberg, *Growth,* 104.

3. William Sullivan, *Familiar Letters on Public Characters and Public Events . . .* (Boston, 1834), 10 (Letter of 27 January 1833), BPL.

4. Ebenezer S. Thomas, *Reminiscences of the Last Sixty-five Years* (Boston, 1840), I:244, BPL.

5. JH, *An Oration: Delivered March 4, 1774, at the Request of the Inhabitants of the Town of Boston to Commemorate the Bloody Tragedy of the Fifth of March, 1770* (Boston: Edes & Gill, 1774), BPL.

6. Adams, II:332.

7. Knollenberg, *Growth,* 105.

8. Ibid., 108.

9. Miller, *Adams,* 300.

10. *DAB,* "Thomas Hutchinson."

11. Scott to JH, February 21, 1774, in Baxter, 285.

12. Committee of Correspondence Papers, June 24, 1774, MHS.

13. Knollenberg, *Growth,* 163–64.

14. William Palfrey to Samuel Adams, September 1774, in First Corps Cadet Papers; cited in Allan, 175.

15. Allan, 164.

16. Knollenberg, *Growth,* 168.

17. Ferling, 126.

18. *Boston Evening Post,* September 19, 1774, BPL.

19. Allan, 164.

20. William Lincoln, ed., *The Journals of Each Provincial Congress of Massachusetts in 1774 and 1775 . . .* (Boston: 1838), 643–44, BPL.

21. Ibid., 29.

22. Circular letter of April 20, 1773, in Knollenberg, *Growth,* 261.

23. [Samuel Johnson], *Taxation No Tyranny* (London, 1775); cited in Knollenberg, *Growth,* 261.

24. Ibid., X:197.

25. John Barker diary, March 6, 1775, in E. E. Dana, ed., *The British in Boston,* 25–26; cited in Allan, 168.

26. MHS *Proceedings,* 1st ser., V (1862): 211.

27. John Andrews to William Barrell, MHS *Proceedings,* 1st ser., VIII (1866): 401.

28. Lincoln, *Journals* (see note 20 above), 509–12.

29. Ibid., 748–50.

30. JH to Dorothy Quincy, March 25, 1775, JH Letter Book, BPL.

31. All four guns served in the Revolutionary War. Two fell into the hands of the enemy, however, and the Adams exploded, leaving the Han-

cock as the only one to serve during the entire conflict. It stands today at the Bunker Hill Monument with this inscription attached:

THE HANCOCK:

SACRED TO LIBERTY.

This is one of four cannon which constituted the
whole train of Field Artillery possessed by the
British colonies of North America
at the commencement of the war on the
19th of April, 1775.

THIS CANNON

and its fellow, belonging to a number of citizens
of Boston, were used in many engagements
during the war. The other two, the
property of the Government of
Massachusetts, were taken by
the enemy.

By order of the United States, in Congress Assembled, May 19, 1788.

32. JH to Samuel Langdon, April 11, 1775, HL.

33. JH to Edmund Quincy, April 7, 1775, HL.

34. James Warren to Mercy Warren, April 6, 1775, in *Warren-Adams Letters*, I:75, MHS.

35. Fowler, 181.

36. Paul Revere to corresponding secretary of MHS, January 1, 1798, in *Collections*, 1st ser., V (1798): 106–07, MHS.

37. Ibid., 107.

38. Ibid.

39. Sumner, 187–88.

40. Knollenberg, *Growth*, 189.

41. Elizabeth Clarke to Lucy W. Allen, April 19, 1841, in Lexington Historical Society *Proceedings* IV (1912):91–92.

42. Ibid., 91.

Chapter 10. President of Congress

1. G. R. Barnes and J. H. Owens, eds., *The Private Papers of John, Earl of Sandwich, First Lord of the Admiralty, 1771–1782* (Naval Records Society *Publications* 69, 71, 75, 78 [1932–38]), I:61; cited in Higginbotham, 61.

2. Although the first shot fired at Lexington is often cited as "the shot heard round the world," the phrase was actually created by Ralph Waldo Emerson for the first stanza of the "Hymn Sung at the Completion of the

Battle Monument" at Concord, July 4, 1837, and it refers to the skirmish at Concord bridge:

By the rude bridge that arched the flood,
Their flag to April's breeze unfurled,
Here once the embattled farmers stood,
And fired the shot heard round the world.

3. Pitcairn to Gage, April 1775, in Clarence E. Carter, ed., *The Correspondence of General Thomas Gage* (New Haven: Yale University Press, 1931–33), II:181; cited in Lancaster, 99.

4. Percy to Gen. Edward Harvey, April 20, 1775, in Charles K. Bolton, ed., *Letters of Hugh Earl Percy . . . 1774–1776* (1902); cited in Knollenberg, *Growth*, 195.

5. *Essex Gazette*, April 25, 1775, BPL.

6. Knollenberg, *Growth*, 267.

7. Sumner, 188.

8. JH to Dorothy Quincy, May 7, 1775, MHS.

9. A strong supporter of the national cause, Witherspoon later became a leading member of the Continental Congress and the only clergyman to sign the Declaration of Independence. He was one of the most influential educators of his era. His graduates from the College of New Jersey included one president of the new nation, James Madison; a vice president, Aaron Burr; ten cabinet officers; sixty members of Congress; and three Supreme Court justices. In effect, Witherspoon, who was a member of the Scottish "common sense" school of philosophy, helped shape the thinking of a new nation.

10. Abigail Adams to Mary Cranch, October 6, 1766, in Ferling, 53.

11. Ferling, 124.

12. Sears, 178–79.

13. Higginbotham, 84.

14. JH to Dorothy Quincy, June 10, 1775, in Allan, 194.

15. Ford, *Journals*, II:77–78.

16. Richard Frothingham, *The Life and Times of Joseph Warren* (Boston, 1865), 495–96; cited in Higginbotham, 95 n.

17. "Proscription of Thomas Gage," June 12, 1775, in Peter Force, ed., *American Archives . . .*, 4th ser., II (1839): 969.

18. Higginbotham, 84–85.

19. Ferling, 124.

20. Adams, II:416–17.

21. Miller, *Adams*, 336.

22. Ibid.

23. JH to Dr. Joseph Warren, June 18, 1775, in Allan, 196.

24. JH to George Washington, July 10, 1775, in Sears, 191.

25. George Washington to JH, July 21, 1775, in Allan, 197.
26. Benjamin Harrison to George Washington, July 21, 1775, in Allan, 201.
27. Sears, 195–96.
28. Ibid., 196–97.
29. John Adams to Abigail Adams, November 4, 1775, in Adams, III: 121–22.
30. John Adams to James Warren, September 19, 1775, in Allan, 205.
31. Sumner, 189.
32. JH to William Palfrey, May 13, 1776, HL.
33. William Palfrey to Sam Adams, October 3, 1775, in Miller, *Adams,* 315.
34. JH to Nicholas Cooke, October 5, 1775, HL.
35. JH to Cooke, November 10, 1775, HL.
36. JH to George Washington, February 12, 1776, HL.
37. Arthur Lee to JH, November 9, 1775, HL.
38. Stirling's great-grandfather was Sir William Alexander (1576–1640), a Scottish courtier, statesman, and poet who founded and colonized the region of Nova Scotia in Canada. A member of the court of James I, Alexander's best-known work was the sonnet "Aurora." In 1621 a grant from the king made him proprietor of New Scotland (Nova Scotia), although the first settlement was not established until eight years later. In 1630 he was created viscount of Stirling and Lord Alexander of Tullibody, and in 1633 the earl of Stirling, viscount of Canada. *EB,* "Stirling, William Alexander, 1st Earl of, Viscount of Canada, Viscount of Stirling, Lord Alexander of Tullibody."
39. Lord Stirling to JH, December 17, 1775, MHS.
40. JH to Philip Schuyler, January 10, 1776, MHS.
41. JH to Thomas Cushing, January 17, 1776, MHS.
42. Allan, 210.
43. JH to George Washington, December 22, 1775, in Force, IV (1843): 379 (see note 17 above).

Chapter 11. *Founding Father*

1. JH to Thomas Cushing, June 12, 1776, MHS. (Although the Massachusetts assembly appointed Hancock in January, his political enemies delayed issuing the commission, and it did not arrive until June.)
2. JH to Thomas Cushing, January 17, 1776, MHS.
3. Thomas Cushing to JH, January 30, 1776, in Allan, 214.
4. JH to Thomas Cushing, March 6, 1776, MHS.
5. JH to Thomas Cushing, March 7, 1776, MHS.
6. Lord Stirling to JH, January 10, 1776, MHS.

7. George Washington to JH, March 19, 1776, in Peter Force, ed., *American Archives* . . . , 4th ser., VI (1846): 420.

8. Isaac Cazneau to JH, April 4, 1776, in W. K. Watkins, "How the British Left the Hancock House," *Old-Time New England* XIII (1923): 194–95; cited in Allan, 219.

9. "A [*sic*] Account of damage done to the Estate of the Honble John Hancock Esq. in the Town of Boston by the British Army since April 19, 1775 taken to Dec, 1776," BPL.

10. See note 8 above.

11. Hart, III:264.

12. *Journal of the Proceedings of the Provincial Congress of North Carolina* (New Bern, N.C., 1776), 9.

13. Hart, III:262.

14. Ford, I:105–13.

15. Julian P. Boyd et al., eds., *The Papers of Thomas Jefferson* (Princeton, N.J.: Princeton University Press, 1950, 60 vols.), I:299; cited in Higginbotham, 117.

16. JH to Thomas Cushing, June 12, 1776, MHS.

17. JH to New Jersey Convention, June 11, 1776, in Theodorus B. Myers, ed., *Letters and Manuscripts of the Signers* (New York, 1871), 217.

18. JH to Massachusetts assembly, July 16, 1776, in Allan, 238.

19. JH to George Washington, May 16, 1776, in Force, VI (1846): 473 (see note 7 above).

20. JH to George Washington, May 21, 1776, in Allan, 222.

21. JH to George Washington, June 3, 1776, in Allan, 222.

22. JH to New Hampshire Convention, June 4, 1776, in Allan, 223.

23. Ford, *Journals*, 5:510–16.

24. "The Unanimous Declaration of the Thirteen United States of America." *EB*, "Declaration of Independence."

25. *DAB*, "Hancock, John."

26. J. H. Hazelton, *The Declaration of Independence* (New York, 1906), 209; cited in Allan, 236, and Fowler, 213.

Chapter 12. President of the United States

1. JH to George Washington, July 6, 1776, in Allan, 234.

2. John Adams to Samuel Chase, July 9, 1776, BPL.

3. JH to Massachusetts assembly, July 16, 1776, in Burnett, I:13–14.

4. JH to Maryland Convention, July 4, 1776, in Burnett, I:526–27.

5. Allan, 236.

6. Ibid., 239.

7. William Palfrey to JH, July 31, 1776, MHS.

8. "Plan of the treaty proposed by Congress, September, 1776," September 30, 1776, HL.

9. All records relating to the baby's birth were lost in the subsequent disorganized flight from Philadelphia.

10. Fowler, 216.

11. JH to Robert Morris, January 14, 1777, NYHS.

12. JH to Maryland assembly, January 31, 1777, in Burnett, II:228.

13. Unnamed delegate, in William Gordon, *History of the United States* (New York, 1801), II:284; cited in Allan, 255–56.

14. Diary entry, February 17, 1777, in Adams, II:435.

15. JH to Robert Morris, February 18, 1777, NYHS.

16. JH to Robert Morris, February 27, 1777, in Burnett, II:286.

17. JH to Dorothy Hancock, March 3, 1777, in Allan, 248.

18. JH to Dorothy Hancock, March 5, 1777, MHS.

19. Ibid., in Allan, 248–49.

20. JH to Dorothy Hancock, March 11, 1777, in Allan, 254.

21. William Palfrey to JH, April, 6, 1777, HL.

22. The frigate *Hancock* would not be the last American fighting ship to bear John Hancock's name. The USS *Hancock* was among the first transports to carry American Expeditionary Force troops and supplies to France in World War I. In 1944 the shipyards at Quincy, Massachusetts, launched the Essex-class aircraft carrier *Hancock,* built at a cost of $60 million, paid for by war bonds sold by the John Hancock Mutual Life Insurance Company. The *Hancock* survived eight months in the Pacific during World War II, despite 140 casualties and the loss of sixteen planes from a direct hit on the flight deck by a Japanese bomb. Two other *Hancock*s sailed under the American flag: a packet that sailed between New York and Newport, Rhode Island, in 1790 and a merchantman called the *John Hancock* in the World War II Liberty fleet.

23. Morris, 95.

24. JH to George Washington, October 17, 1777, in Allan, 260.

25. JH to Dorothy Hancock, October 18, 1777, in NEHGS *Register* XII (1858): 106.

26. An officer who carried the colors.

27. George Washington to JH, October 22, 1777, in Sears, 232–33.

28. Ford, *Journals,* 9:839.

29. Ibid., 9:852–53.

30. JH to William Palfrey, October 19, 1777, HL.

31. German officer's statement, December 10, 1777, in *Massachusetts Magazine* I (1908), BPL.

Chapter 13. A Model Major General

1. John Adams diary, November 17, 1777, in Adams, II:441.

2. Fowler, 225.

3. *Massachusetts Magazine* I (1908):52, BPL.

4. *New York Gazette,* February 1778, NYPL.

5. *Pennsylvania Ledger,* March 11, 1778; cited in Allan, 275.

6. James Warren to Samuel Adams, May 31, 1778, in Ford, *Letters,* II: 13–14, MHS.

7. Ibid.

8. Samuel Holten journal, June 3, 1778, in Allan, 279.

9. JH to Dorothy Quincy Hancock, June 20, 1778, MHS.

10. "Diary of the Honorable William Ellery of Rhode Island, June 28– July 23, 1778," *Pennsylvania Magazine of History and Biography* 11:477–78; cited in Fowler, 231.

11. James Warren to Samuel Adams, August 18, 1778, in Ford, *Letters,* II: 42–43, MHS.

12. JH to Dorothy Quincy Hancock, August 18, 1778, MHS.

13. JH to Dorothy Quincy Hancock, August 19, 1878, BPL.

14. Laco [Stephen Higginson], *Massachusetts Centinel,* March 25, 1789, BPL.

15. Vera B. Lawrence, *Music for Patriots, Politicians and Presidents* (New York, 1975), 79.

16. JH to Jeremiah Powell, August 28, 1778, NYPL.

17. James Warren to Samuel Adams, August 25, 1778, in Ford, *Letters,* II:44.

18. Sumner, 189.

19. Abigail Adams to John Adams, September or October 1778, in Charles F. Adams, ed., *Letters of John Adams, Addressed to His Wife* (Boston, 1841), I:342.

20. James Warren to Samuel Adams, September 30, 1778, in Ford, *Letters,* II:48.

21. Samuel Phillips Savage to Samuel Adams, October 1778, and Samuel Adams to Samuel Phillips Savage, November 1, 1778, in Fowler, 240.

22. James Murray, in Sears, 243.

23. Jensen, 269–70.

24. Sears, 243.

25. Hart, *Commonwealth,* III:266–72.

26. JH to Henry Quincy, August 30, 1779, in Fowler, 242–43.

27. James Warren to Samuel Adams, September 17, 1780, in Ford, *Letters,* II:138.

28. Sears, 230 (no date or other specifications).

Chapter 14. His Excellency the Governor

1. S. Adams to John Scollay, December 30, 1780, in Sears, 273, and Allan, 303.

2. Miller, *Adams,* 365.

3. Although servants were not slaves in the legal sense, they usually were indentured, with few legal rights. Historians often refer to them as "unfree," rather than as slaves.

4. William Palfrey to John Hancock, December 18, 1780, HL.

5. JH, speech delivered in Latin, December 19, 1781, in Brandes, 259–61.

6. William Sullivan, *Familiar Letters on Public Characters and Public Events* . . . (Boston, 1834), 12–13; cited in Allan, 308.

7. Catherine Wendell Davis to J. Wendell, November 1782, in B. Wendell, "A Gentlewoman of Boston," American Antiquarian Society *Proceedings* XXIX (1919): 266–67; cited in Allan, 310.

8. JH to Joseph Willard, October 20, 1783, in Harvard Archives; cited in Sears, 309.

9. Joseph Willard to JH, 1791, in Harvard Archives; cited in Sears, 310.

10. Morris, 111.

11. JH to George Washington, October 15, 1783, MHS.

12. JH to James Scott, November 14, 1783, MHS.

13. *Boston Independent Chronicle,* April 8, 1785, BPL.

14. *Massachusetts Centinal,* January 19, 1785, BPL.

15. Ibid., January 15, 1785.

16. JH to General Court, January 29, 1785, in Brandes, 289.

17. Samuel Adams to John Adams, July 2, 1785, in Cushing, IV:316.

Chapter 15. Hancock! Hancock! Even to the End

1. James Warren to Elbridge Gerry, October 4, 1785, in Ford, *Warren-Adams Letters,* II:265.

2. William Gordon to John Adams, October 3, 1785, MHS.

3. JH to Rufus King, November 30, 1785, in Allan, 321.

4. Rufus King to JH, December 4, 1785, in Allan, 321.

5. Samuel Adams, *Columbian Sentinel,* April 2, 1794; cited in Miller, *Adams,* 374.

6. JH to Henry Knox, March 14, 1787, MHS.

7. James Warren to John Adams, May 18, 1887, in Ford, *Warren-Adams Letters,* II:292–93.

8. Charles Gore to Rufus King, June 7, 1789, in Charles R. King, *Life and Correspondence of Rufus King* (New York, 1894), I:361.

9. *Diary of John Quincy Adams* (Boston, 1903), 33, MHS.

10. John Quincy Adams to John Adams, June 30, 1787, in Allan, 326.

11. Rufus King to George Thatcher, January 20, 1788, in Allan, 329.

12. James T. Austin, *Life of Elbridge Gerry*, II:75–76; cited in Allan, 329.

13. The Tenth Amendment to the United States Constitution would read: "The powers not delegated to the United States by the Constitution, nor prohibited by it to the States, are reserved to the States respectively, or to the people."

14. *Debates and Proceedings in the Convention of the Commonwealth of Massachusetts* (Boston, 1856), 279–80, BPL.

15. J.-P. Brissot de Warville, *New Travels in the United States of America, Performed in 1788* (London, 1792), 373.

16. S. Adams to E. Adams, October 10 and 17, 1788, in Allan, 297–98.

17. *Independent Chronicle*, March 27, 1788, BPL.

18. *New Hampshire Gazette*, February 20, 1788, BPL.

19. Unknown person, in Allan, 335.

20. Sparks, IX:557.

21. Dr. Benjamin Rush to Dr. Jeremy Belknap, October 7, 1788, MHS.

22. Gen. Henry Jackson to Henry Knox, January 11, 1789, and February 1, 1789, MHS.

23. Fowler, 277; Brandes, 402.

24. JH to George Clinton, February 21, 1789, in Fowler, 275.

25. Koch and Peden, 763.

26. George Washington to JH, October 23, 1789, in Allan, 344–45.

27. Notebook entry, October 25, 1789, in John C. Fitzpatrick, ed., *Diaries of George Washington* (Boston, 1925), IV: 34–35.

28. JH to George Washington, October 26, 1789, in Sparks, X:293.

29. George Washington to JH, ibid.

30. Notebook entry, October 26, 1789, in Fitzpatrick, *Diaries*, IV:36.

31. Edmund Quincy, *Life of Josiah Quincy* (Boston, 1867), 38.

32. *Acts and Resolves of the State of Massachusetts*, 1791, May session, 567–79, MA.

33. JH, Commencement Address, Harvard University, Cambridge, July 20, 1791, in *Boston Gazette*, July 25, 1791, BPL.

34. *Boston Gazette*, November 29, 1790, BPL.

35. JH, Commencement Address, Harvard University, Cambridge, July 19, 1792, in *Boston Gazette*, July 23, 1792, BPL.

36. Burglary was a capital offense in Massachusetts on the theory that when a burglar "breaks & enters a dwelling House in the night time with a felonious intention, [he] would probably commit myrder if he should meet with resistance." JH to General Court, January 30, 1793, in Brandes, 292.

37. The Eleventh Amendment was ratified on February 7, 1795.

38. Remarks, September 18, 1793, in *Boston Gazette,* September 23, 1793. No copy of Hancock's last words to the General Court was ever found, and it is assumed he delivered them extemporaneously, as reprinted in the *Gazette.* BPL.

39. *Independent Chronicle,* October 10, 1793, BPL.

40. "Biographical Sketch of the Life and Character of His Late Excellency Governor John Hancock," *Independent Chronicle,* October 1793, BPL.

Epilogue

1. Miller, *Adams,* 392.

2. Ibid., 398.

3. John Adams to Richard Rush, July 31, 1812, in Allan, 364.

4. John Adams to William Tudor, June 1, 1817, in Adams, X:259.

5. The Brattle Square Church was later demolished. It stood on the land now occupied by the Boston City Hall and Government Center in downtown Boston.

6. Towns in Berkshire County (Massachusetts), in what later became Vermont, and in New Hampshire were named for him in 1776, 1778, and 1779, respectively. Sears, 293.

7. Ibid., 327.

Selected Bibliography
of Principal Sources

Biographies of John Hancock

Allan, Herbert S. *John Hancock, Patriot in Purple*. New York: Beechurst Press, 1953.
Baxter, W. T. *The House of Hancock: Business in Boston, 1724–1775*. New York: Russell & Russell, 1965.
Brandes, Paul D. *John Hancock's Life and Speeches*. Lanham, Md.: Scarecrow Press, 1996.
Fowler, William M., Jr. *The Baron of Beacon Hill: A Biography of John Hancock*. Boston: Houghton Mifflin Company, 1980.
Sears, Lorenzo. *John Hancock, the Picturesque Patriot*. Boston: Little, Brown, and Company, 1913.

Additional Historic Works

Adams, Charles F., ed. *The Works of John Adams, Second President of the United States: With a Life of the Author*. 10 vols. Boston, 1850–56.
Alden, John R. *History of the American Revolution*. New York: Alfred A. Knopf, 1969.
Ayling, Stanley. *George the Third*. New York: Alfred A. Knopf, 1972.
Brooke, John. *King George III, America's Last Monarch*. New York: McGraw-Hill Book Company, 1972.
Burnett, Edmund C., ed. *Letters of Members of the Continental Congress*. 8 vols. Washington, D.C., 1921–38.
Cullop, Floyd G. *The Constitution of the United States: An Introduction*. New York: New American Library, 1984.

Cushing, Harvey Alonzo, ed. *The Writings of Samuel Adams.* 4 vols. Boston, 1904–8.

Ferling, John. *John Adams: A Life.* New York: Henry Holt and Company, 1992.

Fisher, David Hackett. *Paul Revere's Ride.* New York: Oxford University Press, 1994.

Fitzpatrick, John C., ed. *The Writings of Washington.* 39 vols. Washington, D.C., 1931–44.

Ford, Worthington C., ed. *Journals of the Continental Congress.* 34 vols. Washington, D.C., 1904–36.

———, ed. *Warren-Adams Letters.* 2 vols. Boston, 1917–25.

Gipson, Henry Lawrence. *The Coming of the Revolution, 1763–1775.* New York: Harper & Brothers, 1954.

Hart, Albert Bushnell, ed. *Commonwealth History of Massachusetts.* 5 vols. New York: Russell & Russell, 1966.

Higginbotham, Don. *The War of American Independence: Military Attitudes, Policies, and Practice, 1763–1789.* New York: Macmillan Company, 1971.

Hutchinson, Thomas. *The History of the Province of Massachusetts-Bay, 1749–74.* 3 vols. Cambridge, 1936.

Jensen, Merrill. *The New Nation: A History of the United States During the Confederation, 1781–1789.* New York: Alfred A. Knopf, 1967.

Knollenberg, Bernhard. *Growth of the American Revolution, 1766–1775.* New York: Free Press, 1975.

———. *Origin of the American Revolution, 1759–1766.* New York: Free Press, 1960, 1961.

Koch, Adrienne, and William Peden, eds. *The Selected Writings of John and John Quincy Adams.* New York: Alfred A. Knopf, 1946.

Labaree, Benjamin Woods. *The Boston Tea Party.* New York: Oxford University Press, 1964.

Lancaster, Bruce. *From Lexington to Liberty: The Story of the American Revolution.* Garden City, N.Y.: Doubleday & Company, 1955.

Miller, John C. *The Federalist Era, 1789–1801.* New York: Harper & Brothers, 1960.

———. *Sam Adams: Pioneer in Propaganda.* Boston: Little, Brown, and Company, 1936.

Morison, Samuel Eliot. *Three Centuries of Harvard, 1636–1936.* Cambridge, Mass.: Belknap Press, 1936.

Morris, Richard B. *Encyclopedia of American History.* New York: Harper & Brothers, 1953.

Smith, Page. *John Adams.* 2 vols. Garden City, N.Y.: Doubleday & Company, 1962.

Sparks, Jared, ed. *The Writings of George Washington.* 12 vols. Boston, 1834–1837.

Sumner, Gen. Wm. H. "Reminiscences." *New England Historical and Genealogical Register* VIII (1854):187–91.

Tudor, William. *The Life of James Otis.* Boston, 1823.

Wells, W. V. *The Life and Public Services of Samuel Adams.* 3 vols. Boston, 1865.

Zobel, Hiller B. *The Boston Massacre.* New York: W. W. Norton & Company, 1970.

Manuscript Collections

Boston Public Library
Bostonian Society
Houghton Library, Harvard University
Massachusetts Historical Society, Boston
Massachusetts State Archives
New England Historical and Genealogical Society
New-York Historical Society
New York Public Library

Newspapers

Boston Evening Post
Boston Gazette
Boston Independent Chronicle
Boston News-Letter
Connecticut Courant
Massachusetts Centinal
Massachusetts Spy
New England Chronicle
New Hampshire Gazette
New York Gazette
New York Journal
Pennsylvania Gazette
Pennsylvania Ledger

General Reference Works

Dictionary of American Biography
Dictionary of National Biography
Encyclopaedia Britannica, 10th ed.
Encyclopedia of American Education
Webster's American Biographies
Webster's New Biographical Dictionary

Index